Interconnecting Cisco Network Devices, Part 2 (ICND2)

Foundation Learning Guide, Fourth Edition

John Tiso

Cisco Press

800 East 96th Street

Indianapolis, IN 46240

Interconnecting Cisco Network Devices, Part 2 (ICND2) Foundation Learning Guide, Fourth Edition

John Tiso

Copyright© 2014 Cisco Systems, Inc.

Published by:
Cisco Press
800 East 96th Street
Indianapolis, IN 46240 USA

Printed in the United States of America 1 2 3 4 5 6 7 8 9 0

First Printing September 2013

Library of Congress Control Number: 2013946147

ISBN-13: 978-1-58714-377-9

ISBN-10: 1-58714-377-1

Warning and Disclaimer

This book is designed to provide information about interconnecting Cisco network devices, the ICND2 portion of the CCNA exam. Every effort has been made to make this book as complete and as accurate as possible, but no warranty or fitness is implied.

The information is provided on an "as is" basis. The author, Cisco Press, and Cisco Systems, Inc., shall have neither liability nor responsibility to any person or entity with respect to any loss or damages arising from the information contained in this book or from the use of the discs or programs that may accompany it.

The opinions expressed in this book belong to the author and are not necessarily those of Cisco Systems, Inc.

Trademark Acknowledgments

All terms mentioned in this book that are known to be trademarks or service marks have been appropriately capitalized. Cisco Press or Cisco Systems, Inc. cannot attest to the accuracy of this information. Use of a term in this book should not be regarded as affecting the validity of any trademark or service mark.

Corporate and Government Sales

The publisher offers excellent discounts on this book when ordered in quantity for bulk purchases or special sales, which may include electronic versions and/or custom covers and content particular to your business, training goals, marketing focus, and branding interests. For more information, please contact:

U.S. Corporate and Government Sales
1-800-382-3419
corpsales@pearsontechgroup.com

For sales outside of the U.S. please contact:

International Sales
international@pearsoned.com

Feedback Information

At Cisco Press, our goal is to create in-depth technical books of the highest quality and value. Each book is crafted with care and precision, undergoing rigorous development that involves the unique expertise of members from the professional technical community.

Readers' feedback is a natural continuation of this process. If you have any comments regarding how we could improve the quality of this book, or otherwise alter it to better suit your needs, you can contact us through email at feedback@ciscopress.com. Please make sure to include the book title and ISBN in your message.

We greatly appreciate your assistance.

Publisher: Paul Boger	Business Operation Manager, Cisco Press: Jan Cornelssen
Associate Publisher: Dave Dusthimer	Executive Editor: Brett Bartow
Development Editor: Marianne Bartow	Managing Editor: Sandra Schroeder
Project Editor: Mandie Frank	Technical Editors: Marjan Bradeško and Diane Teare
Copy Editor: Bill McManus	Editorial Assistant: Vanessa Evans
Proofreader: Dan Knott	Cover Designer: Mark Shirar
Indexer: Larry Sweazy	Compositor: Bronkella Publishing

CISCO

Americas Headquarters
Cisco Systems, Inc.
San Jose, CA

Asia Pacific Headquarters
Cisco Systems (USA) Pte. Ltd.
Singapore

Europe Headquarters
Cisco Systems International BV
Amsterdam, The Netherlands

Cisco has more than 200 offices worldwide. Addresses, phone numbers, and fax numbers are listed on the Cisco Website at www.cisco.com/go/offices.

CCDE, CCENT, Cisco Eos, Cisco HealthPresence, the Cisco logo, Cisco Lumin, Cisco Nexus, Cisco StadiumVision, Cisco TelePresence, Cisco WebEx, DCE, and Welcome to the Human Network are trademarks; Changing the Way We Work, Live, Play, and Learn and Cisco Store are service marks; and Access Registrar, Aironet, AsyncOS, Bringing the Meeting To You, Catalyst, CCDA, CCDP, CCIE, CCIP, CCNA, CCNP, CCSP, CCVP, Cisco, the Cisco Certified Internetwork Expert logo, Cisco IOS, Cisco Press, Cisco Systems, Cisco Systems Capital, the Cisco Systems logo, Cisco Unity, Collaboration Without Limitation, EtherFast, EtherSwitch, Event Center, Fast Step, Follow Me Browsing, FormShare, GigaDrive, HomeLink, Internet Quotient, IOS, iPhone, iQuick Study, IronPort, the IronPort logo, LightStream, Linksys, MediaTone, MeetingPlace, MeetingPlace Chime Sound, MGX, Networkers, Networking Academy, Network Registrar, PCNow, PIX, PowerPanels, ProConnect, ScriptShare, SenderBase, SMARTnet, Spectrum Expert, StackWise, The Fastest Way to Increase Your Internet Quotient, TransPath, WebEx, and the WebEx logo are registered trademarks of Cisco Systems, Inc. and/or its affiliates in the United States and certain other countries.

All other trademarks mentioned in this document or website are the property of their respective owners. The use of the word partner does not imply a partnership relationship between Cisco and any other company. (0812R)

About the Author

John Tiso, CCIE #5162, holds a variety of industry certifications in addition to his Cisco CCIE. These include the Cisco CCDP, Cisco CCNP-Voice, Cisco CCT, and several specializations from Cisco. He is a Microsoft MCSE and also holds certifications from CompTIA, Nortel Networks, Novell, Sun Microsystems, IBM, and HP.

John has a Graduate Citation in Strategic Management from Harvard University and a B.S. degree from Adelphi University. His writing has been published in a variety of industry journals and by Cisco Press. He has served as a technical editor for McGraw-Hill and Cisco Press. John is a past Esteemed Speaker for Cisco Networkers (Live!) and was a speaker at the National CIPTUG Conference. He has been an expert on Cisco's "Ask the Expert" NetPro forum and a question developer for the CCIE program.

John's current role is as a senior engineer at a Cisco Partner. He has a quarter of a century experience in the technology industry, after deciding to stop carrying refrigerators in the family business. Prior to his current position, he held multiple roles while working at Cisco, including TAC Engineer, Systems Engineer, and Product Manager. While at Cisco, one of John's last projects was as a member of the team that developed the recent updates to the CCNA program. Prior to joining Cisco, he was a lead architect and consultant for a Cisco Gold Partner.

John currently resides in Amherst, New Hampshire, with his wife Lauren and their three children, Kati, Nick, and Danny. John is a nine-time marathon finisher and also a Therapy Dog International certified handler of his therapy dog and running partner, Molly. He can be reached at johnt@jtiso.com.

About the Technical Reviewers

Marjan Bradeško has always practiced this principle: If you know something, if you experienced something, if you learned something—tell. That's exactly what he has done throughout his many years at NIL Ltd., and he continues to strive to do it today in his role of Content Development Manager.

Marjan was involved in learning services even prior to joining NIL in 1991. He came from the Faculty of Computer and Information Science at the University of Ljubljana, where he achieved his M.Sc. in computer science and was a teaching assistant. Soon after he joined NIL, the company became a Cisco Systems VAR, and Marjan's subsequent years are all "flavored" with Cisco. In all his various roles—from network engineer, consultant, or instructor to various management positions—Marjan's major goal has always been to educate, teach, and help people to achieve competencies in whatever they do. He has always been passionate about the importance of enthusiastic presentation of high-quality content to motivated people. He has long aided NIL employees in excelling at presentation skills and creating content to help NIL customers achieve competencies in IT and communications technologies. Marjan has also been heavily involved in promoting networking, Internet, cloud, and similar new technologies and publishing articles in numerous magazines.

Through his transitions from software engineer to his current position selling learning services as Content Development Manager, Marjan has gained broad knowledge and many competencies that he gladly shares with customers and coworkers. Marjan became a CCIE in 1995, stayed a CCIE for 16 years, and is now CCIE Emeritus. As a networking veteran, he has seen frequent technology reinventions, and he has had to learn and relearn repeatedly as innovative solutions have revolutionized the industry.

Marjan's passion for sharing his experiences is reflected in his private life as well. As an enthusiastic traveler and nature lover, especially of mountains, he has published many articles and books on nature and beautiful places of the world. In addition, he writes articles and books on presentation skills and sales, showing everyone that competencies are not given, but rather are a merging of talent, learning, and hard work.

Diane Teare, CCNP, CCDP, PMP, is a professional in the networking, training, project management, and e-learning fields. She has more than 25 years of experience in designing, implementing, and troubleshooting network hardware and software, and has been involved in teaching, course design, and project management. She has extensive knowledge of network design and routing technologies, and is an instructor with one of the largest authorized Cisco Learning Partners. She was the director of e-learning for the same company, where she was responsible for planning and supporting all the company's e-learning offerings in Canada, including Cisco courses. Diane has a bachelor's degree in applied science in electrical engineering and a master's degree in applied science in management science.

Dedication

To everyone who helped me find my way back.

Acknowledgments

I'd like to thank the crew at Cisco Press. This includes Brett Bartow, Chris Cleveland, Marianne Bartow (who was my savior, yet again), and Mandie Frank. Your support and sticking with me through the difficulties and challenges I faced during this project meant a lot to me, and was much appreciated. Thank you.

I'd like to thank the technical editors, Marjan and Diane. I'm happy I had the opportunity to meet you in person before I left Cisco and ask you to work on this project. I found your experience with the ICND2 course, your industry experience, and your diligent attention to detail invaluable. I really made you earn your money on this one! Thanks so much!

Lauren, Danny, Nick, and Kati; Thank you for bearing with me under both our normal day-to-day life, as well as when I had to disappear to work on this project. I'd also like to thank Lauren for her photography on several of the photos as well.

I'd also like to thank you, the reader and certification candidate, for your selection of this book.

For everyone else who I did not directly mention, thanks for everything. I keep the words of "The Boss" in my head, "It ain't no sin to be glad you're alive."

Contents at a Glance

Chapter 1   Implementing Scalable Medium-Sized Networks   1

Chapter 2   Troubleshooting Basic Connectivity   47

Chapter 3   Implementing an EIGRP Solution   91

Chapter 4   Implementing a Scalable Multiarea Network with OSPF   143

Chapter 5   Understanding WAN Technologies   185

Chapter 6   Network Device Management   269

Chapter 7   Advanced Troubleshooting   339

Appendix A   Answers to Chapter Review Questions   363

Appendix B   Basic L3VPN MPLS Configuration and Verification   369

Glossary of Key Terms   375

Index   403

Contents

Introduction   xviii

Chapter 1   **Implementing Scalable Medium-Sized Networks   1**

Understanding and Troubleshooting VLANs and VLAN Trunking   2

VLAN Overview   2

Trunk Operation   6

Configuring Trunks   7

Dynamic Trunking Protocol   8

VLAN Troubleshooting   9

Trunk Troubleshooting   10

Building Redundant Switch Topologies   11

Understanding Redundant Topologies   12

BPDU Breakdown   15

STP Types Defined   20

Per-VLAN Spanning Tree Plus   21

Analyzing and Reviewing STP Topology and Operation   24

Examining Spanning-Tree Failures   26

STP Features: PortFast, BPDU Guard, Root Guard, UplinkFast, and
BackboneFast   28

Improving Redundancy and Increasing Bandwidth with EtherChannel   29

EtherChannel Protocols   31

Port Aggregation Protocol   31

Link Aggregation Control Protocol   32

Configuring EtherChannel   33

Checking EtherChannel Operation   34

Understanding Default Gateway Redundancy   36

Hot Standby Router Protocol   37

HSRP Interface Tracking   38

HSRP Load Balancing   39

HSRP in Service Deployments   39

HSRP in IPv6   40

Gateway Load-Balancing Protocol   40

Chapter Summary   42

Review Questions   42

Chapter 2   Troubleshooting Basic Connectivity   47

Troubleshooting IPv4 Basic Connectivity   48

Components of End-to-End IPv4 Troubleshooting   48

Verification of Connectivity   51

Cisco Discovery Protocol   58

Verification of Physical Connectivity Issues   60

Identification of Current and Desired Path   63

Default Gateway Issues   66

Name Resolution Issues   68

ACL Issues   71

Understanding Networking in Virtualized Computing Environments   72

Troubleshooting IPv6 Network Connectivity   75

Understanding IPv6 Addressing   75

IPv6 Unicast Addresses   76

Components of Troubleshooting End-to-End IPv6 Connectivity   78

Verification of End-to-End IPv6 Connectivity   79

Neighbor Discovery in IPv6   80

Identification of Current and Desired IPv6 Path   82

Default Gateway Issues in IPv6   82

Name Resolution Issues in IPv6   83

ACL Issues in IPv6   84

IPv6 in a Virtual Environment   86

A Last Note on Troubleshooting   86

Chapter Summary   88

Review Questions   88

Chapter 3   Implementing an EIGRP Solution   91

Dynamic Routing Review   92

Routing   92

Routing Domains   92

Classification of Routing Protocols   93

Classful Routing Versus Classless Routing   94

Administrative Distance   95

EIGRP Features and Function   98

EIGRP Packet Types   100

EIGRP Path Selection   101

Understanding the EIGRP Metric   103

EIGRP Basic Configuration   105

Verification of EIGRP Configuration and Operation   106

EIGRP Passive Interfaces   108

Load Balancing with EIGRP   111

Variance   112

Traffic Sharing   113

EIGRP Authentication   114

Troubleshooting EIGRP   115

Components of Troubleshooting EIGRP   115

Troubleshooting EIGRP Neighbor Issues   118

Troubleshooting EIGRP Routing Table Issues   121

Issues Caused by Unadvertised Routes   121

Issues Caused by Route Filtering   122

Issues Caused by Automatic Network Summarization   123

Implementing EIGRP for IPv6   124

EIGRP IPv6 Theory of Operation   124

EIGRP IPv6 Feasible Successor   128

EIGRP IPv6 Load Balancing   129

EIGRP for IPv6 Command Syntax   130

Verification of EIGRP IPv6 Operation   131

EIGRP for IPv6 Configuration Example   133

Troubleshooting EIGRP for IPv6   135

Chapter Summary   136

Review Questions   137

Chapter 4   Implementing a Scalable Multiarea Network with OSPF   143

Understanding OSPF   143

Link-State Routing Protocol Overview   144

Link-State Routing Protocol Data Structures   145

Understanding Metrics in OSPF   146

Establishment of OSPF Neighbor Adjacencies   147

Building a Link-State Database   149

OSPF Area Structure   150

OSPF Area and Router Types   150

Link-State Advertisements   153

Multiarea OSPF IPv4 Implementation   154

Single-Area vs. Multiarea OSPF   155

Stub Areas, Not So Stubby Areas, and Totally Stub Areas   155

Planning for the Implementation of OSPF   158

Multiarea OSPF Configuration   158

Multiarea OSPF Verification   160

Troubleshooting Multiarea OSPF   162

OSPF Neighbor States   162

Components of Troubleshooting OSPF   166

Troubleshooting OSPF Neighbor Issues   168

Troubleshooting OSPF Routing Table Issues   172

Troubleshooting OSPF Path Selection   174

Examining OSPFv3   176

OSPFv3 Key Characteristics   176

OSPFv3 LSAs   177

Configuring OSPFv3   178

OSPFv3 Verification   179

Chapter Summary   180

Review Questions   181

Chapter 5   **Understanding WAN Technologies   185**

Understanding WAN Technologies   186

WAN Architecture   188

Hub-and-Spoke Networks   188

Partial-Mesh Networks   189

Full-Mesh Networks   189

Point-to-Point Networks   191

WAN Devices   192

Serial WAN Cabling   195

WAN Layer 2 Protocols   197

Other WAN Protocols   199

Integrated Services Digital Network   199

X.25   199

Multiprotocol Label Switching   200

Service Provider Demarcation Points   200

T1/E1   200

DSL Termination   201

Cable Termination   202

Other WAN Termination   203

WAN Link Options   203

Private WAN Connection Options   204

Public WAN Connection Options   205

Metropolitan-Area Networks   207

Extranet   209

Configuring Serial Interfaces   209

Configuration of a Serial Interface   213

Integrated CSU/DSU Modules   214

Back-to-Back Routers with an Integrated CSU/DSU   217

HDLC Protocol   218

Point-to-Point Protocol   220

PPP Authentication: PAP   222

PPP Authentication: CHAP   222

PPP Configuration   223

Configuring PPP Authentication with CHAP   225

Verifying CHAP Configuration   227

Configuring Multilink PPP over Serial Lines   228

Verifying Multilink PPP   230

Troubleshooting Serial Encapsulation   232

Establishing a WAN Connection Using Frame Relay   233

Understanding Frame Relay   233

Frame Relay Topologies   236

Frame Relay Reachability and Routing Protocol Issues   237

Frame Relay Signaling   239

Frame Relay Address Mappings   240

Configuring Frame Relay   243

Point-to-Point and Multipoint Frame Relay   244

Configuring Point-to-Point Frame Relay Subinterfaces   245

Configuring Point-to-Multipoint Frame Relay   247

Verifying Frame Relay Configuration   249

Introducing Cisco VPN Solutions   252

Introducing IPsec   255

GRE Tunnels   256

Configuring a GRE Tunnel   258

GRE Tunnel Verification   260

Understanding MPLS Networking   261

Basic Troubleshooting of MPLS Services   263

Chapter Summary   264

Review Questions   265

Chapter 6   Network Device Management   269

Configuring Network Devices to Support Network Management
Protocols   270

SNMP Versions   270

Obtaining Data from an SNMP Agent   271

Monitoring Polling Data in SNMP   272

Monitoring TRAPs in SNMP   273

Sending Data to an SNMP Agent   274

SNMP MIBs   275

Basic SNMP Configuration and Verification   276

Syslog Overview   279

Syslog Message Format   281

Syslog Configuration   281

NetFlow Overview   283

NetFlow Architecture   285

NetFlow Configuration   286

Verifying NetFlow Operation   287

Router Initialization and Configuration   288

Router Internal Component Review   289

ROM Functions   291

Router Power-Up Sequence   292

Configuration Register   293

Changing the Configuration Register   294

Locating the Cisco IOS Image to Load   295

Loading a Cisco IOS Image File   297

Selecting and Loading the Configuration   300

Cisco IOS File System and Devices   302

Managing Cisco IOS Images   305

Interpreting Cisco IOS Image Filenames   305

Creating a Cisco IOS Image Backup   306

Upgrading the Cisco IOS Image   308

Managing Device Configuration Files   311

Cisco IOS Password Recovery   313

Cisco IOS Licensing   315

Licensing Overview   315

Cisco IOS Licensing and Packaging Prior to Cisco IOS 15   316

Cisco IOS 15 Licensing and Packaging   317

Obtaining Licensing   318

License Verification   320

Permanent License Installation   321

Evaluation License Installation   322

Backing Up Licenses   325

Uninstalling Permanent Licenses   325

Rehosting a License   327

Cisco IOS-XR, IOS-XE, and NX-OS   328

Cisco IOS-XR   329

Cisco IOS-XE   330

Cisco NX-OS   331

Chapter Summary   332

Review Questions   333

Chapter 7   Advanced Troubleshooting   339

Advanced Router Diagnostics   340

Collecting Cisco IOS Device Diagnostic Information   340

Using the Output Interpreter to Detect Issues   341

Researching Cisco IOS Software Defects   343

Device Debugging   345

Capturing Debugging Output   345

Verifying and Disabling Debugging   350

Limiting Debugging Output   351

ACL Triggered Debugging   351

Conditionally Triggered Debugging   356

Troubleshooting an Issue with Debugging   357

Verifying Protocol Operation with Debugging   359

Chapter Summary   361

Review Questions   361

Appendix A   Answers to Chapter Review Questions   363

Appendix B   Basic L3VPN MPLS Configuration and Verification   369

Glossary of Key Terms   375

Index   403

Icons

Wan
Switch

NetFlow
Collector

WAN Switch

Telecommuter

Mobile /Remote
Worker

End User,
CiscoWorks

Wireless
Router

Wireless
Connectivity

Access
Server

CSU/DSU

Nexus
(NX-OS) Device

Firewall

NetFlow
Router

Network
Management
(NMS)
Workstation

MAN

Route/Switch
Processor

Network Cloud,
White

Cisco SBC
Portfolio

PC

Host (generic)

File Server

Router

Workgroup
Switch

Branch Office

PIX Right

Layer 3
Remote Switch

Printer

Headquarters

IBM Mini
(AS400)

Home Office

Modem
(old)

Modem
(new)

Laptop

Command Syntax Conventions

The conventions used to present command syntax in this book are the same conventions used in the Cisco IOS Command Reference. The Command Reference describes these conventions as follows:

- **Boldface** indicates commands and keywords that are entered literally, as shown. In actual configuration examples and output (not general command syntax), boldface indicates commands that are manually input by the user (such as a **show** command).

- *Italics* indicates arguments for which you supply actual values.

- Vertical bars (|) separate alternative, mutually exclusive elements.

- Square brackets ([ ]) indicate optional elements.

- Braces ({ }) indicate a required choice.

- Braces within brackets ([{ }]) indicate a required choice within an optional element.

Introduction

The purpose of this book is to enable readers to obtain a higher level of foundational knowledge beyond the ICND1 books and course. This book provides numerous illustrations, examples, photographs, self-check questions, and additional background information for reinforcement of the information presented. I have drawn on real-world experience and examples for some of the information.

Cisco develops the career certifications, such as CCNA, to align to job roles. Cisco Press introduced the Foundation Learning Guide Series as a learning tool and a parallel resource for the instructor-led Cisco courses. This book is intended both to teach the fundamentals that a CCNA needs in their job role and to provide the knowledge required to pass the ICND2 exam (or the ICND2 components in the CCNA Composite exam).

In my last role at Cisco, I was involved in the development of the updates to the CCNA program. Based on this experience, I have included some fundamental information in this book that is not directly part of the current ICND2 or CCNA composite exams or the ICND2 instructor-led training (however, it may very well be included in subsequent updates to the CCNA). I included this information (that you will not find in any other CCNA book) to help create and support the foundation necessary for both the job role and to obtain the certification. Areas that I have included that are not necessarily part of the CCNA certification are: MPLS, virtualization, and advanced troubleshooting techniques such as information on IOS debugging.

Debugging is a useful skill for diagnosing network problems. It is also key to understanding how protocols and features work, by using debugging in a lab environment (examples of both uses are given in Chapter 7, "Advanced Troubleshooting"). Improper use of debugging can also cripple a network (also discussed in Chapter 7). Therefore, this type of supplemental knowledge helps support both the job role of a CCNA and the use of alternate techniques and technologies as a study tool.

If you are a certification candidate, I strongly suggest you check the exam blueprints on the Cisco Learning Network (https://learningnetwork.cisco.com/) before embarking on your studying adventure.

Thanks for selecting this book as part of your library, and all the best of luck in your quest for knowledge and certification.

Who Should Read This Book?

There are four primary audiences for this text:

- The network engineer who needs to review key technologies that are important in today's networks

- The reader who is interested in learning about computer networking but might lack any previous experience in the subject

- The reader in the job role targeted for a CCNA who needs to obtain and update fundamental knowledge

- The reader who is interested in obtaining the Cisco CCNA certification

How This Book Is Organized

Certainly, this book may be read cover to cover. But it is designed to be flexible and to allow you to easily move between chapters and sections of chapters to cover only the material you need to learn or would like to revisit. If you do intend to read all of the chapters, the order in which they are presented is an excellent sequence.

Chapter 1: Implementing Scalable Medium Sized Networks. This chapter explores the basic foundational topics of internetworking. VLANs, EtherChannel, Spanning-Tree Protocol, and router redundancy (HSRP, VRRP, GLBP).

Chapter 2: Troubleshooting Basic Connectivity. Tools, techniques, and understanding basic error messaging and using host based and Cisco IOS Software are reviewed. IPv4, IPv6, and Virtualization are explored.

Chapter 3: Implementing an EIGRP Solution. EIGRP theory, operation, and troubleshooting for both IPv4 and IPv6 are discussed.

Chapter 4: Implementing a Scalable Multiarea Network with OSPF. The OSPF routing protocol is introduced. OSPF terminology, operation, configuration, and troubleshooting are explored.

Chapter 5: Understanding WAN technologies. WAN technologies are explored. This includes terminology, theory, configuration, and basic troubleshooting. VPNs are included as part of the chapter. This includes their comparison and integration with traditional WAN technology.

Chapter 6: Network Device Management. This chapter explores the various protocols such as SNMP, SYSLOG, and Cisco Flexible NetFlow. The architecture of the Cisco Integrated Service Routers is discussed. The management of configurations, Cisco IOS Software images, and licensing is explored.

Chapter 7: Advanced Troubleshooting. This chapter explores fundamental theory around advanced troubleshooting. It involves advanced diagnostics, Cisco IOS Software bugs, and Cisco IOS Debugging. The topics in this chapter are all directly outside the scope of the CCNA exam. However, understanding these topics will help the reader in both the job role as a CCNA and in exam preparation.

Appendix A: This appendix contains answers to the end of chapter questions.

Appendix B: This appendix contains information on very basic (customer side) configuration and troubleshooting of the MPLS WAN protocol. Again, the topics in this appendix are all directly outside the scope of the CCNA exam. However, understanding these topics will help the reader in both the job role as a CCNA and in exam preparation.

Glossary: Internetworking terms and acronyms are designed to assist the reader in the understanding of the text.

Chapter 1

Implementing Scalable Medium-Sized Networks

This chapter includes the following sections:

- Understanding and Troubleshooting VLANs and VLAN Trunking

- Building Redundant Switch Topologies

- Improving Redundancy and Increasing Bandwidth with EtherChannel

- Understanding Default Gateway Redundancy

- Chapter Summary

- Review Questions

This chapter begins with a review of virtual LAN (VLAN) trunk technology. Understanding how VLANs and trunks operate and which protocols are associated with them is important for configuring, verifying, and troubleshooting VLANs and trunks on Cisco access switches. Switched networks introduce redundancy, so a Spanning Tree Protocol (STP) loop-avoidance mechanism is needed to prevent undesirable loops in the network. EtherChannel technology, which groups several physical interfaces into one logical channel, and the router redundancy process, which solves problems in local networks with redundant topologies, are also explained. Default gateway and router redundancy methods are also covered.

Chapter Objectives

- Develop an understanding of VLANs

- Configure VLANs

- Troubleshoot Common VLAN issues

- Develop an understanding of redundant switch topologies

- Understand and configure EtherChannel
- Understand the operation and configuration of Spanning Tree Protocol
- Develop an understanding of layer 3 and default gateway redundancy

Understanding and Troubleshooting VLANs and VLAN Trunking

This section discusses the concepts, operation, configuration, and troubleshooting of VLANs and VLAN trunking.

VLAN Overview

A VLAN is a group of devices with a common set of requirements, independent of their physical location. The attributes of a VLAN are similar to those of a physical LAN, except that a VLAN allows the grouping of end stations on the same LAN, even when they are not physically located on the same LAN segment. Because a VLAN acts as an independent LAN, ports can be grouped on a switch and assigned to the VLAN. This allows the limiting of unicast, multicast, and broadcast traffic flooding throughout the switch. If the saying "What happens in Vegas, stays in Vegas" is true, then a VLAN is the Las Vegas of networking. Flooded traffic originating from a specific VLAN stays in that VLAN, and floods only to the ports in that VLAN.

In a VLAN, a switch port has one of two roles. It can act as an access port. An access port is considered a standard port in a specific LAN on the network (in this case, the LAN is *virtual*—a VLAN). This can be considered a "standard" Ethernet port that any end devices would normally be connected to. A switch port in a VLAN can also act as a VLAN trunk. A VLAN trunk port is key to VLAN operation. It is a specialized port designed to link switches, which allows the interconnection of the switch to multiple VLANs. So, more than one VLAN runs across a VLAN trunk, primarily for switch-to-switch connections. However, a VLAN trunk can have other uses, as discussed further in this chapter.

As stated earlier, a VLAN is a logical broadcast domain that can span multiple physical LAN segments. Figure 1-1 shows a three-floor office building in which three VLANs are defined, with each VLAN present on each floor. Notice that within the switched inter-network, VLANs provide segmentation and organizational flexibility. You can design a VLAN structure that allows you to group devices that are segmented logically by functions, access requirements, and device types without regard to the physical location of the users. Containing flooded traffic within a VLAN improves the overall performance of the network.

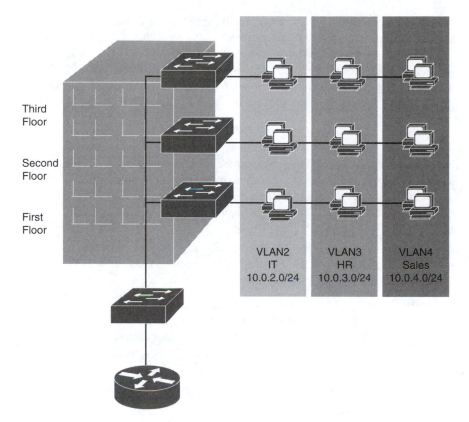

Figure 1-1   *VLANs Are Not Dependant on Physical Location*

Each VLAN that is configured on the switch implements address learning, forwarding, and filtering decisions and loop-avoidance mechanisms, just as though each individual VLAN was on a unique physical switch.

VLANs are implemented by restricting traffic being forwarded to destination ports that are in the same VLAN as the originating ports. When a frame arrives on a switch port, the switch must retransmit the frame only to the other ports that belong to the same VLAN. In essence, a VLAN that is operating on a switch limits transmission of unicast, multicast, and broadcast traffic.

A VLAN can exist on a single switch or span multiple switches. VLANs can include stations in a single building or in multiple-building infrastructures.

VLANs can be connected just like physical LANs. The process of forwarding network traffic from one VLAN to another VLAN using a router is called *inter-VLAN routing*. The main difference between inter-VLAN routing and routing between LANs is that LANs require physical interfaces, while VLANs do not use a physical interface. Instead, they use a logical interface per VLAN.

Cisco Catalyst switches have a factory default configuration in which various default VLANs are preconfigured to support different media and protocol types. There is also a default VLAN for system management. The default Ethernet VLAN is VLAN 1. This is also the default VLAN for management. The switch is assigned an IP address in this management VLAN and it is used for remote communication and configuration. The default VLAN cannot be modified or changed. However, the management VLAN can be changed.

> **Note**   Early Cisco Catalyst switches ran an operating system called *CatOS* (Catalyst Operating System). CatOS and the switch models that ran it are End of Life. Another, current class of Cisco switches, Nexus, run an operating system called *NX-OS* (Nexus Operating System). Features such as VLANs are implemented, configured, and validated differently.
>
> In the scope of both this book and the CCNA certification, the focus is specifically on switches running standard Cisco IOS Software. You should be aware of CatOS and NX-OS if you are reviewing other documentation.
>
> For more information:
>
> "Cisco NX-OS/IOS Configuration Fundamentals Comparison": http://docwiki.cisco. com/wiki/Cisco_NX-OS/IOS_Configuration_Fundamentals_Comparison
>
> "Comparison of the Cisco Catalyst and Cisco IOS Operating Systems for the Cisco Catalyst 6500 Series Switch": http://www.cisco.com/en/US/prod/collateral/switches/ ps5718/ps708/prod_white_paper09186a00800c8441.html

Creating VLANs and Verifying the Configuration

For newer Cisco Catalyst switches, use the **vlan** global configuration command to create a VLAN and enter VLAN configuration mode. Use the **no** form of this command to delete the VLAN. Example 1-1 shows how to add VLAN 50 to the VLAN database, name it HQ50, and add a port to it.

Example 1-1   *Cisco IOS Configuration of a VLAN*

```
HQ# configure terminal
HQ(config)# vlan 50
HQ(config-vlan)# name HQ50
HQ(config-vlan)# interface FastEthernet0/1
HQ(config-if)# switchport access vlan 50
```

To add a VLAN to the VLAN database, assign a number and name to the VLAN. As previously noted, VLAN 1 is the factory default VLAN. Normal-range VLANs are identified with a number between 1 and 1001.

To add an Ethernet VLAN, you must specify at least a VLAN number. If no name is entered for the VLAN, the default is to append the VLAN number to the word VLAN. For example, VLAN0004 would be the default name for VLAN 4 if no name is specified. VLAN names must be unique in the administrative domain and must be an ASCII string from 1 to 32 characters.

When an end system is connected to a switch port, it should be associated with a VLAN in accordance with the network design. To associate a device with a VLAN, the switch port to which the device connects is assigned to a single VLAN and thus becomes an access port. A switch port can become an access port through static or dynamic configuration.

If additional configuration is necessary for VLAN 50, the IOS command **vlan 50** is entered again to configure or reconfigure additional options, such as changing the VLAN name. As shown in Example 1-1, the configuration mode for adding a switch port to a VLAN is in the switch port interface configuration mode.

The VLAN port assignment is configured in interface configuration mode using the **switchport access vlan** command. To assign a group of contiguous interfaces to a VLAN, use the **interface range** command. Use the **vlan** *vlan_number* command to set static access membership.

After you configure the VLAN, use the **show vlan** command to validate the parameters for that VLAN. As shown in Example 1-2, the command displays all VLANs, including any system default VLAN.

Use the **show vlan id** *vlan_number* or **show vlan name** *vlan-name* command to display information about a particular VLAN.

Example 1-2 *Displaying VLAN Information*

```
HQ# show vlan


VLAN Name                             Status    Ports
---- -------------------------------- --------- -----------------------
1    default                          active    Fa0/2,    Fa0/3,
                                                Fa0/4,    Fa0/6,
                                                Fa0/6,    Fa0/7,  Fa0/8,
                                                Fa0/9,    Fa0/10, Fa0/11,
                                                Fa0/12,   Gi0/1,  Gi0/2
50   HQ50                             active    Fa0/1

<<Output Truncated>>
```

Note that the default configuration for a port is in VLAN 1. An interface range is an option to configure a group of contiguous interfaces with the **interface range** command. Given that interfaces all default into VLAN 1, the **range** option is a good choice when configuring VLANs. Remember that a port that is not a trunk port can be in only a single VLAN. Trunk ports are discussed in the next section.

Trunk Operation

As mentioned earlier, a standard port is used for the connection of an end device (such as a PC). Therefore, a standard port can only be in one VLAN at a time. So, the question arises, how are switches interconnected to allow for multiple VLANs per switch? In a traditional LAN environment, different LAN segments must be on different devices, each with its own physical links. So, to permit the connection of VLANs, a trunk port is used. It carries traffic for multiple VLANs. A trunk is generally used for switch-to-switch connectivity.

A trunk is a point-to-point link between one or more Ethernet switch interfaces and another networking device that needs to access multiple VLANs, such as a router or a switch. Ethernet trunks carry the traffic of multiple VLANs over a single link and allow you to extend the VLANs across an entire network. A trunk does not belong to a specific VLAN; rather, it is a conduit for VLANs between switches and routers. In Figure 1-2, the link in the center is a trunk. It carries traffic for all the VLANs in the network.

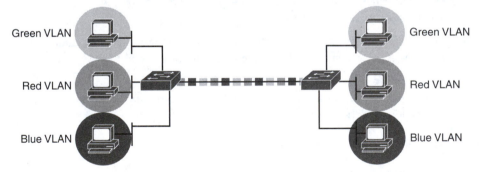

Figure 1-2   *Trunk Port Operation*

A special protocol is used to carry multiple VLANs over a single link between two devices, making it a trunk. Cisco supports the IEEE 802.1Q trunking protocol. A trunk can also be used between a network device and a server or another device that is equipped with an appropriate 802.1Q-capable network interface card (NIC).

Ethernet trunk interfaces support various trunking modes. You can configure an interface as trunking or nontrunking, or have it negotiate trunking with the neighboring interface.

By default on a Cisco Catalyst switch, all configured VLANs are carried over a trunk interface. On an 802.1Q trunk port, there is one native VLAN, which is untagged (by default, VLAN 1). All other VLANs are tagged with a VLAN ID (VID).

When Ethernet frames are placed on a trunk, they need additional information regarding the VLANs they belong to. This task is accomplished by using the 802.1Q encapsulation header. IEEE 802.1Q uses an internal tagging mechanism that inserts a 4-byte tag field into the original Ethernet frame between the Source Address and Type or Length fields. Because 802.1Q alters the frame, the trunking device recomputes the Frame Check Sequence (FCS) on the modified frame. It is the responsibility of the Ethernet switch to look at the 4-byte tag field and determine where to deliver the frame.

Configuring Trunks

Trunks are configured using interface mode on the interface that is to be the trunk port. 802.1Q trunk ports use a native VLAN. The VLAN is untagged and is VLAN 1, by default. It can be reset when configuring the trunk and must be the same on both peer devices. Example 1-3 shows the configuration of the trunk port and the subsequent validation with the **show** command.

Example 1-3   *Trunk Port Configuration*

```
HQ# configure terminal
HQ(config)# interface fa0/11
HQ(config-if)# switchport mode trunk
HQ(config-if)# switchport trunk native vlan 99
<Control-D>

HQ# show interfaces FastEthernet0/11 switchport
Name: Fa0/11
Switchport: Enabled
Administrative Mode: trunk
Operational Mode: trunk
Administrative Trunking Encapsulation: dot1q
Negotiation of Trunking: On
Access Mode VLAN: 99
Trunking Native Mode VLAN: 99
<output omitted>

HQ# show interfaces FastEthernet0/11 trunk
Port          Mode      Encapsulation    Status        Native vlan
Fa0/11        on        802.1q           trunking      99
<output omitted>
```

When using the **show interfaces** command, the **switchport** option verifies the configuration of the port. The **trunk** option verifies that the interface is trunking. These two options to the command display the trunk parameters and VLAN information of the port.

Dynamic Trunking Protocol

Cisco Catalyst switches support the Dynamic Trunking Protocol (DTP), which manages automatic trunk negotiation. It is a Cisco proprietary protocol. Switches from other vendors do not support DTP. It is automatically enabled on a switch port when certain trunking modes are configured on the switch port. DTP manages trunk negotiation only if the port on the other switch is configured in a mode that supports DTP.

A best practice is to configure trunks statically, as this makes operation and troubleshooting cleaner. The default DTP mode is dependent on the Cisco IOS Software version and the platform. Table 1-1 shows which trunking mode is negotiated based on the settings of the two peer trunk ports. The shaded areas in Table 1-1 indicate the suggested settings for a trunk and access port when both sides use the preferred method of manual configuration.

Table 1-1   *Trunk Mode Negotiation*

	Dynamic Auto	Dynamic Desirable	Trunk	Access
Dynamic Auto	Access	Trunk	Trunk	Access
Dynamic Desirable	Trunk	Trunk	Trunk	Access
Trunk	Trunk	Trunk	Trunk	Limited connectivity
Access	Access	Access	Limited connectivity	Access

The current DTP mode is determined with the **show dtp interface** command. You can configure DTP mode to turn the protocol off or instruct it to negotiate a trunk link under only certain conditions, as described in Table 1-2.

Table 1-2   *Definitions of DTP Modes*

DTP Mode	Function
Dynamic auto	Creates the trunk based on the DTP request from the neighboring switch.
Dynamic desirable	Communicates to the neighboring switch via DTP that the interface is attempting to become a trunk if the neighboring switch interface is able to become a trunk.
Trunk	Automatically enables trunking regardless of the state of the neighboring switch and any DTP requests sent from the neighboring switch.
Access	Trunking is not allowed on this port regardless of the state of the neighboring switch interface and any DTP requests sent from the neighboring switch.
Nonegotiate	Prevents the interface from generating DTP frames. This mode can be used only when the interface switch port mode is access or trunk. You must manually configure the neighboring interface as a trunk interface to establish a trunk link.

The **switchport nonegotiate** interface command specifies that DTP negotiation packets are not sent. The switch does not engage in DTP negotiation on this interface. This command is valid only when the interface switchport mode is access or trunk (configured by using the switchport mode access or switchport mode trunk interface configuration command, respectively). This command returns an error if you attempt to execute it in dynamic (auto or desirable) mode. Use the **no** form of this command to return to the default setting. When you configure a port with the **switchport nonegotiate** command, the port trunks only if the other end of the link is specifically set to trunk. The **switchport nonegotiate** command does not form a trunk link with peer ports in either dynamic desirable mode or dynamic auto mode.

VLAN Troubleshooting

This section examines troubleshooting VLANs. VLAN problems usually manifest themselves as devices unable to connect to the network, even though the Layer 3 configuration looks correct and the devices have a physical link.

To troubleshoot VLAN issues when you do not have connection between Ethernet devices, follow these high-level steps:

Step 1.   Use the **show vlan** command to check whether the port belongs to the expected VLAN. If the port is assigned to the wrong VLAN, use the **switchport access vlan** command to correct the VLAN membership.

Step 2.   Use the **show mac address-table** command to check which addresses were learned on a particular port of the switch and to which VLAN that port is assigned.

If the VLAN to which the port is assigned is deleted, the port becomes inactive. Use the **show vlan** or **show interfaces switchport** command to verify that the VLAN is present in the VLAN database.

Figure 1-3 provides a high-level flowchart depicting the preceding steps.

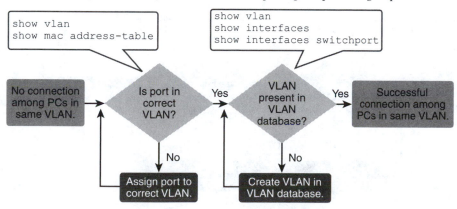

Figure 1-3   *Suggested Troubleshooting Flow for VLAN Issues*

To display the MAC address table, use the **show mac-address-table** command in privileged EXEC mode. This command displays the MAC address table for the switch. Specific views can be defined by using the optional keywords and arguments. Example 1-4 shows MAC addresses that were learned on the FastEthernet0/1 interface. MAC address 000c.296a.a21c was learned on the interface FastEthernet0/1 in VLAN 10. If this number is not the expected VLAN number, change the interface's port VLAN membership using the **switchport access vlan** command.

Example 1-4 *Verifying the VLAN Using the MAC Address Table*

```
JT1# show mac address-table interface FastEthernet0/1

Mac Address Table
-------------------------------------------

Vlan    Mac Address       Type            Ports
------  ----------------  --------------  ---------
10      000c.296a.a21c    DYNAMIC         Fa0/1
10      000f.34f9.9181    DYNAMIC         Fa0/1


Total Mac Addresses for this criterion: 2
```

If the VLAN to which the port belongs is deleted, the port becomes inactive.

Use the command **show interface** *interface* **switchport** to check whether the port is inactive. If the port is inactive, it will not be functional until the missing VLAN is re-created using the **vlan** *vlan_id* command.

Trunk Troubleshooting

When VLAN trunk establishment fails, the configuration must be checked. Figure 1-4 provides a sample troubleshooting flow for VLAN trunking issues.

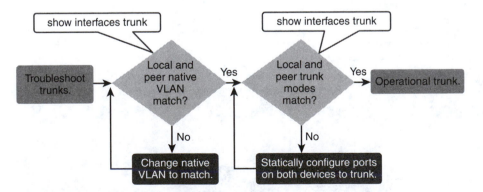

Figure 1-4 *Troubleshooting Trunk Issues*

VLAN leaking occurs when frames are inadvertently leaving one VLAN to go to another. Troubleshoot trunk issues during VLAN leaking by reviewing the **show interfaces trunk** command output, as displayed in Example 1-5.

Use the **show interfaces trunk** command to check whether a trunk has been established between switches. Then confirm that the local and peer native VLANs match. If the native VLAN does not match on both sides, VLAN leaking occurs.

Example 1-5 shows that the native VLAN on one side of the trunk link was changed to VLAN 2. If one end of the trunk is configured as native VLAN 1 and the other end is configured as native VLAN 2, a frame sent from VLAN 1 on one side is received on VLAN 2 on the other. VLAN 1 "leaks" into the VLAN 2 segment. This behavior is never required. Connectivity issues occur in the network if a native VLAN mismatch exists. Change the native VLAN to the same VLAN on both sides of the VLAN to avoid this behavior.

Example 1-5 *Two Switches: HQ and Branch with Trunk Type Mismatch*

```
HQ# show interfaces FastEthernet0/3 trunk

Port    Mode    Encapsulation    Status          Native vlan
Fa0/3   auto    802.1q           not-trunking    1


<output omitted>


SW2# show interfaces FastEthernet0/3 trunk

Port    Mode    Encapsulation    Status          Native vlan
Fa0/3   auto    802.1q           not-trunking    2


<output omitted>
```

The CDP process in the switch detects the VLAN mismatch and notifies via the following logging message:

```
Aug 31 08:34:48.714: %CDP-4-NATIVE_VLAN_MISMATCH: Native VLAN
mismatch  discovered on FastEthernet0/3 (2), with Branch
FastEthernet0/3 (1).
```

DTP can determine the operational trunking mode and protocol on a switch port when it is connected to another device that is also capable of dynamic trunk negotiation. If both ends of a trunk are set to dynamic auto trunk mode, a trunk will not be established. Example 1-5 shows the status of the link as "not-trunking."

Building Redundant Switch Topologies

Most complex networks include redundant devices, to avoid single points of failure. Although a redundant topology eliminates some issues, it can introduce other problems. Spanning Tree Protocol (STP) is a Layer 2 link management protocol that provides path redundancy while preventing undesirable loops in a switched network. This section introduces STP and how it facilitates the development of a redundant topology without creating loops in the internetwork.

Understanding Redundant Topologies

Redundancies in computer networks are an important part of design. Figure 1-5 depicts a traditional Cisco three-tiered architecture. It has three layers: core, distribution, and access.

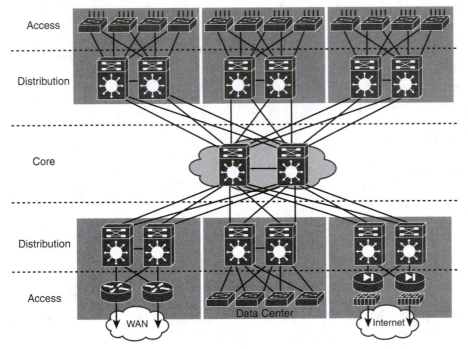

Figure 1-5   *Redundant Hierarchical Switch Topology*

The core layer is the high-speed switching center of the network. The distribution layer contains network services, such as servers. The access layer is where end-user devices are connected.

> **Note**   A detailed discussion of network design is beyond the scope of the CCNA certification exam and this text.

It is important to note that there are redundant links between all components and layers in the network.

Redundant designs can eliminate the possibility of a single point of failure causing a loss of function for the entire switched network. But you must consider some of the problems that redundant designs can cause:

- **Broadcast storms:** Without some loop-avoidance process, each switch floods broadcasts endlessly. This situation is commonly called a *broadcast storm*.

- **Multiple frame transmission:** Multiple copies of unicast frames may be delivered to destination stations. Many protocols expect to receive only a single copy of each transmission. Multiple copies of the same frame can cause unrecoverable errors.

- **MAC database instability:** Instability in the content of the MAC address table results from copies of the same frame being received on different ports of the switch. Data forwarding can be impaired when the switch consumes the resources that are coping with instability in the MAC address table. Stateless Layer 2 LAN protocols, such as Ethernet, lack a mechanism to recognize and eliminate endlessly looping frames. Some Layer 3 protocols implement a Time to Live (TTL) mechanism that limits the number of times a Layer 3 networking device can retransmit a packet. Lacking such a mechanism, Layer 2 devices continue to retransmit looping traffic indefinitely. Both the MAC address table and the Cisco Discovery Protocol (CDP) can also have inconsistent output on the devices that are attached to ports.

A loop-avoidance mechanism solves these problems. STP was developed to address them. It provides loop resolution by managing the physical paths to given network segments, which allows physical path redundancy while preventing the undesirable effects of active loops in the network. STP is an IEEE committee standard defined as 802.1D.

STP behaves in the following ways:

- STP uses bridge protocol data units (BPDU), the OSI Layer 2 packets used for inter-switch communications.

- STP forces certain ports into a standby state so that they do not listen to, forward, or flood data frames. The overall effect is that there is only one path to each network segment that is active at any time, even though the link is physically connected and receives BPDUs.

- If there is a problem with connectivity to any of the segments within the network, STP reestablishes connectivity by automatically activating a previously inactive path, if one exists.

Figure 1-6 shows a redundant topology where a link is deactivated by STP to avoid a loop in the network.

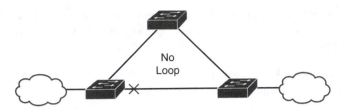

Figure 1-6 *STP Preventing Looped Network*

STP places ports in the network into the following different roles depending on the location and function in the network:

- **Root port (RP):** This port exists on each non-root bridge and is the switch port with the best path to the root bridge. Root ports forward traffic toward the root bridge with the source MAC address of frames.

- **Designated port (DP):** This port type exists on root bridges and non-root bridges. For root bridges, all switch ports are designated ports. For non-root bridges, a designated port is the switch port that receives and forwards frames toward the root bridge as needed. Only one designated port is allowed per segment. If multiple switches exist on the same segment, an election process determines the designated switch, and the corresponding switch port begins forwarding frames for the segment. Designated ports are capable of populating the MAC table.

- **Nondesignated port (NDP):** A nondesignated port is a switch port that is not forwarding (blocking) data frames and is not populating its MAC address table with the source addresses of frames that are seen on the attached segment.

- **Disabled port:** A disabled port is a switch port that is shut down or disabled due to an operational issue with the switch and/or port. STP also places ports in different operating states. These operating states are transitioned by the system as STP converges:

  - **Blocking:** A port is blocking when STP has determined that a better path to the root exists. BPDUs are received but not sent.

  - **Listening:** The switch is listening on the port and processing BPDUs but *is not updating* the MAC address table. A switch stays in listening mode before transitioning to learning using the forwarding timer (default: 15 seconds).

  - **Learning:** The switch is listening on the port and processing BPDUs and *is updating* the MAC address table. A switch stays in learning mode before transitioning to learning using the forwarding timer (default: 15 seconds).

These are the steps of the spanning-tree algorithm:

Step 1. Elect a root bridge. The root bridge becomes the switch with the lowest bridge ID (BID). There can be only one root bridge per network. BID is a combination of bridge priority and MAC address of the switch. Bridge priority is a number between 0 and 65535 and the default is 32768. Figure 1-7 shows a graphic representation of a BID.

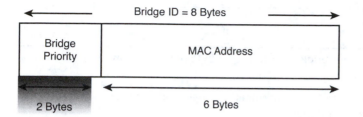

Figure 1-7 *Bridge ID*

Step 2.   Elect a root port for each non-root switch, based on lowest root path cost. The root bridge does not have root ports. Each non-root switch has one root port. The root port is the port through which the non-root bridge has its best path to the root bridge. Therefore, root port shows the direction of the best path to the root bridge.

Step 3.   Elect a designated port for each segment, based on the lowest root path cost. Each link will have one designated port.

Step 4.   The root ports and designated ports transition to the forwarding state, and the other ports stay in the blocking state.

The main point is that STP forces certain ports into a blocking state. These ports do not forward data frames. The overall effect is that only one path to each network segment is active at any time. If there is a problem with connectivity to any of the segments within the network, STP reestablishes connectivity by automatically activating a previously inactive path, if one exists.

BPDU Breakdown

The BPDU frame contains information on the topology of the spanning tree. It determines how the switch calculates the states of ports. The contents of a BPDU are outlined in Table 1-3.

Table 1-3 *Description of BPDU Components*

BPDU Component	Description
Protocol Identifier	Indicates the type of protocol. This field contains the value 0.
Version	Indicates the version of the protocol. This field contains the value 0.
Message type	Indicates the protocol. This field contains the value 0.
Flags	Indicates whether or not the BPDU is a topology change (TC) notification or a topology change acknowledgement (TCA) by setting the TC or TCA bit. A TC signals a change in the topology, while the TCA acknowledges the receipt of a TC notification.

BPDU Component	Description
Root ID	Indicates the root bridge by listing its 2-byte priority followed by its 6-byte ID.
Root Path Cost	Indicates the cost of the path from the bridge sending the configuration message to the root bridge.
Bridge ID	Indicates the priority and ID of the bridge sending the message.
Port ID	Indicates the port number from which the configuration message was sent. This field allows loops created by multiple attached bridges to be detected.
Frame Control	This field is always set to 01.
Destination Address (DA)	Indicates the destination address as specified in the Bridge Group Address table.
Source Address (SA)	Indicates the base MAC address used by the switch.

The first step in the spanning-tree algorithm is the election of a root bridge. Initially, all switches assume that they are the root. They start transmitting BPDUs with the Root ID field containing the same value as the Bridge ID field. Thus, each switch essentially claims that it is the root bridge on the network. Figure 1-8 shows a sample switched topology with bridge priority and MAC addresses.

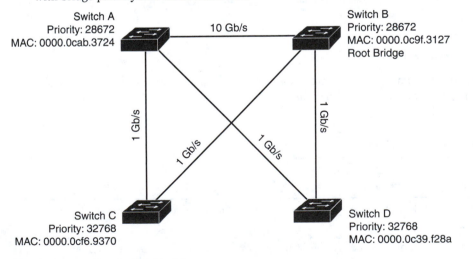

Figure 1-8   *Sample STP Topology*

As soon as the switches start receiving BPDUs from the other switches, each switch compares the Root ID in the received BPDUs against the value that it currently has recorded as the current Root ID. If the received value is lower than the recorded value (which was originally the BID of that switch), the switch replaces the recorded value with the received value and starts transmitting this value in the Root ID field in its own BPDUs.

Eventually, all switches learn and record the BID of the switch that has the lowest BID, and the switches all transmit this ID in the Root ID field of their BPDUs.

Switch B in the example becomes the root bridge because it has the lowest BID. Switch A and Switch B have the same priority, but Switch B has a lower MAC address.

As soon as a switch recognizes that it is not the root (because it is receiving BPDUs that have a Root ID value that is lower than its own BID), it marks the port on which it is receiving those BPDUs as its root port.

BPDUs could be received on multiple ports. In this case, the switch elects the port that has the lowest-cost path to the root as its root port. If two ports have an equal path cost to the root, the switch looks at the BID values in the received BPDUs to make a decision (where the lowest BID is considered best, similar to root bridge election) as to which port will become the root port. If the root path cost and the BID in both BPDUs are the same, because both ports are connected to the same upstream switch, the switch looks at the Port ID field in the BPDUs and selects its root port based on the lowest value in that field. Figure 1-9 shows the root port selection, indicated by "RP."

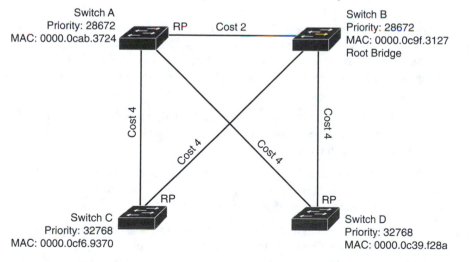

Figure 1-9   *Root Port Election*

The cost associated with each port is, by default, related to its speed (the higher the interface bandwidth, the lower the cost), but the cost can be manually changed. The default costs are as follows:

Bandwidth	Link Cost
10 Mbps	100
100 Mbps	19
1-Gigabit Ethernet	4
10-Gigabit Ethernet	2

In this case, the direct link between Switch A and Switch B is a 10-Gigabit link, and the other links are 1 Gigabit. Switches A, C, and D mark the ports directly connected to Switch B (which is the root bridge) as the root port. These directly connected ports on Switches A, C, and D have the lowest cost to the root bridge.

After electing the root bridge and root ports, the switches determine which switch will become the designated bridge for each Ethernet segment. This process has similarities to the root bridge and root port elections. Each switch connected to a segment sends BPDUs out the port that is connected to that segment, essentially claiming to be the designated bridge for that segment. At this point, it considers its port to be a designated port.

As soon as a switch starts receiving BPDUs from other switches on that segment, it compares the received values of the Root Path Cost, BID, and Port ID fields (in that order) against the values in the BPDUs that it is sending out its own port. The switch stops transmitting BPDUs on the port and marks it as a nondesignated port if the other switch has lower values.

In Figure 1-10, all ports on the root bridge (Switch B) are designated ports (noted by "DP"). The ports on Switch A connecting to Switch C and Switch D become designated ports, because they have a lower root path cost on each segment.

To prevent bridging loops during the time that STP needs to execute its algorithm, all ports start out in the blocking state. As soon as STP marks a port as either a root port or a designated port, the algorithm begins to transition that port to the forwarding state.

Classic (802.1D-1998) and rapid (802.1w/802.1D-2004) versions of STP both execute the same algorithm in the decision-making process (spanning-tree types are explained in more detail in the next section). However, in the transition of a port from the blocking (or discarding, in rapid spanning-tree terms) state to the forwarding state, there is a big difference between those two spanning-tree versions. Classic 802.1D STP takes 30 seconds to transition the port to forwarding. This is because STP keeps a port in listening state and then learning state for the forwarding timer. The default forwarding timer is 15 seconds. The rapid spanning-tree algorithm can leverage additional mechanisms to transition the port to forwarding in less than a second.

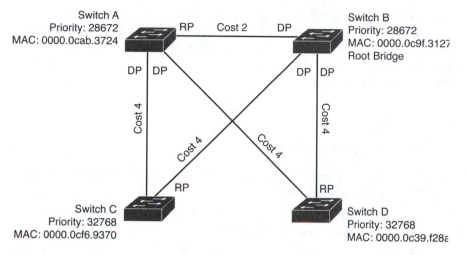

Figure 1-10   *Designated Port Selection*

Although it seems that STP executes steps in a coordinated, sequential manner, that is not actually the case. If you look back at the description of each step in the process, you see that each switch goes through these steps in parallel and that it might adapt its selection of root bridge, root ports, and designated ports as new BPDUs are received. As the BPDUs are propagated through the network, all switches eventually have a consistent view of the topology of the network. Figure 1-11 shows the operational state after STP has completed its calculations. The X denotes the blocking mode ports.

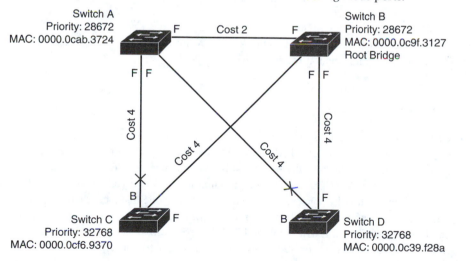

Figure 1-11   *STP Transitioned to a Fully Operational State*

When this stable state is reached, BPDUs are transmitted only by designated ports.

There are two loops in the sample topology, meaning that two ports should be in the blocking state to break both loops. The port on Switch C that is not directly connected to Switch B (root bridge) is blocked because it is a nondesignated port. The port on Switch D that is not directly connected to Switch B (root bridge) is also blocked because it is a nondesignated port.

STP Types Defined

There are several varieties of the Spanning Tree Protocol:

- The original specification of STP, defined in 802.1D, provides a loop-free topology in a network with redundant links.

- Common Spanning Tree (CST) assumes one spanning-tree instance for the entire bridged network, regardless of the number of VLANs.

- Per-VLAN Spanning Tree Plus (PVST+) is a Cisco enhancement of STP that provides a separate 802.1D spanning-tree instance for each VLAN configured in the network.

- Rapid STP (RSTP), or IEEE 802.1w, is an evolution of STP that provides faster convergence of STP.

- Rapid PVST+ is a Cisco enhancement of RSTP that uses PVST+. Rapid PVST+ provides a separate instance of 802.1w per VLAN.

Other than the original 802.1D implementation of Spanning Tree Protocol, all of the protocols mentioned operate over VLAN trunks.

> **Note**   When Cisco documentation or this book refers to implementing RSTP, it is referring to the Cisco RSTP implementation, Rapid PVST+.

These are characteristics of the various STP varieties:

- CST assumes one 802.1D spanning-tree instance for the entire bridged network, regardless of the number of VLANs. 802.1D was originally designed before the advent of VLANs, which is why there is only one instance of STP. Because there is only one instance, the CPU and memory requirements for this version are lower than for the other protocols. However, because there is only one instance, there is only one root bridge and one tree. Traffic for all VLANs flows over the same patch, which can lead to suboptimal traffic flows and inability to load-balance VLAN traffic. Because of the limitations of 802.1D, this version is slow to converge.

- PVST+ is a Cisco enhancement of STP that provides a separate 802.1D spanning-tree instance for each VLAN that is configured in the network. The separate instance supports the following features:

  - PortFast

  - UplinkFast

- BackboneFast

- BPDU guard

- BPDU filter

- Root guard

- Loop guard

These features are explained later in the chapter. Creating an instance for each VLAN increases the CPU and memory requirements but allows for per-VLAN root bridges. This design permits the STP tree to be optimized for the traffic of each VLAN. Convergence of this version is similar to the merging of 802.1D. However, convergence is per VLAN.

- RSTP, or IEEE 802.1w, is an evolution of STP that provides faster STP convergence. This version addresses many convergence issues, but because it still provides a single instance of STP, it does not address the suboptimal traffic flow issues. To support that faster convergence, the CPU usage and memory requirements of this version are slightly higher than those of CST but less than those of Rapid PVST+.

- Rapid PVST+ is a Cisco enhancement of RSTP that uses PVST+. It provides a separate instance of 802.1w per VLAN. The separate instance supports PortFast, BPDU guard, BPDU filter, root guard, and loop guard features. This version addresses both the convergence issues and the suboptimal traffic flow issues. However, this version has the largest CPU and memory requirements.

Note   The default spanning-tree mode for Cisco Catalyst switches is PVST, which is enabled on all ports. PVST+ has much slower convergence after a topology change than does Rapid PVST+.

Per-VLAN Spanning Tree Plus

PVST+ defines a spanning-tree protocol that has several instances running for each case in the network. Figure 1-12 shows an example topology of PVST+. Alternatively in PVST+, load sharing can be configured by having a different topology of root bridge and/or root ports. However, one STP instance per VLAN is kept, which uses more CPU cycles. Looking back at Figure 1-11, notice that there is a root bridge per VLAN and the forwarding/blocking ports are reversed per VLAN. This allows the more efficient use of links.

In describing PVST+, load balancing was mentioned. In a PVST+ environment, you can tune the spanning-tree parameters so that half the VLANs forward on each uplink trunk. The network must be correctly designed. The configuration defines a different root bridge for each half of the VLANs and/or different STP port values per VLAN.

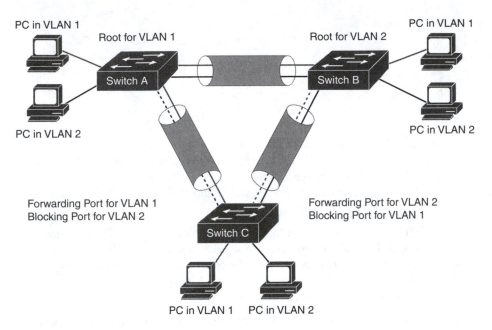

Figure 1-12 *Example PVST+ Network*

Spanning-tree operation requires that each switch have a unique BID. In the original 802.1D standard, the BID was composed of the bridge priority and the MAC address of the switch. PVST+ requires that a separate instance of spanning tree that is run for each VLAN, and the BID field must carry VID information. This functionality, as shown in Figure 1-13, is accomplished by using a portion of the Priority field as the extended system ID to carry the VLAN number.

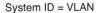

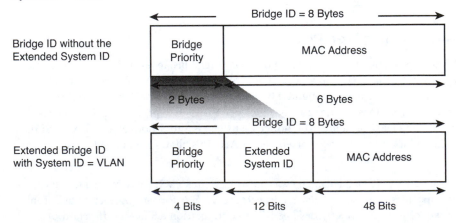

Figure 1-13 *Bridge ID Comparison Between 802.1D and PSVT+*

To accommodate the extended system ID, the original 802.1D 16-bit Bridge Priority field is split into two fields.

The BID includes the following fields:

■ **Bridge Priority:** A 4-bit field is still used to carry bridge priority. However, the priority is conveyed in discrete values in increments of 4096 rather than discrete values in increments of 1, because only the first 4 most-significant bits are available from the 16-bit field, even though it is still written as a 16-bit number. In other words, in binary: priority 0 = [0000|<sys-id-ext #>], priority 4096 = [0001|<sys-id-ext #>], and so on. Increments of 1 would be used if the complete 16-bit field is available. The default priority, in accordance with IEEE 802.1D, is 32,768, which is the midrange value.

■ **Extended System ID:** A 12-bit field carrying, in this case, the VID for PVST+.

■ **MAC Address:** A 6-byte field with the MAC address of a single switch.

By virtue of the MAC address, a BID is always unique. When the priority and extended system ID are prepended to the switch MAC address, each VLAN on the switch can be represented by a unique BID. Referring back to Figure 1-10, the VLAN 2 default BID would be 32770 (priority 32768 plus the extended system ID of 2).

The root bridge is elected based on the BID. Because the priority part of the BID is by default the same for all switches (32768), the root bridge will be the switch with the lowest MAC address. For load balancing between switches (e.g., you want one switch to be the root bridge for VLAN 1 and the other switch to be the root bridge for VLAN 2), modify the priority of the bridge. The easiest way to make a switch the root bridge for a VLAN is to use the **spanning-tree vlan** *vlan_number* **root primary** command. When you enter this command, the switch checks the switch priority of the root switches for each VLAN. Because of the extended system ID support, the switch sets its own priority for the specified VLAN to 24576 if this value causes the switch to become the root for the specified VLAN.

Although STP does not define a secondary root bridge, you can use the **spanning-tree vlan** *vlan_number* **root secondary** command. This modifies the priority so that in case of a failure of the root bridge, this switch becomes the root bridge. Adding the **secondary** option, causes the command to function similarly. However, it sets the bridge priority to one increment above the current root bridge. This switch would then have the next lowest BID in the network. The result is that it would become the root bridge if the existing root bridge fails.

In a production network, it is not uncommon for the candidate root bridge and the secondary root bridge to have the priorities manually set to 0 for the root and 1 for the secondary. Additional candidate root bridges may be defined as 2 or 3. This usually forces the designation of the root bridge in a deterministic manner.

Analyzing and Reviewing STP Topology and Operation

In many networks, the optimal STP topology is determined as part of the network design and then implemented through manipulation of STP priority and cost values. You might run into situations where STP was not considered in the design and implementation, or where it was considered only initially, before the network underwent significant growth and change. In such situations, it is important to know how to analyze the actual STP topology in the operational network.

In addition, a big part of troubleshooting consists of comparing the actual state of the network against the expected state of the network and spotting the differences to gather clues about the problem. You should be able to examine the switches and determine the actual topology, in addition to knowing what the spanning-tree topology is supposed to be. Figure 1-14 shows a flowchart with ideas on how to begin this process.

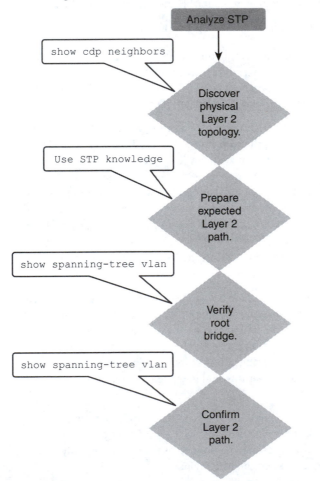

Figure 1-14   *Suggested Troubleshooting Flow for STP*

To analyze the STP topology, follow these steps:

Step 1.   Discover the physical Layer 2 topology. Use network documentation, if it exists, or use the **show cdp neighbors** command.

Step 2.   After you have discovered the physical topology, use your knowledge of STP to determine the expected Layer 2 path. To accomplish this, you will need to know which switch is the root bridge.

Step 3.   Use the **show spanning-tree vlan** command to determine which switch is the root bridge.

Step 4.   Use the **show spanning-tree vlan** command on all switches to find out which ports are in blocking state or forwarding state, thereby confirming your expected Layer 2 path.

Using the **show spanning-tree** command without specifying any additional options is a good way to get a quick overview of the status of STP for all VLANs that are defined on a switch. If you are interested only in a particular VLAN, you can limit the scope of this command by designating that specific VLAN as an option. Example 1-6 shows the output when running the command on VLAN 100.

Example 1-6   show spanning tree vlan *Command*

```
SwitchA# show spanning-tree vlan 100
VLAN0100
  Spanning tree enabled protocol ieee
  Root ID     Priority    28772
              Address     0000.0c9f.3127
              Cost 2
              Hello Time   2 sec  Max Age 20 sec  Forward Delay 15 sec

  Bridge ID  Priority 28772   (priority 28672 sys-id-ext 100)
             Address     0000.0cab.3724
             Hello Time   2 sec  Max Age 20 sec  Forward Delay 15 sec
             Aging Time   300 sec


Interface           Role  Sts  Cost       Prio.Nbr    Type
-------------------  ----  ---  ---------  ----------  -------------------------
Gi3/1               Desg  FWD  4          128.72      P2p
Gi3/2               Desg  FWD  4          128.80      P2p
Te9/1               Root  FWD  2          128.88      P2p
```

Use the **show spanning-tree vlan** *vlan_id* command to get STP information for a particular VLAN. This command allows you to obtain information about the role and status of each port on the switch. The example output on Switch A (root bridge) shows all three ports in the forwarding state (FWD) and the role of the three ports as either designated ports or root ports. Any ports being blocked have status BLK in the output.

The output also gives information about the BID of the local switch and the root ID, which is, in fact, the BID of the root bridge.

Examining Spanning-Tree Failures

With many protocols, a malfunction only means that you lose the functionality that the protocol was providing. For example, if Open Shortest Path First (OSPF) is malfunctioning on one of your routers, you might lose connectivity to networks that are reachable via that router, but it would generally not affect the rest of your OSPF network. If you still have some way to connect to that router, you can perform your troubleshooting routines to diagnose and fix the problem.

With STP, there are two types of failure. The first is similar to the OSPF problem: STP might erroneously decide to block ports that should have gone into the forwarding state. You might lose connectivity for traffic that would normally pass through this switch, but the rest of the network is unaffected, and you can troubleshoot the switch as long as you still have a way to access it. The second type of failure is much more disruptive. It happens when STP erroneously decides to move one or more ports into the forwarding state.

Frames that have a destination address recorded in the MAC address table of the switches are simply forwarded to the port that is associated with the MAC address and do not enter a loop. However, any frame that is flooded by a switch—broadcasts, multicasts, and unicasts with an unknown destination MAC address—enters a loop. Figure 1-15 displays a bridge loop failure.

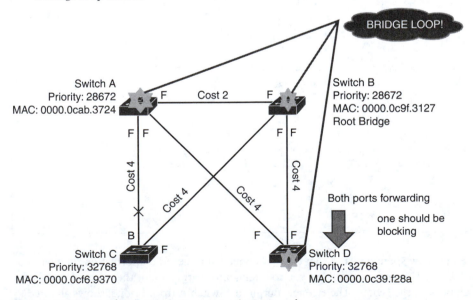

Figure 1-15 *Bridging Loop Occurs in the Network*

What are the consequences and corresponding symptoms of STP failure?

- The load on all links in the switched LAN quickly starts to increase as more and more frames enter the loop. This problem is not limited to the links that form the loop but also affects any other links in the switched domain, because the frames are flooded on all links. When the spanning-tree failure is limited to a single VLAN, only links in that VLAN are affected. Switches and trunks that do not carry that VLAN operate normally.

- If the spanning-tree failure has caused more than one bridging loop to exist, traffic increases exponentially. This is because frames not only start to circle but also begin to duplicate. This problem happens because, with multiple loops, there are switches that receive a frame on a port and then flood it out on multiple ports, which essentially creates a copy of the frame every time a switch forwards it.

- The switches experience very frequent MAC address table changes. This problem occurs because frames usually start to loop in both directions. This causes a switch to see a frame with a certain source MAC address coming in on a port. Then it identifies a frame with the same source MAC address coming in on a different port just a fraction of a second later.

- Because of the combination of very high load on all links and the switch CPUs running at maximum load, these devices typically become unreachable, making it nearly impossible to diagnose the problem while it is happening.

A viable approach is to take over the role of the failing spanning tree by manually removing redundant links in the switched network, either physically or through configuration (if that is still possible), until all loops are eliminated from the topology. When the loops are broken, the traffic and CPU loads should quickly drop to normal levels, and you should regain connectivity to your devices. The following example output from **show processes cpu** demonstrates a growing CPU load potentially from a bridging loop:

```
Switch# show processes cpu
CPU utilization for five seconds: 98%/10%; one minute: 96%; five minutes: 96%
PID  Runtime(ms)  Invoked  uSecs   5Sec   1Min  5Min TTY Process
<Output Omitted>
55       2050     959972    3791   32.63% 30.03% 17.35%   0 Spanning Tree
<Output Omitted>
```

Although this intervention restores connectivity to the network, you cannot consider it the end of your troubleshooting process. You have removed all repetition from your switched network, but you need to restore the redundant links.

Of course, if the underlying cause of the spanning-tree failure has not been fixed, chances are that restoring the redundant links will trigger a new broadcast storm. Before you restore the redundant links, spend sufficient time investigating what happened the moment that the broadcast storm began. When you eventually start restoring the redundant links, carefully monitor the network and have an emergency plan to fall back on if you see a new broadcast storm developing.

STP Features: PortFast, BPDU Guard, Root Guard, UplinkFast, and BackboneFast

PortFast is a Cisco technology. When a switch port that is configured with PortFast is configured as an access port, that port transitions from the blocking state to the forwarding state immediately, bypassing the typical STP listening and learning states. You can use PortFast on access ports that are connected to a single workstation or to a server to allow those devices to connect to the network immediately rather than waiting for STP to converge.

In a valid PortFast configuration, BPDUs should never be received, because that would indicate that another bridge or switch is connected to the port, potentially causing a spanning-tree loop. Cisco switches support to a feature called BPDU guard. When it is enabled, BPDU guard puts the port in an error-disabled state (effectively shut down) on receipt of a BPDU.

Note   Because the purpose of PortFast is to minimize the time that access ports connecting to user equipment and servers must wait for spanning tree to converge, it should be used only on access ports. If you enable PortFast on a port connecting to another switch, you risk creating a spanning-tree loop. The only exception is when a trunk connects to a non-switch device, typically a server.

Root guard is a Cisco proprietary technology. BPDU guard and root guard are similar, but their impact is different. BPDU guard disables the port upon BPDU reception if PortFast is enabled on the port. The disablement effectively denies devices behind such ports from participation in STP. You must manually reenable the port that is put into errdisable state (using **shutdown** and **no shutdown** commands) or configure **errdisable-timeout**.

Root guard allows the device to participate in STP as long as a port attached to the device with root guard does not attempt to seize the root bridge role. If root guard blocks the port, subsequent recovery is automatic. Recovery occurs as soon as the offending device ceases to send BPDU packets indicating superiority.

There can be a unidirectional link failure between two bridges in a network. Because of this, one bridge does not receive the BPDUs from the root bridge. With such a failure, the root switch receives frames that other switches send, but the other switches do not receive the BPDUs that the root switch sends. This can lead to an STP loop. Because the other switches do not receive any BPDUs from the root, these switches believe that they are the root and start to send BPDUs.

When the real root bridge starts to receive BPDUs, the root discards the BPDUs because they are not superior. The root bridge does not change. Therefore, root guard does not help to resolve this issue. The UniDirectional Link Detection (UDLD) and loop guard features address this issue by detecting and disabling down unidirectional links.

BPDU guard and PortFast can be enabled globally or on a specific interface. Root guard can only be enabled on a specific interface.

To configure PortFast globally, enter the command **spanning-tree portfast default** in global configuration mode. On a specific interface, enter **spanning-tree portfast** in interface configuration mode.

To enable BPDU guard globally, enter **spanning-tree portfast bpduguard default** in global configuration mode. To enable it on a specific interface, enter **spanning-tree bpduguard enable** on a port in interface configuration mode.

UplinkFast is another Cisco-proprietary fast-convergence option. It is configured on a switch with one or more blocked ports. The ports are grouped, and a secondary path to the root is calculated in the blocked ports. Upon a failure of a root port, the secondary port is immediately unblocked before STP recalculates.

BackboneFast is also a Cisco proprietary technology that is used for fast convergence. It allows a faster convergence from indirect link failures in the path to the root bridge. This means that a switch between the root and another switch fails. The switch's root port is still active, but it no longer has a path to the root.

BackboneFast must run on all switches, because it sends out proprietary frames called Root Link Query (RLQ) BPDUs. These are sent out ports that receive BPDUs. The switch then uses the RLQs to determine alternate paths to the root, so that if the root becomes unreachable through an intermediate switch, it can start forwarding in an alternate path, rather than waiting for STP to recalculate.

Note   There is an alternative to STP for avoiding topology loops: Transparent Interconnection of Lots of Links (TRILL). TRILL is beyond the scope of the CCNA and this text. For more information, see the Internet Protocol Journal article "Introduction to TRILL" (by Radia Perlman and Donald Eastlake) at http://www.cisco.com/web/about/ac123/ac147/archived_issues/ipj_14-3/143_trill.html.

Improving Redundancy and Increasing Bandwidth with EtherChannel

In hierarchical network design, some links between access and distribution switches may be heavily utilized as well as oversubscribed. The speed of these links can be increased, but only to a certain degree. EtherChannel is a technology that allows you to circumvent this restriction by creating logical links made up of several physical links.

Figure 1-16 shows a sample network topology with EtherChannel. The ovals represent links logically bonded together with EtherChannel. STP recognizes the EtherChannel links as a single port. The X marks the EtherChannel placed in blocking mode.

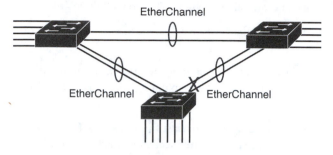

Figure 1-16 *Network Topology with EtherChannel*

EtherChannel is a technology that was originally developed by Cisco as a LAN switch-to-switch technique of grouping Fast Ethernet or Gigabit Ethernet ports into one logical channel. The ports in a channel must be of the same type (for example, Fast Ethernet, Gigabit Ethernet, or 10-Gigabit Ethernet).

This technology has many benefits, such as:

■ Most configuration tasks can be done on the EtherChannel interface instead of on each individual port, ensuring configuration consistency throughout the links.

■ It relies on the existing switch ports. There is no need to upgrade the link to a faster and more expensive connection to increase bandwidth.

■ Load balancing is possible between links that are part of the same EtherChannel. Depending on the hardware platform, you can implement one or several methods across the physical links, such as source MAC address-to-destination MAC address load balancing or source IP address-to-destination IP address load balancing.

■ EtherChannel creates an aggregation that is recognized as one logical link. When several EtherChannel bundles exist between two switches, STP may block one of the bundles to prevent redundant links. When STP stops one of the redundant links, it prevents one EtherChannel, thus blocking all the ports belonging to that EtherChannel link. Where there is only one EtherChannel link, all physical links in the EtherChannel are active because STP sees only one (logical) link.

■ EtherChannel provides redundancy. The overall link is seen as one logical connection, the loss of one physical link does not create a change in the topology. A spanning-tree recalculation does not need to take place. As long as at least one physical link is present, the EtherChannel is functional, even if its overall throughput decreases.

EtherChannel can be implemented by grouping from two to eight physical links into a logical EtherChannel link. You cannot mix interface types (for example, Fast Ethernet and Gigabit Ethernet) within a single EtherChannel. Keep in mind that the point of

EtherChannel is to increase the speed between switches. This concept was extended as the EtherChannel technology became more popular, and some hardware devices other than switches support link aggregation into an EtherChannel link. In any case, EtherChannel creates a one-to-one relationship. You can create an EtherChannel link between two switches or between an EtherChannel-enabled server and a switch, but you cannot send traffic to two different switches through the same EtherChannel link. One EtherChannel link always connects two devices only. The exception is to switch clustering technologies, such as Multichassis EtherChannel (MEC) with virtual switching system (VSS) or virtual port channel (vPC).

vPC and MEC/VSS are technologies that allow two switches to be configured to appear as a logical, single switch. vPC and VSS are beyond the scope of the CCNA.

Note   For more information on vPC, VSS, and MEC, see *Cisco Catalyst 6500 VSS and Cisco Nexus 7000 vPC Interoperability and Best Practices* at: http://www.cisco.com/en/US/prod/collateral/switches/ps5718/ps708/white_paper_c11_589890.html.

When using EtherChannel, the individual EtherChannel group member port configuration must be consistent on both devices. If the physical ports of one side are configured as trunks, the physical ports of the other side must also be designed as trunks. Each EtherChannel has a logical port channel interface. A configuration applied to the port channel interface affects all physical interfaces that are assigned to that interface.

EtherChannel Protocols

This section examines two EtherChannel protocols for the creation of EtherChannel groups: Port Aggregation Protocol (PAgP), which is a Cisco proprietary protocol, and the Link Aggregation Control Protocol (LACP), which is a standards-based protocol.

Port Aggregation Protocol

PAgP is a Cisco proprietary protocol that aids in the automatic creation of EtherChannel links. When an EtherChannel link is configured using PAgP, PAgP packets are sent between EtherChannel-capable ports to negotiate the forming of a channel. When PAgP identifies matched Ethernet links, it groups the links into an EtherChannel. The EtherChannel is then added to the spanning tree as a single bridge port.

When enabled, PAgP also manages the EtherChannel. PAgP packets are sent every 30 seconds. They check for configuration consistency and manage link additions and failures between two switches. PAgP ensures that when an EtherChannel is created, all ports have the same type of configuration. In EtherChannel, it is mandatory that all ports have the same speed, duplex setting, and VLAN information. Any port modification after the creation of the channel changes all the other channel ports.

Table 1-4 provides the PAgP available port settings and the effect of the settings. The table is a matrix of the settings of each side of the link. For example, the first row indicates that when each side is set to "on," each link has PAgP on. The resulting Yes indicates that a channel will be established.

Table 1-4   *PAgP SModes*

Channel Establishment	On	Desirable	Auto
On	Yes	No	No
Desirable	No	Yes	Yes
Auto	No	Yes	No

The PAgP modes are as follows:

- **Auto:** Places an interface in a passive negotiating state in which the interface responds to the PAgP packets that it receives but does not initiate PAgP negotiation.

- **Desirable:** Places an interface in an active negotiating state in which the interface initiates negotiations with other interfaces by sending PAgP packets.

- **On:** Forces the interface to channel without PAgP. Interfaces configured in the on mode do not exchange PAgP packets.

The modes must be compatible on each side. If you configure one side to be in auto mode, it is placed in a passive state, waiting for the other side to initiate the EtherChannel negotiation. If the other side is also set to auto, the negotiation never starts and the EtherChannel does not form. If you disable all modes by using the **no** command, or if no mode is configured, then the interface is placed in the off mode and EtherChannel is disabled.

Note that the on mode manually places the interface in an EtherChannel, without any negotiation. It works only if the other side is also set to on. If the other side is set to negotiate parameters through PAgP, no EtherChannel will form, because the side that is set to on mode will not negotiate.

Link Aggregation Control Protocol

LACP is part of an IEEE specification (802.3ad) that allows several physical ports to be bundled to form a single logical channel. LACP permits a switch to negotiate an automatic bundle by sending LACP packets to the peer. It performs a function similar to PAgP with Cisco EtherChannel. Because LACP is an IEEE standard, you can use it to facilitate EtherChannels in multivendor environments. On Cisco devices, both protocols are supported.

PAgP helps create the EtherChannel link by detecting the configuration of each side and confirming that they are compatible so that the EtherChannel link can be enabled when needed.

LACP has three modes of operation to build a channel:

- **LACP passive:** Places a port in a passive negotiating state. In this state, the port responds to the LACP packets that it receives but does not initiate LACP packet negotiation.

- **LACP active:** Places a port in an active negotiating state. In this state, the port initiates negotiations with other ports by sending LACP packets.

- **LACP on:** Forces the interface to channel without LACP. Interfaces configured in the on mode do not exchange LACP packets.

Similar to Table 1-4 for PAgP, Table 1-5 shows how the LACP settings on both links effect channel establishment.

Table 1-5   *LACP Modes*

Channel Establishment	On	Active	Passive
On	Yes	No	No
Active	No	Yes	Yes
Passive	No	Yes	No

Configuring EtherChannel

Follow these guidelines and observe the restrictions when configuring EtherChannel interfaces:

- **EtherChannel support:** All Ethernet interfaces on all modules support EtherChannel (maximum of eight interfaces). It is not required that interfaces be physically contiguous or on the same module.

- **Speed and duplex:** Configure all interfaces in an EtherChannel to operate at the same speed and in the same duplex mode.

- **VLAN match:** All interfaces in the EtherChannel bundle must be assigned to the same VLAN or be configured as a trunk.

- **Range of VLANs:** An EtherChannel supports the same allowed range of VLANs on all the interfaces in a trunking Layer 2 EtherChannel.

If you have to change these settings, configure them in EtherChannel interface configuration mode. After you configure the EtherChannel interface, any configuration that you apply to the port channel interface affects individual interfaces as well. The opposite does not apply and will cause interface incompatibility in the EtherChannel.

Example 1-7 provides the configuration of a two-port EtherChannel. It also shows the design of the EtherChannel as a VLAN trunk. One point to note is that an EtherChannel can be configured as an access port, as a trunk port, or as both. In this example, it is configured as both. When configured as both, it will fall back to the access port configuration if LACP or PAgP fails to form a channel.

Example 1-7   *Configuring EtherChannel*

```
HQ#(config)# interface range FastEthernet0/1 - 2
HQ#(config-if)# channel-group 1 mode active
HQ#(config-if)# interface port-channel 1
HQ#(config-if)# switchport mode trunk
HQ#(config-if)# switchport trunk allowed vlan 1,2,20
```

As shown in Example 1-7, configuring EtherChannel is a two-step process. Also, Example 1-7 shows that FastEthernet0/1 and FastEthernet0/2 are bundled into EtherChannel interface port channel 1. To change Layer 2 settings on the EtherChannel interface, enter EtherChannel interface configuration mode using the **interface port-channel** command, followed by the interface identifier. In the example, the EtherChannel is configured as a trunk interface with allowed VLANs as specified.

Checking EtherChannel Operation

You can use one of several commands to verify an EtherChannel configuration. First, use the **show interface port-channel** command to display the general status of the EtherChannel interface. In Example 1-8, the Port-channel1 interface is up.

Example 1-8   *Verifying Interface Status*

```
HQ# show interface port-channel1
Port-channel1 is up, line protocol is up (connected)
  Hardware is EtherChannel, address is 000f.34f9.9182 (bia
000f.34f9.9182)   MTU 1500 bytes, BW 200000 Kbit, DLY 100 usec,
     reliability 255/255, txload 1/255, rxload 1/255   Encapsulation ARPA, loopback
not set
<output omitted>
```

When several port channel interfaces are configured on the same device, use the **show etherchannel summary** command, as demonstrated in Example 1-9, to simply display one line of information per port channel. In this example, the switch has one EtherChannel configured; group 1 uses LACP. The interface bundle consists of the FastEthernet0/1 and FastEthernet0/2 interfaces. You can see that the group is Layer 2 EtherChannel and that it is in use (indicated by the letters SU next to the port channel number).

Example 1-9 *One-Line Summary per Channel Group*

```
HQ# show etherchannel summary
Flags:      D    - down            P - bundled in port-channel
                  I - stand-alone    s - suspended
                  H - Hot-standby  (LACP only)
                  R - Layer3          S - Layer2
                  U - in use              f - failed to allocate aggregator
                  M - not in use, minimum links not met
                  u - unsuitable for bundling
                  w - waiting to be aggregated
                  d - default port
Number of channel-groups in use: 1
Number of aggregators:                    1
Group Port-channel Protocol Ports
--------+-------------+-----------+-----------------------------------------
1          Po1(SU)      LACP Fa0/1(P) Fa0/2(P)
```

Use the **show etherchannel port-channel** command to display information about a specific port channel interface. In Example 1-10, the Port-channel1 interface consists of two physical interfaces, FastEthernet0/1 and FastEthernet0/2. It uses LACP in active mode. It is properly connected to another switch with a compatible configuration. This is why the port channel is said to be in use.

Example 1-10 *Display of Port Channel Information*

```
HQ# show etherchannel port-channel
                                Channel-group listing:
                                ----------------------------

Group: 1
------------
                                Port-channels in the group:
                                ----------------------------------
port-channel:     Po1    (Primary Aggregator)
----------------
Age of the Port-channel   = 4d:01h:29m:00s
<output omitted>
  Protocol            =    LACP
  <output omitted>
Ports in the Port-channel:
Index Load Port   EC state         No of bits
------+------+------+------------------+-----------
0        55 Fa0/1  Active            4
1        45 Fa0/2  Active            4
Time since last port bundled:        0d:00h:00m: 18s     Fa0/2
Time since last port Un-bundled: 0d:00h:00m:32s      Fa0/2
```

Understanding Default Gateway Redundancy

This section explains how to solve routing problems in a local network with a redundant default gateway topology. One solution to these problems is explained through the router redundancy process. This section identifies Hot-Standby Routing Protocol (HSRP), Virtual Router Redundancy Protocol (VRRP), and Gateway Load Balancing Protocol (GLBP) as Layer 3 redundancy protocols.

If TCP/IP devices require the capability to communicate to networks other than the local subnet the device is attached to, a route to the remote network is needed. A default gateway removes the device's need to hold a gateway for each route it needs to take. If the default gateway is no longer reachable, the device will not be able to communicate past its local subnet.

With the type of router redundancy that is shown in Figure 1-17, a set of routers works together to present the illusion of a single router to the hosts on the LAN by sharing an IP (Layer 3) address and a MAC (Layer 2) address. Two or more routers can act as a single "virtual" router.

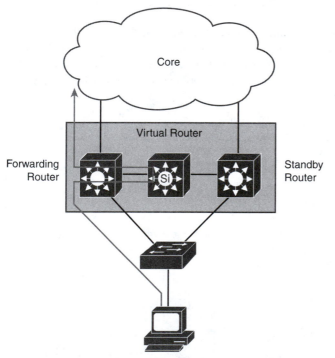

Figure 1-17 *Redundancy Through Virtual Routers*

The IP address of the virtual router is configured as the default gateway for the workstations on a specific IP segment. When frames are sent from the workstation to the default gateway, the workstation uses ARP to resolve the MAC address that is associated with the IP address of the default gateway. The ARP resolution returns the MAC address of the virtual router. Frames that are sent to the MAC address of the virtual router can then be physically processed by any active or standby router that is part of that virtual router group.

A protocol is used to identify two or more routers as the devices that are responsible for processing frames that are sent to the MAC or IP address of a single virtual router. Host devices send traffic to the address of the virtual router. The physical router that forwards this traffic is transparent to the end stations.

The redundancy protocol provides the mechanism to determine which router should take the active role in forwarding traffic and when that role must be taken over by a standby router. The transition from one forwarding router to another is transparent to the end devices.

These are the steps that take place when a router fails:

Step 1.   The standby router stops seeing hello messages from the forwarding router.

Step 2.   The standby router assumes the role of the forwarding router.

Step 3.   Because the new forwarding router assumes both the IP and MAC addresses of the virtual router, the end stations do not recognize a disruption in service.

Hot Standby Router Protocol

HSRP defines a standby group of routers, with one router designated as the active router. HSRP provides gateway redundancy by sharing IP and MAC addresses between redundant gateways. The protocol consists of virtual MAC and IP addresses that are shared between two routers that belong to the same HSRP group. This section examines HSRP and how to validate its operation.

HSRP terms include the following:

- **Active router:** The current device that acts as the virtual router and provides service.

- **Standby router:** The primary backup router. The function of the HSRP standby router is to monitor the operational status of the HSRP group and to quickly go into service if the active router becomes inoperable.

- **Standby group:** The set of routers participating in HSRP that jointly emulates a virtual router.

Note   HSRP is a Cisco proprietary protocol, and VRRP is a standard protocol. Beyond that, the functional differences between HSRP and VRRP are very slight, such as the IOS configuration and **show** commands.

To display HSRP information, use the **show standby** command in privileged EXEC mode. Example 1-11 displays the HSRP state on the R1 router. The IP of the virtual router is 10.1.1.100, and R1 is actively routing traffic.

Example 1-11 *Viewing the HSRP State*

```
R1# show standby
Vlan1 - Group 1
  State is Active
    2 state changes, last state change 00:00:10
  Virtual IP address is 10.1.1.100
  Active virtual MAC address is 0000.0c07.ac01
      Local virtual MAC address is 0000.0c07.ac01 (v1 default)
  Hello time 3 sec, hold time 10 sec
    Next hello sent in 2.800 secs
  Preemption disabled
Active router is local
Standby router is unknown
Priority 100 (default 100)
  Group name is "hsrp-Vl1-1" (default)
```

HSRP Interface Tracking

Interface tracking enables the priority of a standby group router to be automatically adjusted, based on the availability of the router interfaces. When a tracked interface becomes unavailable, the HSRP tracking feature ensures that a router with an unavailable key interface relinquishes the active router role.

Figure 1-18 shows the HSRP group tracking the uplink interface. If the active router fails, the standby router becomes the active device. In Figure 1-18, assume the router on the right is configured with a higher priority and, because of that, is handling the traffic toward the core. As soon as the uplink interface on the right of the router fails, the host is unable to reach the core network. HSRP makes the router on the left the active router.

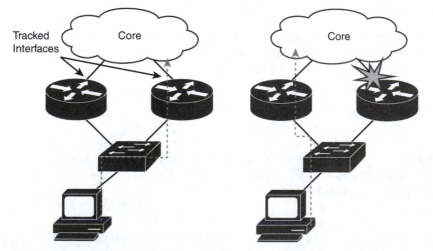

Figure 1-18 *HSRP Interface Tracking*

HSRP Load Balancing

Routers can simultaneously provide redundant backup and perform load sharing across different subnets. In the case of Figure 1-19, the active HSRP router for each VLAN is not on the same router. Running HSRP over trunks allows users to configure redundancy among multiple routers.

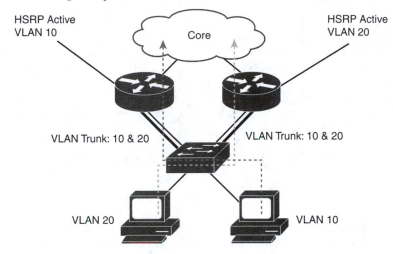

Figure 1-19   *HSRP Load Balancing*

By configuring HSRP over VLAN trunks, you can eliminate situations in which a single point of failure causes traffic interruption. This feature inherently provides some improvement in overall networking resilience by providing load-balancing and redundancy capabilities between subnets and VLANs.

HSRP in Service Deployments

A router can be utilized for more than just a packet forwarder. Historically, Cisco routers were only employed as data networking packet forwarders. As time went on, they provided additional network services. This section examines a VoIP solution that does not need to route packets to provide service.

> **Note** This is not a VoIP discussion; rather, it is another example usage of HSRP. Focus on the application of the router, not the VoIP aspect.

HSRP can also be used in "one-armed" deployment (only one network interface is connected to the network) of routers as service engines. The router provides network services only.

An example would be the use of HSRP for the redundancy of a VoIP application Cisco Unified Border Element (CUBE), which terminates VoIP Session Initiation Protocol (SIP) trunks. Figure 1-20 shows how HSRP is used to create redundancy in a CUBE environment, where CUBE is "one-armed" and provides this service without routing packets.

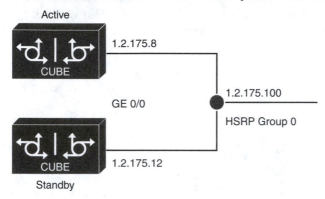

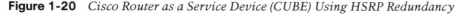

Figure 1-20   *Cisco Router as a Service Device (CUBE) Using HSRP Redundancy*

HSRP in IPv6

HSRP can be used in IPv6 environments as well. However, the implementation and deployment is slightly different because IPv6 addressing and interface configuration is slightly different from IPv4 addressing.

An HSRP IPv6 group has a virtual MAC address that is derived from the HSRP group number and a virtual IPv6 link-local address that is, by default, derived from the HSRP virtual MAC address. Periodic router advertisements (RA) are sent from the HSRP virtual IPv6 link-local address when the HSRP group is active. These RAs stop after a final RA is sent when the group leaves the active state.

> **Note**   For more information on HSRP in IPv6, see http://www.cisco.com/en/US/tech/
> tk648/tk362/technologies_configuration_example09186a0080b9119e.shtml.

Gateway Load-Balancing Protocol

Although HSRP and VRRP provide gateway resiliency, for the standby members of the redundancy group, the upstream bandwidth is not used while the device is in standby mode. Only the active router in HSRP and VRRP groups forwards traffic for the virtual MAC address. Resources that are associated with the standby router are not fully utilized. You can accomplish some load balancing with these protocols by creating multiple groups and assigning various default gateways, but this configuration creates an administrative burden and is considered "static load balancing." So if a single VLAN has imbalance of traffic, it requires manual monitoring and intervention if the imbalance must be remediated. GLBP helps to avoid this.

GLBP is a Cisco proprietary solution that allows automatic selection and simultaneous use of multiple available gateways in addition to automatic failover between those gateways. Multiple routers share the load of frames that, from a client perspective, are sent to a single default gateway address.

With GLBP, you can fully utilize resources without the administrative burden of configuring multiple groups and managing multiple default gateway configurations.

To display GLBP information, use the **show glbp** command in privileged EXEC mode, as shown in Example 1-12.

Example 1-12   *Output from the* **show glbp** *Command*

```
HQ# show glbp
FastEthernet0/1 - Group 1
  State is Active
    1 state change, last state change 00:02:34
  Virtual IP address is 192.168.2.100
  <output omitted>
Active is local
Standby is 192.168.2.2, priority 100 (expires in 8.640 sec)
Priority 100 (default)
Weighting 100 (default 100), thresholds: lower 1, upper 100
Load balancing: round-robin
  Group members:
    001e.7aa3.5e71 (192.168.2.1) local
    001e.7aa3.5f31 (192.168.2.2)
There are 2 forwarders (1 active)
  Forwarder 1
    State is Active
      1 state change, last state change 00:02:23
    MAC address is 0007.b400.0101 (default)
    Owner ID is 001e.7aa3.5e71
    Redirection enabled
    Preemption enabled, min delay 30 sec
    Active is local, weighting 100
Forwarder 2
    State is Listen
  <output omitted>
```

In Example 1-12, the output confirms that the virtual router's IP address is 192.168.2.100 and that one router is in Active state and the other router is in Listen state. "Active" indicates that this router is responsible for responding to ARP requests for the virtual IP address. "Listen" indicates that the router is receiving hello packets and is ready to be activated if there is a failure in the active router.

Chapter Summary

VLANs are an important Layer 2 concept and component of internetworking. They extend the initial concept of a LAN to create location-independent LAN segments. VLANs are interconnected by VLAN trunks, which are device-to-device connections using normal switch ports and cabling. The ports for VLAN trunks differ in configuration from an access port because they use a trunking protocol, 802.1Q. Trunking allows the carrying of the traffic of multiple VLANs simultaneously while maintaining Layer 2 separation between each VLAN.

Redundancy in LANs is necessary to create a stable and reliable network. It is created by using a loop-avoidance protocol. Spanning Tree Protocol (STP) is a loop-avoidance mechanism. STP has many variants, each of which has unique attributes that dictate how it operates and converges. These include Cisco proprietary extensions.

EtherChannel is a protocol that allows the Layer 2 binding, through a port channel, of multiple interfaces of the same speed and type to create higher aggregate bandwidth through load balancing. EtherChannel also creates redundancy. When one or more of the underlying links fails, the remaining operational links continue to forward traffic. EtherChannel links appear as a single logical interface. This means that they can be access ports or trunk ports. They also appear as a single link to both Layer 3 and STP.

Default gateway and router redundancy allows end devices to maintain connectivity in the case of a router failure. This is important because end devices generally do not have any entries in the routing table other than the default gateway. Any packets that have a destination beyond the local subnet need to traverse the default gateway. Three protocols exist for creating router redundancy. HSRP is a Cisco proprietary protocol that creates an active/standby backup for the default gateway. HSRP offers a unique feature that the other redundancy protocols do not support. HSRP also allows non-packet-forwarding router features to be redundant (such as VoIP features). VRRP is an industry-standard protocol that is very similar to HSRP. GLBP is an active/active default gateway protocol that allows load balancing between devices.

Review Questions

Use the questions here to review what you learned in this chapter. The correct answers are located in Appendix A, "Answers to Chapter Review Questions."

1. Which feature is required for multiple VLANs to span multiple switches? (Source: "Understanding and Troubleshooting VLANs and VLAN Trunking")

   a. A trunk to connect the switches

   b. A router to connect the switches

   c. A bridge to connect the switches

   d. A VLAN configured between the switches

2. What are two reasons for using 802.1Q? (Choose two.) (Source: "Understanding and Troubleshooting VLANs and VLAN Trunking")

   a. To allow switches to share a trunk link with nontrunking clients
   b. To allow clients to see the 802.1Q header
   c. To provide inter-VLAN communication over a bridge
   d. To load-balance traffic between parallel links using STP
   e. To provide trunking between Cisco switches and other vendor switches

3. Which term commonly describes the endless flooding or looping of frames? (Source: "Building Redundant Switch Topologies")

   a. Flood storm
   b. Loop overload
   c. Broadcast storm
   d. Broadcast overload

4. How does STP provide a loop-free network? (Source: Introducing LANs)

   a. By placing all ports in the blocking state
   b. By placing all bridges in the blocking state
   c. By placing some ports in the blocking state
   d. By placing some bridges in the blocking state

5. Which port marks the lowest-cost path from the non-root bridge to the root bridge? (Source: Troubleshooting Layer 2 Loops and STP)

   a. Root
   b. Blocking
   c. Designated
   d. Nondesignated

6. Which configuration will actually form an EtherChannel link? (Source: "Improving Redundancy and Increasing Bandwidth with EtherChannel")

   a. Switch A: Auto; Switch B: Auto
   b. Switch A: Desirable; Switch B: Active
   c. Switch A: On; Switch B: On
   d. Switch A: Passive; Switch B: On

7. Which two protocol choices do you have when you are implementing an EtherChannel bundle? (Choose two.) (Source: "Improving Redundancy and Increasing Bandwidth with EtherChannel")

   a. PAgP
   b. PAgD
   c. LACP
   d. LAPD

8. How does STP select the designated port on a segment? (Source: Troubleshooting Layer 2 Loops and STP)

   a. Highest-cost path to the closest non-root bridge

   b. Lowest-cost path to the closest non-root bridge

   c. Lowest-cost path to the root bridge

   d. Highest-cost path to the root bridge

9. With STP, what is the state of a nondesignated port? (Source: Troubleshooting Layer 2 Loops and STP)

   a. Forwarding

   b. Blocking

   c. Listening

   d. Learning

10. What is the major difference between VRRP and HSRP? (Source: "Understanding Layer 3 Redundancy")

   a. HSRP is a standard protocol, while VRRP is Cisco proprietary.

   b. HSRP is configured at the global level, while VRRP is configured at the interface level.

   c. VRRP offers Layer 2 first-hop redundancy, while HSRP offers Layer 3 first-hop redundancy.

   d. VRRP is a standard protocol, while HSRP is Cisco proprietary.

11. What is a characteristic of STP PortFast? (Source: "STP Features: PortFast, BPDU Guard, Root Guard, UplinkFast, and BackboneFast")

   a. Can't be enabled on any port of the root bridge

   b. Must be enabled on a port-by-port basis

   c. It is a Cisco proprietary technology

   d. Can only be enabled with BPDU guard

12. Which of the following is true about EtherChannel? (Source: "EtherChannel Protocols")

   a. Speed of ports does not have to be the same

   b. Duplex of ports does not have to be the same

   c. Can only be enabled on trunk ports

   d. Can use PAgP or LACP to form channels

13. What does BPDU guard do? (Source: "STP Features: PortFast, BPDU Guard, Root Guard, UplinkFast, and BackboneFast")

   a. If it receives a BPDU on a port with PortFast on, it disables PortFast.

   b. If it receives a BPDU on a port with PortFast on, it disables the port.

   c. If it receives a BPDU on a port with PortFast on, it puts the port in blocking mode.

   d. If it receives a BPDU on a port with PortFast on, it does nothing.

   e. If it receives a BPDU on a port with PortFast on, it changes the port to a root port.

14. Which is not a step in the spanning-tree algorithm? (Source: Spanning tree operation)

   a. Elect a root bridge

   b. Elect a secondary root bridge

   c. Elect a root port for each non-root switch

   d. Transition ports to blocking or forwarding state

15. True or False: HSRP requires a minimum of two interfaces to operate in the standby group. (Source: "HSRP in Service Deployments")

16. HSRP cannot be used in which configuration? (Source: "Understanding Layer 3 Redundancy")

   a. IPv6 deployments

   b. In a service deployment with only one interface

   c. Active-active load balancing

   d. Between two different router models

Chapter 2

Troubleshooting Basic Connectivity

This chapter includes the following sections:

- Troubleshooting IPv4 Basic Connectivity

- Troubleshooting IPv6 Network Connectivity

- A Last Note on Troubleshooting

- Chapter Summary

- Review Questions

Troubleshooting is standard practice for network engineers. The network is the core of the environment, with all points connecting at some spot. Understanding the components of networking is critical for troubleshooting. Sometimes solving a problem can be as simple as proving the network is *not* the problem. However, as is often said, "It is only simple if you know the answer."

This chapter examines connectivity troubleshooting in IPv4 and IPv6 environments. Important key concepts on problem isolation and other tips will be discussed. Virtualized computing environments will be explored. Various tools and other information from both host operating systems (such as Microsoft Windows and Mac-OS) will be explored as well.

Chapter Objectives

- Troubleshooting connectivity in an IPv4 and IPv6 environment

- Reviewing and isolating failures to proper source and OSI layer

- Understanding operating system and Cisco IOS tools and counters used for troubleshooting

Troubleshooting IPv4 Basic Connectivity

This section covers troubleshooting basic IPv4 connectivity and the tools that are employed. It includes information on basic Layer 2 and Layer 3 testing. Connectivity is examined from the router, switch, and end device perspectives.

Components of End-to-End IPv4 Troubleshooting

It is impossible to present a set of troubleshooting procedures that will solve all problems. The troubleshooting process can be guided by structured methods, but the exact steps that are taken at each point along the way cannot be prescribed because they depend on many different factors. Each network is unique, each problem is exclusive, and the skill set and experience of each engineer involved in a troubleshooting process are different.

Figure 2-1 is an example of a typical troubleshooting problem. The user on PC1 needs to access an application on the server. The desirable and suboptimal paths are outlined in Figure 2-1. Figure 2-1 is used in several examples in this section.

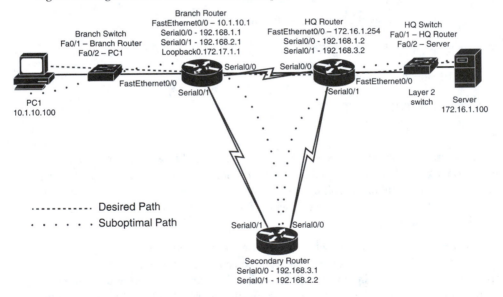

Figure 2-1   *Desirable Path vs. Suboptimal Path*

There are five distinct scenarios that can occur in Figure 2-1:

1. The packets take the desirable path and the application performs properly.

2. The packets take the suboptimal path and the application appears to function normally, but the users report performance issues.

3. The packets do not reach the server and the users can't access the application.

4. The packets take either path and reach the server, but the users can't access the application because the application is not working at all.

5. The packets reach the server using the desirable path, but the users report performance issues because the application is not working properly.

6. The users report performance problems. Packets are taking the suboptimal path (causing performance problems) *and* the application is experiencing performance problems.

As the network administrator, you may be called on to troubleshoot scenarios 2 through 6. Looking at scenarios 4 and 5, your initial reaction might be that neither is a network issue for you to fix. However, network administrators are commonly called upon to troubleshoot issues 4 and 5 to validate that it is not a "network" problem.

When connectivity fails or does not behave properly, you must begin a troubleshooting process. The tendency is to log into the first device and start diving in. However, you should first devise a good problem statement. Start by identifying the following:

■ What is the overall problem? Be sure to look at it from a functional level. The problem statement should not be "I can't ping the server." A good example would be: "The users in accounting can't process payroll checks."

■ What does the problem look like? What data is available? Example: A user sends the screenshot shown in Figure 2-2 to you.

■ What has the user done to try to circumvent the issue?

■ What are the affected component(s)?

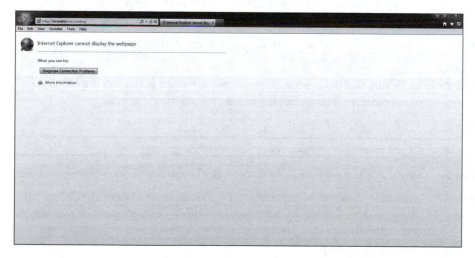

Figure 2-2 *User-Reported Error*

After you have formulated a good problem statement and have determined that you must troubleshoot, you need to begin looking into the end-to-end problem resolution. Figure 2-3 gives a suggested flowchart.

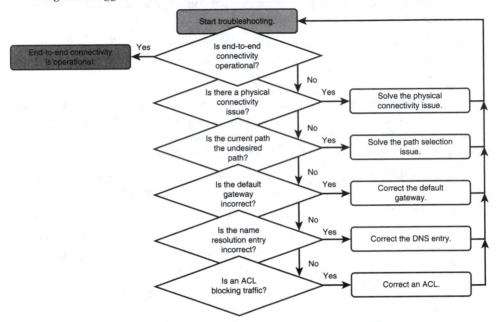

Figure 2-3   *A Sample Troubleshooting Process*

When there is no end-to-end connectivity, the suggested flowchart provides a starting point. The following sections examine each of the following steps:

Step 1.   If you have physical access to the cabling, check the cables to rule out a faulty cable or interface.

Step 2.   Make sure that devices are determining the correct path from the source to the destination. Manipulate the routing information if needed.

Step 3.   Verify that the default gateway is correct.

Step 4.   Check for proper Domain Name Server (DNS) settings.

Step 5.   Verify that there are no ACLs that are blocking traffic.

Step 6.   After every failed troubleshooting step, a solution should be provided to make the step successful. The outcome of this process is operational, end-to-end connectivity.

Verification of Connectivity

Ping is probably the most widely known connectivity-testing tool in networking and has been part of Cisco IOS Software from the beginning. The **ping** command is used for testing IP connectivity between hosts. It sends out requests for responses from a specified host address. The **ping** command uses a Layer 3 protocol that is a part of the TCP/IP suite called Internet Control Messaging Protocol (ICMP), and it employs the ICMP echo request and ICMP echo reply packets. If the host at the specified address receives the ICMP echo request, it responds with an ICMP echo reply packet.

Traceroute is a utility that allows observation of the path between two hosts. Use the **traceroute** Cisco IOS command or the **tracert** Windows command to observe the path between two hosts. The trace generates a list of hops that are successfully reached along the path. This list provides important verification and troubleshooting information. If the data reaches the destination, the trace lists the interface on every router in the path. If the data fails at some hop along the way, the address of the last router that responded to the trace is known. This address is an indication of where the problem is located or the security restrictions reside.

Note   Traceroute is not always enabled in all networks, for security purposes. Traceroute is represented as **tracert** on PCs and as **traceroute** on Linux/UNIX, Mac, and Cisco IOS Software.

First test for basic connectivity. Example 2-1 is based on the network shown previously in Figure 2-1. The example demonstrates the initial sample **ping** command from PC 1 to the default gateway. It is successful. Once the connectivity to the default gateway is verified, a **ping** runs to the server. It fails. Now run **ping** from the Branch router to the server. In Example 2-1, following the tests from the PC, a **ping** is run from the router.

Note   Devices sometimes show an 80 percent success rate in ping. The first ping will sometimes fail because the device needs to resolve the Layer 2 MAC address to the IP address. The first ping times out. This is accomplished by using the Address Resolution Protocol (ARP). ARP is discussed later in the section.

Example 2-1   *The ping Command in Microsoft Windows*

```
C:\windows\system32> ping 10.1.10.1
Pinging 10.1.10.1 with 32 bytes of data:
Reply from 10.1.10.1: bytes=32 time=8ms TTL=254
Reply from 10.1.10.1: bytes=32 time=1ms TTL=254
Reply from 10.1.10.1: bytes=32 time=1ms TTL=254
Reply from 10.1.10.1: bytes=32 time=1ms TTL=254
```

```
Ping statistics for 10.1.10.1:
    Packets: Sent = 4, Received = 4, Lost = 0 (0% loss),
Approximate round-trip times in milliseconds:
    Minimum = 1ms, Maximum = 8ms, Average = 2ms


C:\windows\system32> ping 172.16.1.100


Pinging 172.16.1.100 with 32 bytes of data:
Request timed out.
Request timed out.
Request timed out.
Request timed out.


Ping statistics for 172.16.1.100:
    Packets: Sent = 4, Received = 0, Lost = 4 (100% loss),
Branch# ping 172.16.1.100


Type escape sequence to abort.
Sending 5, 100-byte ICMP Echos to 172.16.1.100, timeout is 2 seconds:
.!!!!
Success rate is 80 percent (4/5), round-trip min/avg/max = 8/9/12 ms
```

Example 2-2 displays the **tracert** command in Windows executing a test from the PC to the server. This is followed by a test from the Branch router to the server.

Example 2-2   *Running a traceroute*

```
C:\windows\system32> tracert 172.16.1.100
Tracing route to 172.16.1.100 over a maximum of 30 hops
     1        1  ms        <1 ms        <1 ms    10.1.10.1
     2        1  ms        <1 ms        <1 ms    192.168.1.2
     3        1  ms        <1 ms        <1 ms    172.16.1.100
Trace complete.


Branch# traceroute 172.16.1.100


Type escape sequence to abort.
Tracing the route to 172.16.1.100


  1 10.1.10.1        0 msec 0 msec 0 msec
  2 192.168.1.2      0 msec *   0 msec
```

In Example 2-2, if the suboptimal path was taken in the trip, you would see the traceroute pass through the secondary router.

Cisco IOS Software also supports a concept of *extended* **ping** and *extended* **traceroute**. Entering more options on the Cisco IOS command line or via just typing the **ping** or **traceroute** command without options can access the extended mode. Example 2-3 shows an extended **ping** and then an extended **traceroute** to the server:

Example 2-3   *Extended ping*

```
Branch# ping
Protocol [ip]:
Target IP address: 172.16.1.100
Repeat count [5]:
Datagram size [100]:
Timeout in seconds [2]:
Extended commands [n]: y
Source address or interface: loopback 0
Type of service [0]:
Set DF bit in IP header? [no]:
Validate reply data? [no]:
Data pattern [0xABCD]:
Loose, Strict, Record, Timestamp, Verbose[none]:
Sweep range of sizes [n]:
Type escape sequence to abort.
Sending 5, 100-byte ICMP Echos to 172.16.1.100, timeout is 2 seconds:
Packet sent with a source address of 172.17.1.1
!!!!!
Success rate is 100 percent (5/5), round-trip min/avg/max = 1/1/4 ms

Branch# traceroute
Protocol [ip]:
Target IP address: 172.16.1.100
Source address: 172.17.1.1
Numeric display [n]: y
Timeout in seconds [3]:
Probe count [3]:
Minimum Time to Live [1]:
Maximum Time to Live [30]:
Port Number [33434]:
Loose, Strict, Record, Timestamp, Verbose[none]:
Type escape sequence to abort.
Tracing the route to 172.16.1.100
  1 10.1.10.1       0 msec 0 msec 0 msec
  2 192.168.1.2     0 msec *  0 msec
```

Note Extended **ping** and extended **traceroute** allow more granular and advanced testing. In Example 2-3, the tests are run using the source interface that is not directly connected to the next-hop router. This can test for situations where the next-hop network is not being properly inserted into routing tables in the packet path. Other options available that can be used for testing are increase the number of ping attempts, protocol used, data sent, and so forth.

For more information on the use and operation of extended **ping** and **traceroute**, see the following technical document: http://www.cisco.com/en/US/tech/tk365/technologies_tech_note09186a0080093f22.shtml.

Ping usually results in either a dot (.), indicating a timeout, or a !, indicating success. Ping can also deliver additional output for analysis. Table 2-1 defines these characters.

Table 2-1 *Ping Output Characters*

Code	Description
!	Success.
.	Timeout.
U	A destination unreachable error was sent by a remote router because it did not know where to route the packet. If a router is configured with **no ip unreachables**, the ping will just time out.
Q	Destination too busy (Source Quench). This code is rarely seen.
M	A router in the packet path could not fragment the ICMP packet, even though it needs to be fragmented.
N	Similar to U, except the remote router is reporting it can't reach the network/subnet. This code is rarely seen.
&	Packet lifetime exceeded. This means the TTL (Time to Live) was exceeded. TTL is used to make sure packets do not run in infinite circles.
?	An unknown packet type was returned.

Traceroute can also return additional codes. However, traceroute codes other than * for a timeout or a trip time are rarely seen.

While ping and traceroute can be used to test network layer connectivity, they can't test beyond the network layer. For instance, assume that you are troubleshooting a problem where someone cannot send email through a particular SMTP server. You ping the server, and it responds. This means that the network layer between you and the server is operational. Now, how do you verify the transport layer? Of course, you could configure a client and start a top-down troubleshooting procedure, but it would be better if you could first establish that Layer 4 is operational. So how can you do this?

Although the Telnet server application runs on its own well-known port number 23 and Telnet clients connect to this port by default, you can establish a specific port number on the client and connect to any TCP port that you want to test. At a minimum, this will display if the connection is accepted, is refused, or times out. Example 2-4 shows three connection attempts. The first is into the SMTP e-mail port (25), followed by the standard Telnet port (first refuses connection, second times out), and then port 80 (HTTP). In the Telnet example, a device is used that does not permit Telnet. From any of those responses, you can draw further conclusions concerning the connectivity. Certain applications, if they use a text-based session protocol, might even display an application banner, or you might be able to trigger some responses from the server by typing in some keywords. Example 2-4 uses a computer connected to a live Internet connection to employ resolvable DNS names. It then issues a few keywords to each protocol that connects (www/http and mail/smtp).

Note   Using hostnames can validate if name resolution (DNS) is operating. Devices can be reached by hostnames only if they are included in the name resolution (usually DNS, static hosts file, or **ip host** command in Cisco IOS Software). Additional information on name resolution is provided later in the chapter.

Example 2-4   *Telnet to IP Ports*

```
! Telnet to port 25 (email):
JT-Mac:~ johnny$ telnet mail.spanlink.com 25
Trying 72.21.254.30...
Connected to mail.spanlink.com.
Escape character is '^]'.
helo jtiso.com
554 splkspam4.spanlink.com ESMTP not accepting messages
250 splkspam4.spanlink.com Hello c-75-67-255-225.hsd1.nh.comcast.net
[75.67.255.225], pleased to meet you
quit
221 2.0.0 splkspam4.spanlink.com closing connection

! Standard Telnet (port 23) - connection refused:
JT-Mac:~ johnny$ telnet mail.jtiso.com
Trying 205.178.146.249...
telnet: connect to address 205.178.146.249: Connection refused
telnet: Unable to connect to remote host

! Standard Telnet (port 23) - connection time out:
JT-Mac:~ johnny$ telnet nohost.jtiso.com
Trying 208.91.197.27...
```

```
telnet: connect to address 208.91.197.27: Operation timed out
telnet: Unable to connect to remote host


! Telnet to port 80 (http):


JT-Mac:~ johnny$ telnet www.cisco.com 80
Trying 23.48.112.170...
Connected to e144.dscb.akamaiedge.net.
Escape character is '^]'.
GET http://www.cisco.com/ HTTP/1.0
HTTP/1.0 408 Request Time-out
Server: AkamaiGHost
Mime-Version: 1.0
Date: Sat, 23 Mar 2013 19:00:10 GMT
Content-Type: text/html
Content-Length: 218
Expires: Sat, 23 Mar 2013 19:00:10 GMT


<HTML><HEAD>
<TITLE>Request Timeout</TITLE>
</HEAD><BODY>
<TITLE>Request Timeout</TITLE>
</HEAD><BODY>
<H1>Request Timeout</H1>
The server timed out while waiting for the browser's request.<P>
Reference&#32;&#35;2&#46;b26d19b8&#46;1364065210&#46;0
</BODY></HTML>
Connection closed by foreign host.
```

Note   In some cases, a network or destination may have deployed a security feature or device in the packet path that detects that a normal client is not in use. It is crucial that you understand the network topology.

The **arp** Windows command displays and modifies entries in the ARP cache that are used to store the mapping between the Layer 3 IP addresses and their resolved Layer 2 Ethernet physical (MAC) addresses. As shown in Example 2-5, the **arp** Windows command and then the **show arp** Cisco IOS command list all devices that are currently in the ARP cache.

Example 2-5   *Viewing the ARP Cache in a PC and in a Router*

```
C:\windows\system32> arp -a
Interface: 10.1.10.100 --- 0xd
Internet Address          Physical Address       Type
10.1.10.1                      54-75-d0-8e-9a-d8     dynamic
224.0.0.22       01-00-5e-00-00-16     static
224.0.0.252                    01-00-5e-00-00-fc       static
255.255.255.255        ff-ff-ff-ff-ff-ff-ff          static
Branch# show arp
Protocol   Address          Age (min)   Hardware Addr   Type    Interface
Internet   10.1.10.100              1   00d0.e4c3.47ff   ARPA   FastEthernet0/0
Internet   192.168.1.2              -   0013.c4b8.8660   ARPA   FastEthernet0/0
Internet   192.168.1.222            -   0013.aaaa.bbbb   ARPA   FastEthernet0/0
```

The information displayed for each device includes the IP address, physical (MAC) address, and the addressing type (static or dynamic). The cache can be cleared by using the **arp -d** Windows command if you want to repopulate the cache with updated information. In Cisco IOS Software, the **clear arp-cache** command clears the ARP cache. Be aware, any connections to the router will get dropped.

A static ARP entry can cause issues. Because ARP maps MAC addresses to IP addresses, an incorrect static entry can cause reachability problems. Static ARP entries are manually created in the system. In Windows, the **arp –s** entry adds static entries to the ARP table. In Cisco IOS Software, static entries are entered in global configuration mode using the **arp** command.

Take another look at Example 2-4. Notice the static entries in Windows with the key word *static*. In Cisco IOS Software, looking at the output, you see static entries marked with an age of –, but there isn't an interface associated with that entry. In the router, a – indicates a static entry if there is no interface assigned, as in the last line. If an entry is notated with – and has an associated interface, it is the MAC address entry for that physical interface in the router.

Ping and traceroute operate at Layer 3. To examine Layer 2, begin at the switch. A switch forwards a frame only to the port where the destination is connected. The switch consults its MAC address table to accomplish this. The MAC address table lists which MAC address is connected to which port. Use the **show mac address-table** command to display the MAC address table on the switch, as shown in Example 2-6.

Example 2-6 show mac address-table *Output from Branch Switch*

```
SW1# show mac address-table

          Mac Address Table
-------------------------------------------
Vlan      Mac Address      Type       Ports
All       0100.0ccc.cccc   STATIC     CPU
All       0100.0ccc.cccd   STATIC     CPU
1         5475.d08e.9ad8   DYNAMIC    Fa0/2
1         000c.29bc.4654   DYNAMIC    Fa0/1
Total Mac Addresses for this criterion: 4
```

Looking at the MAC address table, you can determine the port and VLAN that a particular MAC address is mapped to in a switch. This helps verify if the device is on the network and in the correct VLAN, or if there is an invalid static entry. In this case, PC1's MAC address, 5475.d08e.9ad8, is shown connected to Fa0/2, as shown earlier in Figure 2-1.

Cisco Discovery Protocol

Cisco Discovery Protocol (CDP) is a Cisco proprietary protocol that can be used for connectivity troubleshooting. It is a media-independent, device-discovery protocol that runs most Cisco-manufactured equipment, such as:

■ Routers

■ Access servers

■ Switches

■ Wireless access points

■ VoIP devices

CDP can also run on non-Cisco equipment. A few examples are some HP ProCurve switches (HP removed most of the support for CVP in 2006), Mitel VoIP phones, and third-party software (cvp-tools for Linux, and other commercial and free tools). Using CDP allows a device to advertise its presence on the network and listen for the existence of any devices that are directly connected to the same network segment, LAN or WAN. Examples of media that support CDP are Ethernet, Frame Relay, HDLC, and ATM media. CDP is protocol independent and runs over the data link layer. It operates on the multi-cast address, 01-00-0c-cc-cc-cc.

You can find out many interesting things by using CDP, such as:

■ Devices connected at Layer 2 without a valid IP address

■ Device types

- Device capabilities

- A duplex mismatch

- A mismatch on a VLAN trunk

Example 2-7 shows basic CDP output. The only CDP neighbor is a 3745 router named HQ. The local interface is Serial0/0, and the interface on HQ is Serial0/0.

Example 2-7   show cdp neighbors *Command Output*

```
Branch# show cdp neighbors
Capability Codes: R - Router, T - Trans Bridge, B - Source Route Bridge
                  S - Switch, H - Host, I - IGMP, r - Repeater


Device ID        Local Intrfce     Holdtme     Capability  Platform   Port ID
HQ               Serial0/0         174           R S I     3745       Serial0/0
```

The **show cdp neighbors detail** command in Example 2-8 provides more information, such as the source and destination ports, the Cisco IOS version, and the IP address.

Example 2-8   show cdp neighbors detail *Command Output*

```
Branch# show cdp neighbors detail
-------------------------
Device ID: HQ
Entry address(es):
  IP address: 172.16.1.254
Platform: Cisco 3745,  Capabilities: Router Switch IGMP
Interface: Serial0/0,  Port ID (outgoing port): Serial0/0
Holdtime : 141 sec

Version :

Cisco IOS Software, 3700 Software (C3745-ADVENTERPRISEK9-M), Version 12.3(4)T4,
RELEASE SOFTWARE (fc2)
Technical Support: http://www.cisco.com/techsupport
Copyright (c) 1986-2004 by Cisco Systems, Inc.
Compiled Thu 11-Mar-04 16:52 by eaarmas

advertisement version: 2
VTP Management Domain: ''
```

CDP also provides interesting messages in the router log/console. Example 2-9 shows two example console messages. The first shows a VLAN mismatch. The second shows a duplex mismatch.

Example 2-9   *CDP Messages at the Console*

```
Mar 22 17:53:41.303: %CDP-4-NATIVE VLAN_MISMATCH: Native VLAN mismatch discovered
on  FastEthernet0/0  (100), with JAB032700M2(old-switch) 2/1 (200).


Mar 22 17:53:41.303: %CDP-4-DUPLEX_MISMATCH: duplex mismatch discovered on
FastEthernet0/0 (not half duplex), with JAB032700M2(old-switch) 2/1 (half duplex)
```

Verification of Physical Connectivity Issues

Inevitably, troubleshooting processes involve a hardware component. In the end, there are really only three main categories that could cause a failure on the network: hardware failures, software failures (bugs), and configuration errors. One could argue that performance problems form a fourth category, but they are not really a problem cause, but a symptom. Having a performance issue means that there is a difference between the expected behavior and the observed behavior. This can mean one of two things:

- **The expectation was not in line with reality:** The system is functioning as it should, but the result is not what was expected or promised. In this case, the problem is not technical but organizational in nature and cannot be resolved through technical means.

- **The system is not functioning as could be reasonably expected:** There must be an underlying reason that causes the system to behave differently from what was expected, such as a hardware failure, a software failure, or a configuration error.

In essence, any network device is a specialized computer. At a minimum this would consist of a CPU, RAM, and storage that permit it to boot and run the operating system and interfaces. Allowing for the reception and transmission of network traffic. Therefore, if you think that a problem might be hardware related, it is worthwhile to at least verify the operation of these generic components. The most commonly used Cisco IOS commands for this purpose are the **show processes cpu**, **show memory**, and **show interface** commands. This section examines the **show interface** command.

The interfaces that traffic passes through are another component that is always worth verifying when you are troubleshooting performance-related issues and you suspect the hardware to be at fault. In most cases, the interfaces are one of the first things that you should consider while tracing the path between devices.

The output of the **show interface** command lists a number of important statistics that should be checked:

- **Input queue drops:** Input queue drops (and the related ignored and throttle counters) signify that at some point more traffic was delivered to the router than it could process. This does not necessarily indicate a problem, because input queue drops could be normal during traffic peaks. However, input queue drops could be an indication that the CPU cannot process packets in time, so if this number is consistently high, it is worth trying to determine at which moments these counters are increasing and how this relates to CPU usage.

- **Output queue drops:** Output queue drops indicate that packets were dropped due to congestion on the interface. Seeing output drops is normal for any point where the aggregate input traffic is higher than the output traffic. During peaks, packets are dropped if traffic is delivered to the interface faster than it can be sent out. However, even if this is considered normal behavior, it leads to packet drops and queuing delays, so applications that are sensitive to those, such as VoIP, might suffer from performance issues. Consistently seeing output drops can therefore be a good indicator that you might need to research and implement an advanced queuing mechanism to provide good quality of service (QoS) to each application and eliminate unnecessary traffic.

Note   QoS is an advanced topic beyond the CCNA. For additional information on QoS, see the Cisco QoS home page at http://www.cisco.com/en/US/products/ps6558/products_ios_technology_home.html.

- **Input errors:** Input errors indicate failures that are experienced during the reception of the frame, such as cyclic redundancy check (CRC). High numbers of CRC errors could indicate cabling problems, interface hardware problems, or, in an Ethernet-based network, duplex mismatches. On a WAN interface, such as a serial interface, an increasing number of input errors can also be indicative of a noisy telco line.

- **Interface resets:** Interface resets usually indicate a hardware problem outside the device. Check the neighboring port. In WAN environments, check any external channel service unit/data service unit (CSU/DSU) and any telco termination equipment that is on the premises.

- **Carrier transitions:** On a WAN, errors in the connection to the telecommunications provider can occur where the link is going up and down. This can happen due to a variety of events, including a lightning strike or a physical layer problem.

- **CRC errors:** These errors occur when there is excessive noise or collisions. If excessive collisions are not present, check hardware and cabling (damaged or wrong type).

- **Collisions:** In a switched network, collisions are usually indicative of either a speed/duplex problem or traffic that comes into the switch and exceeds the switch backplane capacity.

- **Late collisions:** Check to make sure that the length of the cabling or diameter of the network does not exceed Ethernet specifications.

- **Runts:** Runts are packets that are smaller than the minimum that the media allows. In the case of Ethernet this would be a packet smaller than 64 bytes in length. These are caused by excessive collisions or a malfunctioning network driver or NIC on a host.

- **Framing errors:** Check the WAN line or carrier network for errors.

- **Aborted transmissions:** Check the WAN line or carrier network for errors.

Example 2-10 shows the output from a **show interfaces** command. It shows an interface in proper operating order without failures. However, remember some errors can be normal based on the network operating condition.

Example 2-10   show interfaces *Command Output*

```
Branch# show interfaces GigabitEthernet 0/1
GigabitEthernet0/1 is up, line protocol is up
<output omitted>
  Input queue: 0/75/0/0 (size/max/drops/flushes); Total output drops: 0
  Queueing strategy: fifo
  Output queue: 0/40 (size/max)
<output omitted>
     0 input errors, 0 CRC, 0 frame, 0 overrun, 0 ignored  <output omitted>
     0 output errors, 0 collisions, 1 interface resets
     0 unknown protocol drops  <output omitted>
```

A common cause of errors in Ethernet links is a mismatched duplex mode between two ends of the link. In many Ethernet-based networks, point-to-point connections are now commonplace and the use of hubs and the associated half-duplex operation is becoming unconventional. This means that most Ethernet links today operate in full-duplex mode, and while collisions were seen as normal for an Ethernet link, collisions today often indicate that duplex negotiation has failed, and that the link is not operating in the correct duplex mode.

The IEEE 802.3ab Gigabit Ethernet standard mandates the use of autonegotiation for speed and duplex. In addition, although it is not strictly mandatory, practically all Fast Ethernet NICs also use autonegotiation by default. The use of autonegotiation for speed and duplex is the current recommended practice.

However, if duplex negotiation fails for some reason, it might be necessary to set the speed and duplex manually on both ends. Typically, this means setting the duplex mode to full duplex on both ends of the connection. However, if unsuccessful, running half duplex on both ends is always preferred over a duplex mismatch. A network supporting legacy devices is a likely candidate for this process.

In the earlier days of switched Ethernet, many network engineers believed that hard-setting the speed and duplex on both sides of every link was best practice to avoid mismatches, because they were quite common and time consuming.

Serial lines are main connection types to a telco provider. In a serial line WAN interface, the interface status can also be useful to determine network status. The status of a serial interface might be any of the following:

- **UP/UP:** Normal operation.

- **DOWN/DOWN:** Nothing is detected on the other end. The link is down or equipment is disconnected.

- **UP/DOWN:** The interface is up, but there is no connection to the remote end. May be a configuration problem, carrier problem, or hardware failure.

- **UP/UP (looped):** A loop exists in the topology. A loop in a serial line interface occurs when the circuit transmit and receive have been crossed somewhere at the physical layer (Layer 1). If the router or CSU/DSU is not physically looped at the local end, the telco carrier has the line looped. This usually occurs when the telco provider is running circuit diagnostics.

- **UP/DOWN (disabled):** The interface has been disabled due to either a hardware failure or a high error rate on the line.

- **Administratively DOWN/DOWN:** The interface has been shut down in the configuration or has detected a duplicate IP address.

Identification of Current and Desired Path

To troubleshoot Layer 3 connectivity, you need to have a good understanding of the processes that are involved in routing a packet from a host across multiple routers to the final destination. For example, the topology in Figure 2-1, at the beginning of the section, shows the attempt of PC1 to contact the server. The correct path is denoted by the dotted line. Look at the edge and see how the packets will be sent. Then, consider the following:

- Which decisions will PC1 make? Which information does it need? Which actions will it perform to successfully send a packet that is destined for Server to first-hop router Branch?

- Which decisions will the Branch router make? Which information does it need? Which actions will it perform to successfully send the packets from PC1 that are destined for the server to the HQ router1?

As shown in Example 2-11, use the **show ip route** command to examine the routing table. In this case, the routing table on the Branch router does not have the route to the server's network (172.16.1.0).

Example 2-11 *Looking at the Unicast Routing Table*

```
Branch# show ip route
Codes: C - connected, S - static, R - RIP, M - mobile, B - BGP
       D - EIGRP, EX - EIGRP external, O - OSPF, IA - OSPF inter area
       N1 - OSPF NSSA external type 1, N2 - OSPF NSSA external type 2
       E1 - OSPF external type 1, E2 - OSPF external type 2
       i - IS-IS, su - IS-IS summary, L1 - IS-IS level-1, L2 - IS-IS level-2
       ia - IS-IS inter area, * - candidate default, U - per-user static route
       o - ODR, P - periodic downloaded static route

Gateway of last resort is not set

     172.17.0.0/32 is subnetted, 1 subnets
C       172.17.1.1 is directly connected, Loopback0
     10.0.0.0/24 is subnetted, 1 subnets
C       10.1.10.0 is directly connected, FastEthernet0/0
C    192.168.1.0/24 is directly connected,Serial0/0
C    192.168.2.0/24 is directly connected, Serial0/1
```

The routing tables can be populated by the following methods:

■ **Directly connected networks:** This entry comes from having directly connected router interfaces that are attached to network segments. This is the most certain method of populating a routing table. This includes loopback interfaces configured in the router. If the interface fails or is administratively shut down, the entry for that network is removed from the routing table.

■ **Local host routes:** These entries are taken from the local IP address on the directly connected router interfaces. The subnet mask of 255.255.255.255 represents the host route.

■ **Static routes:** A system administrator manually enters static routes directly into the configuration of a router.

■ **Dynamic routes:** The router learns dynamic routes automatically when the routing protocol is configured and a neighbor relationship to other routers is established. The information is responsive to changes in the network and updates constantly. There is, however, always a lag between the time that a network changes and all of the routers become aware of the change. The time delay for a router to match a network change is called *convergence time*. A shorter convergence time is better for users of the network. Routing protocols perform differently in this regard. Larger networks require the dynamic routing method because there are usually many networks with multiple routes that may change dynamically.

- **Default routes:** A default route is an optional entry that is used when no explicit path to a destination is found in the routing table. The default route can be manually inserted or can be populated from a dynamic routing protocol.

When identical routes come from different sources, the router uses a concept called *administrative distance* to choose the route to insert in the routing table. Administrative distance determines how well a router "trusts" the routing sources. Connected interfaces are the most trusted, followed by static routes and then dynamic routes. Dynamic routes are assigned an administrative distance by protocol. Administrative distances are discussed later in the chapter.

The **show ip route** command displays the routing table in a router. The first part of the output explains the codes, presenting the following letters and the associated source of the entries in the routing table:

- **L:** Reserved for the local host route

- **C:** Reserved for directly connected networks

- **S:** Reserved for static routes

- **R:** Reserved for the Routing Information Protocol (RIP)

- **O:** Reserved for the Open Shortest Path First (OSPF) Protocol

- **D:** Reserved for the Enhanced Interior Gateway Protocol (EIGRP); *D* stands for DUAL, the update algorithm that is used by EIGRP

- **B:** Reserved for the Border Gateway Protocol (BGP)

- **I:** Reserved for the Intermediate System-to-Intermediate System (IS-IS) Protocol

The full definition of the routing table can be found by executing the command **show ip route** on the branch router. Examine the beginning of the output as seen in Example 2-12.

Example 2-12   show ip route *Output*

```
Branch# show ip route
Codes: C - connected, S - static, R - RIP, M - mobile, B - BGP
       D - EIGRP, EX - EIGRP external, O - OSPF, IA - OSPF inter area
       N1 - OSPF NSSA external type 1, N2 - OSPF NSSA external type 2
       E1 - OSPF external type 1, E2 - OSPF external type 2
       i - IS-IS, su - IS-IS summary, L1 - IS-IS level-1, L2 - IS-IS level-2
       ia - IS-IS inter area, * - candidate default, U - per-user static route
       o - ODR, P - periodic downloaded static route
```

You can expect different results depending on the destination address in a packet, as described in these scenarios:

- If the destination address in a packet does not match an entry in the routing table, then the default route is used. If a default route is not configured, the packet is discarded.

- If the destination address in a packet matches a single entry in the routing table, then the packet is forwarded through the interface that is defined in this route.

- If the destination address in a packet matches more than one entry in the routing table and the routing entries have the same prefix (network mask), then the router sends the packets through one of the routes.

- If the destination address in a packet matches more than one entry in the routing table and the routing entries have different prefixes (network mask), then the packets for this destination are forwarded out of the interface that is associated with the route that has the longer prefix match.

Default Gateway Issues

End devices, such as PC1 and the server in Figure 2-1, should have a destination for unknown packets. Otherwise, a route to every network must be inserted into the device. This is not feasible for many end-user devices, and a default gateway should be set in this instance. PC1 can have its default gateway set to the Branch router. The server can have its default gateway set to the HQ router. This allows the routers to make the decisions.

Routers may also need a default destination for unknown packets. This is referred to as the "gateway of last resort," which does not need to be set. If the router has a route to every network in the environment, it is not necessary. However, having this set in a router can be important. In the case of the Internet, every device connecting private networks needs the full Internet routing table (roughly 7 million routes), which would be completely excessive, create instability, and waste resources (think of every device having 7 million routes).

Note   There are many public route servers, accessible by Telnet, that can give you an indication of the enormous size of the Internet. These devices are either routers (Cisco or Juniper) or Linux. Use a search engine and enter "Route Servers." These systems allow low-level command-line access. The Cisco routers offer some limited **show** commands. The **show ip bgp** command demonstrates every route in the global Internet.

Cisco devices have the **ip default-gateway** and **ip default-network** commands. The **ip default-gateway** command is used on routers that are not actively routing packets (such as a terminal server for Telnet/SSH or other service device). The **ip default-network** command is used to set a gateway of last resort. However, this is unnecessary. The preferred way to set up a default gateway is to have either a routing protocol or a static route set to 0.0.0.0/0. This route is used for any packet that does not match a route in the router. Referencing the network in Figure 2-1, to set a default route statically from the Branch router to the HQ router, use the following configuration:

```
Branch# configure terminal
Enter configuration commands, one per line.  End with CNTL/Z.
Branch(config)# ip route 0.0.0.0 0.0.0.0 192.168.1.2
```

Note For more information about default routing in Cisco routers, see http://www.cisco.com/en/US/tech/tk365/technologies_tech_note09186a0080094374.shtml.

As stated earlier, end devices should have a default gateway set. Use the **route print** command in Windows to locate the default route. You can also see it in the Control Panel, as well as in the Mac settings under the current active interface. In Linux and UNIX operating systems, the **netstat** command prints the routing table. Looking at the routing table on PC1 from Figure 2-1, the Branch router is set as its default route. as shown in Example 2-13.

Example 2-13 *Display the PC IP Routing Table*

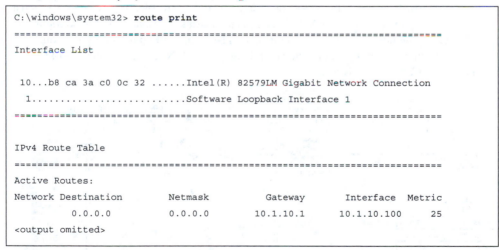

```
C:\windows\system32> route print
===========================================================================
Interface List

 10...b8 ca 3a c0 0c 32 ......Intel(R) 82579LM Gigabit Network Connection
  1...........................Software Loopback Interface 1
===========================================================================

IPv4 Route Table
===========================================================================
Active Routes:
Network Destination        Netmask          Gateway       Interface  Metric
          0.0.0.0          0.0.0.0        10.1.10.1      10.1.10.100     25
<output omitted>
```

Note A common practice is to assign default gateways to end devices through DHCP when assigning an IP address.

Name Resolution Issues

Name resolution is the mapping of device names to IP addresses which can be accomplished in two ways:

- **Static:** The system administrator creates a text file, called a HOSTS file, and enters each device name and IP address. The file is then distributed on the network. When a connection to another computer is requested, the file is used to resolve the name to the correct IP address. This system works well for simple networks that change infrequently.

- **Dynamic:** The Doman Name System (DNS) protocol controls the domain name server, a distributed database with which you can map hostnames to IP addresses. There are other dynamic methods of name to IP address lookup. These are discussed later in the chapter. DNS is examined because it is the most common lookup method.

Static Name Resolution

The hosts file translates human-friendly hostnames into IP addresses, which identify and locate a host in an IP network. In some operating systems, the hosts file's content is used preferentially for other methods, such as DNS. Unlike DNS, the hosts file is under the direct control of the local computer's administrator. For a Windows operating system, the file is located at c:\windows\system32\drivers\etc\hosts. Other operating systems may have the hosts file in a different location, may use a different file, or may not have such a file at all (for instance Cisco IOS Software maintains this information in the configuration file). Open the hosts file in a text editor such as Notepad. In Figure 2-4, PC1 is equipped with a hosts file, and it pings the Server in Example 2-14. Notice in Example 2-14 the name resolved to the hostname.

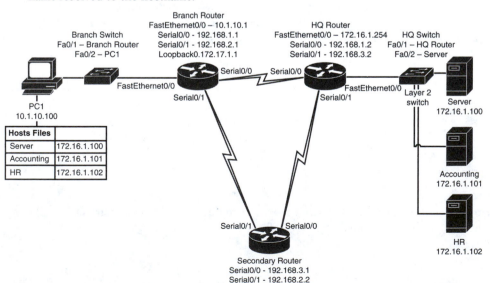

Figure 2-4 *Static Name Resolution*

Example 2-14   *Use the* **ping** *Command with a Hostname*

```
C:\windows\system32> ping Server


Pinging Server [172.16.1.100] with 32 bytes of data:
Reply from 172.16.1.100: bytes=32 time=50ms TTL=127
Reply from 172.16.1.100: bytes=32 time=53ms TTL=127
Reply from 172.16.1.100: bytes=32 time=48ms TTL=127
Reply from 172.16.1.100: bytes=32 time=51ms TTL=127


Ping statistics for 172.16.1.100:
    Packets: Sent = 4, Received = 4, Lost = 0 (0% loss),
Approximate round trip times in milli-seconds:
    Minimum = 48ms, Maximum = 53ms, Average = 50ms
```

To make a static name-resolution entry on a switch or a router, use the **ip host** *name ip_address* command. For example, if you want to add an entry Server that resolves into IP address 172.16.1.100, the syntax is **ip host Server 172.16.1.100**.

When domain (DNS) lookup is enabled, anything typed into the command line that is not identified as a command is assumed to be a hostname and triggers a domain lookup. Many administrators disable domain lookup in Cisco IOS Software. It can be configured by adding the **no ip domain-lookup** command to the configuration.

Note   For more information on name resolution under Cisco IOS Software, see http://www.cisco.com/en/US/tech/tk648/tk362/technologies_tech_note09186a00800c525f.shtml.

Dynamic Name Resolution

DNS defines a hierarchical naming scheme that allows a device to be identified by its location or domain. Domain names are pieced together with periods (.) as the delimiting characters. For example, Cisco is a commercial organization that IP identifies by a .com domain name, so its domain name is cisco.com. As a specific device in this domain, for example, the FTP system is identified as ftp.cisco.com.

To keep track of domain names, IP has defined the concept of a DNS (Domain Name System) server, which holds a cache (or database) of names that is mapped to IP addresses. To map domain names to IP addresses, you must first identify the hostnames, specify the name server that is present on your network, and enable the DNS. In Figure 2-5, some devices are added to the example network. The DNS server has a table. PC1 requests the IP address of the Accounting server and the DNS server returns it.

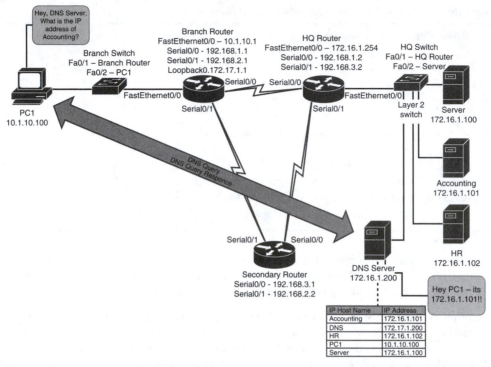

Figure 2-5   *Dynamic Name Resolution with DNS*

Figure 2-5 is a very simplistic example of DNS. DNS on the Internet operates recursively, meaning that a DNS server is configured with one or more parent DNS servers to research unfamiliar hostnames.

Once you configure name resolution on the device, substitute the hostname for the IP address with all IP commands, such as **ping** or **telnet**.

A host-based tool for inspecting DNS records without using an application is called **nslookup**. Example 2-15 shows a simple query using the command from the command line of a Mac.

Example 2-15   nslookup *from a Host*

```
JT-Mac:~ johnny$ nslookup
> www.ciscopress.com
Server:        192.168.220.1
Address:       192.168.220.1#53

Non-authoritative answer:
www.ciscopress.com    canonical name = ciscopress.com.
Name:    ciscopress.com
Address: 159.182.165.54
> exit
```

> **Note**   Other forms of IP name resolution exist, but they are not widely used. These include YP/NIS/NIS+ (Network Information Service, primarily for UNIX), LDAP (Lightweight Directory Access Protocol, which can be used for name resolution, although it is used primarily for authentication), and Microsoft WINS (Windows Internet Name Service).

ACL Issues

Access control lists (ACL) can have a significant impact on what is forwarded in and out of the router. They control traffic flow by permitting or denying certain traffic. It is important to correctly configure/apply an ACL. They are administered directly to an interface in either the inbound or outbound direction. A single ACL can be used more than once.

When configuring and applying ACLs, it is important to understand the traffic flow. Although ACLs are applied in a single direction, you must understand that traffic flows are bidirectional. An example ACL that blocks all IP traffic between two specific hosts is shown in Example 2-16.

Example 2-16   *Reviewing ACLs with the* **show access-lists** *Command*

```
Branch# show access-lists
Extended IP access list 100
    10 deny ip host 10.1.10.100 host 172.16.1.102
    20 permit ip any any
To see how an ACL is applied, the show ip interface command:
Branch# show ip interface FastEthernet0/0
FastEthernet0/0 is up, line protocol is up
  Internet address is 192.168.1.2/24
  <output omitted>
  Outgoing access list is not set
  Inbound  access list is 100
  <output omitted>
```

Figure 2-6 shows this example ACL applied to the Branch router.

In Figure 2-6, PC1 can ping Accounting and the Server, but it can't ping HR.

Remember, when investigating ACLs, traffic must be able to flow in both directions. This book only covers the basics of ACLs in Cisco IOS Software as part of the CCNA curriculum. There are multiple types of non-IP access lists and other IP access lists, such as those used in Cisco IOS Firewall that are beyond the scope of the CCNA.

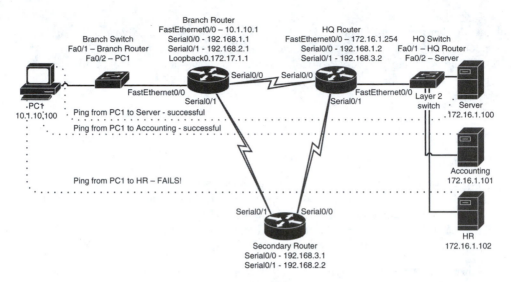

Figure 2-6 *Troubleshooting ACL Issues with* **ping**

> **Note** For more information on ACLs, refer to the *Securing the Data Plane Configuration Guide Library, Cisco IOS Release 15M&T* at: http://www.cisco.com/en/US/docs/ios-xml/ios/security/config_library/15-mt/secdata-15-mt-library.html Also check out *CCNA Security 640-554 Official Cert Guide*, by Keith Barker and Scott Morris from Cisco Press.

Understanding Networking in Virtualized Computing Environments

Virtual machines are a very common configuration in computing environments today. It is a design where software called a *hypervisor* runs one or more independent instances of an operating system. The hypervisor may run directly on hardware and boot as an OS. In other cases, the hypervisor may run under a bootable OS, such as Windows. The physical machine splits its resources between one or more virtual machines. Figure 2-7 displays a single physical server with three virtual servers running on it. Each virtual server has an individual IP address and functions independently.

In Figure 2-8 a hypervisor called *VMware Fusion* is displayed on a Mac OS X computer. Either of two computing instances can be launched, a Microsoft Windows 7 image or a Microsoft Windows XP image.

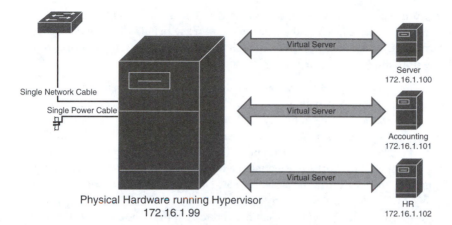

Figure 2-7 *Virtual Servers with a Hypervisor on a Physical Server*

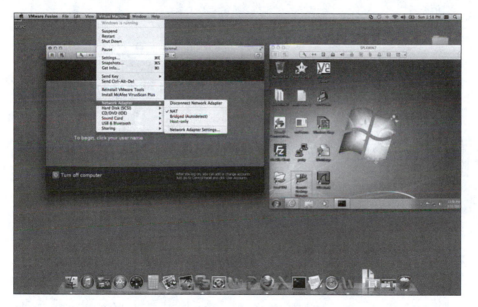

Figure 2-8 *Hypervisor Running Two Distinct Virtual Machines*

Notice in Figure 2-8 that the hypervisor software presents the virtualized hardware configuration to the virtual machine. For instance, there are specific options on how the virtual machine's network adapter will function. Bridged mode allows distinct network addressing and protocol operation from the hypervisor. It is important to note that the physical machine's network adapter will show multiple IP addresses, possibly different protocols (IPv4 and/or IPv6 from each virtual machine running independently, as an example), and additional MAC addresses. Another mode is NAT (Network Address

Translation). When configuring NAT mode on the virtual machine, this places the virtual machines' network address inside and the adapter effectively behind the hypervisor/host operating system. This is similar to what a firewall or home broadband router does with the mapping of multiple devices to a single IP address.

The hypervisor's networking configuration is in addition to the host operating system's networking configuration. Although it is presented virtually by the hypervisor, as you can see in Figure 2-8, the host operating system's network configuration is no different than if it was running directly on the computer "bare metal" without the hypervisor. This includes the VPN client software that is running. The advantage is that you can use the VPN on the virtual machine without affecting the connectivity of the base operating system. In Figure 2-9, the host operating system is Mac OS X and is simultaneously executing an instance of Windows XP and an instance of Windows 7. The Windows XP and Windows 7 instances both have independent networking configuration. The Windows 7 image is running a VPN connection.

Figure 2-9 *Host Network and VPN Appears and Operates Identically to Nonvirtualized Environment*

To add an extra layer of complexity, Cisco offers specific virtual environment networking enhancements as part of the Nexus 1000 line of products.

Note For more information on Cisco Nexus in the virtual environment, refer to http://www.cisco.com/en/US/products/ps9902/index.html.

The process in which networking is implemented in your virtual environment directly affects your troubleshooting of the environment. The key is to fully understand the physical and virtual topology, the configuration, and the features/function of the associated products and devices.

Troubleshooting IPv6 Network Connectivity

IPv6 was developed in 1996, but it is just starting to become widely adopted by enterprises and service providers. As in IPv4 networks, problems also arise in IPv6 networks. Therefore, knowledge of troubleshooting IPv6 is required for a CCNA. With IPv6 you can use the same structured approach to troubleshooting as you use when troubleshooting IPv4 networks. However, because there are differences in the operation of IPv4 and IPv6, troubleshooting IPv6 networks has some nuances that are different from troubleshooting IPv4 networks. These are due to the protocol structure changes. For example, instead of verifying ARP entries in IPv4, you must verify neighbor discovery entries in IPv6.

This section first describes the process of end-to-end IPv6 connectivity verification. It then explains how to confirm the current paths in networks and verify DNS and default gateway settings. The section concludes with verification of IPv6 ACLs.

Understanding IPv6 Addressing

IPv6 addressing is constructed with 16-byte hexadecimal number fields separated by colons (:) to represent the 128-bit addressing format. Here is an example of a valid IPv6 address: 2001:db8:130F:0000:0000:09C0:876A:130B.

IPv6 allows the use of an abbreviated form of the address for easy representation. It uses the following conventions:

- Leading zeros in the address field are optional and can be compressed: 0000 = 0. In the following example, the hexadecimal numbers can be represented in a compressed format:

    - Example of a short form address: 2001:db8:130F:0000:0000:09C0:876A:130B is equivalent to 2001:db8:130F:0:0:9C0:876A:130B (compressed form)

- A pair of colons (::) represents successive fields of 0. However, the pair of colons is allowed just once in a valid IPv6 address.

    - Example 1: 2001:db8:130F:0:0:9C0:876A:130B is equivalent to 2001:db8:130F::9C0:876A:130B

    - Example 2: FF01:0:0:0:0:0:1 is equivalent to FF01::1

An address parser can easily identify the number of missing zeros in an IPv6 address by separating the two parts of the address and filling in the zeros until the 128-bit address is complete. However, if two instances of :: are placed in the same address, there is no way to identify the size of each block of zeros. The use of the :: makes many IPv6 addresses more manageable.

In IPv6 there are references to prefixes. Prefixes are analogous to subnets in IPv4. The IPv6 prefix is made up of the leftmost bits and acts as the network identifier. The IPv6 prefix is represented by using the IPv6-prefix or prefix-length format the way an IPv4 address is represented in the classless interdomain routing (CIDR) notation. The /prefix-length variable is a decimal value that indicates the number of high-order contiguous bits of the address that form the prefix, which is the network portion of the address. For example, 2001:db8:8086:6502::/64 is an acceptable IPv6 prefix. If the address ends in a double colon, the trailing double colon can be omitted. So, the same address can be written as 2001:db8:8086:6502/64. Either way, the prefix length is written as a decimal number 64 and represents the leftmost bits of the IPv6 address. A similar address in IPv4 would be xxx.xxx.xxx.xxx/16.

IPv6 Unicast Addresses

There are several basic types of IPv6 unicast addresses:

- Global

- Reserved

- Private (link-local)

- Loopback

- Unspecified

RFC 4291 specifies 2000::/3 to be a global unicast address space that the Internet Assigned Numbers Authority (IANA) may allocate to the Regional Internet Registries (RIR). A global unicast address is an IPv6 address from the global unicast prefix, as shown in Figure 2-10. The structure of global unicast addresses enables the aggregation of routing prefixes, which limits the number of routing table entries in the global routing table. Global unicast addresses that are used on links are aggregated upward through organizations and eventually to the ISPs.

Note   The RIRs are as follows: AfriNIC (Africa), APNIC (Asia/Pacific), ARIN (United States, Canada, parts of the Caribbean, and Antarctica), LACNIC (Latin America, Mexico, and parts of the Caribbean), and RIPE (Europe, the Middle East, and Central Asia).

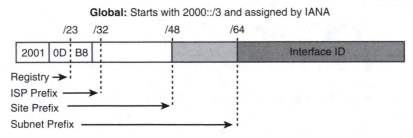

Figure 2-10 *Global Addressing*

Link-local addresses, illustrated in Figure 2-11, are new to the concept of addressing with IP in the network layer. These addresses refer only to a particular physical link. Link-local addresses always begin with FE80::/10. The next digits can be defined manually. If you do not define them manually, the interface MAC address is used based on EUI-64 format, which is discussed ahead.

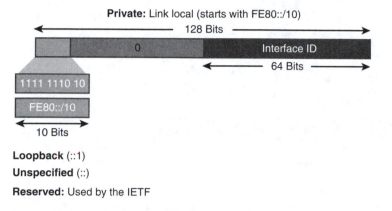

Loopback (::1)

Unspecified (::)

Reserved: Used by the IETF

Figure 2-11 *Link-Local Addressing*

Just as in IPv4, a provision has been made for a special loopback IPv6 address for testing; datagrams that are sent to this address "loop back" to the sending device. However, in IPv6 there is just one address, not a whole block, for this function. The loopback address is 0:0:0:0:0:0:0:1, which is normally expressed as ::1.

In IPv4, an IP address of all zeros has a special meaning; it refers to the host itself, and is used when a device does not know its own address. In IPv6, this concept has been formalized, and the all-zeros address is named the "unspecified" address. It is typically used in the source field of a datagram that is sent by a device that seeks to have its IP address configured.

The EUI-64 standard explains how to stretch IEEE 802 MAC addresses from 48 bits to 64 bits by inserting the 16-bit 0xFFFE in the middle (at the 24th bit) of the MAC address to create a 64-bit, unique interface identifier. In the first byte of the vendor's Organizationally Unique Identifier (OUI) of the MAC address, bit 7 indicates the scope: 0 for global and 1 for local. As most burned-in addresses are globally scoped, bit 7 will usually be 0. The EUI-64 standard also specifies that the value of the 7th bit be inverted. So, for example, MAC address 00-90-27-17-FC-0F becomes 02-90-27-17-FC-0F. The resulting EUI-64 address on network 2001:0DB8:0:1::/64 is 2001:0DB8:0:1:0290:27FF:FE 17:FC0F. Figure 2-12 shows the addressing layout.

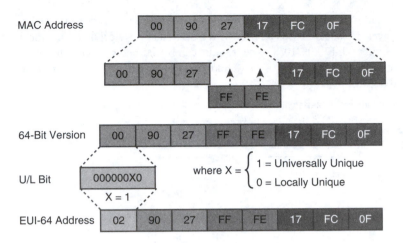

Figure 2-12 *IPv6 Addressing Layout*

Components of Troubleshooting End-to-End IPv6 Connectivity

As with troubleshooting IPv4 connectivity, the process for IPv6 can be guided by structured methods. The overall troubleshooting procedure is the same, with differences that are related to IPv6 specifics. Figure 2-13 shows basically the same sample network as shown in Figure 2-1 earlier in the chapter. The difference is, IPv6 is in use rather than IPv4. In Figure 2-13, PC1 wants to access applications on the server. The desirable path is direct from the Branch router to the HQ router.

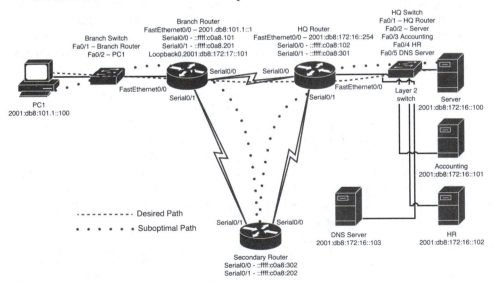

Figure 2-13 *Sample Network with IPv6 Addressing*

When there is no end-to-end connectivity, as with IPv4, these are some items that you should investigate (refer back to Figure 2-3 for a flowchart depicting these steps):

■ Check if there is an issue with physical connectivity; if there is, solve it by adjusting the configuration or changing/modifying the hardware.

■ Make sure that devices are determining the correct path from the source to the destination. Manipulate the routing information if needed.

■ Verify that the default gateway is correct.

■ Confirm that the name resolution settings are correct. There should be a name resolution server that is accessible over IPv4 or IPv6. Depending on the configuration, name resolution can simultaneously support IPv4 and IPv6.

■ Verify that there are no ACLs blocking traffic.

After attempting a step in troubleshooting, the outcome should be noted. Then, the results from the failed step should be used to determine the course of the next step. This should be repeated until operational, end-to-end connectivity is achieved.

Verification of End-to-End IPv6 Connectivity

As shown in Figure 2-14, **ping** and **traceroute** also operate under IPv6. The **ping** utility can be used to test end-to-end IPv6 connectivity by providing the IPv6 address as the destination address. The utilities recognize the IPv6 address when one is provided and use IPv6 as a protocol to test connectivity.

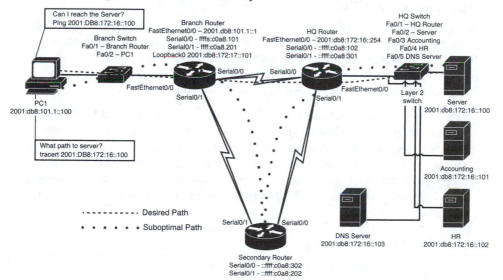

Figure 2-14   *IPv6* **ping** *and* **traceroute**

Similar to IPv4, you can use Telnet to test end-to-end transport layer connectivity over IPv6 using the **telnet** command from a PC, a router, or a switch. When you provide the IPv6 destination address, the protocol stack determines that the IPv6 protocol must be used. If you omit the port number, the client connects to well-known port number 23. You can also specify a specific port number on the client and connect to any TCP port that you want to test.

In Example 2-17, notice two connections from a PC to the Cisco IOS router. The first one connects to port 23 and tests Telnet over IPv6. The second connects to port 80 and tests HTTP over IPv6.

Example 2-17   *Telnet Using IPv6 to Check Connectivity*

```
C:\windows\system32> telnet 2001:db8:172:16::254

HQ#


C:\windows\system32> telnet 2001:db8:172:16::25480

HTTP/1.1 400 Bad Request

Date: Wed, 26 Sep 2012 07:27:10 GMT

Server: cisco-IOS

Accept-Ranges: none

400 Bad Request

Connection to host lost.
```

Neighbor Discovery in IPv6

When troubleshooting end-to-end connectivity, it is useful to verify mappings between destination IP addresses and Layer 2 Ethernet addresses on individual segments. In IPv4, this functionality is provided by ARP. In IPv6, the ARP functionality is replaced by the neighbor discovery process and ICMPv6. The neighbor discovery table caches IP addresses and their resolved Ethernet physical (MAC) addresses.

As shown in Example 2-18, the neighbor discovery table from Figure 2-14 is displayed. The **netsh interface ipv6 show neighbor** Windows command from PC1 and the **show ipv6 neighbors** Cisco IOS command from the Branch router list all devices that are currently in the neighbor discovery table cache. The information displayed for each device includes the IP address, physical (MAC) address, and address type. By examining the neighbor discovery table, you can verify that destination IPv6 addresses map to correct Ethernet addresses.

Example 2-18   *Neighbor Discovery in IPv6*

```
C:\windows\system32> netsh interface ipv6 show neighbor

Interface 13: LAB

Internet Address                              Physical Address    Type

-------------------------------------------   -----------------   ---------

fe80::9c5a:e957:a865:bde9                     00-0c-29-26-fd-f7   Stale

2001:db8:101.1::1                             f8-66-f2-31-72-50   Reachable
```

```
ff02::2                                         33-33-00-00-00-      Permanent
ff02::16                                        33-33-00-00-00-      Permanent
ff02::1:2                                       33-33-00-00-00-      Permanent
ff02::1:3                                       33-33-00-00-00-      Permanent
ff02::1:ff05:f9fb                               33-33-00-00-00-      Permanent
ff02::1:ff31:7250                               33-33-00-00-00-      Permanent
ff02::1:ff65:bde9                               33-33-00-00-00-      Permanent
ff02::1:ff67:bae4                               33-33-00-00-00-      Permanent



Branch# show ipv6 neighbors
IPv6 Address                             Age  Link-layer Addr   State   Interface
::ffff:c0a8:202                          46   000c.2936.fdf7    STALE   SE0/1
2001:db8:101.1::100                       0   001e.7a79.7a81    REACH   FE0/1
2001:DB8:101:1:C31:CD87:7505:F9FB         0   ::ffff:c0a8:102   REACH   SE0/0
```

Example 2-18 also shows the neighbor discovery table on the Cisco IOS router. The neighbor discovery table includes the IPv6 address of the neighbor, the age in minutes since the address was confirmed to be reachable, and the state. Table 2-2 explains the possible states from the State column in the neighbor table under Cisco IOS Software.

Table 2-2   *IPv6 Neighbor Discovery Table Codes from Cisco IOS Software*

State	Description
INCMP (Incomplete)	Address resolution is being performed on the entry. A neighbor solicitation message has been sent to the solicited-node multicast address of the target, but the corresponding neighbor advertisement message has not yet been received.
REACH (Reachable)	Positive confirmation was received within the last ReachableTime milliseconds that the forward path to the neighbor was functioning properly. (The neighbor ReachableTime enables detecting unavailable neighbors.) While in REACH state, the device takes no special action as packets are sent.
STALE	More than ReachableTime milliseconds have elapsed since the last positive confirmation was received that the forward path was functioning properly. While in STALE state, the device takes no action until a packet is sent.
DELAY	More than ReachableTime milliseconds have elapsed since the last positive confirmation was received that the forward path was functioning properly. A packet was sent within the last DELAY_FIRST_PROBE_TIME seconds. If no reachability confirmation is received within DELAY_FIRST_PROBE_TIME seconds of entering the DELAY state, send a neighbor solicitation message and change the state to PROBE.

State	Description
PROBE	A reachability confirmation is actively sought by resending neighbor solicitation messages in RetransTimer milliseconds until a reachability confirmation is received.

Identification of Current and Desired IPv6 Path

To verify that the current IPv6 path matches the desired path to reach destinations, use the **show ipv6 route** command on a router to examine the routing table. In Figure 2-14, the desired path to the server from the Branch router is directly attached to the HQ router. There is a static route to that network, as shown in Example 2-19.

Example 2-19 *Displaying the IPv6 Unicast Routing Table with* **show ipv6 route**

```
Branch# show ipv6 route
IPv6 Routing Table - default - 6 entries
Codes: C - Connected, L - Local, S - Static, U - Per-user Static route
       B - BGP, R - RIP, H - NHRP, I1 - ISIS L1
       I2 - ISIS L2, IA - ISIS interarea, IS - ISIS summary, D - EIGRP
       EX - EIGRP external, ND - ND Default, NDp - ND Prefix, DCE - Destination
       NDr - Redirect, O - OSPF Intra, OI - OSPF Inter, OE1 - OSPF ext 1
       OE2 - OSPF ext 2, ON1 - OSPF NSSA ext 1, ON2 - OSPF NSSA ext 2, l - LISP
S    2001:db8:172:16::0/64 [110/41]
      via ::ffff:c0a8:102, Serial0/0
C    2001:db8:101.1:1::0/127 [0/0]
      via FastEthernet0/0, directly connected
L    2001:db8:101.1::1/128 [0/0]
      via FastEthernet0/1, receive
<output omitted>
```

Default Gateway Issues in IPv6

IPv6 devices, as with IPv4 devices, require a route to destinations in other networks. Unless a host has been configured with a discreet route or default gateway, it is not able to connect to devices in another subnet. It is impractical to have routes to all other subnets on an end device. Therefore, a default gateway is required.

In Example 2-20, the following output is from PC1, assuming it is from the examples in the chapter. PC1 is

Example 2-20   *Looking at the PC IPv6 Configuration*

```
C:\windows\system32>ipconfig

Windows IP Configuration


Ethernet adapter Local Area Connection:


        Connection-specific DNS Suffix  . .:     jtiso.com
        Link-local IPv6 Address . . . . . :      fe80::3472:d687:f82:679c%1
        IPv6 Address. . . . . . . . . . . . .:  2001:db8:101.1::100
        Default Gateway . . . . . . . . . . :    2001:db8:101.1::1%1
```

Notice a percent sign (%), followed by a number, at the end of the IPv6 link-local address
and at the end of the default gateway. The number following the percent sign identifies
an interface on the PC and is not part of the IPv6 address. It should be ignored when
you establish the IPv6 address of the default gateway. The number following the % ID is
used by Windows to determine the zone ID, which is basically the interface to which the
default gateway and link local address belong.

In IPv6, the default gateway can be configured manually or by using stateless autoconfiguration. In the case of stateless autoconfiguration, the default gateway is revealed to
PCs in route advertisements. In IPv6, the IPv6 address that is declared inside route advertisements as a default gateway is the link-local IPv6 address of a router interface. If the
default gateway is configured manually, which is very unlikely, it can be set either to the
global IPv6 address or to the link-local IPv6 address.

Name Resolution Issues in IPv6

As noted, IPv6 addressing is long and difficult to remember. This makes DNS even more
important for IPv6 than it is for IPv4.

Like IPv4, the hosts file serves as the function of translating human-friendly hostnames
into IPv6 addresses that identify and locate a host in an IPv6 network. In some operating systems, the hosts files content is used preferentially to other methods, such as DNS.
Unlike DNS, the hosts file is under the direct control of the local computer's administrator.

For a Windows operating system, the file is located at c:\windows\system32\drivers\etc\
hosts. Other operating systems may have the hosts file in a different location, may use a
different file, or may not have such a file at all (for instance Cisco IOS Software keeps the
static IP to hosts mapping in the running configuration). Open the hosts file in a text editor such as Notepad.

Example 2-21 illustrates how to perform **nslookup** against a site that is running IPv6 and
IPv4.

Example 2-21 nslookup *on a Site Running IPv6 and IPv4*

```
JT-Mac:~ johnny$ nslookup
> set querytype=any
> www.google.com
Server:    192.168.220.1
Address:   192.168.220.1#53

Non-authoritative answer:
Name:   www.google.com
Address: 173.194.75.106
www.google.com has AAAA address 2607:f8b0:400c:c01::69

> exit
```

Note The other, less common types of name resolution (YP/NIS/NIS+, LDAP, and WINS), mentioned in the IPv4 section, also support IPv6.

DNS uses different record types to accommodate IPv6. In Example 2-21, AAAA is a record notation for the IPv6 address record (analogous to the IPv4 A record type).

Note For additional information, see the IANA assigned DNS record types: http://www.iana.org/assignments/dns-parameters/dns-parameters.xml.

ACL Issues in IPv6

The ACL functionality in IPv6 works very much like ACLs in IPv4. Access lists determine which traffic is blocked and forwarded at router interfaces. ACLs filter based on source and destination addresses, inbound and outbound to a specific interface. IPv6 ACLs are defined by deny and permit conditions. These are set using the **ipv6 access-list** command with the **deny** and **permit** keywords in global configuration mode.

IPv6 extended ACLs provide extended ACL functionality to support traffic filtering just like IPv4. IPv6 ACLs operate on IPv6 option headers and optional, upper-layer protocol type information for finer granularity of control. The following information from the packet is used for IPv6 inspection:

- Traffic class
- Flow label
- Payload length

- Next header

- Hop limit

- Source or destination address

All ACLs have **an implicit deny any** rule at the end. In IPv6, there are also explicit **permit** commands to allow neighbor discovery to operate. These are **permit icmp any any nd-na** and **permit icmp any any nd-ns**. This functionality is similar in concept to ARP in IPv4. IPv4 ARP uses a separate data link protocol, so it is not blocked by ACLs unless specifically defined. The respective purposes of ARP and IPv6 neighbor discovery are very similar, to allow local neighbors to be detected or to permit IPv6 neighbor discovery. Example 2-22 lists the implicit standards in an IPv6 access rule.

Example 2-22   *IPv6 ACL Implicit Rules*

```
permit icmp any any nd-na
permit icmp any any nd-ns
deny ipv6 any any
```

As previously stated, IPv6 has additional filtering options over IPv4. These are related to the changes in the protocol structure from IPv4, such as:

- Layer 4 protocol

- Authentication Header Protocol (AHP)

- Encapsulating Security Payload (ESP)

- Payload Compression Protocol (PCP)

- Stream Control Transmission Protocol (SCTP)

- SCTP, TCP, and UDP ports

- ICMP types and codes

- IGMP types (Internet Group Messaging Protocol; primarily used for multicast)

- Flow label

- DSCP value (Differentiated Services Code Point; used for QoS marking)

- TCP packets with the ACK, FIN, PSH, RST, SYN, or URG header bits set

- Established TCP connections

- Packet length

ACL invalid configuration can interfere with connectivity. Use the **show ipv6 access-list** command to verify whether there are any IPv6 ACLs configured on a router. In Example 2-23, there is an ACL named *Outbound* configured on the router. The ACL is applied to the GigabitEthernet0/1 interface in the outbound direction. It permits only ICMP, which allows ping to work. To permit other protocols to pass through, you need to add an entry in the *Outbound* ACL.

Example 2-23   *IPv6 ACL*

```
Branch# show ipv6 interface GigabitEthernet0/1 | include access list
  Outbound access list Outbound
Branch# show ipv6 access-list
IPv6 access list Outbound
    permit icmp any any (44 matches) sequence 10
```

IPv6 in a Virtual Environment

In a virtual environment using IPv6, the concerns and functionalities are pretty much identical to those in an IPv4 environment. One of the key concerns is which protocols are running on the hypervisor versus which are running on the virtual machine(s). Depending on how your hypervisor is configured and operates, you could potentially have IPv4 and/ or IPv6 running on a physical or virtual device, with no instance of that protocol on the corresponding physical or virtual device.

A Last Note on Troubleshooting

A good troubleshooter uses common sense, instinct, knowledge, and method. Figure 2-15 represents a real-life scenario. A technician was dispatched to upgrade a site to a new WAN circuit and a router. The new router was twice the size of the original one, which was clearly installed incorrectly. The technician had the common sense to inform the remote team that the current (unconventional and potentially unsafe) placement of the old router inside a drop ceiling was also unstable for the new, larger router. The ceiling, while it had barely supported the old device, would most likely not support the new one. Her good sense avoided a potentially dangerous situation.

Finally, it is important to keep the data center and wiring closet clean, labeled, and clutter free. Figure 2-16, shows a real-life scenario of a brand new infrastructure that needed troubleshooting. There were various inconsistencies, including how the devices were homed to the core. Multiple cabling issues were causing bridging loops and inoperable EtherChannel links. Unfortunately, it was very difficult to resolve any issues in this cabling nightmare.

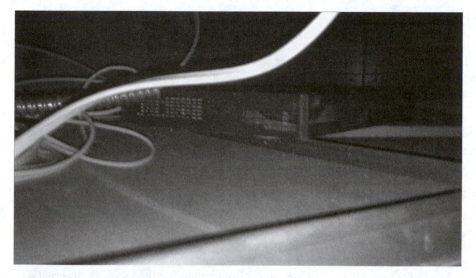

Figure 2-15   *Incorrect Router Placement*

Figure 2-16   *Suboptimal Data Center*

Chapter Summary

This chapter discussed troubleshooting basic connectivity. In troubleshooting, a variety of factors must be considered, including the path packets take, configuration issues, access control lists, and physical layer issues. This chapter also covered the IPv4 and IPv6 protocols and examined their similarities and differences.

As a troubleshooter, you need to have a good understanding of how networks are supposed to operate, both in theory and in practice. You should use a logical and structured method when troubleshooting.

Review Questions

Use the questions here to review what you learned in this chapter. The correct answers are located in Appendix A, "Answers to Chapter Review Questions."

1. Which command would you use to check whether input or output errors exist on a GigabitEthernet0/0 interface? (Source: "Troubleshooting IPv4 Basic Connectivity")

    a. show ip route Gi0/0
    b. show ip interfaces Gi0/0
    c. show interfaces Gigabit0/0
    d. show mac-address-table

2. Connect each of the routing table entries on the left to its description on the right. (Source: "Troubleshooting IPv6 Network Connectivity")

1. Default route	a. Local IP address on router interface
2. Static routing	b. Statically or dynamically learned and used when no other route matches the destination
3. Local host routes	c. Entered manually by a network administrator
4. Dynamic routing	d. An interface on the router directly connects to this network
5. Directly connected	e. Learning routes dynamically through a routing protocol

3. Which command would you use to verify that an ACL is applied to an interface? (Source: "Troubleshooting IPv4 Basic Connectivity")

    a. show access lists GigabitEthernet0/1
    b. show access lists
    c. show ip interface GigabitEthernet0/1
    d. show ip access list

4. Which command would you use to identify the current IPv6 path on a router? (Source: "Troubleshooting IPv6 Network Connectivity")

  a. show ip route
  b. show ipv6 interfaces brief
  c. show arp
  d. show ipv6 route

5. What controls mapping between IPv6 and Layer 2 addressing? (Source: "Verification of End-to-End IPv6 Connectivity")

  a. ARP cache
  b. Neighbor discovery process and ICMPv6
  c. ARP cache and NDP
  d. ICMPv6 and mac-address table

6. Which is not a valid IPv6 address type? (Source: "IPv6 Unicast Addresses")

  a. Global
  b. Reserved
  c. Private
  d. Link-Local
  e. Classful

7. Which statement or statements is/are false concerning networking in a virtualized computing environment? (Source: "Understanding Networking in Virtualized Computing Environments" and "IPv6 in a Virtual Environment")

  a. If a hypervisor runs IPv4, the virtual machine(s) must run IPv4 or dual-stack IPv4/IPv6.
  b. A hypervisor's networking and virtual machines' networking may or may not have unique addressing at Layer 2/3.
  c. Virtualization does not add much complexity to troubleshooting the network.
  d. A hypervisor may run directly on computer hardware or over a host operating system.

8. Which command or commands is/are implicit in an IPv6 access list? (Source: "ACL Issues in IPv6")

  a. permit icmp any any nd-na
  b. permit icmp any any nd-ns
  c. deny any any
  d. All of the above

Chapter 3

Implementing an EIGRP Solution

This chapter contains the following sections:

- Dynamic Routing Review

- EIGRP Features and Function

- Troubleshooting EIGRP

- Implementing EIGRP for IPv6

- Chapter Summary

- Review Questions

EIGRP, Enhanced Interior Gateway Protocol, is an advanced distance vector routing protocol that was developed by Cisco over 20 years ago. It is suited for many different topologies and media. EIGRP scales well and provides extremely quick convergence times with minimal overhead. EIGRP performs in both well-designed networks and poorly designed networks. It is a popular choice for a routing protocol on Cisco devices. EIGRP did have a predecessor, Interior Gateway Protocol (IGRP), which is now obsolete and is not included in Cisco IOS 15.

EIGRP was historically a Cisco proprietary and closed protocol. However, as of this writing, Cisco is in the process of releasing the basic functions to the IETF as an RFC (Request For Comments, a standards document; see http://tools.ietf.org/html/draft-savage-eigrp-00).

This chapter begins with a review of dynamic routing. It then examines the operation, configuration, and troubleshooting of EIGRP for IPv4 and IPv6.

Chapter Objectives:

- Review key concepts for Dynamic Routing Protocols

- Understand how a Cisco Router populates its routing table

- Understand the features, operation, theory, and functions of EIGRP

- Configure and troubleshoot EIGRP for IPv6 and IPv4

Dynamic Routing Review

A dynamic routing protocol is a set of processes, algorithms, and messages that is used to exchange routing and reachability information within the internetwork. Without a dynamic routing protocol, all networks, except those connected directly with the router, must be statically defined. Dynamic routing protocols can react to changes in conditions in the network, such as failed links.

Routing

All routing protocols have the same purpose: to learn about remote networks and to quickly adapt whenever there is a change in the topology. The method that a routing protocol uses to accomplish this purpose depends upon the algorithm that it uses and the operational characteristics of the protocol. The performance of a dynamic routing protocol varies depending on the type of routing protocol.

Although routing protocols provide routers with up-to-date routing tables, there are costs that put additional demands on the memory and processing power of the router. First, the exchange of route information adds overhead that consumes network bandwidth. This overhead can be a problem, particularly for low-bandwidth links between routers. Second, after the router receives the route information, the routing protocol needs to process the information received. Therefore, routers that employ these protocols must have sufficient resources to implement the algorithms of the protocol and to perform timely packet routing and forwarding.

Routing Domains

An autonomous system (AS), otherwise known as a routing domain, is a collection of routers under a common administration. A typical example is an internal network of a company and its interconnection to the network of an ISP. The ISP and a company's internal network are under different control. Therefore, they need a way to interconnect. Static routes are often used in this type of a scenario. However, what if there are multiple links between the company and the ISP? What if the company uses more than one ISP? Static routing protocols would not be suitable. To connect the entities, it is necessary to establish communication with the bodies under different administration. Another example would be a merger, acquisition, or development of a subsidiary that maintains its own IT resources. The networks may need to be connected, but they also may need to be maintained as separate entities. There must be a way to communicate between the two. The third example, which is intimated by the first, is the public Internet. Many different entities are interconnected here as well. Figure 3-1 is a representation of three autonomous systems, one for a private company and two ISPs.

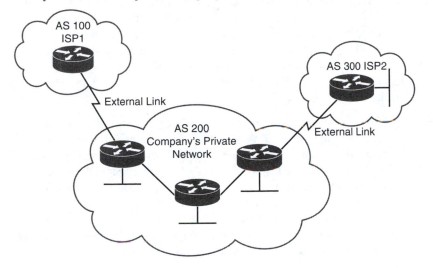

Figure 3-1   *Connection of Three Distinct Autonomous Systems (AS)*

To accommodate these types of scenarios, two categories of routing protocols exist:

- **Interior Gateway Protocols (IGP):** These routing protocols are used to exchange routing information within an autonomous system. EIGRP, IS-IS (Intermediate System-to-Intermediate System) Protocol, RIP (Routing Information Protocol), and OSPF (Open Shortest Path First) Protocol are examples of IGPs.

- **Exterior Gateway Protocols (EGP):** These routing protocols are used to route between autonomous systems. BGP (Border Gateway Protocol) is the EGP of choice in networks today. *The* Exterior Gateway Protocol, designed in 1982, was the first EGP. It has since been deprecated in favor of BGP and is considered obsolete. BGP is the routing protocol used on the public Internet.

Classification of Routing Protocols

EGPs and IGPs are further classified depending on how they are designed and operate. There are two categories of routing protocols:

- **Distance vector protocols:** The distance vector routing approach determines the direction (vector) and distance (hops) to any point in the internetwork. Some distance vector protocols periodically send complete routing tables to all of the connected neighbors. In large networks, these routing updates can become enormous, causing significant traffic on the links. This can also cause slow convergence, as the whole routing table could be inconsistent due to network changes, such as a link down, between updates. RIP is an example of a protocol that sends out periodic updates.

Distance vector protocols use routers as signposts along the path to the final destination. The only information that a router knows about a remote network is the distance or metric to reach that network and which path or interface to use to get there. Distance vector routing protocols do not have an actual map of the network topology. EIGRP is another example of the distance vector routing protocol. However, unlike RIP, EIGRP does not send out full copies of the routing table once the initial setup occurs between two neighboring routers. EIGRP only sends updates when there is a change.

■ **Link-state protocols:** The link-state approach, which uses the shortest path first (SPF) algorithm, creates an abstract of the exact topology of the entire internetwork, or at least of the partition in which the router is situated. Using a link-state routing protocol is like having a complete map of the network topology. Signposts along the way from the source to the destination are not necessary because all link-state routers are using an identical "map" of the network. A link-state router uses the link-state information to create a topology map and select the best path to all destination networks in the topology. Link-state protocols only send updates when there is a change in the network. BGP, OSPF, and IS-IS are examples of link-state routing protocols.

Note   EIGRP was originally classified as a "hybrid" routing protocol, the combination of link state and distance vector. However, it is truly a rich-featured distance vector protocol. A major differentiator to support this is that EIGRP does not have a full picture of the topology in each node.

Classful Routing Versus Classless Routing

IP addresses are categorized in classes: A, B, and C. Classful routing protocols only recognize networks as directly connected by class. So, if a network is subnetted, there cannot be a classful boundary in between. In Figure 3-2, Network A cannot reach Network B using a classful routing protocol because they are separated by a different class network. The term for this scenario is *discontiguous subnets*.

Classful routing is a consequence when subnet masks are not disclosed in the routing advertisements that most distance vector routing protocols generate. When a classful routing protocol is used, all subnetworks of the same major network (Class A, B, or C) must use the same subnet mask, which is not necessarily a default major-class subnet mask. Routers that are running a classful routing protocol perform automatic route summarization across network boundaries. Classful routing has become somewhat obsolete because the classful model is rarely used on the Internet. Because IP address depletion problems occur on the Internet, most Internet blocks are subdivided using classless routing and variable-length subnet masks. You will most likely see classful address allocation inside private organizations that use private IP addresses as defined in RFC 1918 in conjunction with Network Address Translation (NAT) at AS borders.

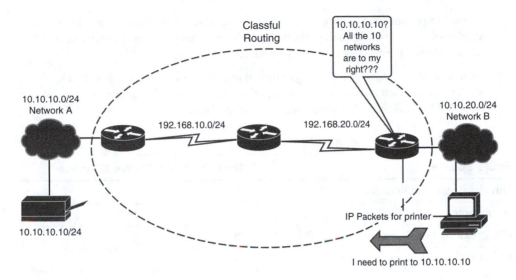

Figure 3-2 *Sample Classful Routing Domain*

Classless routing protocols can be considered second-generation protocols because they are designed to address some of the limitations of the earlier classful routing protocols. A serious limitation in a classful network environment is that the subnet mask is not exchanged during the routing update process, thus requiring the same subnet mask to be used on all subnetworks within the same major network. Another limitation of the classful approach is the need to automatically summarize to the classful network number at all major network boundaries. In the classless environment, the summarization process is controlled manually and can usually be invoked at any bit position within the address. Because subnet routes are propagated throughout the routing domain, manual summarization may be required to keep the size of the routing tables manageable. Classless routing protocols include BGP, RIPv2, EIGRP, OSPF, and IS-IS. Classful routing protocols include Cisco IGRP and RIPv1.

> **Note** RFC 1918 defines the following networks for private use, meaning they are not routed on the public Internet: 10.0.0.0/8, 172.16.0.0/16–172.31.0.0/26, and 192.168.0.0/24–192.168.255.0/24. For more information on RFC 1918, see http://tools.ietf.org/html/rfc1918.

Administrative Distance

Multiple routing protocols and static routes may be used at the same time. If there are several sources for routing information, including specific routing protocols, static routes, and even directly connected networks, an administrative distance value is used to rate the trustworthiness of each routing information source. Cisco IOS Software uses the administrative distance feature to select the best path when it learns about the exact same destination network from two or more routing sources.

An administrative distance is an integer from 0 to 255. A routing protocol with a lower administrative distance is more trustworthy than one with a higher administrative distance. Table 3-1 displays the default administrative distances.

Table 3-1 *Default Administrative Distances*

Route Source	Default Administrative Distance
Directly connected interface	0
Static route	1
eBGP (external BGP; between two different AS)	20
EIGRP	90
OSPF	110
RIP (both v1 and v2)	120
EIGRP External	170
iBGP (internal BGP, inside AS)	200
Unknown/untrusted source	255

Note There are other administrative distances, the discussion of which is beyond the scope of this text. See http://www.cisco.com/en/US/tech/tk365/technologies_tech_note09186a0080094195.shtml for more information.

As shown in the example in Figure 3-3, the router must deliver a packet from Network A to Network B. The router must choose between two routes. One is routed by EIGRP, and the other is routed by OSPF. Although the OSPF route appears to be the logical choice, given that it includes fewer hops to the destination network, the EIGRP route is identified as more trustworthy and is added to the routing table of the router.

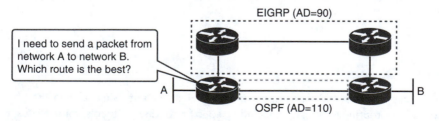

Figure 3-3 *Administrative Distance*

A good way to detect which routing protocols are configured on the router is to execute **show ip protocols**. Example 3-1 gives output from a sample router running OSPF, EIGRP, and BGP. The command provides details regarding each routing protocol, including the administrative distance (Distance), values the routing protocol is using, and other features such as route filtering.

Example 3-1 show ip protocols *Command Output*

```
Branch# show ip protocols
Routing Protocol is "eigrp 1"
  Outgoing update filter list for all interfaces is not set
  Incoming update filter list for all interfaces is not set
  Default networks flagged in outgoing updates
  Default networks accepted from incoming updates
  EIGRP metric weight K1=1, K2=0, K3=1, K4=0, K5=0
  EIGRP maximum hopcount 100
  EIGRP maximum metric variance 1
  Redistributing: eigrp 1
  EIGRP NSF-aware route hold timer is 240s
  Automatic network summarization is in effect
  Automatic address summarization:
    192.200.200.0/24 for Loopback0, Loopback100
    192.168.1.0/24 for Loopback0, Vlan1
    172.16.0.0/16 for Loopback100, Vlan1
      Summarizing with metric 128256
  Maximum path: 4
  Routing for Networks:
    0.0.0.0
  Routing Information Sources:
    Gateway         Distance      Last Update
    (this router)         90      00:00:18
  Distance: internal 90 external 170

Routing Protocol is "eigrp 100"
  Outgoing update filter list for all interfaces is not set
  Incoming update filter list for all interfaces is not set
  Default networks flagged in outgoing updates
  Default networks accepted from incoming updates
  EIGRP metric weight K1=1, K2=0, K3=1, K4=0, K5=0
  EIGRP maximum hopcount 100
  EIGRP maximum metric variance 1
  Redistributing: eigrp 100
  EIGRP NSF-aware route hold timer is 240s
  Automatic network summarization is in effect
  Automatic address summarization:
```

```
      192.168.1.0/24 for Loopback0
      172.16.0.0/16 for Loopback100
        Summarizing with metric 128256
    Maximum path: 4
    Routing for Networks:
      172.16.1.0/24
      192.168.1.0
    Routing Information Sources:
      Gateway           Distance      Last Update
      (this router)           90        00:00:19
    Distance: internal 90 external 170


Routing Protocol is "ospf 100"
    Outgoing update filter list for all interfaces is not set
    Incoming update filter list for all interfaces is not set
    Router ID 172.16.1.100
    Number of areas in this router is 1. 1 normal 0 stub 0 nssa
    Maximum path: 4
    Routing for Networks:
      255.255.255.255 0.0.0.0 area 0
   Reference bandwidth unit is 100 mbps
    Routing Information Sources:
      Gateway           Distance      Last Update
    Distance: (default is 110)


Routing Protocol is "bgp 100"
    Outgoing update filter list for all interfaces is not set
    Incoming update filter list for all interfaces is not set
    IGP synchronization is disabled
    Automatic route summarization is disabled
    Maximum path: 1
    Routing Information Sources:
      Gateway           Distance      Last Update
    Distance: external 20 internal 200 local 200
```

EIGRP Features and Function

EIGRP is a Cisco proprietary routing protocol that combines the advantages of link-state and distance vector routing protocols. EIGRP may act like a link-state routing protocol as it uses a Hello protocol to discover neighbors and form neighbor relationships, and only partial updates are sent when a change occurs. However, EIGRP is still based on the key distance vector routing protocol principle in which information about the rest of the network is learned from directly connected neighbors. EIGRP is an advanced distance vector routing protocol that includes the following features:

- **Rapid convergence:** EIGRP uses the DUAL algorithm to achieve rapid convergence. As the computational engine that runs EIGRP, DUAL is the main computational engine of the routing protocol, guaranteeing loop-free paths and backup paths (called *feasible successors*) throughout the routing domain. A router that uses EIGRP stores all available backup routes for destinations so that it can quickly adapt to alternate routes. If the primary route in the routing table fails, the best backup route is immediately added to the routing table. If no appropriate route or backup route exists in the local routing table, EIGRP queries its neighbors to discover an alternate route.

- **Load balancing:** EIGRP supports both equal and unequal metric load balancing, which allows administrators to better distribute traffic flow in their networks.

- **Loop-free, classless routing:** Because EIGRP is a classless routing protocol, it advertises a routing mask for each destination network. The routing mask feature enables EIGRP to support discontiguous subnets and variable-length subnet masks (VLSM).

- **Reduced bandwidth usage:** EIGRP uses the terms *partial* and *bounded* when referring to its updates. EIGRP does not make periodic updates. *Partial* means that the update includes only information about the route changes. EIGRP sends these incremental updates when the state of a destination changes, instead of sending the entire contents of the routing table. *Bounded* refers to the propagation of partial updates that are sent specifically to those routers that are affected by the changes. By sending only the necessary routing information to those routers that need it, EIGRP minimizes the bandwidth required to send EIGRP updates. EIGRP uses multicast and unicast rather than broadcast. Multicast EIGRP packets employ the reserved multicast address of 224.0.0.10. As a result, end stations are unaffected by routing updates and requests for topology information.

EIGRP has four basic components:

- Neighbor discovery/recovery

- Reliable Transport Protocol

- DUAL finite state machine

- Protocol-dependent modules

Neighbor discovery/recovery is the process that routers use to dynamically learn about other routers on their directly attached networks. Routers must also discover when their neighbors become unreachable or inoperative. This process is achieved with low overhead by periodically sending small hello packets. As long as hello packets are received, a router can determine that a neighbor is alive and functioning. Once this is confirmed, the neighboring routers can exchange routing information.

The reliable transport protocol (not to be confused with Real Time Protocol-RTP, which is used to carry Voice over IP traffic) is responsible for guaranteed, ordered delivery of EIGRP packets to all neighbors. It supports the simultaneous usage of multicast or unicast packets. Only some EIGRP packets must be transmitted perfectly. For efficiency, reliability is provided only when necessary. For example, on a multiaccess network that has multicast capabilities, such as Ethernet, sending hellos reliably to all neighbors individually is not required. So, EIGRP sends a single multicast hello with an indication in the packet informing the receivers that the packet does not need to be acknowledged. Other types of packets, such as updates, require acknowledgment, and that is indicated in the packet. The reliable transport protocol has a provision to send multicast packets quickly when there are unacknowledged packets pending. This ensures that convergence time remains low in the presence of links with varying speed.

The DUAL finite state machine embodies the decision process for all route computations. It tracks all routes advertised by all neighbors. The distance information, known as a *metric*, is used by DUAL to select efficient loop-free paths. DUAL selects routes to be inserted into a routing table based on feasible successors. A successor is a neighboring router used for packet forwarding that has a least cost path to a destination that is guaranteed not to be part of a routing loop. When there are no feasible successors but there are neighbors advertising the destination, a recomputation must occur. This is the process where a new successor is determined. The amount of time it takes to recalculate the route affects the convergence time. Even though the recomputation is not processor-intensive, it is better to avoid it if possible. When a topology change occurs, DUAL tests for feasible successors. If there are feasible successors, it uses any it finds in order to avert any unnecessary recomputation. Feasible successors are defined in detail later in this book.

The protocol-dependent modules are responsible for network layer, protocol-specific requirements. For example, the IP-EIGRP module is accountable for sending and receiving EIGRP packets that are encapsulated in IP. IP-EIGRP is responsible for parsing EIGRP packets and informing DUAL of the new information received. IP-EIGRP asks DUAL to make routing decisions, the results of which are stored in the IP routing table. IP-EIGRP is accountable for redistributing routes learned by other IP routing protocols.

EIGRP Packet Types

EIGRP uses five packet types:

- Hello/ACKs
- Updates
- Queries
- Replies
- Requests

As stated earlier, hellos are multicast for neighbor discovery/recovery. They do not require acknowledgment. A hello with no data is also used as an acknowledgment (ACK). ACKs are always sent using a unicast address and contain a non-zero acknowledgment number.

Updates are used to give information on routes. When a new neighbor is discovered, update packets are sent so that the neighbor can build up its EIGRP topology table. In this case, update packets are unicast. In other cases, such as a link cost change, updates are multicast.

Queries and replies are used for finding and conveying routes. Queries are always multicast unless they are sent in response to a received query. ACKs to queries always unicast back to the successor that originated the query. Replies are always sent in response to queries to indicate to the originator that it does not need to go into Active state because it has feasible successors. Replies are unicast to the originator of the query. Both queries and replies are transmitted reliably.

Note   EIGRP has two other type of packets, but they are insignificant: request packets and IPX SAP packets. Request packets are specialized packets that were never fully implemented in EIGRP. EIGRP for Internet Packet Exchange (IPX) has IPX SAP packets. These packets have an optional code in them, technically making them another packet type.

EIGRP Path Selection

Each EIGRP router maintains a neighbor table. This table includes a list of directly connected EIGRP routers that have an adjacency with this router. Neighbor relationships are used to track the status of these neighbors. EIGRP uses a low-overhead Hello protocol to establish and monitor the connection status with its neighbors.

Each EIGRP router maintains a topology table for each routed protocol configuration. The topology table includes route entries for every destination that the router learns from its directly connected EIGRP neighbors. EIGRP chooses the best routes to a destination from the topology table and places these routes in the routing table.

Figure 3-4 gives an example of the neighbor table, the topology table, and the subsequent derived routing table from the example.

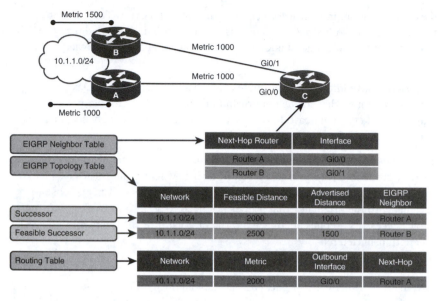

Figure 3-4 *EIGRP Path Selection*

To determine the best route (successor) and any backup routes (feasible successors) to a destination, EIGRP uses the following two parameters:

- **Advertised distance (AD):** The EIGRP metric for an EIGRP neighbor to reach a particular network.

- **Feasible distance (FD):** The AD for a particular network that is learned from an EIGRP neighbor plus the EIGRP metric to reach that neighbor. This sum provides an end-to-end metric from the router to that remote network. A router compares all FDs to reach a specific network and then selects the lowest FD and places it in the routing table.

The EIGRP topology table contains all of the routes that are known to each EIGRP neighbor. As shown in Figure 3-4, Routers A and B sent their routing tables to Router C, whose table is displayed. Both Routers A and B have routes to network 10.1.1.0/24 as well as to other networks that are not shown.

Router C has two entries to reach 10.1.1.0/24 in its topology table. The EIGRP metric for Router C to reach both Routers A and B is 1000. Add this metric (1000) to the respective AD for each route, and the results represent the FDs that Router C must travel to reach network 10.1.1.0/24.

Router C chooses the least FD (2000) and installs it in the IP routing table as the best route to reach 10.1.1.0/24. The route with the least FD that is installed in the routing table is called the *successor route*.

If one or more feasible successor routes exist, Router C chooses a backup route to the successor, called a *feasible successor route*. To become a feasible successor, a route must satisfy this feasibility condition: a next-hop router must have an AD that is less than the FD of the current successor route. (Hence, the route is tagged as a feasible successor, which is a loop-free path to the destination). This rule is used to ensure that the network is loop-free.

If the route via the successor becomes invalid, possibly because of a topology change, or if a neighbor changes the metric, DUAL checks for feasible successors to the destination route. If one is found, DUAL uses it, avoiding the need to recompute the route. A route changes from a passive state to an active state (actively sending queries to neighboring routers for alternative routes) if a feasible successor does not exist and recomputation is necessary to determine the new successor.

Note   In Figure 3-4, values for the EIGRP metric and for FDs and ADs are simplified to make the scenario easier to understand. The metrics in a real-world example would normally be larger.

Understanding the EIGRP Metric

The EIGRP metric can be based on several criteria, but EIGRP uses only two of these by default:

- **Bandwidth:** The smallest bandwidth of all outgoing interfaces between the source and destination in kilobits per second.

- **Delay:** The cumulative (sum) of all interface delay along the route in tenths of micro-seconds.

The following criteria also can be used for the EIGRP metric, but using them is not rec-ommended because they typically result in frequent recalculation of the topology table:

- **Reliability:** This value represents the worst reliability between the source and desti-nation, which is based on keepalives.

- **Load:** This value represents the worst load on a link between the source and destina-tion, which is computed based on the packet rate and the configured bandwidth of the interface.

- **K values:** K values are administratively set parameters that manipulate the value of the EIGRP Metrics. Changing them is not recommended. They are involved in the metric calculation and are set to 1 and 0 to default,. This way, the default K values do not affect the metric(K1, K3 are one – K1, K4, K5 are zero). The K values are

  - K1 = Bandwidth modifier

  - K2 = Load modifier

  - K3 = Delay modifier

- K4 = Reliability modifier

- K5 = Additional Reliability modifier

The composite metric formula is used by EIGRP to calculate metric value. The formula consists of values K1 through K5, which are known as EIGRP metric weights. By default, K1 and K3 are set to 1, and K2, K4, and K5 are set to 0. The result is that only the bandwidth and delay values are used in the computation of the default composite metric. The metric calculation method (K values) and the EIGRP AS number must match between EIGRP neighbors. Figure 3-5 shows a sample metric calculation with default K values and scaled metrics.

EIGRP uses scaled values to determine the total metric: 256 * ([K1 * bandwidth] + [K2 * bandwidth] / [256 – Load] + K3 * Delay) * (K5 / [Reliability + K4]), where if K5 = 0, the (K5 / [Reliability + K4]) part is not used (that is, equals to 1). Using the default K values, the metric calculation simplifies to 256 * (bandwidth + delay). Figure 3-5 gives the metrics in scaled values. Delay and bandwidth are scaled to mathematically fit the equation. 10^7 is used for bandwidth, and 10 is used for delay. This helps keep the metric as a manageable number.

Although a maximum transmission unit (MTU) is exchanged in EIGRP packets between neighbor routers, the MTU is not factored into the EIGRP metric calculation.

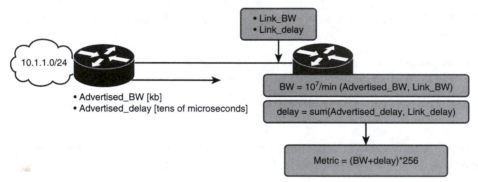

Figure 3-5 *EIGRP Metric*

By using the **show interface** command, you can examine the actual values that are used for bandwidth, delay, reliability, and load in the computation of the routing metric. The output in Example 3-2 shows the values that are used in the composite metric for the Serial0/0/0 interface.

Example 3-2 show interface *to Verify the EIGRP Metric*

```
HQ# show interfaces serial 0/0/0
Serial0/0/0 is up, line protocol is down
  Hardware is GT96K Serial   Description: Link to Branch
    MTU 1500 bytes, BW 1544 Kbit/sec, DLY 20000 usec,
      reliability 255/255, txload 1/255, rxload 1/255
<output truncated>
```

EIGRP Basic Configuration

The **router eigrp** global configuration command enables EIGRP. Use the **router eigrp** and **network** commands to create an EIGRP routing process. Note that EIGRP requires an AS number. The AS parameter is a number between 1 and 65,535 that is chosen by the network administrator and must match all routers in the EIGRP AS. The **network** command is used in the router configuration mode.

Figure 3-6 shows a sample two-node network that is the basis for the following examples explaining how to configure EIGRP.

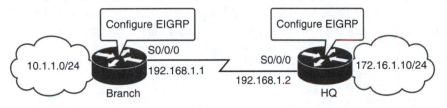

Figure 3-6 *Example Network for EIGRP Configuration*

Example 3-3 shows how to configure EIGRP on the Branch router.

Example 3-3 *Configuring EIGRP on the Branch Router*

```
Branch(config)# router eigrp 100
Branch(config-router)# network 10.1.1.0
Branch(config-router)# network 192.168.1.0
```

Example 3-4 shows how to configure EIGRP on the HQ router.

Example 3-4 *Configuring EIGRP on the HQ Router*

```
HQ(config)# router eigrp 100
HQ(config-router)# network 172.16.1.0 0.0.0.255
HQ(config-router)# network 192.168.1.0 0.0.0.255
```

Table 3-2 describes the EIGRP commands in detail.

Table 3-2 *EIGRP Commands*

Command	Description
router eigrp *as_number*	Enables the EIGRP routing process for the AS number that is specified.
network *network_id wildcard_mask*	Associates the network with the EIGRP routing process. Use of the wildcard mask to match multiple networks is optional.

In Examples 3-3 and 3-4 the **router eigrp** and **network** commands were used to create an EIGRP routing process. Note that EIGRP requires an AS number. In this case, the AS number is 100 on both routers, because the AS parameter must match in all EIGRP routers for the formation of neighbor adjacency and for routes to be exchanged.

The **network** command defines a major network number to which the router is directly connected. Any interface on this router that matches the network address in the **network** command is enabled to send and receive EIGRP updates. The EIGRP routing process searches for interfaces that have an IP address that belongs to the networks specified with the **network** command. The EIGRP process begins on these interfaces. As you can see in Example 3-5, the EIGRP process is running on the interface. However, a second EIGRP process has been configured, but it does not match any interfaces in the **network** command.

Example 3-5   *Reviewing the EIGRP Neighbors*

```
HQ# show ip eigrp neighbors
IP-EIGRP neighbors for process 100
H   Address                 Interface       Hold  Uptime   SRTT   RTO   Q   Seq
                                            (sec)          (ms)        Cnt Num
0   192.168.1.2             FastEthernet0/0  11 00:04:17    8    200   0   2
IP-EIGRP neighbors for process 100
```

Note   For more details regarding the **router eigrp** command, check out the *Cisco IOS IP Routing: EIGRP Command Reference* at http://www.cisco.com/en/US/docs/ios/iproute_eigrp/command/reference/ire_book.html.

For more details regarding the **network** command, see the *Cisco IOS IP Routing: Protocol-Independent Command Reference* at http://www.cisco.com/en/US/docs/ios/iproute_pi/command/reference/iri_book.html.

Verification of EIGRP Configuration and Operation

Use the **show ip eigrp neighbors** command to display the neighbors that EIGRP discovered and determine when they become active and inactive. The command is also useful for debugging when neighbors are not communicating properly.

As you can see in Figure 3-7, the Branch router has a neighbor relationship with the HQ router, which is also shown in the following command output:

```
Branch# show ip eigrp neighbors
IP-EIGRP neighbors for AS(100)
H      Address      Interface     Hold  Uptime    SRTT   RTO   Q    Seq
                                  (sec)           (ms)        Cnt  Num
0      192.168.1.2  S0/0/0         12  00:03:10   1231   4500   0    3
```

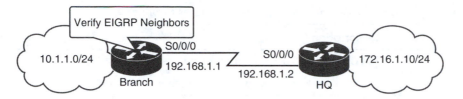

Figure 3-7 *Verification of EIGRP Configuration with* **show ip eigrp neighbors** *Command*

Table 3-3 identifies the key fields in the output of **show ip eigrp neighbors**.

Table 3-3 *Key Output Fields from* **show ip eigrp neighbors** *Command*

Field	Definition
AS	AS identifier for this EIGRP process.
Address	IP address of the neighbor.
Interface	The interface that EIGRP receives hello packets from the neighbor on.
Hold	Length of time (in seconds) that Cisco IOS Software waits to hear from the peer before declaring it down. If the peer is using the default hold time, this number is less than 15. If the peer configures a nondefault hold time, the nondefault hold time is displayed.
Uptime	Elapsed time (in hours:minutes:seconds) since the local router first heard from this neighbor.
Q Cnt	Number of EIGRP packets (update, query, and reply) that the software is waiting to send.
Seq Num	Sequence number of the last update, query, or reply packet that was received from this neighbor.

Use the **show ip eigrp interfaces** command to determine active EIGRP interfaces and learn information regarding those interfaces. If you specify an interface (for example, **show ip eigrp interfaces FastEthernet0/0**), only that interface is displayed. Otherwise, all interfaces on which EIGRP is running are shown. If you specify an AS (for example, **show ip eigrp interfaces 100**), the only thing displayed is the routing process for the specified AS. Otherwise, all EIGRP processes are shown.

Table 3-4 defines the fields in **show ip eigrp interfaces**.

Table 3-4 *Key Output Fields from* **show ip eigrp interfaces** *Command*

Field	Description
Interface	Interface that EIGRP is configured on.
Peers	List of directly connected EIGRP neighbors.
Xmit Queue Unreliable/Reliable	Number of packets remaining in the Unreliable and Reliable queues.
Mean SRTT	Mean smooth round-trip time (SRTT) interval (in milliseconds).
Pacing Time Un/Reliable	Pacing time (how long to wait) used to determine when EIGRP packets should be sent out the interface (Unreliable and Reliable packets).
Multicast Flow Timer	Maximum number of seconds that the router will wait for an ACK packet after sending a multicast EIGRP packet, before switching from multicast to unicast.
Pending Routes	Number of routes in the packets sitting in the transmit queue waiting to be sent.

The **show ip route** command, as seen in the next section, in Example 3-6, displays the current entries in the routing table. EIGRP has a default administrative distance of 90 for internal routes and 170 for routes that are redistributed (redistributed routes are routes brought into a routing protocol from an external source; a routing protocol or static routes). When compared to other IGPs, EIGRP is the most preferred by Cisco IOS Software because it has the lowest administrative distance.

EIGRP Passive Interfaces

Most routing protocols have a passive interface. A passive interface suppresses some routing updates but also allows other updates to be exchanged normally. EIGRP is slightly different from other routing protocols. Routing updates are not received and processed. No neighbor relationships are established via a passive interface.

Passive interfaces are set in EIGRP configuration mode, as shown next, and are not configured on the interface:

```
router eigrp 1
passive-interface FastEthenet0/0
```

This sets passive interface status on FastEthernet0/0. The following sets passive interface status as the default behavior, and explicitly specifies which interfaces should not be "passive":

```
router eigrp 1
passive-interface default
no passive-interface FastEthenet0/0
```

This sets all interfaces to passive, except FastEthernet0/0.

Figure 3-8 displays a sample network for verification using the **show ip route** command.

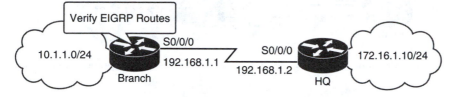

Figure 3-8   *Verification of EIGRP Configuration with* **show ip route** *Command*

The routing table is shown in Example 3-6.

Example 3-6   *Reviewing the Routing Table Using Passive Interfaces*

```
Branch# show ip route
Codes: C - connected, S - static, R - RIP, M - mobile, B - BGP
       D - EIGRP, EX - EIGRP external, O - OSPF, IA - OSPF inter area
       N1 - OSPF NSSA external type 1, N2 - OSPF NSSA external type 2
       E1 - OSPF external type 1, E2 - OSPF external type 2
       i - IS-IS, su - IS-IS summary, L1 - IS-IS level-1, L2 - IS-IS level-2
       ia - IS-IS inter area, * - candidate default, U - per-user static route
       o - ODR, P - periodic downloaded static route


Gateway of last resort is not set

     10.0.0.0/24 is subnetted, 1 subnets
C       10.1.1.0/24 is directly connected, GigabitEthernet0/0
L       10.1.1.1/32 is directly connected, GigabitEthernet0/0
     172.16.0.0/24 is subnetted, 1 subnets
D       172.16.1.0 [90/156160] via 192.168.1.2, 02:02:02, Serial 0/0/0
     192.168.1.0/24 is subnetted, 1 subnets
C       192.168.1.0/24 is directly connected, Serial0/0/0
L       192.168.1.1/32 is directly connected, Serial0/0/0
```

For the example network depicted in Example 3-7, the **show ip eigrp topology** command displays the EIGRP topology table, the active or passive state of routes, the number of successors, and the FD to the destination. Use the **show ip eigrp topology all-links** command to display all paths, even those that are not feasible.

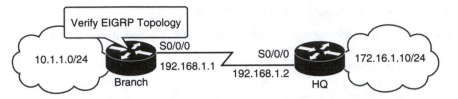

Figure 3-9   *Verification of EIGRP Configuration with* **show ip eigrp topology** *Command*

Example 3-7   *Using the* **show ip eigrp topology** *Command*

```
Branch# show ip eigrp topology
IP-EIGRP Topology Table for AS(100)/ID(192.168.1.1)


Codes: P - Passive, A - Active, U - Update, Q - Query, R - Reply,
       r - reply Status, s - sia Status


P 192.168.1.0/24, 1 successors, FD is 28160
        via Connected, Serial0/0/0
P 172.16.1.0/24, 1 successors, FD is 156160
        via 192.168.1.2 (156160/128256), Serial0/0/0
P 10.1.1.0/24, 1 successors, FD is 28160
        via Connected, GigabitEthernet0/0
```

Table 3-5 defines the fields in the **show ip eigrp topology** command.

Table 3-5   *Key Output Fields from* **show ip eigrp topology** *Command*

Field	Description
Codes	State of this topology table entry. Passive and Active refer to the EIGRP state with respect to this destination; Update, Query, and Reply refer to the type of packet that is being sent.
	P – Passive: No EIGRP computations are being performed for this destination.
	A – Active: EIGRP computations are being performed for this destination.
	U – Update: An update packet was sent to this destination.
	Q – Query: A query packet was sent to this destination.
	R – Reply: A reply packet was sent to this destination.
	r – Reply status Flag that is set after the software has sent a query and is waiting for a reply.

Field	Description
172.16.1.0 /24	Destination IP network number and bits in the subnet mask (/24=255.255.255.0)
successors	Number of successors. This number corresponds to the number of next hops in the IP routing table. If "successors" is capitalized, then the route or next hop is in a transition state.
FD	Feasible distance. The FD is the best metric to reach the destination or the best metric that was known when the route went active. This value is used in the feasibility condition check. If the advertised distance (AD) of the router (the metric after the slash) is less than the FD, the feasibility condition is met and that path is a feasible successor. Once the software determines it has a feasible successor, it does not need to send a query for that destination.
replies	Number of replies that are still outstanding (have not been received) with respect to this destination. This information appears only when the destination is in Active state.
via	IP address of the peer that informed the software about this destination. The first N of these entries, where N is the number of successors, are the current successors. The remaining entries on the list are feasible successors.
(156160/128256)	The first number is the EIGRP metric that represents the cost to the destination. The second number is the EIGRP metric that this peer advertised.
Serial0/0/0	Interface from which this information was learned.

Load Balancing with EIGRP

Every routing protocol supports equal-cost path load balancing, which is the ability of a router to distribute traffic over all of its network ports that are the same metric from the destination address. Load balancing increases the use of network segments and increases effective network bandwidth. EIGRP also supports unequal-cost path load balancing. You use the **variance** n command to instruct the router to include routes with a metric of less than n times the minimum metric route for that destination. The variable n can take a value between 1 and 128. The default is 1, which specifies equal-cost load balancing. Traffic is also distributed among the links with unequal costs, proportionately, with respect to the metric.

Here's a quick comparison of the two types of load balancing offered by EIGRP:

- **Equal-cost load balancing**

  - By default, up to four routes with a metric equal to the minimum metric are installed in the routing table.

  - By default, the routing table can have up to 16 entries for the same destination.

- **Unequal-cost load balancing**

  - By default, it is not turned on.

  - Load balancing can be performed through paths that are 128 times less desirable than the route with the lowest FD.

For IP, Cisco IOS Software applies load balancing across up to four equal-cost paths by default. With the **maximum-paths** router configuration command, up to 32 equal-cost routes can be kept in the routing table, depending on the router type and Cisco IOS version. If you set the value to 1, you disable load balancing. When a packet is process-switched, load balancing over equal-cost paths occurs on a per-packet basis. When packets are fast-switched, load balancing over equal-cost paths occurs on a per-destination basis.

Per-packet load balancing is problematic for applications such as voice and video, which require packets to arrive in order. Per-destination switching is the default and must be changed to per-packet using the interface command **ip load-sharing per-packet**. Unless your network is free of applications that require packets in order, changing this parameter is not recommended.

Variance

This section provides an example of variance for the sample network depicted in Figure 3-10.

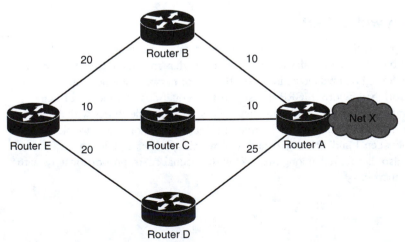

Figure 3-10 *Example Network to Display Metrics*

In Figure 3-10, there are three ways to get from Router E to Network X:

- E-B-A with a metric of 30

- E-C-A with a metric of 20

- E-D-A with a metric of 45

Router E chooses the path E-C-A with a metric of 20 because 20 is better than 30 and 45. To instruct EIGRP to select the path E-B-A as well, you would configure **variance** with a multiplier of 2:

```
router eigrp 1
network x.x.x.x variance 2
```

This configuration increases the minimum metric to 40 (2 * 20 = 40). EIGRP includes all routes that have a metric of less than or equal to 40 and satisfy the feasibility condition. The configuration in this section illustrates that EIGRP now uses two paths to reach Network X, E-C-A and E-B-A, because both paths have a metric of under 40. EIGRP does not use path E-D-A because that path has a metric of 45, which is not less than the value of the minimum metric of 40 because of the variance configuration. Also, the AD of neighbor D is 25, which is greater than the FD of 20 through C. This means that, even if variance is set to 3, the E-D-A path is not selected for load balancing because Router D is not a feasible successor.

Traffic Sharing

EIGRP provides not only unequal-cost path load balancing, but also intelligent load balancing, such as traffic sharing. To control how traffic is distributed among routes when multiple routes for the same destination network have different costs, use the **traffic-share balanced** command. With the keyword **balanced**, the router distributes traffic proportionately to the ratios of the metrics that are associated with different routes. This is the default setting:

```
router eigrp 1
network x.x.x.x   variance 2
traffic-share balanced
```

The traffic share count for the example in Figure 3-10 is

- **For path E-C-A:** 30 / 20 = 3 / 2 = 1

- **For path E-B-A:** 30 / 30 = 1

Because the ratio is not an integer, you round down to the nearest integer. In this example, EIGRP sends one packet to E-C-A and one packet to E-B-A.

If we change the metric between links E and B in the example, the result would be the change in metric between B and A changes to 15. In this case, the E-B-A metric is 40. However, this path will not be selected for load balancing because the cost of this path,

40, is not less than (20 * 2), where 20 is the FD and 2 is the variance. To also include this path in load sharing, the variance should be changed to 3. In this case, the traffic share count ratio is

■ **For path E-C-A:** 40 / 20 = 2

■ **For path E-B-A:** 40 / 40 = 1

In this situation, EIGRP sends two packets to E-C-A and one packet to E-B-A. Therefore, EIGRP provides both unequal-cost path load balancing and intelligent load balancing.

Similarly, when you use the **traffic-share** command with the keyword **min**, the traffic is sent only across the minimum-cost path, even when there are multiple paths in the routing table:

```
router eigrp 1
network x.x.x.x  variance 3
  traffic-share min across-interfaces
```

In this situation, EIGRP sends packets only through E-C-A, which is the best path to the destination network. This is identical to the forwarding behavior without use of the **variance** command. However, if you use the **traffic-share min** command and the **variance** command, even though traffic is sent over the minimum-cost path only, all feasible routes get installed into the routing table, which decreases convergence times.

EIGRP Authentication

Many routing protocols allow the addition of some sort of authentication to protect against accepting routing messages from other routers that are not configured with the same preshared key. If this authentication is not configured, a malicious or misconfigured device can be introduced into the network. This may inject different or conflicting route information into the network, causing loss of service.

To configure EIGRP authentication, the router must first be configured globally with a "key chain," using the **key chain** command in global configuration mode. Then, each interface that uses EIGRP must be configured individually in the device. In Example 3-9, MD5 type key encryption is used.

Example 3-8 *Configuring EIGRP Authentication*

```
Branch# configure terminal
Enter configuration commands, one per line.  End with CNTL/Z.
Branch(config)# key chain 1
Branch(config-keychain)# exit
Branch(config)# key chain key4eigrp
Branch(config-keychain)# key 1
Branch(config-keychain-key)# key-string secureeigrp
Branch(config-keychain-key)# exit
```

With the global key chain configured, other applications, besides EIGRP, such as the RIP version 2 routing protocol, can now use this key chain. Next, apply it to the EIGRP interface configuration. EIGRP authentication is on a per-link basis. Neighboring interfaces must be configured with the same key chain. Other interfaces can be configured with other key chains or can have no authentication, as long as all neighbors are configured similarly. Example 3-9 provides the configuration necessary for application of the key chain to a single interface. The routers that are directly connected neighbors from interface FastEthernet0/0 in Example 3-9 must use the same authentication mode and the same key chain.

Example 3-9   *Placing Authentication on an Interface*

```
Branch# configure terminal
Enter configuration commands, one per line.  End with CNTL/Z.
Branch(config)# interface FastEthernet0/0
Branch(config-if)# ip authentication mode eigrp 100 md5
Branch(config-if)# ip authentication key-chain eigrp 100 key4eigrp
Branch(config-if)# exit
```

Note   For more information on EIGRP authentication, see the Cisco document "EIGRP Message Authentication Configuration Example" at http://www.cisco.com/en/US/tech/tk365/technologies_configuration_example09186a00807f5a63.shtml.

Troubleshooting EIGRP

The ability to troubleshoot problems related to the exchange of routing information and missing information from the routing table is one of the most essential skills for a network engineer who is involved in the implementation and maintenance of a routed enterprise network that uses a routing protocol.

This section provides a suggested troubleshooting flow and explains the Cisco IOS commands that you can use to gather information from the EIGRP data structures and routing processes to detect and correct routing issues.

Components of Troubleshooting EIGRP

In troubleshooting EIGRP, as with any networking issue, follow a structured methodology. Figure 3-11 shows a suggested flowchart.

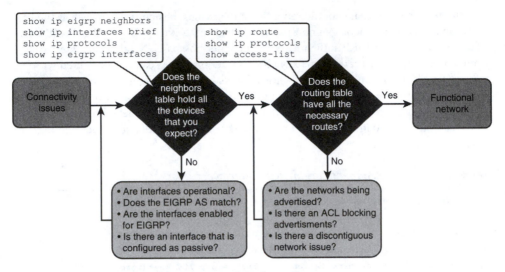

Figure 3-11   *EIGRP Troubleshooting Flowchart*

After configuring EIGRP, first test connectivity to the remote network, using ping. If the ping fails, check that the router has EIGRP neighbors and troubleshoot on a link-by-link basis. Neighbor adjacency might not be running for a number of reasons. Figure 3-12 provides a very basic design with two EIGRP neighbors connected by an Ethernet switch. The HQ router has three loopback interfaces, and both routers have two FastEthernet interfaces. One FastEthernet (0/0) interface from each router is connected to a switch. The switch has only one VLAN for all ports.

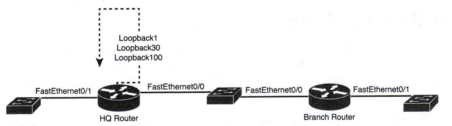

Figure 3-12   *Simple Network Example*

Now let's examine a few potential scenarios, via **show** commands:

- The interface between the devices is down:

```
HQ# show ip interface brief
Interface           IP-Address      OK?  Method  Status      Protocol
FastEthernet0/0     192.168.1.20    YES  NVRAM   down        down
FastEthernet0/1     10.5.0.1        YES  NVRAM   up          up
Loopback1           5.5.5.5         YES  NVRAM   up          up
Loopback30          2.2.2.2         YES  NVRAM   up          up
Loopback100         1.1.1.1         YES  NVRAM   up          up
```

In this case, FastEthernet0/0 is down. Possibilities include a disconnected cable, a down switch, or faulty hardware.

■ The two routers have mismatching EIGRP AS numbers:

```
HQ# show ip protocol
Routing Protocol is "eigrp 1"
<output omitted>


Branch# show ip protocol
Routing Protocol is "eigrp 10"
<output omitted>
```

In this case, the Branch and HQ routers are misconfigured with different EIGRP AS numbers.

■ Proper interfaces are not enabled for the EIGRP process:

```
HQ# show running-config
<output omitted>
router eigrp 1
network 192.168.1.0 255.255.255.0
<output omitted>
```

```
HQ# show ip interface brief
Interface          IP-Address       OK?    Method    Status        Protocol
FastEthernet0/0    192.168.1.20     YES    NVRAM     up            up
FastEthernet0/1    10.5.0.1         YES    NVRAM     up            up
Loopback1          5.5.5.5          YES    NVRAM     up            up
Loopback30         2.2.2.2          YES    NVRAM     up            up
Loopback100        1.1.1.1          YES    NVRAM     up            up
```

In this case, there is only a single interface configured for EIGRP.

■ The interface between the devices is up but can't ping:

```
HQ# show ip interface brief
Interface          IP-Address       OK?    Method    Status        Protocol
FastEthernet0/0    192.168.1.20     YES    NVRAM     up            up
FastEthernet0/1    10.5.0.1         YES    NVRAM     up            up
Loopback1          5.5.5.5          YES    NVRAM     up            up
Loopback30         2.2.2.2          YES    NVRAM     up            up
Loopback100        1.1.1.1          YES    NVRAM     up            up
Branch# show ip interface brief
Interface          IP-Address       OK?    Method    Status        Protocol
FastEthernet0/0    192.168.1.25     YES    NVRAM     up            up
FastEthernet0/1    10.20.0.1        YES    NVRAM     up            up
```

In this case, a potential Layer 2 problem exists. This could be a misconfigured switch port and/or VLAN misconfiguration.

■ An interface is configured as passive:

```
HQ# show running-config
<output omitted>
router eigrp 1
  passive-interface FastEthernet0/0
network 192.168.1.0 255.255.255.0
<output omitted>
```

In this case, a *passive-interface* is configured. The **show ip protocols** command will also identify passive interfaces.

Aside from the issues reviewed here, there are a number of other, more advanced concerns that can prevent neighbor relationships from forming. Two examples are misconfigured EIGRP authentication or mismatched K values, depending on which EIGRP calculates its metric. The next section covers specifically neighbor adjacency.

Troubleshooting EIGRP Neighbor Issues

The previous section examined several possible reasons why EIGRP might not be working properly. This section takes a closer look at troubleshooting EIGRP neighbor relationships. As previously mentioned, a major prerequisite for the neighbor relationship to form between routers is Layer 3 connectivity. By investigating the output of **show ip interface brief**, you can verify that the status and protocol are both up for the interface between the routers. In Figure 3-13 and Example 3-10, the Serial0/0/0 interface that is connected to the Branch router is up. A successful ping then confirms IP connectivity between routers.

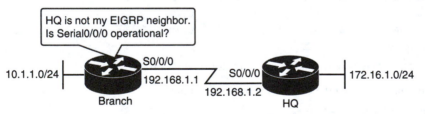

Figure 3-13   *Determining If the Interface Is Operational*

Example 3-10   *Verifying Protocol and Status of Link Between Neighbors*

```
Branch# show ip interface brief
Interface           IP-Address      OK?   Method   Status      Protocol
GigabitEthernet0/0  10.1.1.1        YES   NVRAM    up          up
Serial0/0/0         192.168.1.1     YES   NVRAM    up          up


Branch# ping 192.168.1.1


Type escape sequence to abort.
```

```
Sending 5, 100-byte ICMP Echos to 192.168.1.1, timeout is 2 seconds:
.....
Success rate is 0 percent (0/5)
```

If the ping is not successful, as shown in Example 3-10, you should use the technologies discussed in Chapter 2, "Troubleshooting Basic Connectivity." First, check the cabling and verify that the interfaces on connected devices are on a common subnet.

If you notice a log message such as the following that states that EIGRP neighbors are "not on common subnet," this indicates that there is an improper IP address on one of the two EIGRP neighbor interfaces:

```
*Mar  28 04:04:53.778: IP-EIGRP(Default-IP-Routing-Table:100): Neighbor
192.168.100.1 not on common subnet for Serial0/0/0
```

If this message was received on the Branch router, you can see that the reported IP address of the neighbor does not match what you expected. However, you can still have an IP address mismatch and not see this message.

Next, check that the AS numbers are the same between neighbors. The command that starts the EIGRP process is followed by the AS number, **router eigrp** *as_number*. This AS number is significant to the entire network, as it must match between all the routers within the same routing domain. In other routing protocols, the numbering used to start the process may have only local significance (for instance, the OSPF routing protocol is started with a process-id and does not use an AS number).

In Figure 3-14 and Example 3-11, **show ip protocols** helps to determine if the AS numbers match.

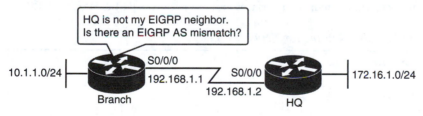

Figure 3-14   *Determining AS Numbers*

Example 3-11   *Using* show ip protocols *to Verify EIGRP AS Numbers*

```
Branch# show ip protocols
Routing Protocol is "EIGRP 1"
<output omitted>


HQ# show ip protocols
Routing Protocol is "EIGRP 2"
<output omitted>
```

Note   For more details about **show ip protocols** and related commands, see the *Cisco IOS IP Routing: Protocol-Independent Command Reference* at http://www.cisco.com/en/US/docs/ios/iproute_pi/command/reference/iri_book.html.

Also confirm that EIGRP is running on the correct interfaces. The **network** command configured under the EIGRP routing process indicates which router interfaces will participate in EIGRP.

The **show ip eigrp interfaces** *interface* command shows you which interfaces are enabled for EIGRP. If connected interfaces are not enabled for EIGRP, then neighbors will not form an adjacency. If an interface is not on the list, that means the router is not communicating EIGRP through that interface. Figure 3-15 shows that EIGRP is running on the Branch router. Run the same command on the HQ router and look for the same results. In this case, both routers are neighbors.

Figure 3-15   *EIGRP Interface Enabled*

You can also check the interface by referring to the "Routing for Networks" section of the **show ip protocols** command output. As shown in Example 3-12, this indicates which networks have been configured; any interfaces in those networks participate in EIGRP.

Example 3-12   *Check the "Routing for Networks" Output*

```
HQ# show ip protocols
<output omitted>
Routing Protocol is "eigrp 1"
 <output omitted>
Routing for Networks:
     172.16.0.0
     192.168.1.0
  Passive Interface(s):
     Serial0/0/0
 <output omitted>
```

With the **show ip protocols** command, you can also confirm if an interface is in passive mode only. The **passive-interface** command prevents both outgoing and incoming routing updates, because the effect of the command causes the router to stop sending and receiving hello packets over an interface. For this reason, routers do not become neighbors. An example where you would need to configure an interface as passive toward a specific LAN. You want to advertise LANs but don't want to have the security risk of transmitting hello packets into the LAN. A final suggestion for checking a failed neighbor relationship is to confirm a mismatch in the authentication parameters. The key authentication configuration must match on both neighbors. The key number and key string should be checked in the running configuration.

Troubleshooting EIGRP Routing Table Issues

This section covers issues that cause missing entries in the routing table when proper connectivity and neighbor relationships exist. The exclusion of routes that should be in the routing table can be caused by routes not being advertised, by route filtering, or by network summarization. Missing routing entries due to these issues can be related to a problem either with a directly connected EIGRP neighbor or with an EIGRP router that is in another section of the network.

Issues Caused by Unadvertised Routes

Routing table issues caused by unadvertised routes are indicated by a failed ping test. Figure 3-16 illustrates the Branch/HQ example that has been implemented. It is established by checking the neighbor adjacency.

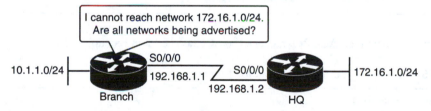

Figure 3-16   *Troubleshooting EIGRP Routing Table Issues with the* **show ip protocols** *Command*

In this case, checking the **show ip protocols** command output from the HQ router indicates the HQ router is not advertising 172.16.1.0/24. Adding the **network** statement to EIGRP, as demonstrated in Example 3-13, should resolve the issue.

Example 3-13   *Adding the Correct Network Command*

```
HQ(config)# router eigrp 1
HQ(config-router)# network 172.16.1.0
```

This should restore the routing table. If it does not, check route filtering. Route filtering can be performed by route maps or ACLs, as discussed in the next section.

Issues Caused by Route Filtering

Routing protocols can be configured to filter routes. This is a powerful tool, especially when connecting different routing domains (different AS). However, a misconfigured filter can be difficult to detect.

> **Note** Route maps and distribute lists are not part of the CCNA curriculum, but are visited as part of the CCNP curriculum. This book contains only brief coverage of distribute lists. For more information on route maps, see Chapter 8, "EIGRP Support for Route Map Filtering," of the *IP Routing EIGRP Configuration Guide, Cisco IOS Release 15S*: http://www.cisco.com/en/US/docs/ios-xml/ios/iproute_eigrp/configuration/15-s/ire-15-s-book.pdf.

When investigating filtering issues, first check the **show ip protocols** command, as demonstrated in Example 3-14.

Example 3-14 *Indentifying Incoming Filtering*

```
Branch# show ip protocols
Routing Protocol is "eigrp 1"
  Outgoing update filter list for all interfaces is not set
  Incoming update filter list for all interfaces is 1
```

As you can see, there is an ACL. Next, check the ACL, as shown in Example 3-15.

Example 3-15 *Identifying Access List Used for Filtering*

```
Branch# show ip access-lists
Standard IP access list 1
    10 deny    172.16.0.0, wildcard bits 0.0.255.255 (2 matches)
    20 permit any (6 matches)
```

The ACL matches the missing network. In this case, remove the ACL from the EIGRP configuration, as demonstrated in Example 3-16.

Example 3-16 *Removing the Distribute List Used for Filtering*

```
Branch# config t
Enter configuration commands, one per line.  End with CNTL/Z.
Branch(config)# router EIGRP 1
Branch(config-router)# no distribute-list 1 in
```

The console output shows the change in the adjacency after changing the configuration, as demonstrated in Example 3-17.

Example 3-17 *Console Reporting Neighbor Change Due to Reconfiguration*

```
*Mar  1 00:17:37.775: %DUAL-5-NBRCHANGE: IP-EIGRP(0) 1: Neighbor 192.168.1.1
(FastEthernet0/0) is down: route configuration changed
*Mar  1 00:17:41.431: %DUAL-5-NBRCHANGE: IP-EIGRP(0) 1: Neighbor 192.168.1.1
(FastEthernet0/0) is up: new adjacency
```

> **Caution** Do not remove an actual ACL without first removing the ACL reference from other configuration/interfaces. Otherwise, you may create instability in the configuration!

Take notice of the "in" on the **distribute-list**. ACLs can be placed in both inbound and outbound directions. Inbound and outbound lists are structured the same, but the transmission or reception of routes is controlled by direction.

Issues Caused by Automatic Network Summarization

EIGRP can be configured to automatically summarize routes at classful boundaries. If you have discontiguous networks, automatic summarization can cause inconsistencies in the routing tables.

In Figure 3-17, Router B is not receiving individual routes for the 172.16.1.0/24 and 172.16.2.0/24 subnets. Both Router A and Router C automatically summarized those subnets to the 172.16.0.0/16 classful boundary when sending EIGRP update packets to Router C.

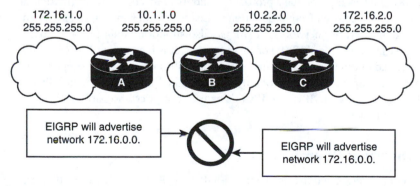

Figure 3-17 *Automatic Summarization Issues*

Router B has two routes to 172.16.0.0/16 in the routing table, which can result in inaccurate routing and packet loss, as shown in Example 3-18.

Example 3-18   *Inaccurate Routing Entries*

```
RouterB# show ip route
<output omitted>

 Gateway of last resort is not set
      10.0.0.0/24 is subnetted, 2 subnets
C     10.1.1.0 is directly connected, Serial0/2/0
C     10.2.2.0 is directly connected, Serial0/3/0
D   172.16.0.0/16 [90/2172416] via 10.1.1.1, 00:03:51, Serial0/2/0
                                [90/2172416] via 10.2.2.3, 00:00:14, Serial0/3/0
```

> **Note**   The behavior of the **auto-summary** command is disabled by default on
> Cisco IOS version 15. Older versions of Cisco IOS Software may have automatic
> summarization enabled by default.

In Example 3-19, automatic summarization is disabled by entering the **no auto-summary**
command in the router eigrp configuration mode:

Example 3-19   *Disable Automatic Summarization*

```
RouterB(config)# router eigrp 1
RouterB(config-if)# no auto-summary
```

Implementing EIGRP for IPv6

Although EIGRP is a Cisco proprietary protocol, it and its predecessor, IGRP (IGRP is an
obsolete protocol and removed from production in Cisco IOS 12.3 and later), have been
widely deployed in enterprise networks. EIGRP has also supported multiple protocols
besides IP (AppleTalk and Novell IPX). For these reasons, it is logical that EIGRP would
continue to be used in the IPv6 world. This section describes Cisco EIGRP support for
IPv6. The theory and operation of EIGRP only differs slightly between IPv6 and IPv4.
The main differences are where IPv6 and IPv4 deviate as a protocol, so parts of this section will serve as a review.

EIGRP IPv6 Theory of Operation

Although the configuration and management of EIGRP for IPv4 and EIGRP for IPv6 are
similar, they are configured and managed separately.

As previously mentioned, EIGRP is inherently a multiprotocol routing protocol because
it has supported non-IP protocols. Novell IPX and AppleTalk were protocols with early
support from EIGRP. As with the non-IP protocols, IPv6 support is added as a separate

module within the router. IPv6 EIGRP is configured and managed separately from IPv4 EIGRP, but the mechanisms and configuration techniques for IPv6 EIGRP will be very familiar to engineers who have worked with EIGRP for IPv4.

EIGRP maintains feature parity across protocols, where appropriate. Due to the differences in protocols, configuration and operation can slightly differ. Much of the theory in key areas such as DUAL and metrics are the same.

The following are a few (not all) examples of similarities shared by IPv4 EIGRP and IPv6 EIGRP:

- DUAL is used for route calculation and selection with the same metrics.

- It is scalable to large network implementations.

- Neighbor, routing, and topology tables are maintained.

- Both equal-cost load balancing and unequal-cost load balancing are offered.

A few (not all) examples of differences include these:

- The **network** command is not used in IPv6; EIGRP is configured via links.

- The **ipv6** keyword is used in many of the EIGRP commands.

- Needs to be explicitly enabled on each interface when configuring EIGRP.

The basic components of EIGRP for IPv6 remain the same as in the IPv4 version. So, this section contains a review of the operation of EIGRP and DUAL.

As in IPv4, EIGRP in IPv6 uses a hello packet to discover other EIGRP-capable routers on directly attached links and to form neighbor relationships. Updates may be acknowledged by using a reliable transport protocol, or they may be unacknowledged—depending on the specific function that is being communicated. The protocol provides the flexibility necessary to unicast or multicast updates, acknowledged or unacknowledged.

Hello packets and updates are set to the well-known, link-local multicast address FF02::A, which Cisco has obtained from the Internet Assigned Numbers Authority (IANA). This multicast distribution technique is more efficient than the broadcast mechanism that is used by earlier, more primitive routing protocols such as RIPv1. EIGRP for IPv4 also uses multicast for update distribution.

Note For more information on IANA numerical assignments, see http://www.iana. org/numbers.

EIGRP sends incremental updates when the state of a destination changes, instead of sending the entire contents of the routing table. This feature minimizes the bandwidth that is required for EIGRP packets.

DUAL, which is an EIGRP algorithm for determining the best path through the network, uses several metrics to select efficient, loop-free paths. Figure 3-18 shows a topology with sample metrics. When multiple routes to a neighbor exist, DUAL determines which route has the lowest metric (the FD) and enters this route into the routing table. Other possible routes to this neighbor with larger metrics are received, and DUAL determines the AD to this network. The AD is defined as the total metric that is advertised by an upstream neighbor for a path to a destination. DUAL compares the AD with the FD, and if the AD is less than the FD, DUAL considers the route to be a feasible successor and enters the route into the topology table. The feasible successor route that is reported with the lowest metric becomes the successor route to the current route if the current route fails. To avoid routing loops, DUAL ensures that the AD is always less than the FD for a neighbor router to reach the destination network; otherwise, the route to the neighbor may loop back through the local router.

When there are no feasible successors to a route that has failed, but there are neighbors advertising the route, a recomputation must occur. This is the process where DUAL determines a new successor. The amount of time that is required to recompute the route affects the convergence time. Recomputation is processor-intensive, so avoiding unneeded recomputation is advantageous. When a topology change occurs, DUAL tests for feasible successors. If there are feasible successors, DUAL uses them to avoid unnecessary recomputation of the topology.

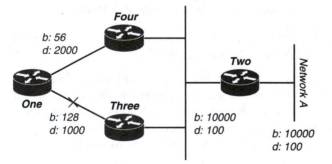

Figure 3-18   *EIGRP Path Selection*

Of these metrics, by default, only minimum bandwidth and delay are used to compute the best path. Unlike most metrics, minimum bandwidth is set to the minimum bandwidth of the entire path, and it does not reflect how many hops or low-bandwidth links are in the path. Delay is a cumulative value that increases by the delay value of each segment in the path. In Figure 3-18, Router One is computing the best path to Network A.

It starts with the two advertisements for this network: one through Router Four, with a minimum bandwidth of 56 and a total delay of 2200; and the other through Router Three, with a minimum bandwidth of 128 and a delay of 1200. Router One chooses the path with the lowest metric.

Let's compute the metrics. EIGRP calculates the total metric by scaling the bandwidth and delay metrics.

■ EIGRP uses the following formula to scale the bandwidth:

bandwidth = (10000000 / bandwidth(i)) * 256

where bandwidth(i) is the least bandwidth (represented in kilobits) of all outgoing interfaces on the route to the destination network.

■ EIGRP uses the following formula to scale the delay:

delay = delay(i) * 256

where delay(i) is the sum of the delays configured on the interfaces, on the route to the destination network, in tens of microseconds. The delay as shown in the **show ipv6 eigrp topology** command or the **show interface** command is in microseconds, so you must divide by 10 before you use it in this formula. Throughout the section, a delay is used as it is configured and shown on the interface.

■ EIGRP uses these scaled values to determine the total metric to the network:

metric = [K1 * bandwidth + (K2 * bandwidth) / (256 − load) + K3 * delay] * [K5 / (reliability + K4)]

Caution   You should not change these K values without first giving the decision careful consideration. Any revisions should be avoided and completed only after careful planning. Mismatched K values prevent a neighbor relationship from being built, which causes the network to fail to converge.

Note   If K5 = 0, the formula reduces to metric = [K1 * bandwidth + (K2 * bandwidth) / (256 − load) + K3 * delay].

The default values for K are

■ K1 = 1

■ K2 = 0

■ K3 = 1

■ K4 = 0

■ K5 = 0

For default behavior, you can simplify the formula as follows:

metric = bandwidth + delay

Cisco routers round down to the nearest integer to properly calculate the metrics. In this example, the total cost through Router Four is

minimum bandwidth = 56 kb total delay = 100 + 100 + 2000 = 2200 [(10000000 / 56) + 2200] x 256 = (178571 + 2200) x 256 = 180771 x 256 = 46277376

And the total cost through Router Three is

> minimum bandwidth = 128kb total delay = 100 + 100 + 1000 = 1200 [(10000000 / 128) + 1200] x 256 = (78125 + 1200) x 256 = 79325 x 256 = 20307200

So to reach Network A, Router One chooses the route through Router Three.

Note that the bandwidth and delay values used are those configured on the interface through which the router reaches its next hop to the destination network. For example, Router Two advertised Network A with the delay configured on its Ethernet interface; Router Four added the delay configured on its Ethernet interface; and Router One added the delay configured on its serial interface.

When a router discovers a new neighbor, it records the neighbor address and interface as an entry in the neighbor table. One neighbor table exists for each protocol-dependent module (as stated earlier, EIGRP runs a protocol-independent module for each protocol running, so IPv4 and IPv6 are calculated independently). When a neighbor sends a hello packet, it advertises a hold time, which is the amount of time that a router treats a neighbor as reachable and operational. If a hello packet is not received within the hold time, the hold time expires and DUAL is informed of the topology change.

The topology table contains all destinations that are advertised by neighboring routers. Each entry in the topology table includes the destination address and a list of neighbors that have advertised the destination. For each neighbor, the entry records the advertised metric, which the neighbor stores in its routing table. An important rule that distance vector protocols must follow is that if the neighbor advertises this destination, the neighbor must use the route to forward packets. Although having a route and using it to forward packets may seem implicit, link-state protocols may advertise a route that is not necessarily a direct path. Explicitly, this can be done with the Border Gateway Protocol (BGP), but that topic is beyond the scope of this text.

Note   As in IPv4, the MTU in IPv6 is carried in the EIGRP hello packets but is not used in the metric calculation.

EIGRP IPv6 Feasible Successor

As previously defined, the feasible distance is the best metric along a path to a destination network, including the metric to the neighbor advertising that path. Reported distance is the total metric along a path to a destination network as advertised by an upstream neighbor. A feasible successor is a path whose AD is less than the FD (current best path). Figure 3-19 illustrates this process.

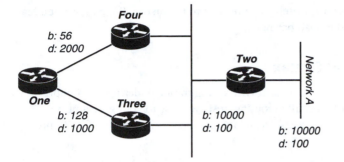

Figure 3-19   *Example Topology for Calculating Metric*

Router One recognizes two routes to Network A, one through Router Three and another through Router Four:

■ The route through Router Four has a cost of 46277376 and an AD of 307200.

■ The route through Router Three has a cost of 20307200 and an AD of 307200.

Note that in each case, EIGRP calculates the AD from the router advertising the route to the network. In other words, the AD from Router Four is the metric to get to Network A from Router Four, and the AD from Router Three is the metric to get to Network A from Router Three. EIGRP chooses the route through Router Three as the best path, and uses the metric through Router Three as the FD. Because the AD to this network through Router Four is less than the FD, Router One considers the path through Router Four a feasible successor.

When the link between Routers One and Three goes down, Router One examines each path it knows to Network A and finds that it has a feasible successor through Router Four. Router One uses this route, using the metric through Router Four as the new FD. The network converges instantly, and updates to downstream neighbors are the only traffic from the routing protocol.

EIGRP IPv6 Load Balancing

Similarly to IPv4, IPv6 supports equal-cost load balancing and unequal-cost load balancing.

Cisco IOS Software has the ability to load balance across up to four equal-cost paths by default. With the **maximum-paths** router configuration command, up to 32 equal-cost routes can be kept in the routing table, depending on the router type and Cisco IOS version. If you set the value to 1, you disable equal-cost load balancing.

EIGRP supports unequal-cost path load balancing. Use the **variance** *n* command to instruct the router to include routes with a metric of less than *n* times the minimum metric route for that destination. The variable *n* can take a value between 1 and 128. The default is 1, which means equal-cost load balancing. Traffic is also distributed among the links with unequal costs, proportionately, with respect to the metric. If a path is not a feasible successor, it is not used in load balancing.

EIGRP for IPv6 Command Syntax

This section covers some of the basics for EIGRP configuration under IPv6. Example 3-20 illustrates the process of basic IPv6 routing. It shows how to configure an IPv6 address and the EIGRP routing protocol on an interface, and verify that the EIGRP process has begun.

Example 3-20 *Configuring and Verifying EIGRP for IPv6*

```
IPv6-router# config terminal
Enter configuration commands, one per line.  End with CNTL/Z.
IPv6-router(config)# interface FastEthernet0/0
IPv6-router(config-if)# ipv6 address 2001:DB8:A00:1::1/32
IPv6-router(config-if)# no shutdown
IPv6-router(config-if)# exit
IPv6-router(config)# ipv6 unicast-routing
IPv6-router(config)# ipv6 router eigrp 1
IPv6-router(config-rtr)# no shutdown
IPv6-router(config-rtr)# interface FastEthernet0/0
IPv6-router(config-if)# ipv6 eigrp 1
IPv6-router(config-if)# exit
IPv6-router(config)# exit
*Apr  8 06:56:18.011: %SYS-5-CONFIG_I: Configured from console by console
IPv6-router# show ipv6 protocol
IPv6 Routing Protocol is "connected"
IPv6 Routing Protocol is "eigrp 1"
  EIGRP metric weight K1=1, K2=0, K3=1, K4=0, K5=0
  EIGRP maximum hopcount 100
  EIGRP maximum metric variance 1
  Interfaces: FastEthernet0/0
  Redistribution:
    None
  Maximum path: 16
  Distance: internal 90 external 170

IPv6-router#
```

Table 3-6 describes the basic commands used in Example 3-20.

Table 3-6 *Commands Used in Example 3-20*

Command(s)	Description
interface FastEthernet0/0	Enter interface mode
ipv6 address 2001:DB8:A00:1::1/32	Assign an IPv6 address on the interface
ipv6 unicast-routing	Enable IPv6 routing
ipv6 router eigrp 1	Configure EIGRP with AS number 1
no shutdown	Enable the EIGRP process
show ipv6 protocol	Verify the EIGRP process has started (more on EIGRP verification/**show** commands in the next section)

Note For more information on configuring IPv6, refer to the *IOS IPv6 Configuration Guide, Cisco IOS Release 15.1.S*: http://www.cisco.com/en/US/docs/ios-xml/ios/ipv6/configuration/15-1s/ipv6-15-1s-book.html.

Verification of EIGRP IPv6 Operation

Example 3-21 shows the EIGRP topology for IPv6. A good point to note is that the command execution and information displayed are similar to the IPv4 version of the command (see Figure 3-7), and are just differentiated by the IPv4 and IPv6 protocol differences.

Example 3-21 *EIGRP Topology for IPv6*

```
IPv6-router# show ipv6 eigrp topology

IPv6-EIGRP Topology Table for AS(1)/ID(2001:0DB8:10::/64)

Codes: P - Passive, A - Active, U - Update, Q - Query, R - Reply,
r - reply Status, s - sia Status

P 2001:0DB8:3::/64, 1 successors, FD is 281600
via Connected, Ethernet1/0
```

The EIGRP neighbors are shown in Example 3-22.

Example 3-22 *Verifying EIGRP Neighbors*

```
IPv6-router# show ipv6 eigrp neighbors
IPv6-EIGRP neighbors for process 1
H   Address                 Interface   Hold   Uptime    SRTT   RTO    Q     Seq
                                        (sec)            (ms)          Cnt   Num
0   Link-local address:     Se0/0        13    15:17:58   44    264    0     12
    FE80::2
```

Example 3-23 displays the associated routing table.

Example 3-23 *Verifying the Routing Table*

```
IPv6-router# show ipv6 route eigrp
IPv6 Routing Table - 12 entries
Codes: C - Connected, L - Local, S - Static, R - RIP, B - BGP
          U - Per-user Static route, M - MIPv6
          I1 - ISIS L1, I2 - ISIS L2, IA - ISIS interarea, IS - ISIS summary
          O - OSPF intra, OI - OSPF inter, OE1 - OSPF ext 1, OE2 - OSPF ext 2
          ON1 - OSPF NSSA ext 1, ON2 - OSPF NSSA ext 2
          D - EIGRP, EX - EIGRP external
D   1000:AB8::/64 [90/2297856]
        via FE80::2, Serial0/0
D   2000:AB8::/64 [90/2297856]
        via FE80::2, Serial0/0
D   3000:AB8::/64 [90/2297856]
        via FE80::2, Serial0/0
```

The **show** commands in Example 3-20 through Example 3-23 have the same role as in EIGRP for IPv4. The differences are related to the protocol output:

- To display entries in the EIGRP for IPv6 topology table, use the **show ipv6 eigrp topology** command in privileged EXEC mode.

- To display the neighbors discovered by EIGRP for IPv6, use the **show ipv6 eigrp neighbors** command.

- The **show ipv6 route eigrp** command reveals the content of the IPv6 routing table that includes the routes specific to EIGRP.

EIGRP for IPv6 Configuration Example

Figure 3-20 along with the configurations in Examples 3-24 and 3-25 provide a simple two-node network with a Branch router and an HQ router.

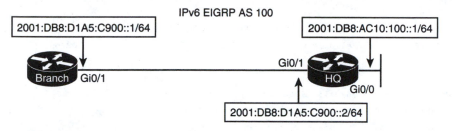

Figure 3-20   *Two-Router IPv6 Network*

On the Branch router, EIGRP for IPv6 is enabled with AS 100. EIGRP is then enabled on the interface GigabitEthernet0/1.

Example 3-24   *Branch Router Configuration*

```
Branch(config)# ipv6 router eigrp 100
Branch(config-router)# no shutdown
Branch(config-router)# exit
Branch(config)# interface GigabitEthernet0/1
Branch(config-if)# ipv6 eigrp 100
```

As displayed in Example 3-25, on the HQ router, first EIGRP for IPv6 is enabled with AS 100. Then interfaces GigabitEthernet0/0 and GigabitEthernet0/1 are enabled for IPv6 EIGRP.

Example 3-25   *HQ Router Configuration*

```
HQ(config)# ipv6 router eigrp 100
HQ(config-router)# no shutdown
HQ(config)# exit
HQ(config)# interface GigabitEthernet0/0
HQ(config-if)# ipv6 eigrp 100
HQ(config-if)# exit
HQ(config)# interface GigabitEthernet0/1
HQ(config-if)# ipv6 eigrp 100
```

In the **show ipv6 eigrp interfaces** command output that follows in Example 3-26 for the Branch router, one neighbor is on the GigabitEthernet0/1 interface, which is the only interface that is included in the EIGRP process.

Example 3-26 *Verifying EIGRP Interface*

```
Branch# show ipv6 eigrp interfaces
IPv6-EIGRP interfaces for AS(100)

                       Xmit Queue    Mean    Pacing Time    Multicast     Pending
Interface     Peers    Un/Reliable   SRTT    Un/Reliable    Flow Timer    Routes
Gi0/1           1         0/0          0        0/10            0            0


Un/reliable mcasts: 0/0 Un/reliable ucasts: 0/0
Mcast exceptions: 0 CR packets: 0 ACKs suppressed: 0
Retransmissions sent: 0 Out-of-sequence rcvd: 0
Authentication mode is not set
```

Example 3-27 shows the output of the **show ipv6 eigrp neighbors** command from the Branch router. The fields in the command output are described in Table 3-7.

Example 3-27 *Reviewing EIGRP Neighbors*

```
IPv6-router# show ipv6 eigrp neighbors
IPv6-EIGRP neighbors for process 1
H   Address                Interface   Hold   Uptime    SRTT   RTO   Q   Seq
                                       (sec)            (ms)         Cnt Num
0   Link-local address:      Gi0/1      12   00:20:48     9    100   0    2
    FE80::FE99:47FF:FEE5:2671
```

Table 3-7 *Significant Fields in the* **show ipv6 eigrp neighbors** *Command from the Branch Router*

Field	Description
Link-local address	The IPv6 interface address used for communication local to a single subnet only. Link-local packets are not routed. EIGRP IPv6 uses this to establish neighbor relationships.
Interface	The EIGRP interface.
Hold	The amount of time an EIGRP neighbor awaits a hello packet from a neighbor before determining that the neighbor relationship should be timed out and broken. The default is three times the hold timer.
Uptime	How long the neighbor relationship has been established.

The **show ipv6 eigrp topology** command displays the topology table of EIGRP for IPv6 routes, as demonstrated in Example 3-28. All the routes are present in the topology table, but only the best ones are in the routing table.

Example 3-28 *IPv6 Topology*

```
Branch# show ipv6 eigrp topology
EIGRP-IPv6 Topology Table for AS(100)/ID(209.165.201.1)
Codes: P - Passive, A - Active, U - Update, Q - Query, R - Reply,
             r - reply Status, s - sia Status
P 2001:DB8:D1A5:C900::/64, 1 successors, FD is 28160
        via Connected, GigabitEthernet0/1
P 2001:DB8:AC10:100::/64, 1 successors, FD is 156160
        via FE80::FE99:47FF:FEE5:2671 (156160/128256), GigabitEthernet0/1
```

Example 3-29 displays output from the **show ipv6 route eigrp** command. Here, you are presented with a route that is learned by the EIGRP routing protocol.

Example 3-29 *Verifying the EIGRP Routes in the Routing Table*

```
Branch# show ipv6 route eigrp
IPv6 Routing Table - default - 4 entries
Codes: C - Connected, L - Local, S - Static, U - Per-user Static route
             B - BGP, R - RIP, I1 - ISIS L1, I2 - ISIS L2
             IA - ISIS interarea, IS - ISIS summary, D - EIGRP, EX - EIGRP external
             ND - ND Default, NDp - ND Prefix, DCE - Destination, NDr - Redirect
             O - OSPF Intra, OI - OSPF Inter, OE1 - OSPF ext 1, OE2 - OSPF ext 2
             ON1 - OSPF NSSA ext 1, ON2 - OSPF NSSA ext 2
D    2001:DB8:AC10:100::/64 [90/156160]
        via FE80::FE99:47FF:FEE5:2671, GigabitEthernet0/1
```

Troubleshooting EIGRP for IPv6

When considering EIGRP for IPv6, there are many similarities to EIGRP for IPv4. The commands are comparable, the algorithm is the same, and the metrics work alike. However, being aware of some of the major differences and key points makes trouble-shooting easier. The following points provide a brief summary:

- EIGRP for IPv6 is directly designed on the interfaces over which it runs. This feature allows EIGRP for IPv6 to be configured without the use of a global IPv6 address. There is no network statement in EIGRP for IPv6.

- In per-interface design at system startup, if EIGRP has been configured on an interface, then the EIGRP protocol may start running before any EIGRP router mode commands have been executed.

- An EIGRP for IPv6 protocol instance requires a router ID before it can start running.

- EIGRP for IPv6 has a shutdown feature. The routing process should be in **no shutdown** mode in order to start running.

- When using a passive-interface configuration, EIGRP for IPv6 does not need to be configured on the interface that is made passive.

- EIGRP for IPv6 provides route filtering using the **distribute-list** command.

Note   As with IPv4 EIGRP, distribute lists are explored in more detail in the Implementing Cisco IP Routing (ROUTE) course and the related texts for preparation for the Implementing Cisco IP Routing (ROUTE) exam.

Chapter Summary

Dynamic routing protocols are defined by type, distance vector or link state. Distance vector protocols use a metric to determine the path through the network on a hop-by-hop basis. Link-state protocols keep a topology of all routers and links in the network. Examples of distance vector protocols are EIGRP and RIP. Examples of link-state protocols are OSPF and BGP.

Dynamic routing protocols are classified as Exterior Gateway Protocol (EGP) or Interior Gateway Protocol (IGP). An EGP is used between different autonomous systems, such as autonomous systems connected to the public Internet. IGPs are used inside a network. The only current EGP for IPv4 and IPV6 is BGP. Examples of IGPs are OSPF, EIGRP, and RIP.

EIGRP is an IGP that is considered an advanced distance vector protocol because it has many added features, such as partial updates. EIGRP uses the DUAL algorithm for its topology and metric calculations. It is suitable for many network designs. It supports multiple protocols through separate processes, called protocol-dependent modules.

EIGRP for IPv4 and EIGRP for IPv6 have very similar operating models, such as configuration and troubleshooting. The main deviations are where IPv4 and IPv6 differ as protocols. The primary differences are that IPv6 uses link-local addressing for EIGRP (IPv6) neighbor establishment; EIGRP for IPv6 is configured on an interface-by-interface basis; and the creation of passive interfaces in IPV6 is done not by configuring an interface but by adding configuration for the passive interface.

Review Questions

Use the questions here to review what you learned in this chapter. The correct answers are located in Appendix A, "Answers to Chapter Review Questions."

1. In which two ways does the configuration of EIGRP on IPv6 differ from the configuration of EIGRP on IPv4? (Choose two.) (Source: "EIGRP for IPv6 Command Syntax")

   a. The **network** command is changed into the **ipv6 network** command for EIGRP for IPv6.

   b. EIGRP for IPv6 can only be explicitly enabled with the **no shutdown** command. There is no **network** command.

   c. EIGRP for IPv6 is configured per interface on Cisco routers.

   d. If you run EIGRP for IPv6, you have to run EIGRP for IPv4; but if you run EIGRP for IPv4, you do not need to run EIGRP for IPv6.

2. Which command can you use to show if EIGRP for IPv6 is running? (Source: "EIGRP for IPv6 Command Syntax")

   a. show ipv6 interface

   b. show ipv6 protocol

   c. show ipv6 eigrp dual

   d. show eigrp ipv6 dual

3. Which is not a valid IPv6 EIGRP command? (Source: EIGRP Basic Configuration)

   a. show ipv6 eigrp topology

   b. show ipv6 route eigrp

   c. show ipv6 eigrp status

   d. show ipv6 eigrp interfaces

4. Which of the following applies to EIGRP AS numbers? (Source: "Troubleshooting EIGRP Neighbor Issues")

   a. Need to match between EIGRP neighbors only

   b. Need to match OSPF area numbers if routes are being redistributed

   c. Need to match between all EIGRP routers in the topology

   d. Don't need to match at all

   e. Must match BGP AS numbers

5. Which command is most useful for determining if an EIGRP neighbor relationship is not established due to a connectivity issue? (Source: "Troubleshooting EIGRP Neighbor Issues")

   a. show ip protocols

   b. show ip eigrp neighbors

   c. show eigrp topology

   d. show ip protocols

   e. show ip interfaces brief

6. Which of the following applies to an EIGRP passive interface? (Source: "Troubleshooting EIGRP Neighbor Issues")

   a. Only makes a neighbor relationship if a neighbor that is on a directly connected subnet initiates the connection

   b. Can be seen by the **show ip eigrp passive-interfaces** command

   c. Can be seen by the **show ip protocols** command

   d. Can have a different AS number assigned to it

7. Route filtering can be done on which of the following? (Source: "Issues Caused by Route Filtering")

   a. Inbound routes only

   b. Outbound routes only

   c. Either inbound or outbound routes

8. Where is automatic summarization performed? (Source: Classful Routing Versus Classless Routing)

   a. At any contiguous network block

   b. At classful network boundaries

   c. Can be performed on the same classful boundary on more than one network segment at the same time

   d. At the intersection of the classful and classless routing protocol.

9. Which command correctly specifies that network 10.0.0.0 is directly connected to a router that is running EIGRP and should be advertised? (Source: "Implementing EIGRP for IPv6")

   a. Router(config)# **network 10.0.0.0**

   b. Router(config)# **router eigrp 10.0.0.0**

   c. Router(config-router)# **network 10.0.0.0**

   d. Router(config-router)# **router eigrp 10.0.0.0**

10. Connect each EIGRP feature on the left with its description on the right. (Source: "Implementing EIGRP for IPv6")

    1. Reduced bandwidth usage

    2. Classless routing

    3. Load balancing

    4. DUAL

    a. EIGRP algorithm by which EIGRP achieves rapid convergence

    b. A direct consequence of using partial updates

    c. EIGRP knows two types: equal and unequal

    d. Routing mask is advertised for each destination network

11. Which two criteria does EIGRP use by default to calculate its metric? (Choose two.) (Source: "Implementing EIGRP for IPv6")

  a. Bandwidth

  b. Reliability

  c. Load

  d. MTU

  e. Delay

12. Connect each term on the left to its description on the right. (Source: "Implementing EIGRP for IPv6")

  1. Feasible distance   a. The best EIGRP metric for an EIGRP neighbor to reach a particular network

  2. Advertised distance   b. The end-to-end metric that is transmitted from the router for a remote network

  3. Administrative distance   c. The end-to-end EIGRP metric from a router to reach a particular network

  4. Composite metric   d. Used to rate the trustworthiness of each routing information source

13. Which letter is used to signify that a route in the **show ip routes** command originates from EIGRP? (Source: "Verification of EIGRP Configuration and Operation")

  a. A

  b. D

  c. E

  d. L

14. Which is not a valid command? (Source: "Verification of EIGRP Configuration and Operation")

  a. **show ip eigrp dual process** *as_number*

  b. **show ip eigrp interfaces**

  c. **show ip route**

  d. **show ip eigrp neighbors**

15. All routing protocols support uneven-cost load balancing. True or False? (Source: "Load Balancing with EIGRP")

16. Which interface(s) on the Branch router does not have an EIGRP neighbor? (Source: "Verification of EIGRP Configuration and Operation")

    a. Gigabit0/0

    b. Gigabit0/1

    c. Gigabit0/2

    d. Gigabit0/3

    e. All interfaces have an EIGRP neighbor

    f. No interfaces have an EIGRP neighbor

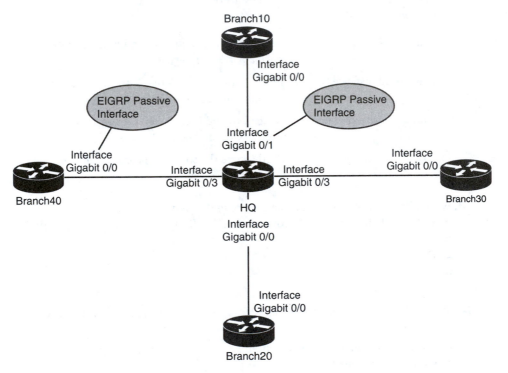

17. Which two choices are *not* a characteristic of EIGRP? (Source: "Dynamic Routing Overview")

    a. Determines distance to any destination in the network

    b. Uses an algorithm called DUAL

    c. Uses an algorithm called SPF

    d. Has a map of every destination in the network

18. Which command would you use to investigate which interfaces are enabled for the EIGRP routing process? (Source: "Troubleshooting EIGRP Neighbor Issues")

    a. show ip eigrp interfaces

    b. show ip eigrp neighbors

    c. show ip interfaces brief

    d. show eigrp enabled interfaces

19. Which of the following statements are false? (Source: "Troubleshooting EIGRP for IPv6")

   a. In per-interface configuration at system startup, if IPv6 EIGRP has been config-ured on an interface, then the IPv6 EIGRP protocol may start running before any EIGRP router mode commands have been executed.

   b. An EIGRP for IPv6 protocol instance does not need a router ID before it can start running. The router ID can be added later.

   c. When using a passive-interface configuration, EIGRP for IPv6 does not need to be configured on the interface that is made passive.

   d. EIGRP for IPv6 is not directly configured on the interfaces over which it runs. In the network statement in EIGRP for IPv6, the interface must be explicitly defined.

   e. EIGRP for IPv6 has a shutdown feature. The routing process must be in **no shut-down** mode in order to start running.

   f. EIGRP for IPv6 provides route filtering using the **distribute-list prefix-list** com-mand. Use of the **route-map** command is not supported for route filtering with a distribute list.

   g. EIGRP uses the advanced DUAL algorithm that maintains a database of every node on the network.

20. Which is not a basic component of EIGRP? (Source: "EIGRP Features and Function")

   a. Topology database

   b. DUAL algorithm

   c. Protocol-dependent modules

   d. Hello packets

21. Which is not a valid dynamic routing protocol classification? (Source: "Dynamic Routing Protocols")

   a. Hybrid

   b. Distance vector

   c. Link state

22. Connect each term on the left with its definition on the right. (Source: "Dynamic Routing Review")

   1. Distance vector protocol   a. Keeps track of all links and routers in the network

   2. EGP   b. Internal routing for a single routing domain

   3. Link-state protocol   c. Tracks the network path on a hop-by-hop basis

   4. IGP   d. Connects routing domains

Chapter 4

Implementing a Scalable Multiarea Network with OSPF

This chapter contains the following sections:

- Understanding OSPF

- Multiarea OSPF IPv4 Implementation

- Chapter Summary

- Review Questions

This chapter explores Open Shortest Path First (OSPF), a complex and highly scalable link-state routing protocol. Although it is complex, it is widely used in both enterprise and service provider large-scale IP networks.

This chapter also explains the benefits of a multiarea OSPF solution compared to a single-area solution. It also covers link-state protocols, OSPF components, the OSPF metric, OSPF operations, and how to configure and verify/monitor multiarea OSPF.

Chapter Objectives:

- Understand the theory of Link State Routing Protocols.

- Understand the design, configuration, and troubleshooting of OSPF for IPv4 and IPv6.

- Distinguish the differences between single area and multiple area OSPF.

Understanding OSPF

OSPF is a link-state routing protocol that is often used in networks for scalability, fast convergence, and multivendor environment support. Understanding OSPF operations and OSPF terms is crucial for network engineers that plan to design, implement, and trouble-shoot scalable networks.

This section includes an overview of link-state routing protocols, OSPF data structures, and OSPF metrics, and then explains the functions of OSPF and its packet types. It describes how the link-state database (LSDB) is built using link-state advertisements (LSA) and neighbor. This section reviews important design limitations and characteristics of OSPF. Link State Protocol and OSPF terminology are also defined.

Link-State Routing Protocol Overview

When a failure occurs in a network, routing protocols should detect the failure as soon as possible and then find another path through the network. Link-state protocols support fast convergence. Link-state protocols also scale well and support multivendor environments. This is why link-state protocols are widely used in enterprise and service provider environments.

Link-state protocols have the following advantages when compared to traditional distance vector routing protocols:

- **They are more scalable:** Link-state protocols use a hierarchical design and can scale to very large networks if properly designed.

- **Each router has a full picture of a topology:** Because each router contains full information regarding all of the routers and links in a network, each router is able to independently select a loop-free and efficient pathway, based on cost, to reach every neighbor in the network.

- **Updates are sent when a topology change occurs and are reflooded periodically:** Link-state protocols send updates of a topology change. By using triggered updates, bandwidth is preserved. Additionally, updates are made on a periodic basis.

- **They respond quickly to topology changes:** Link-state protocols establish neighbor relationships with adjacent routers. The failure of a neighbor is detected quickly, and this failure is communicated by using triggered updates to all routers in the network. This immediate reporting generally leads to fast convergence times.

- **More information is communicated between routers:** Routers that are running a link-state protocol have a common view of the network. This means that each router has full information about other routers and links between them, including the metric on each link.

Link-state protocols have the following disadvantage when compared to traditional distance vector protocols:

- **Higher memory usage:** Link-state protocols keep a map of all endpoints in the network, requiring memory to keep this information in the system RAM.

- **Higher CPU usage:** Although link-state protocols react quickly, they require more calculations for the forwarding database. Because link-state protocols maintain a database of all nodes, a routing change requires the LSDB to be recalculated.

- **Complexity:** Link-state protocols require more-extensive configuration.

Link-State Routing Protocol Data Structures

A router that is running a link-state routing protocol must first recognize other routers and establish a neighbor adjacency with its neighboring routers. This neighbor adjacency is achieved by exchanging hello packets with the neighboring routers. Then a neighbor is put into the neighbor database. As shown in Figure 4-1, Router A recognizes Routers B and D as neighbors. Figure 4-1 also refers to transit networks. A transit network is a term (not unique to OSPF) that indicates a network has more than one router and potentially could be used by traffic as an intermediary path from source to destination. The converse of a transit network is a stub network. A stub network has only one router and one destination in and out.

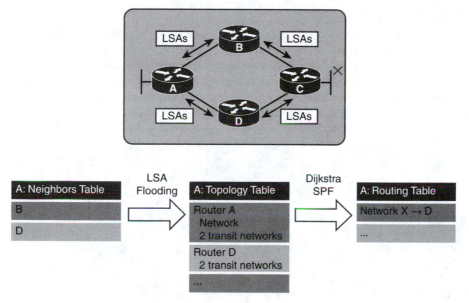

Figure 4-1 *Link-State Routing Protocol Data Structures*

After a neighbor relationship is established between routers, they synchronize their LSDBs by reliably exchanging LSAs. An LSA describes a router and the networks that are connected to that router. Figure 4-1 shows the exchange of LSAs to build the database. LSAs are stored in the LSDB (topology database). By exchanging all LSAs, routers learn the complete topology of the network. Each router in that area should have the same topology database for that area.

After the LSDB is built, each router applies the shortest path first (SPF) algorithm to the topology map. The SPF algorithm uses the Dijkstra calculation (developed by Dutch computer scientist Edsger Dijkstra in 1956). The SPF algorithm builds a tree, where the root of the tree is the router and the leaves are distant networks. The router places itself at the root of a tree and calculates the shortest path to each destination, based on the cumulative cost that is required to reach each destination.

The best choice of path(s) to a destination network are candidate(s) to be placed into the routing table. This will include a destination network, and the next-hop IP address to reach that network.

In Figure 4-1, the routing table on Router A states that a packet should be sent to Router D to reach Network X.

Whenever there is a change in a topology, new LSAs are created and sent throughout the network. All routers in the area change their LSDB at the receipt of the new LSAs, and the SPF algorithm is run again on the updated LSDB to verify new paths to destinations.

Understanding Metrics in OSPF

A metric is an indication of the overhead required to send packets across a certain interface. As shown in Figure 4-2, OSPF uses cost as a metric. A lower cost indicates a better path than a higher cost indicates. In a Cisco router, the cost of an interface is inversely proportional to the bandwidth of that interface. So, a higher bandwidth indicates a lower cost. There is more overhead, higher cost, and latency involved in crossing a 10-Mbps Ethernet line than in crossing a 100-Mbps Ethernet line.

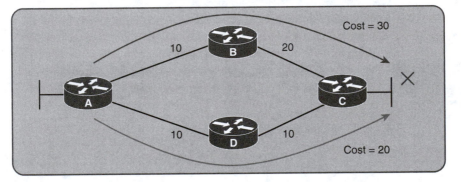

Figure 4-2   *OSPF Metrics*

The formula that is used to calculate OSPF cost is cost = reference bandwidth / interface bandwidth (in bits per second). The default reference bandwidth is 108, which is 100,000,000 bps, or the equivalent of the bandwidth of Fast Ethernet. Therefore, the default cost of a 10-Mbps Ethernet link will be 108 / 107 = 10, and the cost of a 100-Mbps link will be 108 / 108 = 1. OSPF's reference bandwidth is based on the speed of Fast Ethernet (100-Mbps). Higher speed links have a cost of 1, since OSPF cost is represented as a whole number (no fractions). In this case, it is required to change OSPF cost on an interface manually or to adjust the reference bandwidth to a higher value. Example 4-1 shows how to set the reference bandwidth to 1 Gigabit (1000 Mbps).

Example 4-1 *Changing the OSPF Reference Bandwidth Globally*

```
Branch# configure terminal
Enter configuration commands, one per line.  End with CNTL/Z.
Branch(config)# router ospf 100
Branch(config-router)# auto-cost reference-bandwidth 1000
% OSPF: Reference bandwidth is changed.
       Please ensure reference bandwidth is consistent across all routers.
```

In the case of Example 4-1, because the router was set globally to adjust the reference bandwidth to 1000 (Mbps), the value of 1 is Gigabit Ethernet speed. You can also set it on a per-interface basis. Example 4-2 increases the interface cost of a Fast Ethernet interface to 10, which is equal to 10 Megabit Ethernet.

Example 4-2 *Adjusting the OSPF Cost*

```
Branch# configure terminal
Enter configuration commands, one per line.  End with CNTL/Z.
Branch(config)# interface FastEthernet0/0
Branch(config-if)# ip ospf cost 10
```

The cost to reach a distant network from a router is a cumulative cost of all links on the path from the router to the network. In Figure 4-2, the cost from Router A to Network X via Router B is 30 (10 + 20), and the cost via Router D is 20 (10 + 10). The path via Router D is better because it has a lower cost.

Establishment of OSPF Neighbor Adjacencies

Neighbor OSPF routers must recognize each other on the network before they can share information, because OSPF routing depends on the status of the link between two routers. This process is done using the Hello protocol. The Hello protocol uses hello packets, as shown in Figure 4-3, to establish and maintain neighbor relationships by ensuring bidirectional (two-way) communication between neighbors. Bidirectional communication occurs when a router recognizes itself and is listed in the Neighbors field of a hello packet. In Figure 4-3, the parameters marked with a * must match for adjacency to occur.

Figure 4-3 *OSPF Neighbor Adjacencies*

Each interface that is participating in OSPF uses multicast address 224.0.0.5 to periodically send hello packets. A hello packet contains the following information:

- **Network mask:** This is the subnet mask for the interface OSPF is operating on.

- **Router ID:** The router ID is a 32-bit number that uniquely identifies the router. The router ID is set when the router first boots or any time OSPF is reset. The router ID is chosen by OSPF in the following order:

  - The optional **router-id** command is entered into OSPF configuration mode.

  - If the **router-id** command is not configured, the highest IP address out of all loopback interfaces is used.

  - If neither is configured, the highest IP address of the configured physical interfaces is used.

- **Hello and dead intervals:** The Hello interval specifies the frequency, in seconds, at which a router sends hello packets. The default Hello interval on multiaccess networks is 10 seconds. The dead interval is the amount of time, in seconds, that a router waits to hear from a neighbor before declaring the neighboring router out of service. By default, the dead interval is four times the Hello interval. These timers must be the same on neighboring routers; otherwise, an adjacency is not established.

- **Neighbors:** The Neighbors field lists the adjacent routers with established bidirectional communication. This bidirectional communication is indicated when the router recognizes itself as listed in the Neighbors field of the hello packet from the neighbor.

- **Area ID:** To communicate, two routers must share a common segment and their interfaces must belong to the same OSPF area on this segment. The neighbors must also share the same subnet and mask. These routers will all have the same link-state information for that area.

- **Router priority:** The router priority is an 8-bit number that indicates the priority of a router. OSPF uses the priority to select a designated router (DR) and a backup designated router (BDR). In certain types of networks, OSPF elects a DR and BDR. The DR acts as a central point to distribute routing information on the subnet. This is to reduce traffic between routers.

- **DR and BDR IP addresses:** These are the IP addresses of the DR and BDR for the specific network, if they are known.

- **Authentication data:** If router authentication is enabled, two routers must exchange the same authentication data. Authentication is not required, but if it is enabled, all neighboring routers must have the same key configured.

- **Options:** The Options field is a bit that indicates whether the area is a normal area (1) or a stub area (0).

Building a Link-State Database

Figure 4-4 shows the four types of update packets used when building and synchronizing an LSDB, as described in the list that follows.

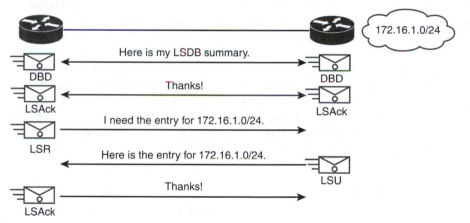

Figure 4-4   *Update Packets Used When Building and Synchronizing LSDBs*

- **DBD (database descriptor) packet:** A DBD packet is used to give a summary description of the network routes of each neighbor. A DBD includes information about the LSA entry header that appears in the LSDB of the router. Each LSA entry header includes information about the link-state type, the address of the advertising router, the cost of the link, and the sequence number. The router uses the sequence number to determine the "newness" of the received link-state information.

- **LSR (link-state request) packet:** After DBD packets are exchanged, the routers request missing information by using LSR packets. Routers compare the information that they receive with the information they already have. If the received DBD packet has a more up-to-date, link-state entry, the router sends an LSR packet to the other router to request the updated link-state entry.

■ **LSU (link-state update) packet:** All missing information is provided to the neighbors by sending LSU packets that contain different LSAs.

■ **LSAck (link-state acknowledgement) packet:** Every packet is acknowledged to ensure reliable transport and exchange of information.

OSPF Area Structure

This section examines the two-tier hierarchy structure of OSPF Backbone and non-backbone (normal) areas. Multi-area OSPF terminology will also be introduced.

In small networks, the web of router links is not complex, and paths to individual destinations are easily deduced. However, in large networks, the web is highly complex, and the number of potential paths to each destination is sizeable. Therefore, the Dijkstra calculations that compare all of these possible routes can be very complex and take a significant amount of time to complete.

A good network design for a link-state routing protocol reduces the size of the Dijkstra calculations by partitioning the network into areas. The number of routers in an area and the number of LSAs that flood within the location are small, which means that the link-state or topology database for an area is minimal. Consequently, the Dijkstra calculation is easier and takes less time. Routers that are inside an area maintain detailed information about the links and maintain only general or summary information about routers and links in other locations. However, summarization is not done by default; it has to be configured. Another advantage of using multiarea OSPF design is that a topology change in an area causes LSA flooding only within that area. SPF recalculations therefore occur only in the zone where the topology change transpired.

OSPF Area and Router Types

Link-state routing protocols use a two-layer hierarchy that consists of the backbone area and the normal (nonbackbone) area, as represented in Figure 4-5.

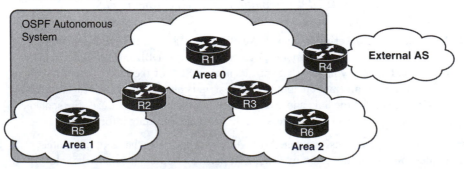

Figure 4-5 *Link-State Routing Two-Layer Hierarchy*

OSPF supports a hierarchical network structure. As shown in Figure 4-5, areas are numbered, as explained next:

- **Backbone or transit area:** The primary function of this OSPF area is to quickly and efficiently move IP packets. In OSPF, the backbone area is known as area 0. The Backbone area interconnects with other OSPF area types. The OSPF hierarchical area structure requires that all areas connect directly to the backbone area. Figure 4-5 shows the multiarea network. In this case, direct links to the backbone area are required. In this scenario, direct links between area 1 and area 2 routers are not allowed. Example 4-3 shows how to configure a router to be in the backbone.

Example 4-3 *Configuration of a Router in the Backbone*

```
R1(config)# router ospf 100
R1(config-router)# network 192.168.1.1 0.0.0.0 area 0
```

In Example 4-3, the **network** command matches the interface 192.168.1.1 and places it in area 0.

- **Normal or nonbackbone area:** The primary function of this type of OSPF area is to connect different areas of the network. Normal areas are usually set up according to functional or geographical groupings. By default, a normal area does not allow traffic from another area to use its links to reach other areas. All traffic from other areas must cross a transit area such as area 0. Normal areas can be of different types regarding the propagation and generation of routing information. Normal area types affect the amount of routing information that is propagated into the normal area. For example, instead of propagating all routes from the backbone area into a normal area, you could propagate only a default route. In Example 4-4, a router is configured to be in area 6, a normal area.

Example 4-4 *Configuration of a Router in a Normal Area*

```
R6(config)# router ospf 100
R6(config-router)# network 192.168.107.1 0.0.0.0 area 6
```

In Example 4-4, the **network** command matches the interface 192.168.107.1 and places it in area 6.

Theoretical limits say that an OSPF router should have a maximum of 50 neighbors in an area, that a single OSPF router should span no more than three areas, and that there should be 60 or fewer OSPF routers per area. When designing a production network, best practice would be to keep the number of areas and number of neighbors on each router as low as possible. Any networks that contain unstable links (poor WAN and/or connectivity) should have as few routers as possible to help support network stability.

Figure 4-6 shows the different roles that routers may have in OSPF.

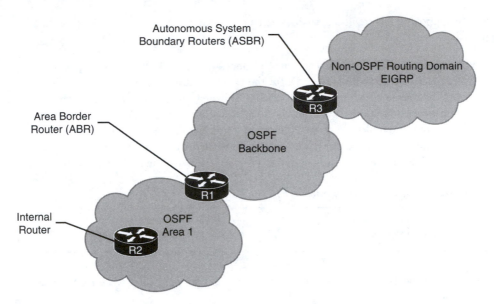

Figure 4-6   *OSPF Router Types as Depicted in an OSPF Autonomous System*

The group of routers that make up the internetwork comprises the OSPF AS (autonomous system). These routers are illustrated in Figure 4-6. As stated earlier, area 0 routers are backbone routers; in Figure 4-6, R1 and R3 are part of the backbone. Routers inside a nonbackbone area are considered to be OSPF internal routers. In Figure 4-6, R2 is an internal router. Routers that connect an area to the backbone are considered Area Boundary Routers (ABR). In Figure 4-6, R1 is an ABR because it is connected to the backbone (area 0) as well as to area 1. Routers that connect to an external routing source (such as BGP, another OSPF AS, or EIGRP) are considered Autonomous System Boundary Routers (ASBR). In Figure 4-6, R3 is an ASBR.

An ABR connects area 0 to the nonbackbone areas. An OSPF ABR plays a very important role in the OSPF infrastructure. It has interfaces in more than one area. An ABR has the following characteristics:

■ It separates LSA flooding zones.

■ It becomes the primary point for area address summarization. It functions as the source for default routes and routes outside of the area.

■ It maintains the LSDB for each area with which it is connected.

Example 4-5 presents a simple ABR configuration. It shows the router with interfaces in the backbone area and another area.

Example 4-5 *Configuring an ABR*

```
R1(config)# router ospf 100
R1(config-router)# network 192.168.1.1 0.0.0.0 area 0
R1(config-router)# network 192.168.107.1 0.0.0.0 area 1
```

An ideal design would have each ABR connected to two areas only: the backbone area and a normal area with only one other normal area connected.

An ASBR connects any OSPF area to another network with different administrative control. The ASBR is the point where external routes are injected into the OSPF autonomous system. Routes are often injected out of OSPF at an ASBR, but it is not necessary or required of an ASBR to inject routes in both directions. Figure 4-6 shows the ASBR connected to EIGRP (although it could be any other routing protocol). In this case, R3 runs OSPF and EIGRP.

In Figure 4-6, assume that the external AS is running the EIGRP routing protocol and you need to inject these routes into OSPF, making the R3 router an ASBR. Use the **redistribute** command, as shown in Example 4-6.

Example 4-6 *Creating an ASBR with the* **redistribute** *Command*

```
R3(config)# router ospf 100
WAN_Core(config-router)# network 192.168.1.1 0.0.0.0 area 0
R3(config-router)# redistribute EIGRP 10
```

Note Redistribution of routing information between routing protocols is a complex activity that requires careful planning. The topic is beyond the scope of this text. For more information, see the "Redistributing Routing Protocols" tech note at http://www.cisco.com/en/US/tech/tk365/technologies_tech_note09186a008009487e.shtml.

Link-State Advertisements

LSAs are the building blocks of the OSPF LSDB. There are many types of LSAs. Some basic types are as follows:

- **Router LSA (Type 1):** Every router generates router LSAs for each area to which it belongs. Router LSAs describe the state of the router's links to the area, and are flooded only within that particular area.

- **Network LSA (Type 2):** Network LSAs are generated by the designated router. They are flooded in the area that contains the network.

- **Summary LSA (Type 3):** The ABR gathers information that it learned in one area and sends it to other areas. It can summarize the routes from the area into summary LSAs.

- **ASBR Summary LSA (Type 4):** This type of LSA is generated by an ABR to inform the rest of the OSPF domain how to access the ASBR.

- **Autonomous system LSA (Type 5):** This type of LSA is an external LSA generated by the ASBRs. Autonomous system LSAs get flooded everywhere, except into stub areas and NSSA areas. Stub areas and NSSA areas are explained later in the chapter, in the "Stub Areas, Not So Stubby Areas, and Totally Stub Areas" section.

Figure 4-7 depicts the basic LSAs. Individually, they act as database records; in combination, they describe the entire topology of an OSPF network or area.

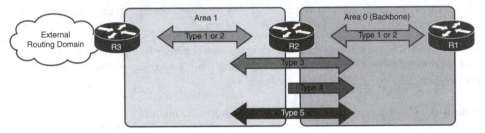

Figure 4-7   *Link-State Advertisements*

In Figure 4-7, R2 is the ABR between areas 0 and 1. As previously explained, area 0 is usually called the backbone area. R3 acts as the ASBR between the OSPF routing domain and an external domain. LSA types 1 and 2 are flooded between routers within an area. Type 3 and type 5 LSAs are flooded within backbone and standard areas. Type 4 LSAs are injected into the backbone area by the ABR so that all routers in the OSPF domain know how to reach the ASBR (R3). This is because we need all routers in OSPF domain to reach the ASBR (R3).

> **Note**   The basic LSA types are described in this book. Advanced LSA types are outside the scope of this book. For more information, see RFC 2328 for OSPF version 2 (http://tools.ietf.org/html/rfc2328 and RFC 5340 for OSPF for IPv6 (http://tools.ietf.org/html/rfc5340).

Multiarea OSPF IPv4 Implementation

The OSPF routing protocol supports a two-tier hierarchical structure. By utilizing a two-tier or multiarea OSPF design you not only can increase the network scalability, but also can reduce the load and utilization on routers because fewer SPF calculations are required and the routing tables are smaller. This section describes the differences between single-area and multiarea OSPF design, how OSPF implementation should be planned, and how to configure and verify multiarea OSPF design in an IPv4 network.

Single-Area vs. Multiarea OSPF

Single-area OSPF design puts all routers into a single OSPF area. This design results in many LSAs being processed on every router and in larger routing tables. In this case the OSPF configuration follows a single-area design, creating a situation where all of the routers are considered internal routers to the area and all of the interfaces are members of this single area.

Multiarea design can be a better solution than single-area design. In a multiarea design, as shown in Figure 4-8, the network is segmented to limit the propagation of LSAs inside an area and to make routing tables smaller by using summarization.

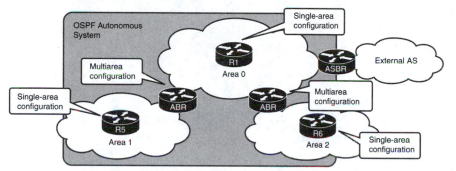

Figure 4-8   *Multiarea OSPF*

In multiarea OSPF, there are two types of routers from the configuration point of view:

- **Routers with single-area configuration:** Internal routers, backbone routers, and ASBRs that are residing in one area

- **Routers with a multiarea configuration:** ABRs and ASBRs that are residing in more than one area

While multiarea OSPF is a very scalable and powerful routing protocol, it can be complex to design, manage, and implement.

Stub Areas, Not So Stubby Areas, and Totally Stub Areas

OSPF has three types of specialized areas: stub areas, not-so-stubby areas (NSSA), and totally stub areas.

Stub Areas

External networks, injected into OSPF from an ASBR, are not allowed to be flooded into a stub area. Routing from these areas to the outside world is based on a default route.

Configuring a stub area reduces the topological database size inside an area and reduces the memory requirements of routers inside that area.

An area is qualified as a stub if there is a single exit point from that area or if routing to outside of the area does not have to take an optimal path. The latter description is just an indication that a stub area that has multiple exit points has one or more BoundaryABRs injecting a default into that area. Routing to the outside world can take a suboptimal path in reaching the destination by going out of the area via an exit point that is farther to the destination than other exit points.

A stub area may not contain an ASBR, and cannot be the backbone area. Figure 4-9 shows the previous example from Figure 4-8 with a stub area added.

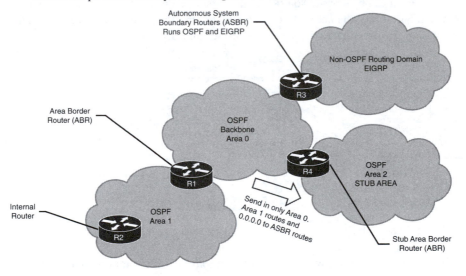

Figure 4-9   *Area 2: OSPF Stub Area*

In area 2, the routes from areas 0 and 1 are sent in, along with a default route for any of the routes.

Not-So-Stubby Areas

The NSSA extends on the concept of a stub area. It allows some external routes to be injected into it. The NSSA is a stub area that permits the existence of an ASBR. It intro- duces another type of LSA, a type 7. The type 7 LSA carries the external routes inside the NSSA instead of a type 5 (type 5 is not permitted in an NSSA). The type 7 LSA stays within the NSSA, and the NSSA ABR then sends it into the backbone as a type 5 LSA. Type 7 LSAs are not found in normal areas, the backbone area, stub areas, or totally stub areas. Totally stub areas are discussed in the next section.

In Figure 4-10, R5 is an ASBR inside the area. Figure 4-10 takes Figure 4-9 and changes the stub area to an NSSA.

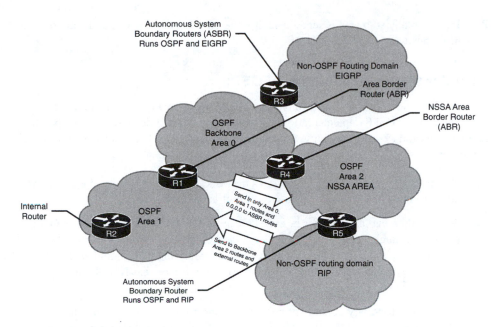

Figure 4-10 *Not-So-Stubby Area*

Totally Stub Area

A totally stub area has only one exit point that is connected to the backbone. The backbone sends in a default route only. Figure 4-11 adds a totally stubby area to the example shown in the previous two figures. R6 is the ABR for area 3, the totally stub area.

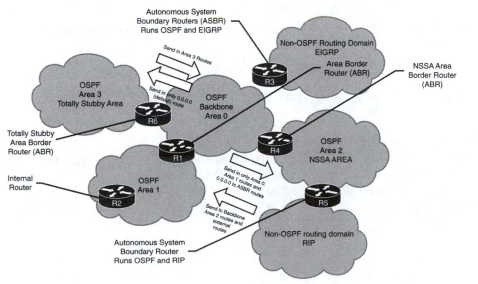

Figure 4-11 *Totally stub area*

Because the totally stub area is sent a default route only, LSA types 3, 4, and 5 are not present in the area.

Planning for the Implementation of OSPF

The OSPF routing protocol can be implemented as a single-area or multiarea infrastructure. The type of OSPF implementation that you choose should depend on your specific requirements and existing topology. When you are planning OSPF, consider the following key points:

- In preparing to deploy OSPF routing in a network, first gather the existing network requirements. Then consider single-area or multiarea deployment.

- The IP addressing plan governs how OSPF can be deployed and how well the OSPF deployment might scale. Thus, a detailed IP addressing plan, along with the IP subnetting information, must be created. A solid IP addressing plan should enable the usage of OSPF multiarea design and summarization to more easily scale the network and optimize OSPF behavior and the propagation of LSAs.

- The network topology consists of links that connect the network equipment and belong to different OSPF areas in a multiarea OSPF design. Network topology is important to determine primary and backup links. Primary and backup links are transport paths that are chosen by OSPF cost. OSPF cost is used to determine the primary (preferred) and secondary paths (and the corresponding links) to be used. This is determined on equal-cost paths by the changing OSPF cost on interfaces.

- A detailed network topology plan should also be used to determine the different OSPF areas, ABRs, and ASBRs, as well as summarization points, if multiarea OSPF is used.

- An implementation plan must be created before configuring OSPF routing in the network.

- After completing the implementation plan, OSPF can actually be administered.

These factors dictate placement of the OSPF areas, ASBRs, ASRs, and internal routers.

Multiarea OSPF Configuration

Multiarea OSPF requires one or more routers connected to the backbone area and a normal (non-backbone) area. A router that connects the backbone and a normal area is an area boundary router (ABR). Figure 4-12 presents three routers. R1 is an internal router in the backbone. R3 is an internal router in area 1. R2 is the ABR connecting area 1 to the backbone.

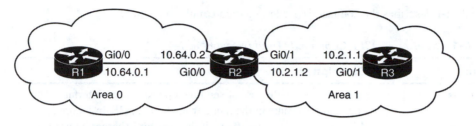

Figure 4-12   *OSPF Configuration on R1*

Example 4-7 gives the configuration of R1, R2, and R3 from figure 4-12.

Example 4-7   *Configuring R1, R2, and R3*

```
R1(config)# interface GigabitEthernet0/0
R1(config-if)# ip address 10.64.0.1 255.255.255.0
R1(config-if)# ip ospf cost 10
R1(config-if)# exit
R1(config)# router ospf 1
R1(config-router)# network 10.64.0.0 0.0.0.255 area 0


R2(config)# interface GigabitEthernet0/0
R2(config-if)# ip address 10.64.0.2 255.255.255.0
R2(config-if)# ip ospf cost 10
R2(config-if)# exit
R2(config)# interface GigabitEthernet0/1
R2(config-if)# ip address 10.2.1.2 255.255.255.0
R2(config-if)# ip ospf cost 10
R2(config-if)# exit
R2(config)# router ospf 1
R2(config-router)# network 10.64.0.0 0.0.0.255 area 0
R2(config-router)# network 10.2.1.0 0.0.0.255 area 1


R3(config)# interface GigabitEthernet0/1
R3(config-if)# ip address 10.2.1.1 255.255.255.0
R3(config-if)# ip ospf cost 10
R3(config-if)# exit
R3(config)# router ospf 1
R3(config-router)# network 10.2.1.0 0.0.0.255 area 1
```

Table 4-1 describes the commands used to configure multiarea OSPF.

Table 4-1   *Multiarea OSPF Commands Used in Example 4-7*

Command	Description
ip ospf cost *cost*	Specifies the OSPF cost of sending a packet on an interface. The cost can be a value in the range from 1 to 65,535. In Example 4-7, the cost is reset to 10 on all the Gigabit Ethernet interfaces, because the OSPF reference bandwidth is 100 Mbps and the example uses Gigabit Ethernet.
router ospf *process_id*	Configures an OSPF routing process. The *process-id* parameter is an internally used identification parameter for the OSPF routing process. It is locally assigned and can be any positive integer. A unique value is assigned for each OSPF routing process in the router.
network *network wildcard_mask* **area** *area_id*	Defines the interfaces on which OSPF runs and defines the area IDs for those interfaces. The *wildcard_mask* parameter determines how to interpret the IP address. The mask has wildcard bits, in which 0 is a match and 1 indicates that the value is not significant. For example, 0.0.255.255 indicates a match in the first two octets.

Multiarea OSPF Verification

To verify multiarea OSPF configuration, use the same commands that you would to verify single-area OSPF. Use the **show ip ospf neighbor** command, as shown in Example 4-8, to verify OSPF neighbors. This command displays the neighbor router ID, neighbor priority, OSPF state, dead timer, neighbor interface IP address, and the interface that the neighbor is accessible through. Router R1 shows a neighbor of 10.2.1.2 and its adjacency state with R2. Note that the IP address listed for R2 is the router ID, the numerically highest interface. So, remember, the router ID will be the same and may not match the interface that the router establishes a neighbor relationship with. Router R2 shows two neighbors (as it is an ABR) and its neighbor status. It is a DR and a BDR for each segment, respectively. R3 is adjacent to R2 and is the BDR. Its router ID is lower than R2's router ID, which causes it to be the BDR, while R2 is the DR on that segment.

Example 4-8   *Determining OSPF Neighbors*

```
R1# show ip ospf neighbor

Neighbor ID     Pri    State      Dead Time   Address        Interface
10.2.1.2          1    FULL/DR    00:00:39    10.64.0.2      GigabitEthernet0/0
```

```
R2# show ip ospf neighbor

Neighbor ID      Pri    State       Dead Time    Address      Interface
10.64.0.1          1    FULL/BDR    00:00:32     10.64.0.1    GigabitEthernet0/0
192.168.1.20       1    FULL/DR     00:00:37     10.2.1.1     GigabitEthernet0/1


R3# show ip ospf neighbor

Neighbor ID      Pri    State       Dead Time    Address      Interface
10.2.1.2           1    FULL/BDR    00:00:35     10.2.1.2     GigabitEthernet0/1
```

Use the **show ip protocols** command to verify the OSPF status. The output of the command reveals which routing protocols are configured on a router and much of the routing protocols configuration. In the case of OSPF, you can see the OSPF neighbors (as Routing Information Sources), number of areas in the router (in the Routing For Networks), and networks for which the router is advertising itself as the source (Routing for Networks). In Example 4-9, the R2 router, which is the ABR, is configured for two areas, with one interface in each area.

Example 4-9 *Verifying Interface Routing*

```
R2# show ip protocols
<output omitted>
  Routing for Networks:
    10.64.0.0 0.0.0.255 area 0
    10.2.1.2 0.0.0.0 area 1
  Routing Information Sources:
    Gateway           Distance    Last Update
    10.64.0.1         110              00:06:07
    10.2.1.1          110              00:06:07
  <output omitted>
```

Use the **show ip route ospf** command to verify the OSPF routes in the IP routing table that are known to the router, as demonstrated in Example 4-10. This command is one of the best ways to determine connectivity between the local router and the rest of the network. It also has optional parameters so that you can further specify the information to be displayed, including the OSPF process ID.

Example 4-10   *OSPF Routing Table*

```
R1# show ip route ospf
Codes: L - local, C - connected, S - static, R - RIP, M - mobile, B - BGP
       D - EIGRP, EX - EIGRP external, O - OSPF, IA - OSPF inter area
       N1 - OSPF NSSA external type 1, N2 - OSPF NSSA external type 2
       E1 - OSPF external type 1, E2 - OSPF external type 2
        i - IS-IS, su - IS-IS summary, L1 - IS-IS level-1, L2 - IS-IS level-2
       ia - IS-IS inter area, * - candidate default, U - per-user static route
        o - ODR, P - periodic downloaded static route, H - NHRP, l - LISP
        + - replicated route, % - next hop override
Gateway of last resort is not set
       10.0.0.0/24 is subnetted, 1 subnets
O IA    10.2.1.0 [110/11 via 10.64.0.2, 00:46:20, GigabitEthernet0/0
<output omitted>
```

In Example 4-10, the 10.2.1.0 subnet is recognized on GigabitEthernet0/0 via neighbor 10.64.0.2. The "O" code represents OSPF routes, and "IA" represents interarea, which means that the route originated from another area. Recall that R1 is in area 0, and the 10.2.1.0 subnet is connected to router R2 in area 1. The entry "[110/11]" in the routing table represents the administrative distance that is assigned to OSPF (110) and the total cost of the route to subnet 10.2.1.0 (cost of 11). Administrative distance is the "trust level" a router holds in a routing protocol. The lower the level, the more trusted it is. A connected interface is assigned "0", static routes are assigned "1," and each routing protocol is assigned a unique value.

Troubleshooting Multiarea OSPF

Because it is a link-state routing protocol, OSPF scales well with a growing network. However, this introduces complexity in design, configuration, and maintenance. This section introduces OSPF neighbor states, which are important when troubleshooting OSPF adjacencies. Then it lists some of the common issues surrounding an OSPF network and provides a flowchart approach to troubleshooting those issues. This section also describes each issue and provides recommendations for troubleshooting.

OSPF Neighbor States

Before you learn how to troubleshoot OSPF, it is of utmost importance that you learn how OSPF routers traverse different OSPF states when adjacencies are being established. This section begins with a description of OSPF neighbor states. In Figure 4-13, notice that hello packets are used to transition between OSPF states. The OSPF state transitions in Figure 4-13 and Figure 4-14 reflect a simplified version. The full state change is listed at the end of the section.

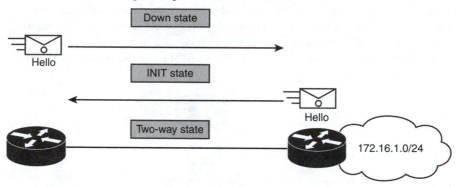

OSPF routers go through different OSPF states:

Figure 4-13 *OSPF Routers Go Through Different States*

When routers that are running OSPF are initialized, an exchange process using the Hello protocol is the first procedure.

Figure 4-13 illustrates the exchange process that happens when routers appear on the network, which is further described in the list that follows:

1. A router is enabled on the LAN and is in a down state because it has not exchanged information with any other router. It begins by sending a hello packet through each of its interfaces that are participating in OSPF, although it does not know the identity of any other routers.

2. All directly connected routers that are running OSPF receive the hello packet from the first router and add the router to their lists of neighbors. After adding the router to the list, other routers are in the INIT state.

3. Each router that received the hello packet sends a unicast reply hello packet to the first router with its corresponding information. The Neighbors field in the hello packet includes all neighboring routers and the first router.

4. When the first router receives these hello packets, it adds all of the routers that had its router ID in their hello packets to its own neighbor relationship database. After this process, the first router is in the two-way state. At this point, all routers that have each other in their lists of neighbors have established bidirectional communication.

If the link type is a broadcast network, such as a LAN link like Ethernet, a DR and BDR must first be selected. The DR acts as a central exchange point for routing information and reduces the amount of routing information that the routers have to exchange. The DR and BDR are selected after routers are in the two-way state. A router with the highest priority becomes the DR. In case of a tie, a router with the highest router ID becomes the DR. Between the routers on a LAN that were not elected as the DR or BDR, the exchange process stops at this point, and the routers remain in the two-way state.

After the DR and BDR have been selected, the routers are considered to be in the exstart state. The routers are then ready to discover the link-state information about the internetwork and create their LSDBs. The exchange of LSAs is used to discover the network routes, and it brings all of the routers from the exchange state to a full state of communication. The first step in this process is for the DR and BDR to establish adjacencies with each of the other routers.

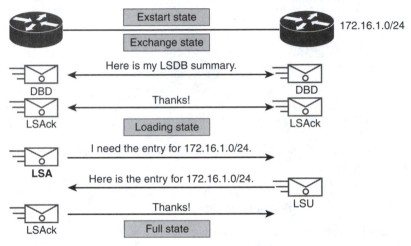

Figure 4-14   *Transition from Exstart to Full State*

As shown in Figure 4-14, the exchange protocol continues as follows:

1. In the exstart state, the DR and BDR establish adjacencies with each router in the network. During this process, a master/slave election is created between each router and its adjacent DR and BDR. The router with the higher router ID acts as the master during the exchange process. The master/slave election dictates which router will start the exchange of routing information. This step is not shown in Figure 4-14.

2. The master and slave routers exchange one or more DBD packets. The routers are in the exchange state.

3. A router compares the DBD that it received with the LSAs that it has. If the DBD has a more up-to-date, link-state entry, the router sends an LSR to the other router. When routers start sending LSRs, they are in the loading state.

4. When all LSRs have been satisfied for a given router, the adjacent routers are considered synchronized and are in the full state.

Table 4-2 defines all of the OSPF states in more detail.

Table 4-2 *OSPF Neighbor States*

OSPF Neighbor State	Definition
Down	This is the first OSPF neighbor state. It means that no information (hellos) has been received from this neighbor, but hello packets can still be sent to the neighbor in this state. During the fully adjacent neighbor state, if a router doesn't receive a hello packet from a neighbor within the RouterDeadInterval or if the manually configured neighbor is being removed from the configuration, then the neighbor state changes from full to down.
Attempt	This state is only valid for manually configured neighbors in a nonbroadcast multiaccess (NBMA)[1] network. In the attempt state, the router sends unicast hello packets every poll interval to the neighbor, from which hellos have not been received within the dead interval.
INIT	This state specifies that the router has received a hello packet from its neighbor, but the receiving router's ID was not included in the hello packet. When a router receives a hello packet from a neighbor, it should list the sender's router ID in its hello packet as an acknowledgment that it received a valid hello packet.
Two-way	This state designates that bidirectional communication has been established between two routers. Bidirectional means that each router has seen the other's hello packet. This state is attained when the router receiving the hello packet sees its own router ID within the received hello packet's Neighbors field. At this state, a router decides whether to become adjacent with this neighbor. On broadcast media and with NBMA networks, a router becomes full with the DR and the BDR; it stays in the two-way state with all other neighbors. On point-to-point and point-to-multipoint networks, a router becomes full with all connected routers.
Exstart	Once the DR and BDR are elected, the actual process of exchanging link-state information can start between the routers and their DR and BDR. In this state, the routers and their DR and BDR establish a master/slave election and choose the initial sequence number for adjacency formation. The router with the higher router ID becomes the master and starts the exchange, and, as master, it is the only router that can increment the sequence number. Note that one would logically conclude that the DR/BDR with the highest router ID will become the master during this process of master/slave election. Remember that the DR/BDR election might be purely by virtue of a higher priority configured on the router instead of highest router ID. Thus, it is possible that a DR plays the role of slave. Also note that master/slave election is on a per-neighbor basis.

OSPF Neighbor State	Definition
Exchange	In the exchange state, OSPF routers exchange DBD packets. Database descriptors contain LSA headers only and describe the contents of the entire LSDB. Each DBD packet has a sequence number which can be incremented only by the master, which is explicitly acknowledged by the slave. Routers also send link-state request packets and link-state update packets (which contain the entire LSA) in this state. The contents of the DBD received are compared to the information contained in the router's LSDB to check if new or more current link-state information is available with the neighbor.
Loading	In this state, the actual exchange of link-state information occurs. Based on the information provided by the DBDs, routers send link-state request packets. The neighbor then provides the requested link-state information in link-state update packets. During the adjacency, if a router receives an outdated or missing LSA, it requests that LSA by sending a link-state request packet. All link-state update packets are acknowledged.
Full	In this state, routers are fully adjacent with each other. All the router and network LSAs are exchanged and the routers' databases are fully synchronized.

Full is the normal state for an OSPF router. If a router is stuck in another state, it's an indication that there are problems in forming adjacencies. The only exception to this is the two-way state, which is normal in a broadcast network. Routers achieve the full state with their DR and BDR only. Neighbors always see each other as two-way. |

1 NBMA is most commonly seen as point-to-multipoint or meshed Frame Relay WANs.

When troubleshooting OSPF neighbors, you should be aware that all states except two-way and full are transitory, and routers should not remain in these states for extended periods of time. However, the most likely problem that you will experience is that you will not see neighbors at all. In this case, verify the OSPF configuration.

This section reviewed the OSPF neighbor adjacencies and how they transition. As stated earlier, understanding these concepts is important when things do not work as anticipated.

Components of Troubleshooting OSPF

This section examines troubleshooting OSPF. Let's begin with Figure 4-15. It is a suggested flowchart for identifying OSPF issues.

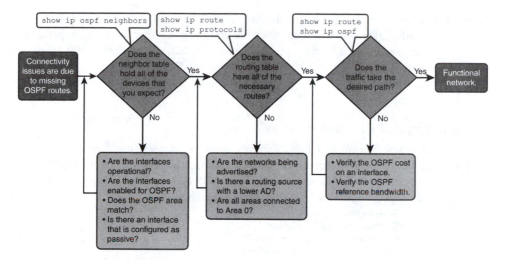

Figure 4-15 *OSPF Troubleshooting Flowhart*

When you are first notified that there are connectivity issues in your network, first test Layer 2/3 connectivity using the methods discussed in Chapter 1, "Implementing Scalable Medium-Sized Networks," and Chapter 2, "Troubleshooting Basic Connectivity." This would most likely involve engaging the **show ip interface brief**, **ping**, and **traceroute** commands. If you believe that the connectivity issues appear to be Layer 3 path related and reachability is compromised, you may need to examine the routing protocol. If the network uses OSPF as the routing protocol, refer to Figure 4-15 and follow the high-level steps indicated to troubleshoot it:

Step 1. Use the **show ip ospf neighbors** command to verify whether your router established adjacency with a neighboring router. If adjacency between two routers is not established, the routers cannot exchange routes. First verify that the interfaces are operational and enabled for OSPF. Use the **show ip protocols** command and check the configuration using **show running-configuration**. Check issues such as access control lists (ACL), passive interfaces, incorrect network commands, and authentication keys.

Step 2. If adjacency between two routers is established but you do not see routes in the routing table using the **show ip route** command, first verify that there is another routing protocol with a lower administrative distance running in the network. In this case, OSPF routes are not considered by the router to be inserted into the routing table. If no other routing protocols are configured, verify that all of the required networks are advertised into OSPF. In the case of multiarea OSPF, also verify if all normal (nonbackbone) areas are connected directly to area 0 (the backbone area). If a normal area is not connected to the backbone area, routers in that normal area cannot send and receive updates to and from other areas.

Step 3.   If you see all of the required routes in the routing table, but the path that traffic takes is not correct, verify the OSPF cost on interfaces on the path. Be careful in cases where you have interfaces that are faster than 100 Mbps, because all interfaces above this bandwidth will have the same OSPF cost by default.

Troubleshooting OSPF Neighbor Issues

To establish an OSPF neighbor relationship, you must have Layer 2 and 3 reachability to the neighbor. Figure 4-16 depicts the **show ip interface brief** output. It verifies that the status and protocol are both up for the Serial0/0/0 interface that is connected to the Branch router. This confirms the link is operational on Layer 2/3.

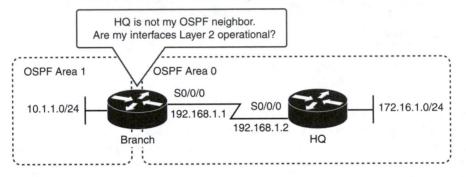

Figure 4-16   *Determining Reachability*

In Figure 4-16, the Branch router shows that both interfaces are up, as illustrated in the following configuration:

```
Branch# show ip interface brief
Interface                 IP-Address      OK? Method   Status         Protocol
GigabitEthernet0/0        10.1.1.1        YES NVRAM     up             up
Seial0/0/0                192.168.1.20    YES NVRAM     up             up
```

In Figure 4-17, a ping from the Branch router to the HQ router is successful. This confirms IP connectivity between the devices. Had the ping failed, you would check the cabling and verify that interfaces on connected devices are operational and are on a common subnet with the same subnet mask.

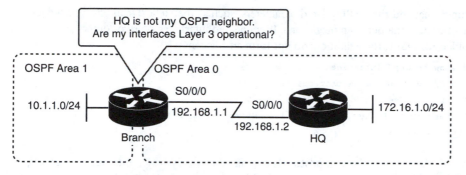

Figure 4-17 *Determining Layer 3 Reachability*

As you can see from the following configuration, you can ping the HQ router:

```
Branch# ping 192.168.1.2
Type escape sequence to abort.
Sending 5, 100-byte ICMP Echos to 10.2.1.1, timeout is 2 seconds:
!!!!!
Success rate is 100 percent (5/5), round-trip min/avg/max = 1/1/1 ms
```

The next step is to make sure that OSPF is operational on the interfaces. In Figure 4-18, the configuration and the interface should be checked for OSPF operation.

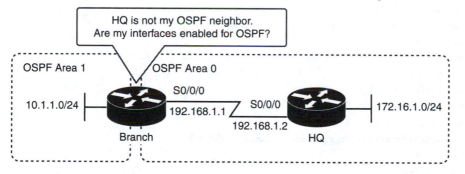

Figure 4-18 *Determining if OSPF Is Running on the Interface*

In the following configuration, notice the **network** command that is configured under the OSPF routing process that indicates which router interface participates in OSPF:

```
Branch# show running-configuration
<output omitted>
router ospf 1
network 10.1.1.0 0.0.0.255 area 1
<output omitted>
```

Use the **show ip ospf interface** command, as shown in the following configuration, to verify which interfaces are enabled for OSPF. The output also shows you which interface is functional and the OSPF-related parameters, such as the Hello/Dead intervals (which must be the same between neighbors). If connected interfaces on two routers are not enabled for OSPF, the neighbors do not form an adjacency.

```
R3# show ip ospf interface
Serial0/0/0 is up, line protocol is up
  Internet Address 192.168.1.1/24, Area 0
  Process ID 1, Router ID 192.168.1.1, Network Type POINT_TO_POINT, Cost: 64
<output omitted>
```

You can also use the **show ip protocols** command to verify which interfaces are configured for OSPF. The output shows you IP addresses or networks that are enabled using the **network** command. If an IP address on an interface falls within a network that has been enabled for OSPF, the interface will be enabled for OSPF. The output of this command also shows you if OSPF is enabled on an interface directly using the **ip ospf** *process_id* area-id *area_id* command. Example 4-11 demonstrates output from the **show ip protocols** command.

Example 4-11   show ip protocols *Command Output*

```
HQ# show ip protocols
*** IP Routing is NSF aware ***
Routing Protocol is "ospf 1"
  Outgoing update filter list for all interfaces is not set
  Incoming update filter list for all interfaces is not set
  Router ID 1.1.1.1
  Number of areas in this router is 1. 1 normal 0 stub 0 nssa
  Maximum path: 4
  Routing for Networks:
    172.16.1.0 0.0.0.255 area 0
    192.168.1.0 0.0.0.255 area 0
  Routing on Interfaces Configured Explicitly (Area 0):
    Loopback0
<output omitted>
```

In Figure 4-19, OSPF is enabled on the Serial0/0/0 interface on both routers.

With OSPF running on a network, the **passive-interface** command stops both outgoing and incoming routing updates. The effect of the command causes the router to stop sending and receiving hello packets over an interface. For this reason, the routers in Figure 4-20 do not become neighbors.

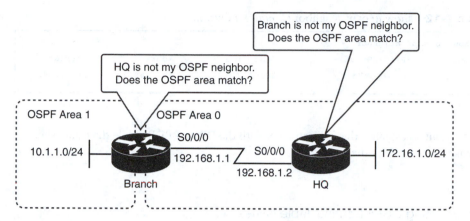

Figure 4-19 *Checking Whether OSPF Areas Match*

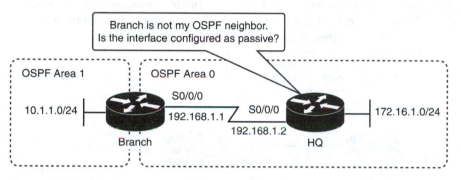

Figure 4-20 *OSPF with Passive Interface Configured*

To verify if any interface on a router is configured as passive, use the **show ip protocols** command in privileged mode.

An example in which you want to configure the interface as passive is an ASBR that may use static routes to connect to the neighboring AS. In this case, you need to advertise this particular link through your own network but not allow the third party to receive hellos or send hellos to your device. That would be a security risk.

To configure an interface as a passive interface in OSPF, you use the **passive-interface** *interface* command in the OSPF router configuration mode. To disable the interface as passive, you use the **no passive-interface** *interface* command.

Once you disable the passive interface, the routers should become adjacent. Recall that two routers should be in the full state in order to exchange LSAs. In Example 4-12, notice an established neighbor relationship after removing the passive interface.

Example 4-12 show ip ospf neighbor *Command Output*

```
HQ# show ip ospf neighbor
Neighbor ID     Pri   State         Dead Time      Address        Interface
192.168.1.2     0     FULL/ -       00:00:31       192.168.1.1    Serial0/0/0
```

Note Routers establish the full state only with the DR and BDR, while the established state is two-way with other routers.

Troubleshooting OSPF Routing Table Issues

In Figure 4-21, the Branch and HQ routers have their neighbor adjacency set up, but a ping test from the Branch router to a host in the 172.16.1.0/24 network is not successful. Checking the routing table of the Branch router leads to the conclusion that there is a route missing to the destination network of 172.16.1.0/24.

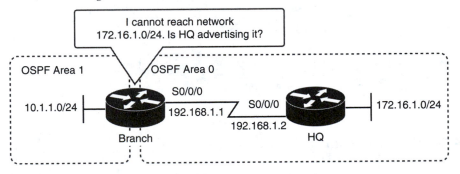

Figure 4-21 *Verification of Network Advertisement Using the* show ip protocols *Command*

You would use the **show ip protocols** command on the HQ router to verify if the 172.16.1.0/24 network is being advertised to OSPF neighbors. In Figure 4-21, the HQ router is not configured to advertise the 172.16.1.0/24 network to the neighbor.

When you have more than one routing protocol configured in a network, you may receive routing information about a network through an undesired routing protocol. Recall that routing protocol administrative distance influences which routes will be installed in the routing table. In Figure 4-22, the routing table is being populated by EIGRP; after the figure, we see the 172.16.1.0/24 route in the **show ip route** command. This may or may not affect connectivity if the routing protocols are routing packets via the same path. However, differences in algorithms, metrics, filtering, and other variables may result in suboptimal routing and asynchronous pathing.

In Figure 4-22, the route about the 172.16.1.0/24 network has been received through EIGRP and OSPF. However, because EIGRP with an administrative distance of 90 is more trustworthy than OSPF with an administrative distance of 110, the EIGRP route will be installed in the routing table.

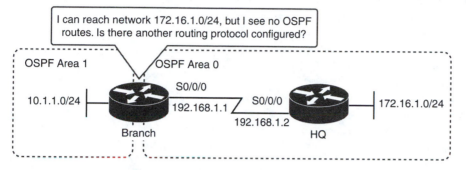

Figure 4-22   *Determining Routing Sources*

In the Branch router in Figure 4-22, the **show ip route** command produces this output:

```
Branch# show ip route 172.16.1.0
Routing entry for 172.16.1.0/24
  Known via "eigrp 1", distance 90, metric 2297856, type internal
  Redistributing via eigrp 1
  Last update from 192.168.1.2 on Serial0/0/0, 00:00:39 ago
<output omitted>
```

The **show ip protocols** command verifies which routing protocols are configured and their administrative distances, as demonstrated in Example 4-13.

Example 4-13   *Verifying Protocol Configuration and Administrative Distance with the show ip protocols Command*

```
Branch# show ip protocols
 Routing Protocol is "ospf 1"
  Outgoing update filter list for all interfaces is not set
  Incoming update filter list for all interfaces is FILTER_OSPF
  Router ID 209.165.201.1
  It is an area Boundary router
  Number of areas in this router is 2. 2 normal 0 stub 0 nssa
  Maximum path: 4
  Routing for Networks:
    10.1.1.0 0.0.0.255 area 1
    192.168.1.0 0.0.0.255 area 0
 Reference bandwidth unit is 100 mbps
  Routing Information Sources:
    Gateway         Distance        Last Update
    1.1.1.1         80              00:02:37
```

```
   Distance: (default is 110)
Routing Protocol is "eigrp 1"
   Outgoing update filter list for all interfaces is not set
   Incoming update filter list for all interfaces is not set
   Default networks flagged in outgoing updates
   Default networks accepted from incoming updates
   EIGRP metric weight K1=1, K2=0, K3=1, K4=0, K5=0
   EIGRP maximum hopcount 100
   EIGRP maximum metric variance 1
   Redistributing: eigrp 1
   EIGRP NSF-aware route hold timer is 240s
   Automatic network summarization is not in effect
   Maximum path: 4
   Routing for Networks:
       10.0.0.0
       192.168.1.0
   Routing Information Sources:
           Gateway           Distance       Last Update
           (this router)        90          00:12:09 00:02:39
           192.168.1.2          90          00:12:09 00:02:39
   Distance: internal 90 external 170
```

Troubleshooting OSPF Path Selection

Incorrect path selection does not always lead to the loss of connectivity. However, certain links in a network should not be used, if possible. This applies, for example, to backup WAN links, which can be charged by the amount of transferred data and can be expensive (for instance, legacy ISDN or 3G/4G). Another example is traffic that is delivery sensitive, such as voice, which should travel only over a specific path and only over links that have a lower latency than originally directed. This section describes how to troubleshoot incorrect path selection caused by OSPF. For example, Figure 4-23 shows two locations that are connected via the primary, high-speed link and via the backup link. In this case, you have to make sure that the backup link is used only when the primary link fails.

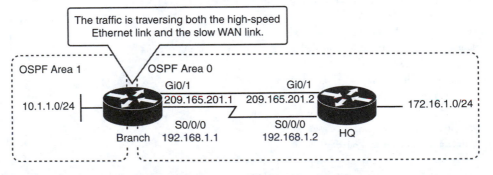

Figure 4-23   *Determining Path*

Figure 4-23 has a network 172.16.0.0/24. It is reachable from the Branch router via the GigabitEthernet0/1 interface and the Serial0/0/0 interface. In this example, both interfaces have the same OSPF cost. This results in load balancing across both. The reason for the same OSPF cost on both interfaces could be that someone manually changed the cost on the interfaces, or that there is an incorrect reference bandwidth when managing interfaces that are faster than 100 Mbps. Recall that the OSPF cost is calculated as interface bandwidth divided by reference bandwidth, which is 100 Mbps by default. For example, with two interfaces, such as 1000 Mbps and 100 Mbps, both will have the same OSPF cost with a value of 1. This case requires either increasing the reference bandwidth to 1000 Mbps or manually changing the OSPF cost on an interface to reflect the actual bandwidth of the interface.

Use the **show ip ospf interface** command to verify the OSPF cost on an interface, as demonstrated in Example 4-14.

Example 4-14   *Verifying OSPF Cost on an Interface with the* **show ip ospf interface** *Command*

```
Branch# show ip ospf interface
 GigabitEthernet0/1 is up, line protocol is up
  Internet Address 209.165.201.2/27, Area 0
  Process ID 1, Router ID 1.1.1.1, Network Type BROADCAST, Cost: 1
<output omitted>

Serial0/0/0 is up, line protocol is up
   Internet Address 192.168.1.2/24, Area 0
  Process ID 1, Router ID 1.1.1.1, Network Type POINT_TO_POINT, Cost: 1
```

Once you increase the OSPF cost on the Serial0/0/0 interfaces on both routers, only the preferred route is installed in the routing table, as Example 4-15 demonstrates.

Example 4-15   *Reviewing the Interface Costs and the Corresponding Route*

```
Branch(config)# interface Serial0/0/0
Branch(config-if)# ip ospf cost 10

Branch# show ip route ospf
172.16.0.0/24 is subnetted, 1 subnets
O 172.16.1.0 [110/2] via 209.165.201.2, 00:14:31, GigabitEthernet0/1
```

The reference bandwidth can be changed from the default of 100 Mbps. You can verify the reference bandwidth using the **show ip ospf** command, as demonstrated in Example 4-16.

Example 4-16   *Verifying the Reference Bandwidth*

```
Branch# show ip ospf
<output omitted>
  Cisco NSF helper support enabled
  Reference bandwidth unit is 100 mbps
    Area BACKBONE(0)
        Number of interfaces in this area is 4
        Area has no authentication
  <output omitted>
```

Manipulating the cost on the interface changes the reference bandwidth. This is covered back in the beginning of the chapter, in the "Understanding Metrics in OSPF" section. Make sure that all the routers within the OSPF autonomous system have the same reference bandwidth by using the **auto-cost reference-bandwidth** *bandwidth_in_Mbits_ per_second* command from the router OSPF configuration mode.

Examining OSPFv3

OSPF version 3 was created to support IPv6. Although there are many similarities between OSPFv2 and OSPFv3, understanding the differences between them is necessary for the successful deployment and operation of an IPv6 network using OSPF for routing. This section describes OSPFv3, the IPv6-capable version of the OSPF routing protocol, including its operations and implementation.

OSPFv3 Key Characteristics

Some of the key points regarding OSPFv3 are

- OSPFv3 is an implementation of the OSPF routing protocol for IPv6.

- OSPFv2 (for IPv4) and OSPFv3 (for IPv6) run independently on the router.

- OSPFv3 has the same key capabilities as OSPFv2 for IPv4 networks:

  - Multiarea network design with BoundaryABRs that segment the network

  - Shortest-path first algorithm for optimum path calculation

- The OSPFv3 metric is still based on interface costing.

- The packet types and neighbor discovery mechanisms are the same in OSPFv3 as they are for OSPFv2.

- LSAs are still flooded throughout an OSPF domain, and many of the LSA types are the same. There are a few new and changed LSA types (as described in the next section).

■ In OSPFv3, the OSPF process no longer requires an IPv4 address for the router ID, but it does require a 32-bit number to be set. This 32-bit number is entered as four octets that are separated by dots (.) and looks like an IP address. The router ID is set using the **router-id** *router_id* command. If it is not manually set, then the router ID will be the same as the highest configured loopback address on the router. If there is also no loopback configured on the device, then it will use the highest IP address of a physical interface. On devices that do not have IPv4 addresses, the router ID must be set manually. A dotted decimal number equivalent to an IPv4 address must be used (for example, 192.168.1.1).

■ OSPFv3 operates on a per-link basis. Adjacencies use link-local addresses to communicate. Router next-hop attributes are neighboring router link-local addresses. Because link-local addresses have the same prefix, OSPF needs to store the information regarding the outgoing interface.

■ OSPFv3 uses IPv6 for transport of LSAs. IPv6 protocol number 89 is used.

■ OSPFv3 takes advantage of IPv6 multicasting by using FF02::5 for all OSPF routers and FF02::6 for the OSPF DR and the OSPF BDR.

Note   OSPFv3 is defined in RFC 5340: http://tools.ietf.org/html/rfc5340.

OSPFv3 LSAs

The following list describes LSA types in OSPFv3:

■ **Router LSA (Type 1):** Describes the link state and costs of a router's links to the area. These LSAs are flooded within an area only. The LSA indicates if the router is a BoundaryABR or an ASBR, and if it is one end of a virtual link. Type 1 LSAs are also used to advertise stub networks. In OSPFv3, these LSAs have no address information and are network protocol independent. In OSPFv3, router interface information may be spread across multiple router LSAs. Receivers must concatenate all router LSAs originated by a given router when running the SPF calculation.

■ **Network LSA (Type 2):** Describes the link-state and cost information for all routers attached to the network. This type of LSA is an aggregation of all the link-state and cost information in the network. Only a designated router tracks this information and can generate a network LSA. In OSPFv3, network LSAs have no address information and are network protocol independent.

■ **Interarea-prefix LSA for ABRs (Type 3):** Advertises internal networks to routers in other areas (interarea routes). Type 3 LSAs may represent a single network or a set of networks summarized into one advertisement. Only ABRs generate summary LSAs. In OSPFv3, addresses for these LSAs are expressed as *prefix, prefix length* instead of *address, mask*. The default route is expressed as a prefix with length 0. This LSA's name has been changed from OSPFv.2.

- **Interarea-router LSA for ASBRs (Type 4):** Advertises the location of an ASBR. Routers that are trying to reach an external network use these advertisements to determine the best path to the next hop. Type 4 LSAs are generated by ABRs on behalf of ASBRs. This LSA's name has been changed from OSPFv.2.

- **Autonomous system external LSA (Type 5):** Redistributes routes from another autonomous system, usually from a different routing protocol, into OSPFv3. In OSPFv3, addresses for these LSAs are expressed as *prefix, prefix length* instead of *address, mask*. The default route is expressed as a prefix with length 0.

Configuring OSPFv3

Figure 4-24 shows a multiarea OSPFv3 network of two routers. Both routers are in area 0. Additionally, the HQ router connects to area 1.

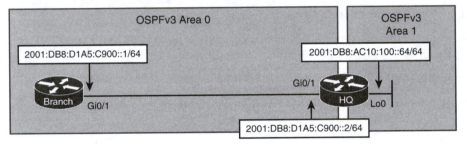

Figure 4-24   *Configuring OSPFv3*

The configuration of Branch and HQ are presented in Example 4-17.

Example 4-17   *Configuration of Branch and HQ Routers from Figure 4-24*

```
Branch(config)# ipv6 router ospf 99
Branch(config-rtr)# router-id 1.1.1.1
Branch(config-rtr)# interface GigabitEthernet0/1
Branch(config-if)# ipv6 address 2001:DB8:D1A5:C900::1/64
Branch(config-if)# ipv6 ospf 99 area 0

HQ(config)# ipv6 router ospf 99
HQ(config-rtr)# router-id 2.2.2.2
HQ(config-rtr)# interface GigabitEthernet0/1
HQ(config-if)# ipv6 address 2001:DB8:D1A5:C900::2/64
HQ(config-if)# ipv6 ospf 99 area 0
HQ(config-if)# interface Loopback 0
HQ(config-if)# ipv6 address 2001:DB8:AC10:100::64/64
HQ(config-if)# ipv6 ospf 99 area 1
```

Table 4-3 defines the important OSPF v3 commands used in Example 4-17.

Table 4-3 *OSPFv3 Commands Used*

Command	Description
ipv6 router ospf *process-id*	Enables OSPF for IPv6 router configuration mode. The *process-id* is internal identification. It is locally assigned and can be a positive integer from 1 to 65,535.
ipv6 ospf *process-id* **area** *area-id*	Enables OSPFv3 on an interface.
router-id *router_id*	Executed in OSPF router configuration mode to statically configure a router ID.

OSPFv3 Verification

The **show ipv6 ospf interface** command displays interfaces with enabled OSPFv3. Figure 4-25 shows the OSPFv3 area, process ID, IPv6 Link-local address, and router ID. Additionally, the output in Example 4-18 displays the adjacent OSPF neighbor that is connected to the interface of the Branch router in this example.

Example 4-18 *Displaying the Configured Interfaces with the* **show ipv6 ospf interface** *Command*

```
Branch# show ipv6 ospf interface
GigabitEthernet0/1 is up, line protocol up
    Link Local Address FE80::21E:7AFF:FEA3:5E71, Interface ID 5
    Area 0.0.0.0, Process ID 99, Instance ID 0, Router ID 1.1.1.1
    Network Type BROADCAST, Cost: 1
    Transmit Delay is 1 sec, State BDR, Priority 2
    Designated Router (ID) 2.2.2.2, local address FE80::21E:7AFF:FEA3:5E31
    Backup Designated Router (ID) 1.1.1.1, local address FE80::21E:7AFF:FEA3:5E71
<output omitted>
      Adjacent with Neighbor 2.2.2.2 (Designated Router)
```

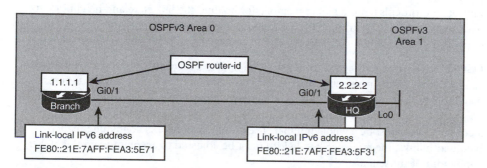

Figure 4-25 *OSPFv3 Network Example*

In Example 4-18, the show ipv6 ospf command displays the OSPFv3 general information for the sample network in Figure 4-26.

The example shows the following:

■ OSPFv3 process ID

■ Router ID

■ Timers

■ Area(s) configured

Note In OSPFv3 the area ID is reported in dotted decimal notation.

■ Reference bandwidth

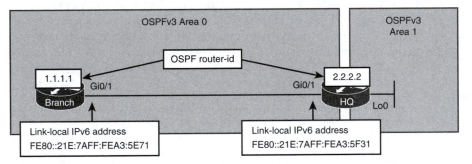

Figure 4-26 *OSPFv3 Area IDs and Link-Local Addressing*

Chapter Summary

Link-state routing protocols develop a shortest-path topology of the network in each router by building a link-state database using Dijkstra's algorithm. Link-state routing protocols converge quickly. However, they need additional resources to accomplish this. Link-state protocols require higher memory for holding the link state and neighbor database and use more CPU to run Dijkstra's algorithm whenever there is a change in the network.

OSPF is a link-state routing protocol that is an open standard that interoperates between vendors. It is used in many enterprise networks. OSPF employs three data structures: neighbors table, topology table, and routing table. Its metric is a cost based on link bandwidth. The reference bandwidth that cost is based off of is Fast Ethernet, which equals a cost of 1 and must be a whole number. Therefore, for networks containing higher-bandwidth links, the reference bandwidth must be adjusted to accommodate the higher bandwidth of those links.

Multiarea OSPF design enables segmentation of a network to limit the propagation of LSAs inside an area, reduce the size of routing tables, and make networks more stable. These areas may have different attributes to control the LSA distribution and the network routing tables.

OSPF supports IPv4 (OSPFv2) and IPv6 (OSPFv3). They both have the same basic algorithm, mechanisms, and data structures.

Troubleshooting OSPF should follow a logical structure. It should include basic Layer 1, Layer 2, and Layer 3 troubleshooting.

Review Questions

Use the questions here to review what you learned in this chapter. The correct answers are located in Appendix A, "Answers to Chapter Review Questions."

1. All of these tables are maintained by a link-state routing protocol except which one? (Source: "OSPF Overview")

   a. Routing

   b. Topology

   c. Update

   d. Neighbor

2. Match each table on the left to its function on the right. (Source: "OSPF Overview")

   1. Topology   **a.** Stores Adjacencies

   2. Routing   **b.** Stores LSAs

   3. Neighbor   **c.** Stores best paths

3. Which is a disadvantage of a link-state routing protocol? (Source: "OSPF Overview")

   a. Slow convergence

   b. Requires more memory and CPU

   c. Less scalable

   d. Does not work as well as a distance vector routing protocol in a poorly designed network topology

4. Which of the following is a metric used by OSPF? (Source: "OSPF Overview")

   a. Cost

   b. Hops

   c. Link state

   d. Administrative distance

5. Which OSPF packet helps form neighbor adjacencies? (Source: "OSPF Overview")

   a. Exchange packet

   b. Hello packet

   c. Neighbor discovery packet

    d. Adjacency packet

6. Which criterion does SPF use to determine the best path? (Source: "OSPF Overview")

    a. Lowest delay

    b. Highest bandwidth

    c. Lowest total cost of the route

    d. Total bandwidth of the route

7. Which of the following describe OSPF areas? (Choose two.) (Source: "Multiarea OSPF IPv4 Implementation")

    a. Are connected by an ASBR

    b. Are connected by an ABR

    c. Can host 100 or more interarea routers

    d. Must connect to area 0

8. Which are the three possible benefits of multiarea design in OSPF? (Choose three.) (Source: "Multiarea OSPF IPv4 Implementation")

    a. Reduced amount of LSA flooding

    b. Reduced number of SPF calculations

    c. Reduced size of the neighbor table

    d. Reduced size of the routing table

9. Which two commands are required for a basic OSPF configuration? (Choose two.) (Source: "Multiarea OSPF IPv4 Implementation")

    a. network *ip-address mask* **area** *area-id*

    b. network *ip-address wildcard-mask* **area** *area-id*

    c. router ospf *process-id*

    d. ip router ospf

10. Which OSPF **show** command describes a list of OSPF adjacencies? (Source: "Multiarea OSPF IPv4 Implementation")

    a. show ip ospf interface

    b. show ip osf

    c. show ip route

    d. show ip ospf neighbor

11. Which two interfaces will have the lowest OSPF cost by default? (Choose two.) (Source: "OSPF v3 Verification")

    a. Fast Ethernet

    b. T1

    c. Gigabit Ethernet

    d. E1

   e. EtherNet

12. Which interface is used as the reference bandwidth for OSPF cost? (Choose one.) (Source: "OSPF v3 Verification")

   a. Fast Ethernet
   b. T1
   c. GigabitEthernet
   d. E1
   e. EtherNet

13. Which LSA type's name changed between OSPFv2 and OSPFv3? (Source: "OSPFv3 LSAs")

   a. Type 1
   b. Type 2
   c. Type 3
   d. Type 5

14. Which LSA type is for bringing routes into OSPF from external sources? (Source: "OSPFv3 LSAs")

   a. Type 1
   b. Type 2
   c. Type 3
   d. Type 5

15. Which of the following is true about OSPFv3 on a router? (Source: "OSPFv3 Key Characteristics")

   a. Runs in OSPF process as a PIM
   b. Shares the SPF tree for IPv4 and IPv6
   c. Runs independently from OSPFv2
   d. Can't coexist with OSPFv2

16. Which of the following can be used for an OSPFv3 router ID? (Source: "OSPFv3 Key Characteristics")

   a. IPv4 loopback address
   b. IPv4 physical interface address
   c. Manually set router ID
   d. All of the above

17. Which command is used to enable OSPFv3? (Source: "Examining OSPFv3")

   a. (config-if)# **ipv6 ospf** *process_id* **area** *area_id*
   b. (config-rtr)# **ipv6 ospf** *process_id* **area** *area_id*

    c. (config-if)# **network** *ipv6_address wildcard_mask* **area** *area_id*

    d. (config-if)# **network** *ipv6_address wildcard_mask*

18. Which command is used to display OSPFv3-related interface information? (Source: "Examining OSPFv3")

    a. show ipv6 ospf interface

    b. show ipv6 interface

    c. show ipv6 ospf

    d. show ipv6 interface

19. What is the algorithm OSPF is based upon? (Source: "OSPF Overview")

    a. DUAL

    b. Dijkstra

    c. Distance vector

    d. Link state

Chapter 5

Understanding WAN Technologies

This chapter contains the following sections:

- Understanding WAN Technologies

- Establishing a WAN Connection Using Frame Relay

- Introducing Cisco VPN Solutions

- Chapter Summary

- Review Questions

Wide-area networks are most often fee-for-service networks, allowing users to access resources across a wide geographical area. Some services are considered Layer 2 connections between the remote locations, typically provided by a telephone company (service provider) over its WAN switches. Some of these technologies include a serial point-to-point (leased line) connection and Frame Relay connections.

Other connections leverage the Internet infrastructure, a Layer 3 alternative, to interconnect the remote locations of an organization. To provide security across the public Internet, you may implement a virtual private network (VPN) solution.

This chapter introduces the components of a VPN solution for WAN connectivity, explains how to configure a Point-to-Point Protocol (PPP) connection, and describes Frame Relay operation, configuration, and troubleshooting. The chapter also introduces the Generic Routing Encapsulation (GRE) tunneling protocol. The chapter concludes with a brief overview of Multiprotocol Label Switching (MPLS).

Chapter Objectives:

- Understand the characteristics and architecture of a WAN.

- Understand differences and similarities between WANs, MANs, and LANs.

- Understand WAN protocols, services, and media types

- Understand and identify "last mile" and demarcation points of WANs

- Configure and troubleshoot leased line and frame relay WANs

- How to utilize public (Internet) networks as a WAN infrastructure

Understanding WAN Technologies

As an enterprise grows beyond a single location, the need to interconnect LANs in various locations arises. This process is achieved with a WAN. There are multiple technologies that are involved in the functioning of WANs, including hardware devices and software functions. This section describes the functions and characteristics of WANs and contrasts them with LANs. It also explores how WANs relate to the OSI reference model in their design and function, and the major hardware components that are typically used in WAN environments.

Figure 5-1 demonstrates the function of a WAN.

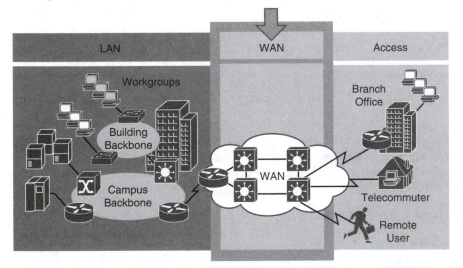

Figure 5-1   *Function of a WAN*

WANs use facilities that are supplied by a service provider, or carrier, such as a telephone or cable company. They connect the locations of an organization to each other, additional organizations, external services, and remote users. WANs carry various traffic types, such as voice, data, and video.

Here are the major characteristics of WANs:

- WANs generally connect devices that are separated by a broader geographical area than a LAN can serve.

- WANs use the services of carriers, such as telephone companies, cable companies, satellite systems, and network providers.

- WANs use connections of various types to provide access to bandwidth over large geographical areas.

- WANs can use the public Internet in conjunction with VPNs.

- WAN service may be dedicated or on-demand.

WAN architectures typically contain the components needed to support a company's business architectures to best support its business requirements. The typical WAN contains some subset, combination, or permutations of the connections shown in Figure 5-2.

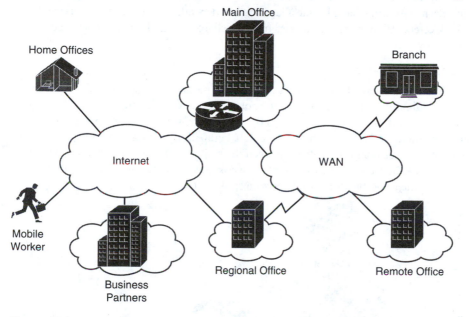

Figure 5-2   *Example WAN*

There are several reasons why WANs are necessary in a communications environment. LAN technologies provide speed and cost efficiency for the transmission of data for organizations in relatively small geographical areas. Sometimes, however, there are additional services that require communication among remote users, including the following:

- People in the regional or branch offices of an organization need to be able to communicate and share data.

- Organizations often want to share information with other businesses across large distances.

- Employees who travel on company business frequently need to access information that resides on their corporate networks.

Because it is not feasible to connect computers across a country or around the world in the same way that computers are connected in a LAN environment with cables, different technologies have evolved to support this need.

Increasingly, the Internet is being used in many different WAN applications. It can be employed as an inexpensive, quickly provisioned alternative to using an enterprise WAN; as a remote-access technology for remote/mobile workers; and as a replacement for dedicated WAN backup.

WAN Architecture

WAN logical circuits can be defined as hub and spoke, partial mesh, full mesh, or point to point. Each WAN type has a business justification, depending on the type of service the network offers. All four have advantages from a technology standpoint, as discussed next.

Hub-and-Spoke Networks

A hub and spoke network defines a "head end" and remote sites (spokes). The head end is the central point of the network (hub). Spokes are the termination points of the remote sites. All traffic flows from the spokes to the hub. There is no spoke-to-spoke direct communication, as the path is through the hub. Figure 5-3 shows a hub-and-spoke topology example. This is an optimal design when the majority of traffic is between the hub and the spoke. Because traffic from spoke to spoke takes a path through the hub, there should be little to no flow of traffic between spoke networks.

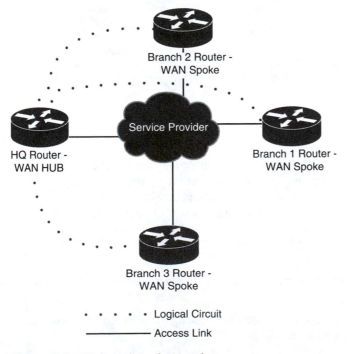

Figure 5-3 *Hub-and-Spoke Topology*

An example of where a hub-and-spoke topology for a business might be useful is a retail chain. This type of application, depending on company policy, requires little to no communication between stores. Typical business applications for the WAN operate on a transaction basis. The two major transactions are polling and credit card authorization. *Polling* is a process where the hub site executes an application. This application notifies the store cash registers or cash register central controller in each store (the registers can be a client/server application with a server that acts as the controller). It then transfers the day's transactions from the store into the hub office for data processing. The second application, credit card authorization, employs the register or store central register controller to contact a credit card authorization vendor on a transaction-by-transaction basis. The majority of retailers perform this process from a WAN to a central site. Sometimes a retailer may have VoIP traffic or video traffic to the hub, with some very low-volume, intermittent VoIP traffic between stores (for example, a store communicating to another store, "Do you have product xyz available for a customer? We are out."). The intermittent nature of these calls does not warrant a high-quality link.

Partial-Mesh Networks

Like a hub-and-spoke topology, a partial-mesh topology has a hub site to which all spokes are connected. However, unlike a hub-and-spoke topology, some spokes have a direct connection to one or more spokes. A partial-mesh topology, as shown in Figure 5-4, is an optimal design when a majority of the remote sites need a connection to a central location, and only a subset of the remote sites require a direct communications path. In Figure 5-4, a connection from Branch 3 to Branch 4 has been added to a hub-and spoke design. This could be a scenario where a business need dictates higher speed/and or lower latency for site-to-site applications between a limited number of sites.

An example of a business case for a partial mesh might be an automotive manufacturer. Figure 5-4 takes a hub-and-spoke architecture and adds an additional direct path between Branch 2 and Branch 3. These branches would represent two R&D facilities engaging in joint collaboration between these branches for product development. The sites would require periodic voice and/or video conferencing (low latency needed) along with the transfer of project files (higher bandwidth needed). A collaborative application with real-time application sharing could also be necessary. However, there would be little to no network traffic to the other (in this case Branch 1) sites, as that site would not be engaged in the joint project.

Full-Mesh Networks

In a full-mesh network, all sites are directly connected to each other. A fully meshed WAN should be carefully considered before being adopted; it requires a large amount of administration, because it requires a link to each site. The formula for figuring out how many links are required is $N * (N - 1)$, where N is the number of sites. In Figure 5-5, for a four-node WAN, the number of links is $4 * (4 - 1) = 12$. So, it would be 12 links for a four-node network. This process can become very unruly with a larger number of sites in the WAN. A fully meshed WAN should be considered for smaller networks that require high-performance connectivity between all sites.

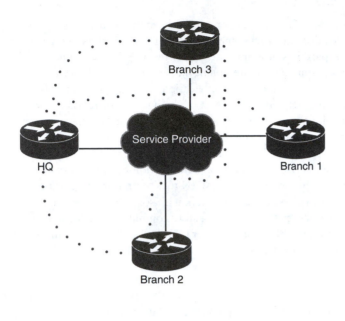

· · · · · Logical Circuit
————— Access Link

Figure 5-4   *Partial-Mesh Topology*

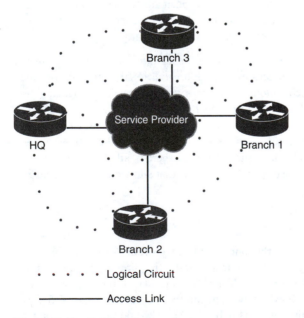

· · · · · Logical Circuit
————— Access Link

Figure 5-5   *Full-Mesh Topology*

Let's use a software development firm as a business case for a full-mesh network. It would require site-to-site collaboration and include the following:

■ Sharing of data

■ Voice and video collaboration

■ Redundant storage of work projects

■ Redundancy of software control systems such as RCS (Real Time Control System)

In this case, the firm is using applications between offices in an any-to-any manner that requires high-quality connections between all offices. The network must be a full mesh.

Point-to-Point Networks

A point-to-point network is the simplest type of WAN. Figure 5-6 shows an interconnection between two remote sites. This network is used by any organization that has only two sites.

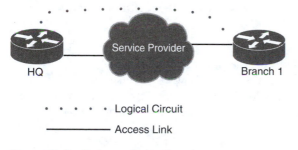

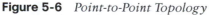

Figure 5-6 *Point-to-Point Topology*

Point-to-point networks have numerous business applications. Some examples are a mail-order/Internet retailer with a main office and a distribution/warehouse facility; a small manufacturer with a headquarters and a manufacturing facility; or a law firm that has two offices that need to exchange documents and e-mail. Point-to-point topology is basically used by any two-site organization that requires network connectivity.

Note   For more information on WAN design, review the Cisco Smart Business Architecture (SBA) "WAN Design Overview" at https://www.cisco.com/en/US/docs/solutions/SBA/February2013/Cisco_SBA_BN_WANDesignOverview-Feb2013.pdf. Be aware that many of the concepts presented in this document are advanced concepts that are beyond the scope of the CCNA certification.

WAN Devices

There are several devices that operate at the physical layer in a WAN. This section describes the devices and functions in a WAN environment. Figure 5-7 shows a set of different WAN devices.

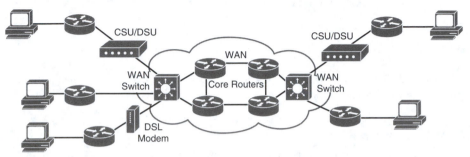

Figure 5-7   *WAN Devices*

WANs use numerous types of devices that are specific to WAN environments, including the following:

- **CSU/DSU (channel service unit/data service unit):** Digital lines, such as T1 or T3 carrier lines, require a CSU and a DSU. The two are often combined into a single piece of equipment that is called the CSU/DSU. The CSU provides termination for the digital signal and ensures connection integrity through error correction and line monitoring. The DSU converts the T-carrier line frames into frames that the LAN can interpret, and vice versa.

> **Note**   T1 and T3 (as well as their European counterparts, E1 and E3) will be covered in more detail in the "Service Provider Demarcation Points" and "Configuring Serial Interfaces" sections.

- **Modem:** Modulates an analog carrier signal to encode digital information, and also demodulates the carrier signal to decode the transmitted information. Modems are primarily used with analog phone lines and cable connections.

- **WAN switch:** A multiport internetworking device that is used in carrier networks.

- **Router:** Provides internetworking and WAN access interface ports that are used to connect to the service provider network. These interfaces may be serial connections or other WAN interfaces. With some types of WAN interfaces, an external device such as a CSU/DSU or modem (analog, cable, or DSL) is required to connect the router to the local point of presence (POP) of the service provider. The latest versions of WAN routers usually have the CSU/DSU integrated into the router.

- **Core router:** A router that resides within the middle or backbone of the WAN, rather than at its periphery. To fulfill this role, a router must be able to support multiple telecommunications interfaces of the highest speed in use in the WAN core. The router also must be able to forward IP packets at wire speed on all of those interfaces. The router must support the routing protocols being used in the core.

Devices on the subscriber premises are referred to as customer premises equipment (CPE). The subscriber owns the CPE or leases the CPE from the service provider.

Whether to lease or purchase CPE is a business decision. Three deciding factors are

- Whether the equipment should be a capital expenditure (CAPEX) or an operating expense (OPEX)

- Whether the enterprise wants to have the service provider manage the CPE

- How the service provider deploys its connection to the customer site

Note   A more detailed discussion regarding leasing versus purchasing can be found at http://www.cisco.com/web/ordering/ciscocapital/emea/assets/pdfs/Capital_Lifecycle_Financing_AAG.pdf.

Connecting the CPE to the provider is accomplished by using a copper or fiber cable to attach the CPE to the nearest exchange or Central Office (CO) of the service provider. This cabling is often called the local loop or "last mile."

In general, there are five WAN connection options, as listed next and shown in Figure 5-8.

The five types are:

- **CSU/DSU:** The router is connected to the CSU/DSU using a serial cable (for example, V.35). The CSU/DSU then connects to the service provider infrastructure using a telephone or coaxial cable (e.g., a T1 or E1 line). Devices that put data on the local loop are called data circuit-terminating equipment (DCE), which is the role of the CSU/DSU in Figure 5-7. The customer devices that pass the data to the DCE are called data terminal equipment (DTE), which describes the router in Figure 5-7. The DCE primarily provides an interface for the DTE into the communication link on the WAN cloud. The DCE is the device that provides the synchronous line clocking for the timing of the data transmission. The DTE receives clocking from the DCE. The CSU/DSU can also be implemented as a module within the router. In that case, you do not need a serial cable.

- **DSL modem:** A router connects to a DSL modem using an Ethernet cable. The modem connects to the service provider network using a telephone cable. It can also be implemented as a router module. In that case, you do not need an Ethernet cable. Often, POTS is run over the same physical cabling, and a type of splitter, called a DSL filter, is used to provide both services.

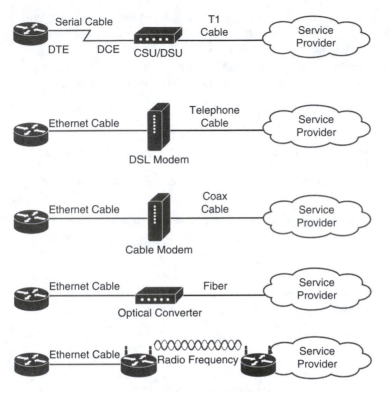

Figure 5-8 *CPE Connections*

- **Cable modem:** A router connects to a cable modem using an Ethernet cable. The modem connects to the cable service provider network using a coax cable. It can also be implemented as a router module. In that case, you do not need an Ethernet cable. Many cable providers often install television and phone service using different frequencies over the same physical cable.

- **Optical fiber converter:** A fiber-optic link terminates and optical signals are converted into electrical signals. The converter can also be implemented as a router or switch module, in which case no Ethernet cable is required.

- **Wireless Networking:** There are a variety of wireless options available. Wireless will be discussed ahead in the chapter starting with the "WAN Layer 2" Protocols section.

There are other types of older, less widely used dial-access methods over the public switched telephone network (PSTN). These include technologies such as analog (plain old telephone service, or POTS) modems and ISDN (Integrated Services Digital Network) modems. ISDN was widely used as a backup to dedicated WANs.

There are also less common WAN access methods. These include high-speed, long-range wireless, satellite, and cellular 3G/4G modems. An extensive dialog on these methods is beyond the scope of this text. One item to note is that cellular modems are becoming more widely used. They are often employed either as a backup to higher-speed WAN (e.g., for mobile workers who need network and/or Internet access on-the-fly) or for low-utilization specialty devices (fire/entry alarms, "smart" vending machines, etc.).

Serial WAN Cabling

WAN physical layer protocols describe how to provide electrical, mechanical, operational, and functional connections for WAN services. The WAN physical layer also determines the interface between the DTE and the DCE. The DTE and DCE interfaces on Cisco routers use various physical layer protocols, including the following (shown in Figure 5-9):

- **V.35:** This is the ITU-T (International Telecommunication Union-Telecommunication Standardization Sector) standard for synchronous communications between a network access device (NAD) and a packet network. Originally specified to support data rates of 48 kbps, it now supports speeds of up to 2.048 Mbps using a 34-pin rectangular connector.

- **EIA/TIA-232:** This protocol from the Electronic Industries Alliance/Telecommunications Industry Association allows signal speeds of up to 64 kbps on a 25-pin D-type connector over short distances.

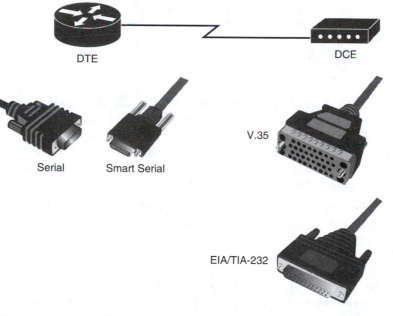

Figure 5-9   *V.35 and EIA/TIA-232 Interfaces*

These protocols establish the codes and electrical parameters that the devices use to communicate with each other. The method of facilitation that is employed by the service provider largely determines the choice of protocol. There are additional protocols other than these two.

When you order a cable, you receive a shielded serial cable that has the appropriate connector for the standard that you specify. The original router end of the shielded serial cable has a DB-60 connector, which connects to the DB-60 port on a serial WAN interface card (WIC). Because five different cable types are supported with this port, the port is sometimes called a five-in-one serial port. The other end of the serial transition cable is available with the connector that is appropriate for the standard that you specify. The documentation for the device to which you want to connect should indicate the standard for that device. To support higher densities in a smaller form factor, Cisco introduced a Smart Serial cable. The serial end of the Smart Serial cable is a 26-pin connector. It is much smaller than the DB-60 connector that is used to connect to a five-in-one serial port. These cables support the same five serial standards, are available in either a DTE or DCE configuration, and are used with two-port serial connections and with two-port asynchronous and synchronous WICs. If you are connecting a DCE and DTE "back-to-back" for a lab or testing environment, you can obtain special DCE-to-DTE cables that basically cross the transmit and receive lines between the DTE and DCE to establish a connection. This is often called a crossover cable.

Note   The term *crossover cable* is also applied to other transmission media (besides serial) that cross the transmit and receive pins. This includes Ethernet. Ethernet crossover cables are less common. Newer Ethernet devices tend to have the ability to auto-detect the pins that should transmit and receive. It is accomplished by using the auto-MDI/MDI-X (media-dependent interface/media-dependent interface crossover) feature. Older Ethernet equipment did not have this capability.

The CPE is a router in this example. The router is the DTE. The data DCE, commonly a modem or a CSU/DSU, is the device that is used to convert the user data from the DTE into a form acceptable to the WAN service provider. The synchronous serial port on the router is configured as DTE or DCE, depending on the attached cable, which is ordered as either DTE or DCE to match the router configuration. If the port is configured as DTE (which is the default setting), it requires external clocking from the DCE device.

In actual production networks, depending on the part of the world, the CSU/DSU functionality can be integrated into the router and only requires an RJ-45 straight-through cable, the same as Ethernet, to integrate with the carrier.

Note   It is very common in North America to use integrated CSU/DSU, whereas in the European Union it is more common for a service provider to provide an external CSU/DSU.

WAN Layer 2 Protocols

In addition to physical layer devices, WANs require data link layer protocols to establish the link across the communication line from the sending device to the receiving device. This section lists and explains different Layer 2 WAN protocols. Figure 5-10 displays five common WAN connections at Layers 1 and 2.

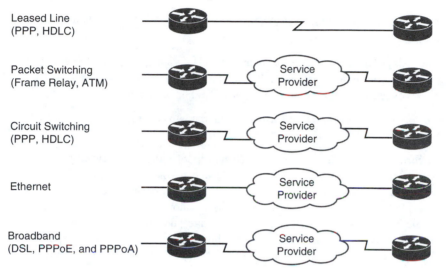

Leased Line
(PPP, HDLC)

Packet Switching
(Frame Relay, ATM)   Service Provider

Circuit Switching
(PPP, HDLC)   Service Provider

Ethernet   Service Provider

Broadband
(DSL, PPPoE, and PPPoA)   Service Provider

Figure 5-10   *WAN Technologies and Associated Layer 2 Protocols*

The technologies shown in Figure 5-10 are described here in detail:

- **High-Level Data Link Control (HDLC) protocol:** This is the Cisco default encapsulation type on point-to-point connections, dedicated links, and circuit-switched connections. HDLC is typically used when two Cisco devices are communicating across a point-to-point connection. It is a bit-oriented synchronous data link layer protocol.

  HDLC is an extension to IBM's Synchronous Data Link Control (SDLC) protocol and is based on multiple industry standards. It allows point-to-point and multipoint connections. However, Cisco's implementation is proprietary and has been streamlined. It has no authentication mechanism or Layer 2 flow control. It also changes the frame structure to add a proprietary field to accommodate Cisco's changes. The added proprietary field contains a protocol control field similar to the Ethernet Type field. Cisco's proprietary field allows HDLC to carry multiple protocols, similar to Ethernet.

  By default, other vendors do not interoperate with Cisco HDLC unless they implement Cisco's proprietary version of HDLC. So, HDLC is not the best choice in multivendor environments.

- **Point-to-Point Protocol (PPP):** This is a standards-based protocol described in RFC 1661. It provides router-to-router and host-to-network connections over synchronous and asynchronous circuits. PPP was designed to work with several network layer protocols, including IP. It also has built-in authentication mechanisms, such as Password Authentication Protocol (PAP) and Challenge-Handshake Authentication Protocol (CHAP).

  PPP can also be run in *Multilink PPP* mode, defined by RFC 1990, allowing the Layer 2 bonding of multiple circuits.

- **Frame Relay:** This is an industry-standard, switched, data link layer protocol. It defines how connections between a DTE and a DCE are maintained for remote terminal access and computer communications in public data networks.

  Cisco routers support the encapsulation in standards-based Frame Relay and Cisco proprietary encapsulation.

- **Asynchronous Transfer Mode (ATM):** This protocol is the international standard for cell relay in which multiple service types, such as voice, video, and data, are conveyed in fixed-length (53-byte) cells. ATM is a cell-switched technology defined in multiple RFCs. It uses fixed-length cells, which allow processing to occur in hardware and reduce transit delays. ATM is designed to take advantage of high-speed transmission media such as T3, E3, and Synchronous Optical Network (SONET). It is also supported in a LAN environment using LAN Emulation (LANE) over ATM.

  ATM in the WAN is also commonly used for Frame-to-ATM internetworking. This allows the transport and conversion of Frame Relay circuits to ATM. It is often used with Frame Relay at remote sites and ATM at the head end in a hub-and-spoke network design. This allows higher-capacity ATM links to terminate a large number of Frame Relay circuits.

- **Ethernet:** The emergence of Ethernet as a viable method of providing both point-to-point and multipoint services has been driven by an abundance of new fiber deployment to business areas. Enterprise customers with years of Ethernet experience in the campus have developed such a comfort level and confidence with Ethernet that they are now asking their service providers for Ethernet as an access option. Ethernet may be the most scalable transport technology ever developed—starting at 10 Mbps, it has now evolved to 100 Gbps.

- **Broadband:** Broadband in data communications refers to information transmission where multiple pieces of data are sent simultaneously to increase the effective rate of transport, regardless of the actual data rate. In network engineering, this term refers to transmission methods where two or more signals share a medium, such as the following technologies:

  - **Digital Subscriber Line (DSL), PPP over Ethernet (PPPoE), and PPP over ATM (PPPoA):** This family of technologies provides digital data transmission over the wires of a local telephone network.

- **Cable Ethernet:** A cable modem provides access to a data signal sent over a cable television infrastructure. It is considered a shared media because local areas are bridged together. Cable data networking is defined by a standard known as Data Over Cable Service Interface Specification (DOCSIS).

- **Wireless:** Wireless can be standard based or proprietary. Transport is over radio frequency. Standards-based wireless can be WiMAX (Worldwide Interoperability for Microwave Access), cellular based, or even Wi-Fi (Wi-Fi, with the right conditions and equipment, can be extended for long distances.)

Other WAN Protocols

This section explores three additional protocols: Integrated Services Digital Network (ISDN), X.25, and Multiprotocol Label Switching (MPLS). Although X.25 is a legacy data protocol, it is a foundational protocol that, due to its historic popularity, is worth a brief mention.

Integrated Services Digital Network

ISDN is a circuit-switched protocol. It is considered a legacy protocol for data applications, but is used pervasively for voice applications. It is an on-demand, dial-by-number digital service through the PSTN. It can be left up for extended periods or used on demand.

Historically, ISDN was used for on-demand applications that required the ability to connect to multiple sites. It was often used for voice, video conferencing, high-end teleworkers, and WAN on-demand backup.

Currently, it is widely used for digital voice, linking private branch exchange (PBX) telephone systems and the PSTN.

ISDN comes in two "flavors." The first is Basic Rate Interface (BRI). This is two bearer (B) channels of 64 kbps and one delta channel (D) of 16 kbps. This is also known as 2B+1D. The D channel is for management and signaling. The B channels are used for data. ISDN offers the flexibility of standard telephone dial lines with a digital interface.

Primary Rate Interface (PRI) is a full T1 or E1 circuit using one channel for signaling. T1 PRI is 23B+D, and E1 PRI is 30B+D. PRI can terminate one or more B channels up to its full capacity. Voice calls generally use one B channel, while data will employ one or more.

X.25

X.25 is a packet-switched technology that is considered to be obsolete. It is an ITU-T protocol standard for WAN communication that defines how user devices and network devices establish and maintain connections. X.25 is highly resistant to errors and poor links. It was considered popular in the 1980s and was used in applications that required high reliability, such as automated teller machines (ATM) used for self-service banking.

Multiprotocol Label Switching

MPLS is a WAN protocol that is becoming a widely used transport for WAN services. It is often referred to as operating at "Layer 2.5" because it utilizes one of the Layer 2 access methods previously mentioned and then encapsulates traffic from the LAN inside IPv4 and attaches a routing label. The encapsulation can occur with Layer 2 frames, such as Ethernet or ISDN. It can also carry Layer 3 protocols, such as IPv4 or IPv6. These labeled packets are TCP/IP packets. This allows a provider to route customer traffic across its backbone in a high-speed and efficient manner without the establishment of permanent circuits or dedicated links. MPLS can be peered across providers and contains all of the benefits of TCP/IP and Layer 2 WAN protocols. It is considered very secure, supports for quality of service (QoS), and permits any-to-any connectivity (mesh). This allows the easy provisioning of hub-and-spoke networks and meshed networks using simple IP routing and label distribution.

Service Provider Demarcation Points

Which termination methods are employed by service providers depends on the circuit type, the type of equipment used, and the region. The location where the service provider terminates its network is called a *demarc* (short for demarcation point). The demarc is the separation point of the service provider's equipment or cabling.

T1/E1

The T1 is one of the more common WAN carrier circuits in North America. Figure 5-11 shows typical service provider demarc points for T1.

Wall Biscuits

Smart Jack Boxes

Figure 5-11 *T1 Demarc Examples*

As shown in Figure 5-11, there are two different methods of termination. The service provider may wire to an RJ-45 jack (aka "biscuit") or to a smart jack. These are usually labeled with a service provider circuit ID. The property owner can also extend the demarc and terminate it into its own patch panel or biscuit if placing equipment in a different area is necessary. However, the service provider's responsibility still ends at the demarc. On a properly wired biscuit or smart jack, a straight-through wired RJ-45 cable is used. This cable is basically the same type that is used to connect an Ethernet device to a switch.

Note   The term "biscuit" is sometimes used in the United States to describe a free-standing RJ-45 jack that the service provider wiring terminates in.

E1 circuits are terminated similarly to T1 circuits. However, most service providers in the European Union provide a device for the CSU/DSU functionality. No matter in which part of the world the WAN terminates, it is best practice to check with the service provider before ordering equipment. This ensures not only the correct termination of the equipment, but also compatibility/support with the service provider's network.

DSL Termination

DSL transmits data over standard analog phones lines. Therefore, the termination process occurs on a standard analog phone line. Figure 5-12 shows a typical demarc for analog telephone service; it uses a network interface jack.

Figure 5-12   *Network Interface for Analog Phone Line*

Depending on the service provider's area facilities, region, and type of building, your analog lines may be terminated differently and split off for telephone service. Figure 5-12 is taken from a U.S. residential analog line termination.

Cable Termination

Cable termination is accomplished with "RG" type coax cabling (RG is a legacy term for Radio Guide). The most common grade used in buildings is RG-6. Cable service is brought into a building, group of buildings, or community of homes. It then is split off to multiple customers and run to their residences. Inside the customer home, it may be split off again for other services (such as television). Figure 5-13 shows the back of a Cisco cable modem.

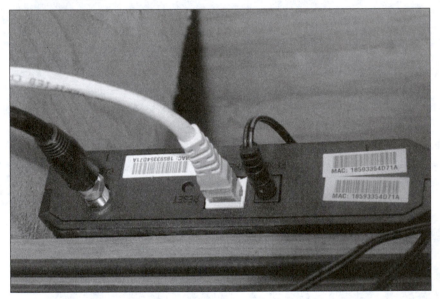

Figure 5-13   *Rear of Cisco Cable Modem*

The back of the cable modem has three connectors:

- Power
- Inbound coax
- Outbound Ethernet

The Ethernet is then run into the customer equipment. The customer may own or lease the modem (when leased, the service provider places it as part of the service). The modem configuration itself is often part of the service provider's network, and the customer does not have access to the configuration. The modem pictured in Figure 5-13 is owned by the service provider (and leased by the customer).

Other WAN Termination

DS3/E3 is usually terminated in a twinax coax cable. Twinax refers to the internal structure of the cable. It is a balanced twisted pair with a cylindrical shield. It is thinner than the RG-6 used in cable TV applications. Figure 5-14 shows a Cisco T3/E3 cable.

Figure 5-14 *Cisco T3/E3 Cable*

Metro Ethernet and other Ethernet-terminating services may be delivered optically (described in the next paragraph) or electrically (copper Ethernet). Often, a provider will terminate its fiber into an Ethernet fiber-to-copper converter (media converter). When using a media converter, be sure to check the speed and duplex settings for the Ethernet. Ethernet auto-detection usually does not work properly over these types of links because of the media conversion.

Optical links are terminated in SC or ST type connectors. SC connectors are rounded and ST connectors are square. Each optical link comes in a pair. One cable is for transmission and the other is for receiving.

Note For more information on optical terminations, see the Cisco document "Inspection and Cleaning Procedures for Fiber-Optic Connections," at http://www.cisco.com/en/US/tech/tk482/tk876/technologies_white_paper09186a0080254eba.shtml. This paper provides not only cleaning and usage tips on optical cabling, but also pictures of all major fiber termination.

Caution Do not look directly into live fiber-optic cable or interfaces. The emissions of the equipment can cause damage to eyes.

WAN Link Options

There are a number of ways in which WANs are accessed, depending on the data transmission requirements. This section describes the major WAN communication link options.

As shown in Figure 5-15, many options for implementing WAN solutions are currently available. They differ in technology, speed, and cost. Familiarity with these technologies is an important part of network design and evaluation.

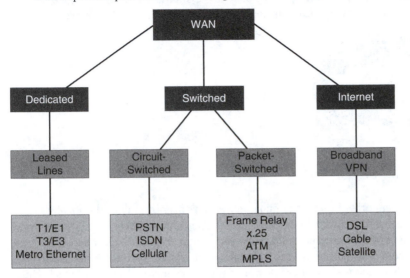

Figure 5-15   *WAN Link Options*

WAN connections can be accessed over a private infrastructure or over a public infrastructure, such as the Internet.

Private WAN Connection Options

Private WAN connections include dedicated and switched communication link options. Each type has its own unique properties:

- **Dedicated communication links:** When permanent dedicated connections are required, point-to-point lines are used with various capacities that are limited only by the underlying physical facilities and the willingness of users to pay for these dedicated lines. A point-to-point link provides a pre-established WAN communications path from the customer premises through the provider network to a remote destination. Point-to-point lines are usually leased from a carrier and thus are also called leased lines. Leased lines can be T1, T3 (in North America), E1, E3 (in Europe), and optical delivery (such as metro Ethernet).

- **Switched communication links:** Switched communication links can be either circuit switched or packet switched:

  - **Circuit-switched communication links:** Circuit switching dynamically establishes a dedicated virtual connection for voice or data between a sender and a receiver. Before communication can begin, it is necessary to create the connection through the network of the service provider. Examples of circuit-switched communication links are analog dialup (PSTN) and ISDN.

■ **Packet-switched communication links:** Many WAN users do not take advantage of the fixed bandwidth that is available with dedicated, switched, or permanent circuits because the data flow fluctuates. Communications providers have data networks that are available to more appropriately service these users. In packet-switched networks, the data is transmitted in labeled frames, cells, or packets. Packet-switched communication links include Frame Relay, ATM, X.25, metro Ethernet, and MPLS.

Public WAN Connection Options

Public connections use the global Internet infrastructure. Until recently, the Internet was not a viable networking option for many businesses because of the significant security risks and lack of adequate performance guarantees in an end-to-end Internet connection. With the development of VPN technology, however, the Internet is now an inexpensive and secure option for connecting to teleworkers and remote offices where performance guarantees are not critical. Internet WAN connection links are available through broadband services such as DSL, cable modem, and broadband wireless, and are combined with VPN technology to provide privacy across the Internet.

Broadband connection options are typically used to connect telecommuting employees to a corporate site over the Internet. Figure 5-16 is a typical teleworker configuration. Cisco has a solution called Cisco Virtual Office (CVO) that uses a router to establish a split-tunnel VPN so that the teleworker's traffic goes through a VPN tunnel while the other users of the Internet use the basic broadband connection. This is shown in Figure 5-16. CVO provides the user with access to the corporate network without being on the premises. The user can perform functions like changing a password, downloading software, and running applications such as an IP phone homed into the corporate system.

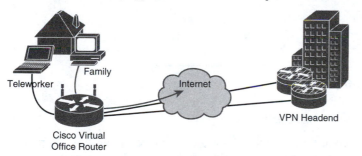

Figure 5-16 *Typical Teleworker Setup Using CVO*

A teleworker can also use a VPN software client. Figure 5-17 shows a sample software client that runs on a PC and connects to a corporate site. Other access methods include "thin client" and Secure Sockets Layer (SSL) clientless browser-based VPNs.

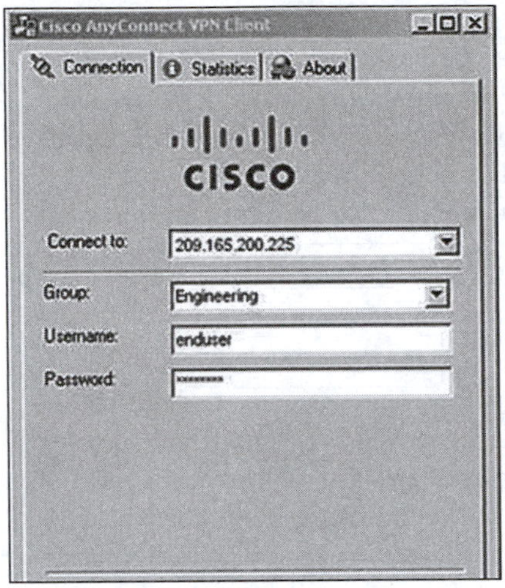

Figure 5-17 *Software VPN*

Figure 5-18 shows a welcome screen in a browser using Cisco's clientless VPN.

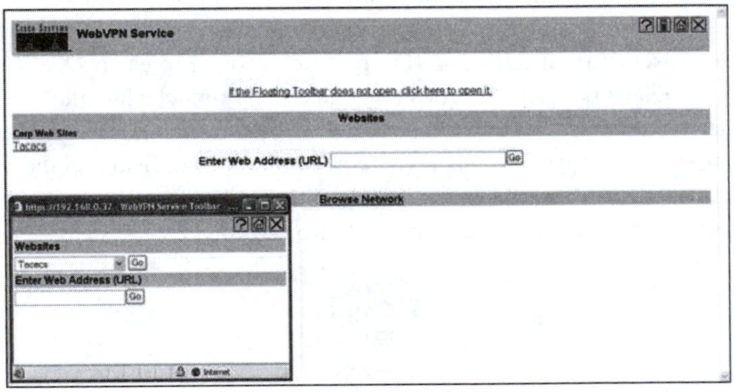

Figure 5-18 *Clientless VPN*

VPNs are explained in more detail later in this chapter.

In general, ISPs use several different WAN technologies to connect their subscribers. The connection types used on the local loop, or last mile, may not be the same as the WAN connection type that is employed within the ISP network or between various ISPs. Figure 5-19 shows a few typical "last mile" scenarios.

Each of these technologies has advantages and disadvantages for the customer. Some technologies are not available in all locations. There is a downside to using a public network for transport. There is usually no guarantee of the type of service that is delivered across the Internet or even across the provider's own network (this is prevalent with cable, because cable is usually delivered as a shared segment between groups of customers). Satellite also has the disadvantage of high latency, because the RF must travel a far distance from Earth to the satellite and back. Older satellite links were also "one way," with the downstream traffic delivered via satellite and the uplink traffic delivered via an analog phone line. This was due to the cost and complexity of the earlier generation of this type of equipment.

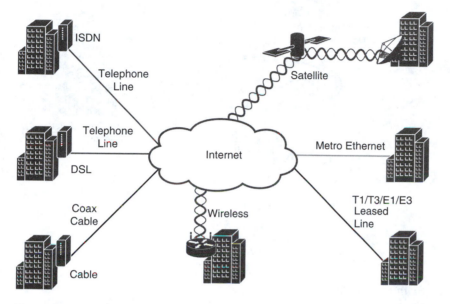

Figure 5-19 *Last-Mile Links*

When a service provider receives data, it must forward that data to other remote sites and/or service providers for final delivery to the recipient. These remote sites connect either to the ISP network or pass from ISP to ISP to the recipient.

Metropolitan-Area Networks

A metropolitan-area network, or MAN, is a very short-distance WAN. When an organization's geographic diversity is just beyond what a LAN can support, a MAN is put in place.

A MAN can use the same technologies as a WAN. However, more often a MAN employs higher-speed technologies that create LAN-like speeds. Due to the short distances, the cost to implement high-speed transports is generally much lower. Like a WAN, a MAN can be meshed, partially meshed, or point to point. Access methods may be mixed. For instance, Figure 5-20 shows a MAN within a city using a combination of wireless and metro Ethernet.

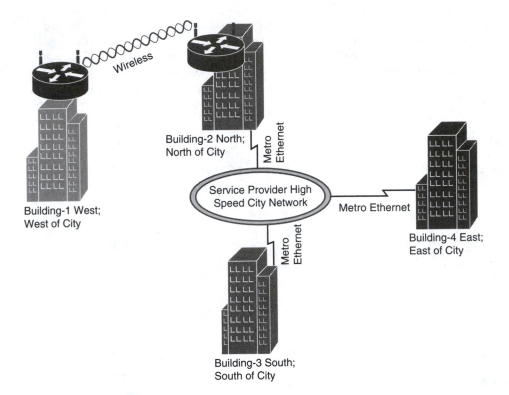

Figure 5-20   *Example Simple MAN*

A MAN can use the same access technology as a WAN. In addition, several other common MAN technologies exist:

■ **Private dark fiber:** An enterprise pulls long-distance fiber-optic cabling across its own property, or in agreement with a neighboring property owner or municipality. The enterprise runs longer-distance optics, such as high-speed Ethernet with long-range optics. In shorter-distance optical applications, generally LEDs (light-emitting diodes) are used. Longer-range optics need lasers, because they are of greater strength to support distance. The term "dark fiber" refers to the fact that the fiber is "dark" when not "lit up" by customer-based equipment.

Note   For more information on fiber communications, see the Cisco white paper "Fiber Types in Gigabit Optical Communications" at http://www.cisco.com/en/US/prod/collateral/modules/ps5455/white_paper_c11-463661.html.

■ **Leased dark fiber:** The same principal as private dark fiber, except the fiber-optic path is leased from a service provider.

- **Wireless technologies:** Can be standards based, such as WiMAX (IEEE 802.16), or proprietary.

- **Metro Ethernet:** A service provider can hand off Ethernet to a customer that is tunneled through the service provider's network. Although this is listed earlier in the chapter as a WAN technology, it is most often associated with a MAN (which is just a short range WAN).

Note   More information on WiMAX is located at the WiMAX Forum, http://www.wimaxforum.org/.

Note   A detailed discussion of MANs is outside the scope of this text. For more information on MANs, check out the case study on the MAN that comprises Cisco's headquarters campus, available at http://www.cisco.com/web/about/ciscoitatwork/network_systems/man_architecture.html.

Extranet

An extranet is defined as a WAN used for specific and secure transport between business partners. Access is allowed only to specific areas of each business's internal resources. Often, this access is over the public Internet, but it could be over dedicated links.

Figure 5-21 shows a simple Internet-based extranet between two businesses, while Figure 5-22 demonstrates a simple extranet between two businesses using dedicated links.

Note   A detailed discussion of extranets is outside the scope of this text. A case study on how Cisco uses extranets to connect to its business partners can be found at http://www.cisco.com/web/about/ciscoitatwork/network_systems/partner_extranet.html.

Configuring Serial Interfaces

One of the most common types of WAN connection is the point-to-point connection. Point-to-point connections are used to link LANs to service provider WANs, and to connect LAN segments within an enterprise network. A LAN-to-WAN point-to-point connection is also referred to as a serial connection or a leased-line connection. Wide-area networking services are typically leased from a service provider. Some WAN services operate as Layer 2 connections between remote locations. These services are typically available through a telephone company over its WAN switches.

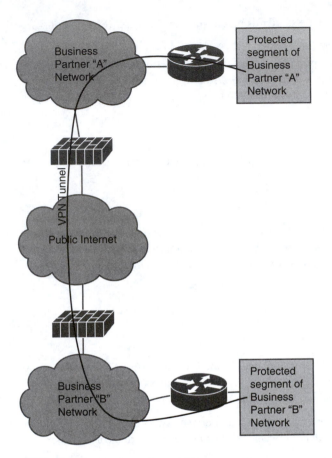

Figure 5-21   *Internet-Based Extranet*

The route of a point-to-point connection begins at the customer premises and then goes through a carrier network to a remote network. Figure 5-23 depicts the functions of point-to-point technology.

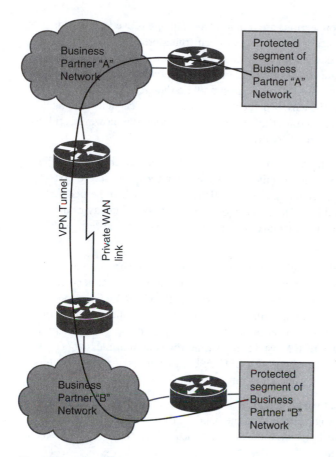

Figure 5-22 *Dedicated Link Extranet*

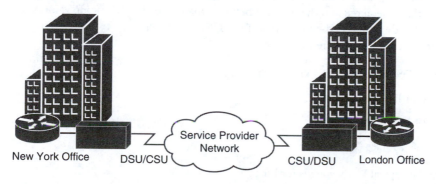

Figure 5-23 *Serial Communication Links*

When permanent dedicated connections are required, a serial line is used to provide a pre-established WAN communications path from the customer premises through the provider network to a remote destination. A serial line can connect two geographically distant sites, such as a corporate office in New York and a regional office in London. Point-to-point lines are usually leased from a carrier and are therefore often called leased lines. For a point-to-point line, the carrier dedicates fixed transport capacity and facility hardware to the line that is leased by the customer. The carrier will, however, still use multiplexing technologies within the network.

Point-to-point links are usually more expensive than shared services such as Frame Relay. The cost of leased-line solutions can become significant when they are used to connect many sites over increasing distances. However, there are times when the benefits outweigh the cost of the leased line. The dedicated capacity removes latency or jitter between the endpoints. Constant availability is essential for some applications, such as VoIP.

A router serial port is required for each leased-line connection. If the underlying network is based on the T-carrier or E-carrier technologies, the leased line connects to the network of the carrier through a CSU/DSU. The purpose of the CSU/DSU is to provide a clocking signal to the customer equipment interface from the DSU and terminate the channelized transport media of the carrier on the CSU. The CSU also provides diagnostic functions such as a loopback test. Most T1 or E1 time-division multiplexing (TDM) interfaces on current routers include approved CSU/DSU capabilities. If using a router-integrated CSU/DSU, the provider's line feeds directly into the router.

Bandwidth refers to the rate at which data is transferred over the communication link. The underlying carrier technology depends on the bandwidth that is available. There is a difference in bandwidth points between the North American (T-carrier) specification and the European (E-carrier) system.

Leased lines are available in different capacities and are generally priced based on the bandwidth that is required and the distance between the two connected points. Normally, carriers sell bandwidth to end customers in T1, T3, E1, and E3 speeds. Typical WAN speeds for the United States are as follows:

- T1 = 24 DS0 channels @ 64 kbps each (1.544 Mbps)

- T2 = 4 T1 lines (6 Mbps)

- T3 = 28 T1 lines (45 Mbps)

- T4 = 168 T1 lines (275 Mbps)

These are the typical WAN speeds for Europe:

- E1 = 30 DS0 channels @ 64 kbps each (2 Mbps)

- E2 = 128 E0 lines (8 Mbps)

- E3 = 16 E1 lines (34 Mbps)

- E4 = 64 E1 lines (140 Mbps)

Leased lines are available in different capacities and are generally priced based on the bandwidth that is required and the distance between the two connected points. Normally, carriers sell bandwidth to end customers in T1, T3, E1, and E3 speeds. A provider can also supply "fractional" service, where only a limited number of channels are delivered. For instance, a fractional T1 can be delivered in increments of DS0s, a T3 can be delivered in increments of T1, and so forth.

Configuration of a Serial Interface

Figure 5-24 shows a "back-to-back" configuration using a fractional T1 (one DS0). RouterA is the DCE and RouterB is the DTE. The **clockrate** command generates a line clocking for DCE based on the bit rate specified (64000 = 64 kbps). The example shows the configuration of RouterA, as shown in Figure 5-24, as the DCE:

```
RouterA(config)# interface serial 0/0/0
RouterA(config-if)# clockrate 64000
RouterA(config-if)# bandwidth 64
RouterA(config-if)# no shutdown
```

RouterB is the DTE in Figure 5-24. It has a standard router DTE configuration, as shown in the following example:

```
RouterB(config)# interface serial 0/0/0
RouterB(config-if)# bandwidth 64
RouterB(config-if)# no shutdown
```

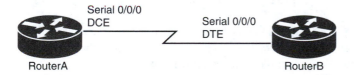

Figure 5-24 *Example of DCE and DTE Serial Routers*

In this case, RouterA's configuration includes the **clockrate** command because the DCE always does the clocking. On both sides, the **bandwidth** command is used. When a serial interface is employed, unless the **bandwidth** command is issued, the routing protocols and **show** commands assume a full T1 of 1544 kbps.

When connecting to a service provider, the router is usually a DTE, and the service provider supplies the clocking. Table 5-1 describes the commands used in the examples based on Figure 5-24.

Table 5-1   *Serial Interface Commands*

Command	Description
interface serial *interface_number*	Selects the serial interface and enters configuration mode.
bandwidth *bandwith_kilobits*	Sets the interface bandwidth metric. Remember, this is a metric, not the actual line speed!
clockrate *clock_rate_bits*	Sets the clocking speed in bps on *DCE* interface that the DCE will generate.
no shutdown	Enables the interface.

Note   The serial cable that is attached determines the DTE or DCE mode of the Cisco router. Choose the cable to match the network requirement. When you are ordering, be aware that the DCE and DTE cables will have different part numbers. For more information on serial cables, see http://www.cisco.com/en/US/products/hw/routers/ps341/products_ tech_note09186a00801a886f.shtml.

The following configuration uses the **show controllers** command to determine cable type:

```
RouterB# show controllers s0/0/0
Interface Serial0/0/0
Hardware is PowerQUICC MPC860
DCE V.35, no clock
idb at 0x81081AC4, driver data structure at 0x81084AC0
```

The information that is displayed is determined when the router initially started and represents only the type of cable that was attached when the router began. If the cable type is changed after startup, the **show controllers** command will not display the type of the new cable.

Integrated CSU/DSU Modules

If your service provider requires a CSU/DSU, Cisco routers support modules that serve this function. It eliminates the need for an external CSU/DSU. These modules come in T1/E1, 56 kbps (a very old leased-line type), and T3/E3. Figure 5-25 shows a one-port T1/ E1 integrated CSU/DSU module.

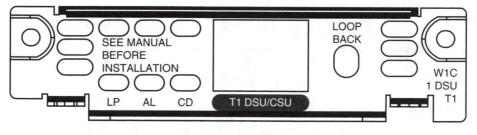

Figure 5-25 *Integrated One-Port CSU/DSU Module*

The integrated CSU/DSU modules are available in multiport versions and also have support for voice, data, and ISDN. Using an integrated CSU/DSU has several advantages, such as:

- Only one device to monitor, manage, and troubleshoot

- Reduced cabling, space, and power requirements—connects demarc directly into the router

- No multiple-vendor compatibility problems

Note   For more information on integrated CSU/DSU products, see *DSU/CSU WAN Interface Cards* at:, http://www.cisco.com/en/US/docs/routers/access/interfaces/ic/hardware/installation/guide/dsu_wic.html

Configuring an Integrated CSU/DSU

Configuring an integrated CSU/DSU for standard data requires additional steps over configuring a serial interface. The controller holds the CSU/DSU functionality. This must be configured before the serial interface. In Example 5-1, port 0 of a two-port T1/E1 card is configured for T1. Then the corresponding serial interface is configured.

Example 5-1   *Configuring an Integrated CSU/DSU*

```
RouterA# configure terminal
RouterA(config)# controller T1 0/0/0
RouterA(config-controller)# cablelength long 0db
RouterA(config-controller)# channel-group 0 timeslots 1-24
RouterA(config-controller)# description <==Circuit ID 46360100 ==>
RouterA(config-controller)# no shutdown
RouterA(config-controller)# exit
RouterA(config)# network-clock-select 1 T1 0/0/0
RouterA(config)# interface Serial0/0/0:0
RouterA(config-if)# ip address 192.168.1.1 255.255.255.0
```

```
RouterA(config-if)# description <==to remote site "B"==>
RouterA(config-if)# no shutdown
```

In Example 5-1, there are a few items to be noted:

■ As stated earlier, the controller and the serial interface must be configured.

■ The description on the controller is a circuit ID assigned by the service provider carrier. The description is completely optional and is used to help identify the circuit. The serial interface also has a description. This, too, is optional and is used to help identify the interface. Using descriptions are best practice when setting up a WAN.

■ The default values are used for bandwidth (full T1), encapsulation, encoding, and so on. Table 5-2 explores the options.

■ The **network-clock-select** command is used to select the clocking source for the T1s in multiple T1 systems.

Table 5-2 describes the integrated CSU/DSU **controller** command options.

Table 5-2   *Integrated CSU/DSU controller Command Options*

Command	Description
controller *type slot/port*	Specifies the controller to be configured.
framing *framing_type*	Specifies the framing type; normally provided by the service provider carrier. Default is **esf**.
linecode *code_type*	Specifies the line coding type; normally provided by service provider carrier. Default is **b8zs**.
channel-group *channel-no* **timeslots** *timeslot-list* **speed**	Specifies the channel group and time slots to be mapped.[1] After you configure a channel group, the serial interface is automatically created. The syntax is as follows: *channel-no*: ID number to identify the channel group. The valid range is from 0 to 30. *timeslot-list*: Timeslots (DS0s) to include in this channel group. The valid time slots are from 1 to 31. **speed {64}**: The speed of the DS0. Example 5-1 configures the channel group and time slots for the T1 controller.

Command	Description
cablelength {**long** [**-15db** | **-22.5db** | **-7.5db** | **0db**] **short** [**110ft** | **220ft** | **330ft**| **440ft** | **550ft** | **600ft**]}	Specifies the cable length. Should usually be **long** with **0db** unless specified by the service provider carrier or the routers are back to back.
network-clock-select *priority t1_or_e1 slot/port*	Specifies the port for the network clock. A priority defines the order in which the defined port is used, when utilizing multiple ports. T1 or E1 interface is selected for circuit type, and slot/port in the router.

1 When you are using the **channel-group channel-no timeslots timeslot-list** {**64**} command to change the configuration of an installed card, you must enter the **no channel-group channel-no timeslots timeslot-list speed** {**64**} command first. Then enter the **channel-group channel-no timeslots timeslot-list** {**64**} command for the new configuration information.

Back-to-Back Routers with an Integrated CSU/DSU

Routers with an integrated CSU/DSU can be placed back to back. Like serial interfaces, a special cable is needed. Unlike serial interfaces, the cable side does not determine DTE or DCE. Clocking is configured only on the DCE, and not on the DTE, with a crossover cable. A T1/E1 crossover cable just crosses the transmit and receive pairs. The CSU/DSU is configured on the DCE side with the **clock source internal** command under the *controller* for the interface used for DCE.

Figure 5-26 shows a graphical representation of a T1 crossover cable pinout. This crosses the transmit and receive pairs (1 and 4 are crossed, 2 and 5 are crossed).

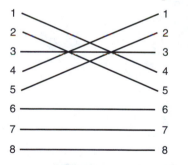

Figure 5-26   *T1 Crossover Cable*

T1 Loopback Plug

A T1 loopback plug creates a looped condition between the transmit and receive pairs. This is often used for diagnostics of local wiring or T1 hardware.

As you can see in Figure 5-27, the transmit and receive pairs are connected to each other (1 and 4 are crossed, 2 and 5 are crossed). As when a service provider loops a circuit, the **show interface** command displays the serial interface *up/down (looped)*.

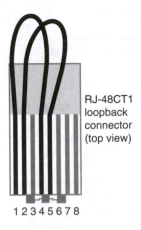

Figure 5-27   *T1 Loopback Plug*

If a demarc is extended, a loopback plug is useful to determine if a connectivity problem is related to the wiring between the router and the demarc.

HDLC Protocol

The HDLC protocol is one of two major data-link protocols that are commonly used with point-to-point WAN connections. This section describes HDLC. Figure 5-28 shows the structure of an HDLC frame, the structure of a Cisco proprietary HDLC frame, and where HDLC is used.

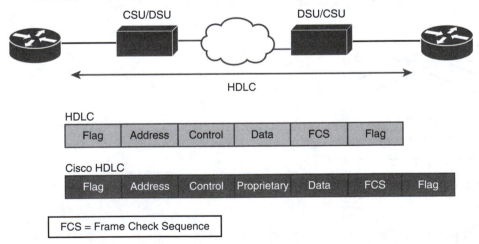

Figure 5-28   *HDLC Protocol*

On each WAN connection, data is encapsulated into frames before crossing the WAN link. To ensure that the correct protocol is used, you need to configure the appropriate Layer 2 encapsulation type. The choice of protocol depends on the WAN technology and the communicating equipment.

The International Organization for Standardization (ISO) developed HDLC as a bit-oriented synchronous data link layer protocol. HDLC uses synchronous serial transmission to provide error-free communication between two points. HDLC defines a Layer 2 framing structure that allows for flow control and error checking by using acknowledgments, control characters, and checksums. Each frame has the same format, whether it is a data frame or a control frame. HDLC may not be compatible, however, between devices from different vendors because of the way that each vendor may have chosen to implement it.

When you want to transmit frames over synchronous or asynchronous links, remember that those links have no mechanism to mark the beginning or end of the frames. HDLC uses a frame delimiter to mark the beginning and the end of each frame.

Cisco's implementation of HDLC is the default encapsulation for serial lines on Cisco routers. Cisco HDLC is very streamlined. It has no windowing or flow control, and only point-to-point connections are allowed. The Cisco HDLC implementation includes proprietary extensions in the data field, as shown Figure 5-28. The extensions allowed multiprotocol support at a time before PPP was specified. Because of the modification, the Cisco HDLC implementation will not interoperate with other HDLC implementations. HDLC encapsulations vary, but PPP should be used when interoperability, authentication, or Layer 2 redundancy is required.

To validate the encapsulation on a serial line, use the **show interfaces** command, as demonstrated in Example 5-2.

Example 5-2   *Validating Encapsulation on a Serial Line*

```
RouterA# show interfaces Serial 0/0/0
Serial0/0/0 is up, line protocol is up
  Hardware is GT96K Serial
  Description: Link to HQ
  Internet address is 192.168.1.1/24
  MTU 1500 bytes, BW 1544 Kbit/sec, DLY 20000 usec,
     reliability 255/255, txload 1/255, rxload 1/255
  Encapsulation HDLC, loopback not set
  Keepalive set (10 sec)
  CRC checking enabled
  Last input 00:00:02, output 00:00:05, output hang never
  Last clearing of "show interface" counters never
  Input queue: 0/75/0/0 (size/max/drops/flushes); Total output drops: 0
  Queueing strategy: weighted fair
  Output queue: 0/1000/64/0 (size/max total/threshold/drops)
     Conversations  0/1/256 (active/max active/max total)
     Reserved Conversations 0/0 (allocated/max allocated)
     Available Bandwidth 1158 kilobits/sec
<output omitted>
```

If the default encapsulation method has been changed, use the **encapsulation hdlc** command in interface configuration mode to reenable HDLC.

Point-to-Point Protocol

This section examines the characteristics of PPP and how it is enabled on a serial interface. Figure 5-29 displays the use of PPP (which fits in the same place as HDLC in the network) and the frame structure.

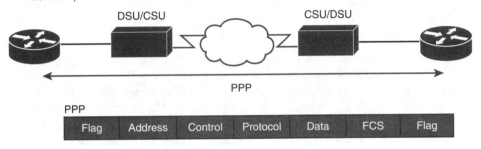

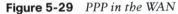

Figure 5-29 *PPP in the WAN*

As mentioned earlier, HDLC is a very efficient protocol, and is a good choice for any leased-line LAN circuits. However, PPP does have features that HDLC lacks:

■ **Vendor interoperability:** PPP is a standards-based protocol, while Cisco's implementation of HDLC is proprietary.

■ **Authentication:** PPP supports PAP and CHAP authentication.

■ **Error detection:** The link-quality monitoring (LQM) feature monitors the quality of the link. If too many errors are detected, PPP takes down the link.

■ **Layer 2 bonding of circuits:** PPP has a multilink option that allows redundancy and increasing of bandwidth at Layer 2. HDLC does not have this capability.

PPP includes the following three main components, which are also shown in Figure 5-30:

■ A method for encapsulating multiprotocol datagrams.

■ Extensible Link Control Protocol (LCP) to establish, configure, and test the WAN data-link connection.

■ Family of Network Control Protocols (NCP) for establishing and configuring different network layer protocols. PPP allows the simultaneous use of multiple network layer protocols.

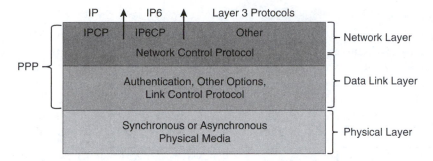

Figure 5-30 *PPP Components*

LCP provides versatility and portability to a wide variety of environments. It negotiates the PPP Maximum Receive Unit (MRU), the authentication protocol, compression of PPP header fields, callback, and multilink options.

NCP configures the network (Layer 3) protocols. PPP can carry other protocols besides TCP/IP. The type of protocol (TCP/IP) and the network options (such as address and subnet mask) are established using NCP.

LQM is used to negotiate link-quality reporting (LQR) between the devices. LQM uses LQR to determine if the link quality is too low, in which case it will tear down the connection.

The authentication options require the calling side of the link to enter authentication information to help ensure that the user has permission from the network administrator to make the call. Peer routers exchange authentication messages.

Figure 5-31 illustrates a high-level flow of PPP activation.

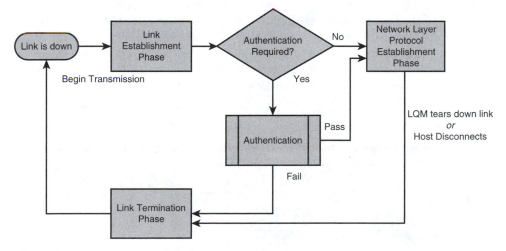

Figure 5-31 *PPP Link Activation*

PPP Authentication: PAP

The Password Authentication Protocol is one of the two PPP authentication protocols (the other, CHAP, is discussed in the next section). As shown in Figure 5-32, PAP is a two-way handshake that provides a simple method for a calling node to establish its identity to a called node. PAP is performed only upon initial link establishment. There is no encryption. The username and password are sent in plaintext. After the PPP link establishment phase is complete, the remote node repeatedly sends a username and password pair to the router until authentication is acknowledged or the connection is terminated.

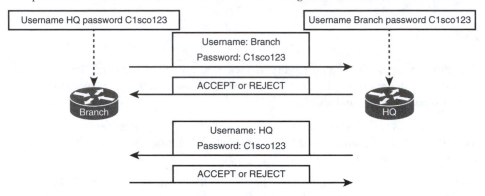

Figure 5-32 *Password Authentication Protocol*

PAP is not a strong authentication protocol, but it may be adequate in environments that use token-type passwords that change with each authentication. It is not secure in most environments. Also, there is no protection from playback or repeated trial-and-error attacks—the calling node is in control of the frequency and timing of the login attempts.

In Figure 5-32, the Branch router first sends its PAP username and password to the HQ router. The HQ router evaluates the Branch router's credentials against its local database. If the credentials match, the HQ router accepts the connection. If not, it rejects the connection. The authentication of the Branch router to the HQ router is the two-way handshake previously mentioned. Then the reverse process occurs: the HQ router authenticates to the Branch router (which is considered a separate two-way handshake).

PPP Authentication: CHAP

The Challenge Handshake Authentication Protocol is the other PPP authentication protocol. Figure 5-33 shows the messaging flow of CHAP.

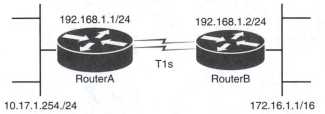

Figure 5-33 *CHAP Messaging Flow*

CHAP is more secure than PAP. It involves a three-way exchange of a shared secret. Once authentication is established with PAP, it is completed and no further authentication occurs. This leaves the network vulnerable to attack. Unlike PAP, which only authenticates once, CHAP conducts periodic challenges to make sure that the remote node still has a valid password value.

After the PPP link establishment phase is complete, the local router sends a challenge message to the remote node. The remote node responds with a value that is calculated using a one-way hash function, typically MD5, based on the password and challenge message. The local router checks the response against its own calculation of the expected hash value. If the values match, the authentication is acknowledged. Otherwise, the connection is terminated immediately.

CHAP provides protection against playback attack using a variable challenge value that is unique and unpredictable, which means that the resulting hash value will also be unique and random. The use of repeated challenges is intended to limit exposure to any single attack. The local router or a third-party authentication server is in control of the frequency and timing of the challenges.

In Figure 5-33, the HQ router sends a challenge message to the Branch router. The Branch router responds to the HQ router by sending a CHAP response, which is a hash of the username and password. The HQ router evaluates the Branch router credentials against its local database. If the credentials match, the HQ router accepts the connection. If not, it rejects the connection. The authentication of the Branch router to the HQ router is considered a three-way handshake. Then, a three-way handshake of the Branch router authenticating the HQ router follows.

PPP Configuration

This section covers the base configuration of a simple PPP link between two routers. Figure 5-34 shows two routers over a leased line, and Example 5-3 provides their corresponding configuration.

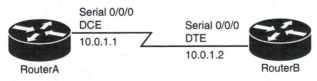

Figure 5-34 *Simple PPP Example*

Example 5-3 *Basic PPP Configuration Example*

```
RouterA(config)# interface serial 0/0/0
RouterA(config-if)# ip address 10.0.1.1 255.255.255.0
RouterA(config-if)# encapsulation ppp
RouterA(config-if)# bandwidth 64
```

```
RouterA(config-if)# clockrate 64000
RouterA(config-if)# no shutdown


RouterB(config)# interface serial 0/0/0
RouterB(config-if)# ip address 10.0.1.2 255.255.255.0
RouterB(config-if)# encapsulation ppp
RouterB(config-if)# bandwidth 64
RouterB(config-if)# no shutdown
```

To set PPP as the encapsulation method to be used by a serial interface, use the **encap-sulation ppp** interface configuration command. The **encapsulation ppp** command has no arguments. Remember that if you do not configure PPP on a Cisco router, the default encapsulation for serial interfaces is HDLC. In Example 5-3, the **bandwidth** value is set to 64 kbps.

Table 5-3 defines the PPP encapsulation commands, many of which are the same as when using HDLC.

Table 5-3   *Commands Used in Example 5-3*

Command	Description
bandwidth *bandwith_kbps*	Sets the bandwidth metric on the interface. This does not change the actual bandwidth of the interface. It sets a metric for routing protocols to use (e.g., OSPF) with best path calcu-lations. Default is 1544, T1 speed.
clockrate *clock_rate_bps*	On the DCE side, sets the clock rate to the specified value.
interface serial *port/mod*	Enters configuration mode for the interface.
encapsulation ppp	Sets the interface to PPP.
ip address *ip_v4_address subnet_mask*	Sets the IP address and the subnet mask.
no shutdown	Enables the interface.

In Example 5-4, PPP encapsulation is enabled on the serial interface. Observe that LCP is running (LCP Open). As stated earlier, PPP does have support for multiple protocols through NCP. Two protocols have been negotiated: IP (IPCP) and Cisco Discovery Protocol (CDPCP).

Example 5-4   *PPP Interface in NCP Established Phase*

```
RouterA# show interfaces Serial 0/0/0
Serial0/0/0 is up, line protocol is up
  Hardware is GT96K Serial
```

```
    Description: Link to RouterB
    Internet address is 10.0.1.1/24
    MTU 1500 bytes, BW 512 Kbit, DLY 20000 usec,
        reliability 255/255, txload 1/255, rxload 1/255
    Encapsulation PPP, LCP Open
    Open: IPCP, CDPCP, loopback not set
    Keepalive set (10 sec)
    CRC checking enabled
    Last input 00:00:36, output 00:00:01, output hang never
    Last clearing of "show interface" counters 00:01:09
    Input queue: 0/75/0/0 (size/max/drops/flushes); Total output drops: 0
    Queueing strategy: weighted fair
    Output queue: 0/1000/64/0 (size/max total/threshold/drops)
        Conversations  0/1/256 (active/max active/max total)
        Reserved Conversations 0/0 (allocated/max allocated)
        Available Bandwidth 384 kilobits/sec
<output omitted>
```

Configuring PPP Authentication with CHAP

This section examines how authentication is used with PPP. Figure 5-35 provides a check-list of the items that must be configured when running CHAP with PPP.

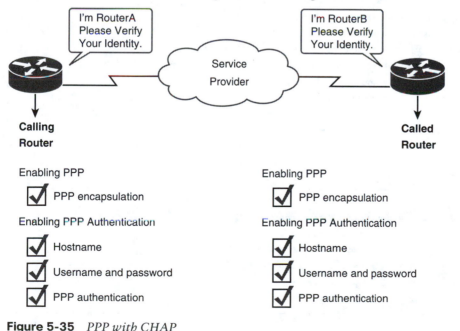

Figure 5-35 *PPP with CHAP*

As depicted in Figure 5-35, here are the steps for configuring PPP with CHAP:

Step 1. Enable PPP encapsulation as the Layer 2 protocol of an interface.

Step 2. Enable PPP authentication by completing the following:

    a. Configure the router hostname for identification.

    b. Configure the username and password to authenticate the PPP peer.

    c. Choose CHAP as the authentication technique.

Figure 5-36 explores the two-node PPP network reviewed earlier.

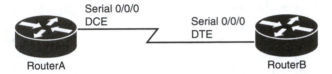

Figure 5-36 *Simple Example for CHAP Authentication*

The sample configurations of both routers using PPP with CHAP authentication are shown in Examples 5-5 and 5-6.

Example 5-5 *Configuring CHAP Authentication: RouterA Side*

```
RouterA(config)# hostname RouterA
RouterA(config)# username RouterB password C1sco123
RouterA(config)# interface serial 0/0/0
RouterA(config-if)# ip address 10.0.1.1 255.255.255.0
RouterA(config-if)# encapsulation ppp
RouterA(config-if)# ppp authentication chap
RouterA(config-if)# bandwidth 64
RouterA(config-if)# clockrate 64000
RouterA(config-if)# no shutdown
```

Example 5-6 *Configuring CHAP Authentication: RouterB Side*

```
RouterB(config)# hostname RouterB
RouterB(config)# username RouterA password C1sco123
RouterB(config)# interface serial 0/0/0
RouterB(config-if)# ip address 10.0.1.2 255.255.255.0
RouterB(config-if)# encapsulation ppp
RouterB(config-if)# bandwidth 64
RouterB(config-if)# no shutdown
```

The following are the key points when configuring PPP with CHAP:

- The hostname on one router must match the username that the other router has configured.

- The same password must be configured on both routers.

- Both routers must be configured for the same PPP authentication type.

Table 5-4 reviews the PPP commands used to set up a link with CHAP.

Table 5-4 *Configuring CHAP Authentication Commands*

Command	Description
hostname *hostname*	Sets a hostname for the router.
username *username* password *password*	Sets a username and password for the authentication. These are case sensitive.
interface serial *port/mod*	Enters configuration mode for the interface.
ip address *ip_v4_address subnet_mask*	Sets the IP address and the subnet mask.
encapsulation ppp	Sets the interface to PPP.
ppp authentication chap	Enables CHAP on the interface.
shutdown	Disables the interface.

Verifying CHAP Configuration

Use the **show interfaces** command to verify proper configuration. Example 5-7 shows that PPP encapsulation is configured and LCP has established a connection, as indicated by "LCP Open" in the command output. In the command output, "Open: IPCP, CDPCP" indicates that NCP was able to successfully configure IPv4 and CDP as network layer protocols.

Example 5-7 *Verifying LCP and NCP*

```
RouterA# show interfaces Serial 0/0/0
Serial0/0/0 is up, line protocol is up
<output omitted>
  Encapsulation PPP, LCP Open
  Open: IPCP, CDPCP, loopback not set
  Keepalive set (10 sec)
<output omitted>
```

> **Note**   A username/password combination does not need to reside in the local router if
> an authentication server (such as RADIUS or TACACS+) exists. For more information on
> TACACS+ and RADIUS, see http://www.cisco.com/en/US/tech/tk59/technologies_tech_
> note09186a0080094e99.shtml.

Configuring Multilink PPP over Serial Lines

As discussed earlier, Multilink PPP allows the bonding of multiple interfaces at Layer 2
for redundancy and increase of bandwidth. This creates a virtual interface in the router
for the multilink bundle. Figure 5-37 shows a typical application of WAN routers over
leased T1 lines.

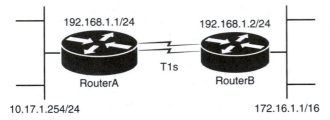

192.168.1.1/24   192.168.1.2/24

T1s

RouterA   RouterB

10.17.1.254/24   172.16.1.1/16

Figure 5-37   *Multilink PPP Example*

Let's examine the steps for configuring Multilink PPP on RouterA (without authentication) from Figure 5-37:

Step 1.   If using an integrated CSU/DSU, configure the controller and **network-clock-
select** commands as shown in the following configuration:

```
Router-A# configure terminal
Router-A(config)# controller T1 0/0/0
Router-A(config-controller)# cablelength long 0db
Router-A(config-controller)# channel-group 0 timeslots 1-24
Router-A(config-controller)# description <==Circuit ID 46360100 ==>
Router-A(config-controller)# no shutdown
Router-A(config-controller)#exit
Router-A(config)# controller T1 0/0/1
Router-A(config-controller)# cablelength long 0db
Router-A(config-controller)# channel-group 0 timeslots 1-24
Router-A(config-controller)# description <==Circuit ID 46360101 ==>
Router-A(config-controller)# no shutdown
Router-A(config-controller)# exit
Router-A(config)# network-clock-select 1 T1 0/0/0
```

Step 2.   Create a multilink virtual interface with the IP addressing used on the WAN:

```
Router-A(config)# interface Multilink1
Router-A(config-if)# ip address 192.168.1.1 255.255.255.0
Router-A(config-if)# ppp multilink
Router-A(config-if)# ppp multilink group 1
Router-A(config-if)# exit
```

Step 3.   Configure the serial interfaces for PPP encapsulation and bond to the multilink virtual interface:

```
Router-A(config)# interface Serial0/0/0:0
Router-A(config-if)# no ip address
Router-A(config-if)# encapsulation ppp
Router-A(config-if)# ppp multilink
Router-A(config-if)# ppp multilink group 1
Router-A(config-if)# description <=to site "B" MPPP Group 1 =>
Router-A(config-if)# no shutdown
Router-A(config-if)# exit
Router-A(config)# interface Serial0/0/1:0
Router-A(config-if)# no ip address
Router-A(config-if)# encapsulation ppp
Router-A(config-if)# ppp multilink
Router-A(config-if)# ppp multilink group 1
Router-A(config-if)# description <=to site "B" MPPP Group 1 =>
Router-A(config-if)# no shutdown
Router-A(config-if)# exit
```

There are several points to note about the preceding steps:

- The IP address exists on the multilink virtual interface.

- The multilink interface is where any interface settings, including authentication, would be placed that would normally be used on a physical interface.

- The serial interface is configured for PPP encapsulation and to the multilink group (bundle).

- The default bandwidth of the virtual multilink interface is the sum of the bandwidth of the included interfaces. In this case, because the **bandwidth** commands were not used, it would be equal to 2 – T1s.

- In this example, RouterB's configuration is almost identical. IP addressing, interface naming (if different interface numbers and/or types are used), and the description would change to meet the site.

- **show** commands can be run on the controllers, serial interfaces, and multilink virtual interface.

Note For more information on configuring Multilink PPP, see the "Using Multilink PPP over Serial Interface Links" section of the *QoS: Latency and Jitter Configuration Guide, Cisco IOS Release 15M* at http://www.cisco.com/en/US/docs/ios-xml/ios/qos_latjit/configuration/15-mt/qos-mlppp-sl.html.

Verifying Multilink PPP

Let's begin the verification process by executing a few **show** commands. The first command, **show ip interface brief**, confirms whether the interfaces are operational, as shown in Example 5-8.

Example 5-8 *Displaying the Interfaces*

```
Router_A# show ip interface brief
Interface              IP-Address      OK? Method Status                 Protocol
GigabitEthernet0/0     10.17.1.254     YES NVRAM  up                     up
GigabitEthernet0/2     unassigned      YES NVRAM  administratively down  down
Serial0/0/0:0          unassigned      YES unset  up                     up
Serial0/0/1:0          unassigned      YES unset  up                     up
Multilink1             192.168.1.1     YES NVRAM  up                     up
```

Notice that one of the LAN interfaces is configured. The other one is unused and shut down. The two serial interfaces are operational, and the multilink interface has the correct IP address and is in working order. Now execute **show interface** on the multilink interface to verify whether it is configured properly, as shown in Example 5-9.

Example 5-9 *Verifying the Multilink Interface*

```
Router_A# show interface multilink 1
Multilink1 is up, line protocol is up
  Hardware is multilink group interface
  Internet address is 192.168.1.1/24
  MTU 1500 bytes, BW 3072 Kbit/sec, DLY 20000 usec,
     reliability 255/255, txload 1/255, rxload 4/255
  Encapsulation PPP, LCP Open, multilink Open
  Stopped: CDPCP
  Open: IPCP, loopback not set
  Keepalive set (10 sec)
  DTR is pulsed for 2 seconds on reset
  Last input 00:00:00, output never, output hang never
  Last clearing of "show interface" counters 00:46:41
  Input queue: 0/75/0/0 (size/max/drops/flushes); Total output drops: 0
```

```
Queueing strategy: Class-based queueing
Output queue: 0/1000/0 (size/max total/drops)
5 minute input rate 54000 bits/sec, 21 packets/sec
5 minute output rate 18000 bits/sec, 19 packets/sec
    37181 packets input, 11824776 bytes, 0 no buffer
    Received 0 broadcasts (0 IP multicasts)
    0 runts, 0 giants, 0 throttles
    0 input errors, 0 CRC, 0 frame, 0 overrun, 0 ignored, 0 abort
    20988 packets output, 7682171 bytes, 0 underruns
    0 output errors, 0 collisions, 0 interface resets
    0 unknown protocol drops
    0 output buffer failures, 0 output buffers swapped out
    0 carrier transitions
```

In Example 5-9, the multilink bundle (multilink virtual interface) is running with the proper encapsulation in multilink mode with no errors. Now check the serial interfaces, as shown in Example 5-10. In this case, you need to look at only one of the serial interfaces in the multilink bundle, as in normal operating conditions the output should be almost identical.

Example 5-10 *Verifying the Serial Interface*

```
Router_A# show interfaces serial 0/0/1:0
Serial0/0/1:0 is up, line protocol is up
  Hardware is DSX1
  MTU 1500 bytes, BW 1536 Kbit/sec, DLY 20000 usec,
      reliability 255/255, txload 2/255, rxload 3/255
  Encapsulation PPP, LCP Open, multilink Open
  Link is a member of Multilink bundle Multilink1, crc 0, loopback not set
  Keepalive set (10 sec)
  Last input 00:00:00, output 00:00:00, output hang never
  Last clearing of "show interface" counters 00:47:41
  Input queue: 0/75/0/0 (size/max/drops/flushes); Total output drops: 0
  Queueing strategy: fifo
  Output queue: 0/40 (size/max)
  5 minute input rate 19000 bits/sec, 10 packets/sec
  5 minute output rate 15000 bits/sec, 13 packets/sec
    31766 packets input, 8056299 bytes, 0 no buffer
    Received 0 broadcasts (0 IP multicasts)
    0 runts, 0 giants, 0 throttles
    0 input errors, 0 CRC, 0 frame, 0 overrun, 0 ignored, 0 abort
    18631 packets output, 4583993 bytes, 0 underruns
```

```
0 output errors, 0 collisions, 0 interface resets

0 unknown protocol drops

0 output buffer failures, 0 output buffers swapped out

0 carrier transitions
```

Notice that the interface has PPP encapsulation and is a member of Multilink Bundle 1.

Troubleshooting Serial Encapsulation

Figure 5-38 provides a brief flowchart on troubleshooting serial link encapsulation.

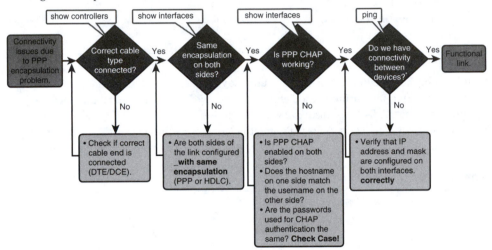

Figure 5-38 *Troubleshooting Serial Link Flowchart*

To troubleshoot link issues due to misconfigured encapsulation and authentication on the serial interface, follow these high-level steps:

Step 1. Check if the correct type of cable is connected to the device (DTE/DCE).

Step 2. Verify that both sides of the serial connection are configured with the same encapsulation: PPP, Multilink PPP, or HDLC. HDLC is the Cisco default.

Step 3. If PPP encapsulation is correctly configured on both sides of the link, verify that CHAP authentication is successful. The CHAP authentication may not be successful when the hostname on one side does not match the username on the other side, or the password is not the same on both sides. The password is often misconfigured due to an additional space character at the end of the password string. Also, make sure that the same authentication method (PAP or CHAP) is selected on both sides of the link.

Step 4. If CHAP authentication is successful, the link should be operational. If a ping still does not work, verify that the IP address and mask are correctly set on both sides of the link.

Establishing a WAN Connection Using Frame Relay

Frame Relay is a standards-based data link layer protocol for the transmission of data through a service provider's network. It has been a pervasive WAN technology for a long period of time, so a large number of established Frame Relay networks exist. Currently Frame Relay is falling out of favor as newer technologies, such as MPLS, are adopted. Understanding Frame Relay is important both for supporting legacy Frame Relay networks and for converting Frame Relay networks to other technologies.

This section examines the basic functionality of Frame Relay, including topologies, reachability issues, and LMI signaling. It also describes basic Frame Relay configuration and Frame Relay over point-to-point and multipoint subinterfaces. The section concludes with a discussion of how to verify Frame Relay operations.

Understanding Frame Relay

Frame Relay was originally designed for use across ISDN interfaces. Today, it is employed over various network interfaces as well, primarily T1/E1 and T3/E3. Frame Relay is a connection-oriented data-link technology that is streamlined to provide high performance and efficiency. For error protection, it relies on upper-layer protocols and dependable fiber and digital networks. Frame Relay is an example of a packet-switched technology. Packet-switched networks enable end stations to dynamically share the network media and the available bandwidth.

Frame Relay defines the interconnection process between the router and the local access switching equipment of the service provider. It does not define how the data is transmitted within the Frame Relay service provider cloud. Figure 5-39 shows a basic picture of Frame Relay.

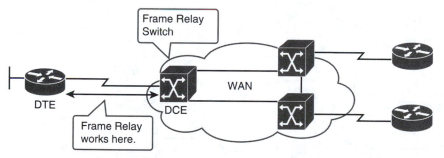

Figure 5-39 *Frame Relay*

Devices that are attached to a Frame Relay WAN fall into two categories:

- **Data terminal equipment:** Generally considered to be the terminating equipment for a specific network. DTE devices are typically located on the customer premises and may be owned by the customer. Examples of DTE devices are Frame Relay access devices (FRAD), routers, and switches. Routers are the most common device.

Note   A FRAD is also referred to as a Frame Relay assembler/disassembler. A standalone FRAD is rarely seen, as FRAD functionality is integrated into routers. Standalone FRADs are usually only seen in legacy applications such as a non-LAN attached asynchronous SNA (Systems Network Architecture, a legacy networking protocol) device. So, you will most likely never see a FRAD.

■ **Data circuit-terminating equipment:** Service provider–owned internetworking devices. The purpose of DCE devices is to provide clocking and switching services in a network and transmit data through the WAN. In most cases, the switches in a WAN are Frame Relay switches.

Note   Cisco routers can act as Frame Relay switches, but this functionality is primarily used in lab environments.

Frame Relay provides a means for statistically multiplexing many logical data conversations, referred to as virtual circuits (VC), over a single physical transmission link by assigning connection identifiers to each pair of DTE devices. The service provider switching equipment constructs a switching table that maps the connection identifier to outbound ports. When a frame is received, the switching device analyzes the connection identifier and delivers the frame to the associated outbound port. The complete path to the destination is established before transmission of the first frame.

The following list defines certain terms that are used frequently in Frame Relay circuit discussions. Figure 5-40 visually depicts several of these terms in an example Frame Relay network.

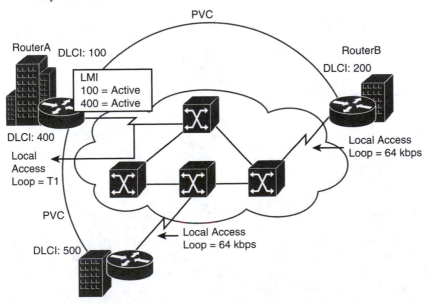

Figure 5-40   *Frame Relay Example*

- **Local access rate:** Clock speed (port speed) of the connection (local loop) to the Frame Relay cloud. The local access rate is the rate at which data travels into or out of the network, regardless of other settings.

- **Virtual circuit (VC):** A logical circuit, uniquely identified by a data-link connection identifier (DLCI), that is created to ensure bidirectional communication from one DTE device to another. A number of VCs can be multiplexed into a single physical circuit for transmission across the network. This capability often reduces the complexity of the equipment and network required to connect multiple DTE devices. A VC can pass through any number of intermediate DCE devices (Frame Relay switches). Multiple VCs may terminate on a single access link. This is a common configuration.

- **Permanent virtual circuit (PVC):** Provides permanently established connections that are used for frequent and consistent data transfers between DTE devices across the Frame Relay network.

- **Switched virtual circuit (SVC):** Provides on-demand connections that are used for demand-driven data transfers between DTE devices across the Frame Relay network.

Note   SVCs are not common in real-world scenarios. Most carriers never deployed SVCs in their networks, and not all Frame Relay equipment supports this function, due to its lack of acceptance.

- **Data-link connection identifier (DLCI):** Frame Relay VCs are identified by DLCIs. The Frame Relay service providers (for example, telephone companies) typically assign DLCI values. A DLCI contains a 10-bit number in the Address field of the Frame Relay frame header that identifies the VC. DLCIs have local significance because the identifier references the point between the local router and the local Frame Relay switch to which the DLCI is connected. Therefore, devices at opposite ends of a connection can use different DLCI values to refer to the same VC. Although the DLCI has only local significance for the circuit, many service providers will facilitate both sides of the PVC with the same DLCI to make it easier to follow the VC.

- **Committed information rate (CIR):** Specifies the maximum average data rate that the network undertakes to deliver under normal conditions. When subscribing to a Frame Relay service, specify the local access rate (for example, 56 kbps or T1). Typically, you are also asked to specify a CIR for each DLCI. If you send information faster than the CIR on a given DLCI, the network marks some frames with a DE (Discard Eligible) bit. The network does its best to deliver all packets but discards DE packets first if there is congestion. Many inexpensive Frame Relay services are based on a CIR of zero. A CIR of zero means that every frame is a DE frame, and the network throws away any frame when it deems necessary.

■ **Inverse ARP:** A method of dynamically associating the network layer address of the remote router with a local DLCI. Inverse ARP (Address Resolution Protocol) allows a router to automatically discover the network address of the remote DTE device that is associated with a VC.

■ **Local Management Interface (LMI):** A signaling standard between the router (DTE device) and the local Frame Relay switch (DCE device) that is responsible for managing the connection and maintaining status between the router and the Frame Relay switch. Basically, the LMI is a mechanism that provides status information regarding Frame Relay connections between the router (DTE) and the Frame Relay switch (DCE). Every 10 seconds or so, the end device polls the network, requesting either a dumb sequenced response or channel status information. If the network does not respond with the requested information, the DTE device may consider the connection to be down.

As shown in Figure 5-40, Router A has two PVCs that are configured on one physical interface. A DLCI of 100 identifies the PVC that connects to Router B. A DLCI of 400 identifies the PVC that connects to Router C. At the other end, a different DLCI number is used to identify the PVC. LMI at Router A allows the router to learn DLCIs for PVCs that are available from the local Frame Relay switch.

Frame Relay Topologies

A Frame Relay network provides nonbroadcast multiaccess (NBMA) connectivity between remote sites. An NBMA environment is treated like other broadcast media segments, such as Ethernet, where all the routers are on the same subnet. So, there could be multiple DLCIs that terminate on the same access link. However, unlike Ethernet, Frame Relay has no facility to generate a broadcast or multicasts at Layer 2. So, broadcasts and multicasts must be simulated by Layer 3 mappings (TCP/IP addresses) to the DLCIs, and the Layer 3 protocol uses the mappings to send out unicasts across all PVCs.

Figure 5-41 shows the Frame Relay topologies that can be used. They follow the basic guidelines that are explained in the "WAN Architecture" section, earlier in the chapter. In that section, a point-to-point topology is discussed. However, no Frame Relay point-to-point topology is provided. Although, it is technologically possible to have a two-site Frame Relay network, this type of service would not be provisioned by a carrier. Instead, a point-to-point dedicated circuit would be used.

The following list discusses the topologies shown in Figure 5-41 in more detail:

■ **Full-mesh topology:** All routers have VCs to all other destinations. A full-mesh topology, although costly, provides direct connections from each site to all other sites and allows for redundancy. When one link goes down, a router can reroute traffic through another site. As the number of nodes in this topology increases, a full-mesh topology can become very expensive. Use the n $(n - 1)$ / 2 formula to calculate the total number of links required to implement a full-mesh topology, where n is the number of nodes. For example, to fully mesh a network of 10 nodes, 45 PVCs are required: 10 (10 − 1) / 2.

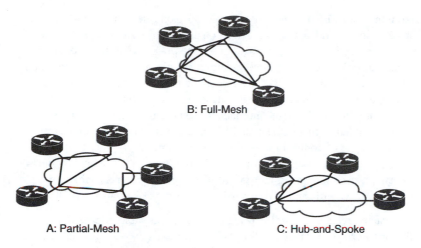

Figure 5-41 *Frame Relay Topologies*

- **Partial-mesh topology:** Not all sites have direct access to other sites. Depending on the traffic patterns in the network, you may want to have additional PVCs connect to remote sites that have large data traffic requirements.

- **Hub-and-spoke topology:** Remote sites are connected to a central site that generally provides a service or an application. The hub-and-spoke topology is the most popular Frame Relay network topology. It is the least expensive because it requires the fewest PVCs. In Figure 5-41, the central router provides a multipoint connection because it uses a single interface to interconnect multiple PVCs. This is the most commonly deployed topology.

Frame Relay Reachability and Routing Protocol Issues

In any Frame Relay topology, when a single multipoint interface is used to interconnect multiple sites, reachability issues can result due to the NBMA nature of Frame Relay. The Frame Relay NBMA topology can cause the problems illustrated in Figure 5-42 and described in the list that follows.

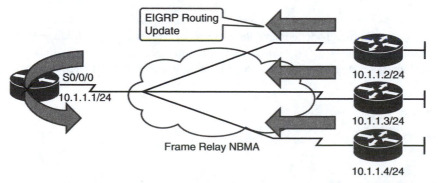

Figure 5-42 *Issues Caused by Frame Relay NBMA*

■ **Split horizon:** In case of EIGRP and RIP, the split-horizon rule reduces routing loops by preventing a routing update that is received on an interface from being forwarded out the same interface. In a scenario using a hub-and-spoke Frame Relay topology, a remote router (a spoke router) sends an update to the headquarters router (the hub router) that is connecting multiple PVCs over a single physical interface. The headquarters router receives the broadcast on its physical interface but cannot forward that routing update through the same interface to other remote (spoke) routers. Split horizon is not a problem if there is a single PVC on a physical interface or logical subinterface. This type of connection would be point to point. So, EIGRP split horizon is not a concern in this case. However, EIGRP split horizon is disabled by default on Frame Relay physical interfaces. However, EIGRP split-horizon is enabled by default on Frame Relay with subinterfaces (which should be okay, also).

So, this issue can be resolved by either using point-to-point subinterfaces or disabling split horizon. Subinterfaces are discussed in more detail following this list and in the "Point-to-Point and Multipoint Frame Relay" section later in this chapter.

■ **Neighbor discovery and DR and BDR election:** OSPF over NBMA networks operates in nonbroadcast network mode by default. Therefore, neighbors are not automatically discovered. You can statically configure neighbors. However, be sure that the hub router becomes a DR. Recall that an NBMA network behaves like Ethernet, and on Ethernet, a DR is needed to exchange routing information between all routers on a segment. Therefore, only the hub router can act as a DR, because it is the only router that has PVCs with all other routers.

Note   When configuring OSPF over Frame Relay, you can also use broadcast and point-to-multipoint OSPF network mode to overcome the neighbor discovery problem.

■ **Broadcast and multicast replication:** With routers that support multipoint connections over a single interface that terminate many PVCs, the router must replicate broadcast packets, such as routing update broadcasts/multicasts, on each PVC to the remote routers. These replicated broadcast packets consume bandwidth and cause significant latency variations in user traffic.

Figure 5-43 displays the concept of subinterfaces. To enable forwarding of broadcast routing updates in a hub-and-spoke Frame Relay topology, configure the hub router with logically assigned interfaces, called *subinterfaces*. *Subinterfaces* are logical subdivisions of a physical interface. A subinterface requires configuration of a physical interface that includes

■ IP address

■ Subnet mask

■ DLCI

■ Routing protocol configuration

No IP address is configured on the main interface, but the encapsulation type is (Frame Relay in this case).

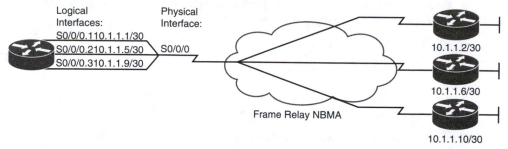

Figure 5-43 *Using Subinterfaces to Avoid NBMA Issues*

In split-horizon routing environments, routing updates that are received on one subinterface can be sent out to another subinterface.

In subinterface configuration, each VC can be configured as a point-to-point connection, which allows each subinterface to act like a leased line. When you use a Frame Relay point-to-point subinterface, each subinterface is on its own subnet.

Frame Relay Signaling

LMI is a standard for signaling between a router and a Frame Relay switch. It is responsible for managing the connection and maintaining the status between the devices. The LMI type is set by the service provider at the Frame Relay switch.

Although LMI is configurable, the Cisco router can autosense which LMI type the Frame Relay switch is using. The router sends one or more complete LMI status requests to the Frame Relay switch. The Frame Relay switch responds with one or more LMI types, and the router configures itself with the last LMI type that was received.

Figure 5-44 illustrates the placement of LMI.

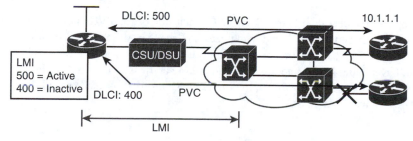

Figure 5-44 *LMI Operation*

Cisco routers support three LMI types:

- **Cisco:** Developed jointly by Cisco, StrataCom (acquired by Cisco in 1996), Northern Telecom (Nortel), and Digital Equipment Corporation

- **ANSI:** ANSI T1.617 Annex D

- **Q.933A:** ITU-T Q.933 Annex A

You can also manually configure the appropriate LMI type from the three supported types to ensure proper Frame Relay operation.

When the router receives LMI information, it updates its VC status to one of three states:

- **Active:** Indicates that the VC connection is active and that routers can exchange data over the Frame Relay network

- **Inactive:** Indicates that the local connection to the Frame Relay switch is working but the router can't connect to the remote end of the PVC

- **Deleted:** Indicates that either no LMI is being received from the Frame Relay switch or there is no service between the router and the local Frame Relay switch

Frame Relay Address Mappings

A Frame Relay local DLCI must be mapped to a destination network layer address, such as an IP address. Routers can automatically discover their local DLCI from the local Frame Relay switch using the Inverse ARP protocol.

On Cisco routers, the local DLCI can be dynamically mapped to the remote router network layer addresses with Inverse ARP. Inverse ARP associates a given DLCI to the next-hop protocol address for a specific connection. Inverse ARP is described in RFC 1293. Instead of using Inverse ARP to automatically map the local DLCIs to the remote router network layer addresses, you can manually configure a static Frame Relay map in the map table.

Figure 5-45 depicts an end-to-end Frame Relay PVC. Each side of the PVC knows its local DLCI to the other end. So, each end recognizes its Layer 3 address and the remote Layer 2 address (the DLCI). This is the inverse of an Ethernet segment, where each end knows its own Layer 2 and Layer 3 address. To find remote addresses, it uses ARP. In this case, the inverse information is known. So, the Inverse ARP protocol is used to find the remote IP address (Layer 3 address).

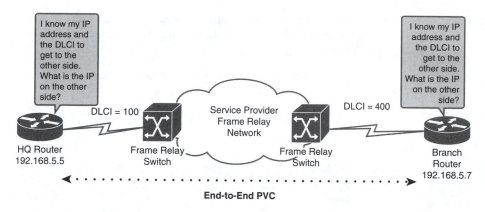

Figure 5-45   *Use Case for Frame Relay Inverse ARP*

Figure 5-46 illustrates how the first four steps of Inverse ARP and LMI signaling work.

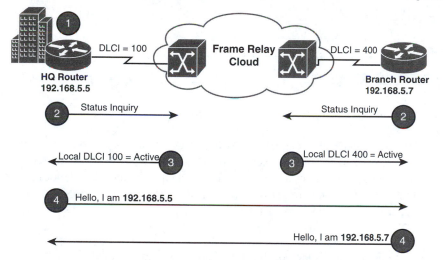

Figure 5-46   *Inverse ARP and LMI Signaling Steps 1 to 4*

The following steps provide more detail to the signaling steps:

Step 1.   Each router connects to the service provider's Frame Relay cloud through an access circuit.

Step 2.   When Frame Relay is configured on an interface, the router sends an LMI status inquiry message to the Frame Relay switch. The message notifies the switch of the router status and asks the switch for the connection status of the router VCs.

Step 3. When the Frame Relay switch receives the request, it responds with an LMI status message that includes the local DLCIs of the PVCs to the remote routers to which the local router can send data.

Step 4. For each active DLCI, each router sends an Inverse ARP packet with its own IP address.

Figure 5-47 shows how steps 5 through 7 of Inverse ARP and LMI signaling work.

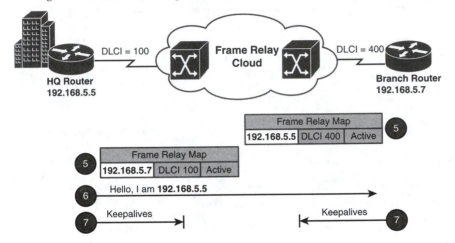

Figure 5-47 *Inverse ARP and LMI Signaling Steps 5 to 7*

Step 5. When a router receives an Inverse ARP message, it creates a map entry in its Frame Relay map table that includes the local DLCI and the remote router network layer address. Note that the router DLCI is the local DLCI, not the DLCI that the remote router is using. Any of the three connection states can appear in the Frame Relay map table.

> **Note** If Inverse ARP is not working or the remote router does not support Inverse ARP, you must manually configure static Frame Relay maps, which map the local DLCIs to the remote network layer addresses.

Step 6. Every 10 seconds, the router exchanges LMI information with the switch (keepalives).

Step 7. The router changes the status of each DLCI to active, inactive, or deleted, based on the LMI response from the Frame Relay switch.

If the remote router does not support Inverse ARP, the Frame Relay peers have different Frame Relay encapsulation types. Additionally, to control broadcast and multicast traffic over the PVC, you must statically map the local DLCI to the remote router network layer address. These static Frame Relay map entries are referred to as *static maps*. Configure a Frame Relay static map in these situations:

- A Frame Relay peer does not support Inverse ARP.

- You want to control broadcast traffic across a PVC.

- You want to have different Frame Relay encapsulations across PVCs.

Configuring Frame Relay

Figure 5-48 depicts a basic Frame Relay configuration across a WAN.

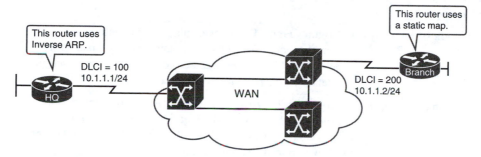

Figure 5-48   *Basic Frame Relay*

Examples 5-11 and 5-12 show the configuration on each of the routers in Figure 5-48.

Example 5-11   *Configuration of the HQ Router with Inverse ARP*

```
HQ# configure terminal
HQ(config)# interface Serial0/0/0
HQ(config-if)# ip address 10.1.1.1 255.255.255.0
HQ(config-if)# encapsulation frame-relay
```

Example 5-12   *Configuration of the Branch Router Without Inverse ARP*

```
Branch# configure terminal
Branch(config)# interface Serial0/0/0
Branch(config-if)# ip address 10.1.1.1 255.255.255.0
Branch(config-if)# encapsulation frame-relay
Branch(config-if)# frame-relay map ip 10.1.1.1 200
Branch(config-if)# frame-relay interface-dlci 200
```

A basic Frame Relay configuration assumes that you want to configure Frame Relay on one or more physical interfaces and that the routers support LMI and Inverse ARP. Inverse ARP is enabled by default on Cisco routers. Table 5-5 describes the Frame Relay configuration commands used in Examples 5-11 and 5-12.

Table 5-5 *Frame Relay Commands from Examples 5-11 and 5-12*

Command	Description
interface *interface*	Enters interface configuration mode for the specified interface.
ip address *ip_address subnet_mask*	Sets the IP address on the interface.
encapsulation frame-relay [cisco | ietf]	Configures Frame Relay encapsulation on an interface. Optionally, you can specify the Frame Relay encapsulation type. You can choose between **cisco** and **ietf**, where **cisco** is the default and **ietf** is an IETF standard.
frame-relay map *protocol protocol-address dlci*	Creates a static mapping between a DLCI and a remote device. *protocol* is a Layer 3 protocol (**ip**, **ipv6**, etc.). *protocol-address* is the network address (IP address). *dlci* is the DLCI used to map to the remote address.
frame-relay interface-dlci *dlci*	Statically assigns the DLCI to the interface.

In Figure 5-48, both routers are configured with Frame Relay on the Serial0/0/0 interface. The HQ router uses Inverse ARP to learn the IP address of the Branch router, while the Branch router uses static mapping.

Point-to-Point and Multipoint Frame Relay

You can configure subinterfaces in either of two modes:

- **Point to point:** A single point-to-point subinterface is used to establish one PVC connection to another physical interface or subinterface on a remote router. In this case, each pair of the point-to-point subinterface is on its own subnet, and each point-to-point subinterface has a single DLCI. In a point-to-point environment, because each subinterface acts like a point-to-point interface, update traffic is not subject to the split-horizon rule.

- **Multipoint:** A single multipoint subinterface is used to establish multiple PVC connections to multiple physical interfaces or subinterfaces on remote routers. In this case, all the participating interfaces are in the same subnet. Because the subinterface acts like a regular NBMA Frame Relay interface, update traffic is subject to split horizon.

Configuring Point-to-Point Frame Relay Subinterfaces

In Figure 5-49, a sample Frame Relay point-to-point network is shown along with the router configurations of the HQ at the hub, with the two branch routers as spokes.

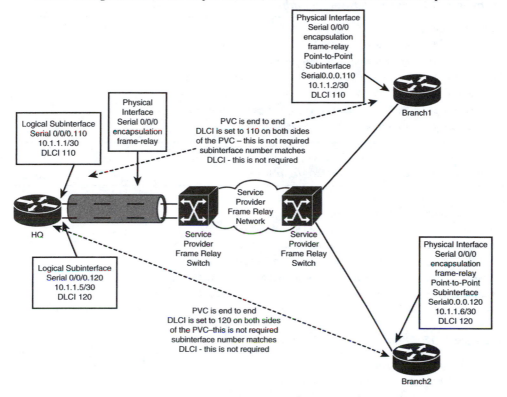

Figure 5-49 *Configuring Point-to-Point Frame Relay*

To configure Frame Relay point-to-point subinterfaces, first enable Frame Relay encapsulation on the physical interface. Then create a point-to-point subinterface and assign an IP address, bandwidth, and DLCI to it. On point-to-point subinterfaces, you do not need to use the **frame-relay map** command to perform static address mapping, because it is always assumed that the end point of the point-to-point connection automatically resides on the same subnet as the start point. Enabling or disabling Inverse ARP is also not required, because there is only a single remote destination on a point-to-point PVC and thus discovery is not necessary.

In Figure 5-49, the HQ router is configured with two point-to-point subinterfaces. One subinterface uses DLCI 110 to reach the Branch1 router, and the other subinterface uses DLCI 120 to reach the Branch2 router. The BR1 router has one subinterface to reach the HQ router. It uses DLCI 110 to reach the HQ router. The Branch2 router has one subinterface to reach the HQ router. It uses DLCI 120 to reach the HQ router.

Examples 5-13, 5-14, and 5-15 provide the configuration of the HQ, Branch1, and Branch2 routers, respectively, from Figure 5-49.

Example 5-13 *HQ Router Configuration*

```
HQ# configure terminal
HQ(config)# interface serial0/0/0
HQ(config-if)# encapsulation frame-relay
HQ(config-if)# interface serial0/0/0.110 point-to-point
HQ(config-if)# ip address 10.1.1.1 255.255.255.252
HQ(config-if)# interface serial0/0/0.120 point-to-point
HQ(config-if)# ip address 10.1.1.5 255.255.255.252
```

Example 5-14 *Branch1 Router Configuration*

```
Branch1# configure terminal
Branch1(config)# interface serial0/0/0
Branch1(config-if)# encapsulation frame-relay
Branch1(config-if)# interface serial0/0/0.110
Branch1(config-if)# ip address 10.1.1.2 255.255.255.252
Branch1(config-if)# frame-relay map ip 10.1.1.1 110
Branch1(config-if)# frame-relay interface-dlci 110
```

Example 5-15 *Branch2 Router Configuration*

```
Branch2# configure terminal
Branch2(config)# interface serial0/0/0
Branch2(config-if)# encapsulation frame-relay
Branch2(config-if)# interface Serial0/0/0.120
Branch2(config-if)# ip address 10.1.1.6 255.255.255.252
Branch2(config-if)# frame-relay map ip 10.1.1.5 120
Branch2(config-if)# frame-relay interface-dlci 120
```

Note DLCIs are of local significance. However, providers can map the DLCIs to the same value on both sides of the PVC to make it easier to identify the PVC. By the same note, subinterface numbers do not need to match DLCI numbers, but this can be mapped in the configuration of the router to make it easier to identify the PVC.

Table 5-6 describes the commands used in Examples 5-13, 5-14, and 5-15.

Table 5-6 *Commands for Configuring Point-to-Point Frame Relay*

Command	Description
encapsulation frame-relay	Sets Frame Relay encapsulation on the interface.
interface *interface.subinterface* **point-to-point**	Creates a point-to-point subinterface and enters subinterface configuration mode.
frame-relay interface-dlci *dlci*	Statically maps a DLCI to a subinterface.
frame-relay map *protocol protocol_address dlci*	Creates a static mapping between a DLCI and a remote device. *protocol* is a Layer 3 protocol (**ip**, **ipv6**, etc.), *protocol_address* is the network address (IP address), and *dlci* is the DLCI used to map to the remote address.

Configuring Point-to-Multipoint Frame Relay

In Figure 5-50, a sample Frame Relay point-to-multipoint network is shown along with the router configurations of the HQ at the hub, with the two branch routers as spokes.

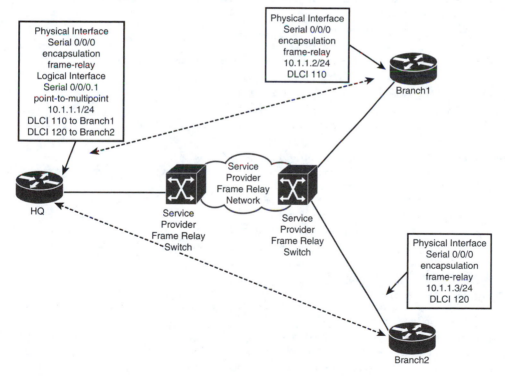

Figure 5-50 *Configuring Point-to-Multipoint Frame Relay*

To configure Frame Relay point-to-multipoint subinterfaces, enable Frame Relay encapsulation on the physical interface. Then create a multipoint subinterface and assign an IP address bandwidth. Map the DLCIs to the remote IP addresses. When you use static mappings between IP addresses and DLCIs using the **frame-relay map** command, the **frame-relay interface-dlci** command is not needed, because the **frame-relay map** command also assigns the DLCI.

In Figure 5-50, the HQ router has a point-to-multipoint interface. It uses DLCI 110 and DLCI 120 mapped to the remote IP address. The **broadcast** keyword is used to permit the NBMA media to act like broadcast media (using Layer 3 to emulate Layer 2 broadcasts).

Although DLCIs are local identifiers, it is a good idea to have the service provider carrier set the same DLCI on each side of the PVC. This keeps the configuration easier to understand.

Examples 5-16, 5-17, and 5-18 provide the configuration of the HQ, Branch1, and Branch2 routers, respectively, from Figure 5-50.

Example 5-16 *HQ Router Configuration*

```
HQ# configure terminal
HQ(config)# interface serial0/0/0
HQ(config-if)# encapsulation frame-relay
HQ(config-if)# interface serial0/0/0.1 point-to-multipoint
HQ(config-if)# ip address 10.1.1.1 255.255.255.0
HQ(config-if)# frame-relay map ip 10.1.1.2 110 broadcast
HQ(config-if)# frame-relay map ip 10.1.1.3 110 broadcast
```

Example 5-17 *Branch1 Router Configuration*

```
Branch1# configure terminal
Branch1(config)# interface serial0/0/0
Branch1(config-if)# encapsulation frame-relay
Branch1(config-if)# ip address 10.1.1.2 255.255.255.0
Branch1(config-if)# frame-relay map ip 10.1.1.1 110 broadcast
```

Example 5-18 *Branch2 Router Configuration*

```
Branch1# configure terminal
Branch1(config)# interface serial0/0/0
Branch1(config-if)# encapsulation frame-relay
Branch1(config-if)# ip address 10.1.1.3 255.255.255.0
Branch1(config-if)# frame-relay map ip 10.1.1.1 120 broadcast
```

Table 5-7 describes the commands used in Examples 5-16, 5-17, and 5-18.

Table 5-7   *Commands for Configuring Point-to-Multipoint Frame Relay*

Command	Description
encapsulation frame-relay	Sets Frame Relay encapsulation on the interface.
interface *interface.subinterface* point-to-multipoint	Creates a point-to-multipoint subinterface and enters subinterface configuration mode.
frame-relay map *protocol protocol_address dlci*	Creates a static mapping between a DLCI and a remote device. *protocol* is a Layer 3 protocol (**ip**, **ipv6**, etc.), *protocol_address* is the network address (IP address), and *dlci* is the DLCI used to map to the remote address.

Verifying Frame Relay Configuration

This section examines the **show** commands involved in verifying the Frame Relay configuration.

Example 5-19 presents the **show interfaces** command to verify the status of Frame Relay and Layer 1 and Layer 2. Confirm that the encapsulation is set to Frame Relay. The command also displays information about the LMI type and the LMI DLCI.

Example 5-19   *Using the* **show interface** *Command to Check LMI*

```
Branch# show interfaces Serial0/0/0
Serial0/0/0 is up, line protocol is up
  Hardware is WIC MBRD Serial
  Internet address is 192.168.1.1/24
  MTU 1500 bytes, BW 1544 Kbit/sec, DLY 20000 usec,
     reliability 255/255, txload 1/255, rxload 1/255
  Encapsulation FRAME-RELAY, loopback not set
  Keepalive set (10 sec)
  LMI enq sent 630, LMI stat recvd 616, LMI upd recvd 0, DTE LMI up
  LMI enq recvd 15, LMI stat sent 0, LMI upd sent 0
  LMI DLCI 1023 LMI type is CISCO frame relay DTE
  Broadcast queue 0/64, broadcasts sent/dropped 9/0, interface broadcasts 0
  Last input 00:00:04, output 00:00:04, output hang never
  Last clearing of "show interface" counters 01:45:04
  Input queue: 0/75/0/0 (size/max/drops/flushes); Total output drops: 0
  Queueing strategy: weighted fair
<output omitted>
```

The output also displays the Frame Relay DTE or DCE type. Normally, the router is the DTE and the service provider is the DCE. However, a Cisco router can be configured as the Frame Relay switch. In that case, the type is DCE.

Use the **show frame-relay lmi** command to display LMI traffic statistics. This command shows the number of status messages that are exchanged between the local router and the local Frame Relay switch. This command output helps isolate the problem to a Frame Relay communications issue between the service provider switch and the router, as demonstrated in Example 5-20.

Example 5-20 *Using* **show frame-relay lmi** *to Check the Local Communication*

```
Branch# show frame-relay lmi
LMI Statistics for interface Serial0/0/0 (Frame Relay DTE) LMI TYPE = CISCO
  Invalid Unnumbered info 0 Invalid Prot Disc 0
  Invalid dummy Call Ref 0 Invalid Msg Type 0
  Invalid Status Message 0 Invalid Lock Shift 0
  Invalid Information ID 0 Invalid Report IE Len 0
  Invalid Report Request 0 Invalid Keep IE Len 0
  Num Status Enq. Sent 3834 Num Status msgs Rcvd 7820
  Num Update Status Rcvd 0 Num Status Timeouts 14
  Last Full Status Req 00:07:21 Last Full Status Rcvd 00:07:21
```

Table 5-8 defines the important fields in the output of the command.

Table 5-8 *Key Fields in show frame-relay lmi Command Output*

Field	Description
(Frame Relay DTE)	The local router is the DTE.
LMI TYPE	Signaling or LMI specification. The options are Cisco, ANSI, or ITU-T.
Num Status Enq. Sent	Number of LMI status inquiry messages that were sent.
Num Status Msgs Rcvd	Number of LMI status messages that were received

As demonstrated in Example 5-21, the **show frame relay pvc** command indicates the statistics for each PVC in the router. Each DLCI is listed followed by its individual information.

Example 5-21   *Examining the PVCs*

```
Branch# show frame-relay pvc
PVC Statistics for interface Serial0/0/0 (Frame Relay DTE)
                Active      Inactive      Deleted       Static
Local             1            0             0             0
Switched          0            0             0             0
Unused            0            0             0             0
DLCI = 120, DLCI USAGE = LOCAL, PVC STATUS = ACTIVE, INTERFACE = Serial0/0/0
input pkts 18              output pkts 18           in bytes 962
out bytes 962             dropped pkts 0            in pkts dropped 0
out pkts dropped  0     out bytes dropped 0
in FECN pkts 0            in BECN pkts           0 out FECN pkts 0
out BECN pkts 0          in DE pkts             0 out DE pkts 0
out bcast pkts 13         out bcast bytes 442
5 minute input rate 0 bits/sec, 0 packets/sec
5 minute output rate 0 bits/sec, 0 packets/sec
pvc create time 02:32:29, last time pvc status changed 02:32:29
```

Table 5-9 defines the notable fields in the **show frame relay pvc** command.

Table 5-9   *Key Fields in* **show frame-relay pvc** *Command Output*

Field	Description
DLCI	The DLCI identifier for the PVC.
DLCI Usage	Lists SWITCHED when the router or access server is used as a switch; lists LOCAL when the router or access server is used as a DTE device. This should be LOCAL most of the time.
PVC Status	Status of the PVC. The DCE device reports the status, and the DTE device receives the status. When you disable the LMI mechanism on the interface by using the **no keepalive** command, the PVC status is STATIC. Otherwise, the PVC status is exchanged using the LMI protocol: STATIC: LMI is disabled on the interface. ACTIVE: The PVC is operational and can transmit packets. INACTIVE: The PVC is configured but is down. DELETED: The PVC is not present (DTE device only), which means that no status is received from the LMI protocol.
Interface	Router interface the PVC is mapped to.

As demonstrated in Example 5-22, the **show frame-relay map** command displays the current map entries and information about the connections. With this output, the IP address, DLCI, and interface can all be correlated.

Example 5-22 *Using the* **frame-relay map** *Command to See the Connections*

```
Branch# show frame-relay map
Serial0/0/0 (up): ip 192.168.1.2 dlci 120(0x78,0x1C80), dynamic, broadcast,
CISCO, status defined, active
```

The following list explains the **show frame-relay map** output that appears in Example 5-22.

- **120:** The local DLCI number, in decimal

- **0x78:** Trivial output; the hexadecimal conversion of the DLCI number (0 * 78 = 120 decimal)

- **0x1C80:** Trivial output; the value as it would appear "on the wire" because of the way that the DLCI bits are spread out in the address field of the Frame Relay frame

- **192.168.1.2:** The remote router IP address (a dynamic entry that is learned via the Inverse ARP process)

- **broadcast:** Indicates broadcasts and multicasts are enabled on the PVC

- **active:** The PVC status

Introducing Cisco VPN Solutions

Enterprises need secure, reliable, and cost-effective networks to connect corporate headquarters, branch offices, remote employees, and suppliers. With the shift to more people working in small office/home office (SOHO) locations and other remote locations, the need for secure remote access has dramatically increased.

Cisco VPN solutions were discussed briefly at the beginning of the chapter. They provide an Internet-based WAN infrastructure for connecting branch offices, home offices, business partner sites, and remote telecommuters to all or portions of a private enterprise network. When utilizing high-bandwidth Internet connectivity that is secured by encrypted VPN tunnels, you can reduce WAN bandwidth costs while increasing connectivity speeds.

Figure 5-51 illustrates some of the possible remote connection topologies of networks. In some cases, in the Internet "cloud," the remote locations connect only to the headquarters location, while in other cases, some remote locations connect to multiple sites. The regional (branch) office in Figure 5-51 connects to the headquarters and partner sites, through the Internet cloud, while the mobile worker has a single connection to the headquarters.

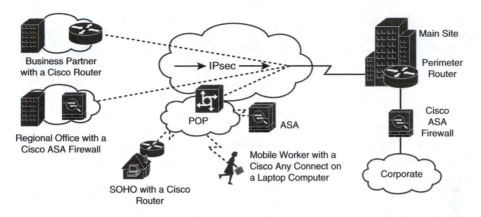

Figure 5-51 *Typical VPN Deployments*

VPNs offer flexible, on-demand, and scalable connectivity. Site-to-site connections can provide a secure, fast, and reliable remote connection. This is the most common option for teleworkers. It is usually combined with remote access over broadband, to establish a secure VPN over the public Internet.

With a VPN, traffic from a private network is transported over a public network, such as the Internet. This forms a virtual network instead of using a dedicated Layer 2/3 connection. The traffic is encrypted to keep the data confidential. For our purposes, a VPN is defined as an encrypted connection between private networks over the Internet.

There are two types of VPN networks:

■ **Site-to-site VPNs:** They provide the services of a classic WAN. Devices send and receive traffic through a VPN device. This could be a router or a Cisco Adaptive Security Appliance (ASA). The device used to establish the VPN is responsible for encapsulating and, optionally, encrypting outbound traffic for all of the traffic from a particular site and sending it through a VPN tunnel to a peer VPN device on the target site. Upon receipt, the peer VPN gateway encapsulates and/or decrypts the traffic and directs it into the site network.

■ **Remote-access VPNs:** They can support the needs of telecommuters, mobile users, and others who need on-demand access. In a remote-access VPN, each VPN client has software installed. In a remote-access VPN, whenever the device sends any traffic, the VPN client software encapsulates and encrypts (if encryption is used) that traffic before sending it over the Internet to the VPN gateway at the edge of the target network. Upon receipt, the VPN gateway behaves as it does for site-to-site VPNs.

Cisco ASA is a network security device that acts as a VPN endpoint (concentrator) as well as a firewall. The ASA supports both site-to-site and remote-access VPNs.

Note   Cisco previously manufactured dedicated VPN appliances, such as the VPN 3000 and 5000 series of VPN concentrators. These have all been declared end-of-life (EOL) status in favor of rolling this function into the ASA and Cisco IOS (in routers).

Figure 5-52 is the composite of a traditional WAN integrated with site-to-site and remote-access VPNs. Site-to-site VPNs can be used alongside traditional WANs, as a backup for a traditional WAN, or the WAN itself. Remote-access VPNs are often integrated with traditional WANs as well.

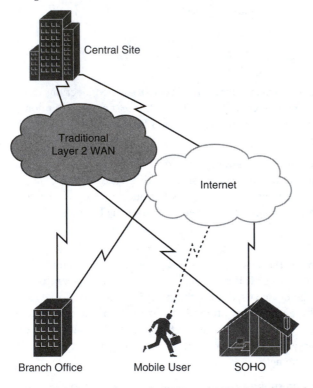

Figure 5-52   *Traditional WAN and VPN Side by Side*

The benefits of a VPN include the following:

- **Cost savings:** VPNs enable enterprises to use cost-effective, third-party Internet transport to connect remote offices and remote users to enterprise resources and sites, therefore eliminating expensive, dedicated WAN links.

- **Scalability and flexibility:** VPNs enable enterprises to use the Internet infrastructure within ISPs and devices. This allows location independence, provides capacity on demand, and eliminates long-term technology requirements.

- **Compatibility with any transport:** VPNs allow mobile workers, telecommuters, and other individuals to use any connectivity, such as DSL, cellular, and cable ISPs, to gain access to the resources that they need to access securely.

- **Security:** VPNs can provide the highest level of security by using advanced encryption and authentication protocols that protect resources from unauthorized access.

There are multiple protocols, devices, and methods for establishing VPNs. Often, tunneling and encryption technologies are combined to create a VPN solution. The encryption technologies include Secure Sockets Layer (SSL) and Internet Protocol Security (IPsec), and the tunneling technologies include Generic Routing Encapsulation (GRE) and Multiprotocol Label Switching (MPLS).

Cisco IOS SSL VPN is displayed in Figure 5-53. This is a technology that provides remote-access connectivity from almost any Internet-enabled location using a web browser and its native SSL encryption or using Cisco AnyConnect VPN Client.

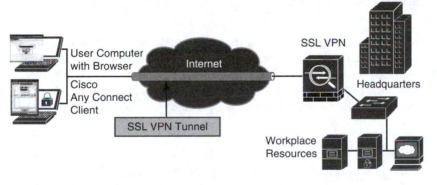

Figure 5-53 *Cisco IOS SSL VPN*

Introducing IPsec

IPsec is an IETF standard that defines the foundation for configuring VPNs using the TCP/IP protocol. IPsec is not bound to any specific encryption, authentication, or keying technology, nor is it bound to any specific set of security algorithms. It is a framework of open standards that defines the scope for secure communications. IPsec relies on existing algorithms to implement the encryption, authentication, and key exchange. Because IPsec does not rely on any specific set of algorithms, newer and better algorithms can be implemented without altering the existing IPsec standards.

IPsec provides data confidentiality, data integrity, and origin authentication between participating peers at the IP layer. IPsec secures a path between a pair of devices. IPsec works at the network layer, protecting and authenticating IP packets between participating IPsec devices (peers). As a result, IPsec can protect virtually all application traffic because the protection can be implemented from Layer 4 through Layer 7. All implementations of IPsec have a plaintext Layer 3 header, like any other IP packet. This ensures that there are no issues with routing IPsec packets through a network. IPsec functions over all Layer 2 protocols, such as Ethernet, ATM, and Frame Relay. IPsec security services provide four critical functions:

- **Confidentiality (encryption):** The sender can encrypt the packets before transmitting them across a network. By doing so, no one can eavesdrop or intervene in the communication. If the communication is intercepted, it cannot be read.

- **Data integrity:** The receiver can verify that the data was transmitted through the Internet without being changed or altered in any way. IPsec ensures data integrity by using checksums, which is a simple redundancy check.

- **Authentication:** Authentication ensures that the connection is made with the desired communication partner. The receiver can authenticate the source of the packet by guaranteeing and certifying the source of the information. IPsec uses Internet Key Exchange (IKE) to authenticate users and devices that can carry out communication independently. IKE uses several types of authentication, including username and password, one-time password, biometrics, preshared keys (PSK), and digital certificates.

- **Antireplay protection:** Antireplay protection verifies that each packet is unique and not duplicated. IPsec packets are protected by comparing the sequence number of the received packets with a sliding window on the destination host or security gateway. A packet that has a sequence number that is before the sliding window is considered to be either late or a duplicate packet. Late and duplicate packets are dropped.

Note A detailed discussion of IPSec, including configuration, is beyond the scope of this text. For more information, the Cisco Validated Design (CVD) Program is a good starting point. The CVDs explain the design and implementation of most Cisco solutions, and several VPN design guides are available. See http://www.cisco.com/go/cvd.

GRE Tunnels

Generic Routing Encapsulation (GRE) is an IP tunneling protocol that encapsulates a wide variety of protocol packet types inside IP tunnels, creating a virtual point-to-point link to Cisco routers at remote points over an IP internetwork. It connects multiprotocol subnets in a single-protocol backbone environment. IP tunneling using GRE enables network expansion across a single-protocol backbone environment. GRE allows the passing of network traffic through a tunnel, as if the networks were directly connected. This includes management information, such as routing protocols. Figure 5-54 shows a representation of GRE location and the packet structure.

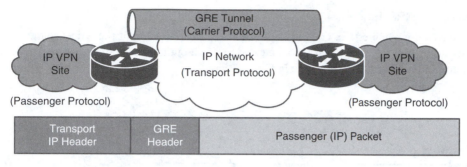

Figure 5-54 *Generic Routing Encapsulation*

GRE is a simple, general-purpose protocol that is designed to manage the transportation of multiprotocol and IP multicast traffic between two or more sites that may only have IP connectivity. It is designed to encapsulate any type of network layer packets inside arbitrary types of network layer packets as defined in RFC 1701, "Generic Routing Encapsulation (GRE)" (Informational), RFC 1702, "Generic Routing Encapsulation over IPv4 Networks" (Informational), and RFC 2784, "Generic Routing Encapsulation (GRE)" (Proposed Standard). GRE was originally developed by Cisco and then submitted to the IEEE as a standard.

A tunnel interface supports a header for each of the following:

- A passenger protocol or encapsulated protocol, such as IPv4 or IPv6. This protocol is the one being encapsulated.

- A carrier or encapsulation protocol (GRE in this case).

- A transport delivery protocol, such as IP, which is the protocol that carries the encapsulated protocol.

GRE has these characteristics:

- GRE encapsulation uses a Protocol Type field in the GRE header to support the encapsulation of any OSI Layer 3 protocol.

- GRE is stateless. It does not include any flow-control mechanisms by default.

- Tunneling and encryption are often combined (as noted earlier). GRE does not include any strong security mechanisms to protect its payload, so when encryption is needed, IPsec is combined with GRE.

- The GRE header, together with the tunneling IP header, creates at least 24 bytes of additional overhead for tunneled packets.

Configuring a GRE Tunnel

To create a tunnel interface, you must first know the IP addressing of the tunnel source, destination, and the tunnel. It is recommended that you outline a plan of action prior to the configuration process, as shown in Figure 5-55.

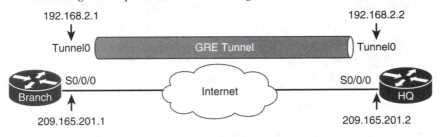

Figure 5-55   *Tunnel Diagram*

Once you have made a diagram, proceed by designing a small table or chart. Table 5-10 shows a sample that matches the example in Figure 5-55. This type of documentation is helpful in both the deployment and troubleshooting of a GRE solution. It is important to note that the tunnel is treated as an IP subnet that is separate from the physical subnets.

Table 5-10   *Designing a Tunnel Solution*

Router	Tunnel Source IP	Tunnel Destination IP	Tunnel Interface
HQ	209.165.202.2	209.165.202.1	Tunnel0:192.168.2.2/24
Branch	209.165.202.1	209.165.202.2	Tunnel0:192.168.2.1/24

Now that you have appropriated the data for the tunnel, it is time to configure it. This is performed on both routers terminating the tunnel by using the following steps:

Step 1.   Configure and test the Layer 2/3 connectivity for the connection the tunnel will be operating over.

Step 2.   Create the tunnel interface.

Step 3.   Specify the tunnel source and destination IP addresses.

Step 4.   Configure an IP address for the tunnel interface.

The sample configurations in Examples 5-23 and 5-24 illustrate a basic GRE tunnel design on the routers Branch and HQ in Figure 5-55. The minimum configuration requires specification of the tunnel source and destination IP addresses. As with a physical or loopback interface, you must also configure an IP subnet to provide IP connectivity across the tunnel link, as shown in Figure 5-55.

Example 5-23 *Branch Router Tunnel Configuration*

```
Branch(config)# interface tunnel0
Branch(config-if)# tunnel mode gre ip
Branch(config-if)# ip address 192.168.2.1 255.255.255.0
Branch(config-if)# tunnel source 209.165.201.1
Branch(config-if)# tunnel destination 209.165.201.2
```

Example 5-24 *HQ Router Tunnel Configuration*

```
HQ(config)# interface tunnel0
HQ(config-if)# tunnel mode gre ip
HQ(config-if)# ip address 192.168.2.2 255.255.255.0
HQ(config-if)# tunnel source 209.165.201.2
HQ(config-if)# tunnel destination 209.165.201.1
```

Table 5-11 provides description of the commands used in Examples 5-23 and 5-24.

Table 5-11 *Tunneling Commands*

Command	Description
interface tunnel*<tunnel_number>*	Creates the tunnel interface and enters interface configuration mode.
tunnel mode *gre ip*	Sets the tunnel mode to GRE with IPv4. Other options exist, including IPv6 as a tunnel type.
tunnel source *ip_address*	Identifies the source address to use as the originating IP address of the tunnel.
tunnel destination *ip_address*	Identifies the destination address to direct the tunnel packets to.

Note An extensive discussion of tunneling is outside the scope of this text; see the "Implementing Tunnels" section of the *Interface and Hardware Component Configuration Guide, Cisco IOS Release 15SY* at http://www.cisco.com/en/US/docs/ios-xml/ios/interface/configuration/15-sy/ir-impl-tun.html.

Each of the tunnel interfaces has the tunnel source set as the local Serial0/0/0 interface and the tunnel destination set as the peer router Serial0/0/0 interface. The IP address is assigned to the tunnel interfaces on both routers.

> **Note**   If you are connecting through the tunnel from other subnets, routes to the tunnel subnet, the source/destination interface, and the subnet(s) connected must be included in the routing tables in the network.

GRE Tunnel Verification

To determine whether the tunnel interface is up or down, use the **show ip interface brief** command. Verify the state of a GRE tunnel by using the **show interface tunnel** command. The line protocol on a GRE tunnel interface is up as long as there is a route to the tunnel destination. Example 5-25 presents the **show ip interface brief** command, with a reminder to search for the "up up" status. Example 5-26 provides more details using the **show ip interface command** (without the **brief** option). This output includes the verification of the tunnel source and destination, the IP address of the tunnel, and the tunnel type.

Example 5-25   *Verifying Tunnel Up/Down Status Using* **show ip interface brief**

```
Branch# show ip interface brief | include Tunnel
Tunnel0 192.168.2.1 YES manual up up
```

> **Note**   The **include** command strips all output in a command except lines containing the string following the **include** command.

Example 5-26   *Verifying Tunnel Status Using* **show ip interface**

```
Branch# show interface Tunnel 0
Tunnel0 is up, line protocol is up
Hardware is Tunnel
Internet address is 192.168.2.1/24
MTU 17916 bytes, BW 100 Kbit/sec, DLY 50000 usec,
reliability 255/255, txload 1/255, rxload 1/255
Encapsulation TUNNEL, loopback not set
Keepalive not set
Tunnel source 209.165.201.1, destination 209.165.201.2
Tunnel protocol/transport GRE/IP
<output omitted>
```

By issuing the **show ip route** command, as shown in Example 5-27, you can identify the route between the Branch and HQ routers. Because a tunnel is established between the two routers, the path is seen as directly connected. In order for the tunnel to be established, the route to the tunnel destination must also appear in the routing table.

Example 5-27 *Verifying the Route Through the Tunnel Interface*

```
Branch# show ip route
<output omitted>
192.168.2.0/24 is variably subnetted, 2 subnets, 2 masks
C 192.168.2.0/24 is directly connected, Tunnel0
L 192.168.2.1/32 is directly connected, Tunnel0
209.165.202.0/24 is variably subnetted, 2 subnets, 2 masks
C 209.165.201.0/24 is directly connected, Serial0/0/0
L 209.165.201.1/32 is directly connected, Serial0/0/0

<output omitted>
```

Understanding MPLS Networking

MPLS is a networking protocol that was introduced earlier in this chapter. It is an advanced subject. This section covers only the fundamental infrastructure and basic verification points from the MPLS customer perspective. As a CCNA, you should be aware of basic MPLS terms and operation from the customer/enterprise network perspective. The Cisco Service Provider certification portfolio (CCNA SP, CCNP SP, etc.) focuses more on the configuration and operation of core MPLS.

MPLS was originally designed by Cisco as Tag Switching, to create an infrastructure for a service provider that forwards the switching packets at higher speed. The tagging permits the routers to advance the packets without a routing table lookup or being dependent on routing table convergence times. Tag Switching later became MPLS and an industry standard.

MPLS has become a widespread offering and infrastructure for service providers. It allows them to reduce the cost of the network while providing additional services that improve existing networks. Service providers can use all the benefits and features of an IP backbone, rather than a Layer 2 backbone. An example of a benefit for service providers is the ability for the path and service level through the service provider network to be tightly and dynamically controlled though MPLS Traffic Engineering (MPLS TE). This allows for better utilization of the links and more granular service-level agreement (SLA) control.

In Figure 5-56, a simplified and high-level MPLS infrastructure shows the three types of MPLS routers.

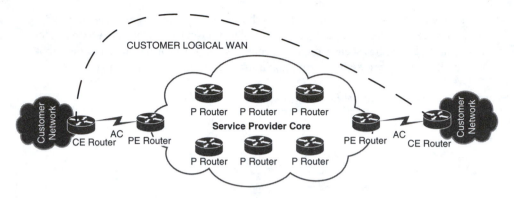

Figure 5-56 *Simplified MPLS Infrastructure*

MPLS router types, as defined by the role and placement of the router in the network, are as follows:

■ **Customer Edge (CE) router:** The demarcation point between the service provider's MPLS infrastructure and the customer's infrastructure. It is the connection point of the customer LAN infrastructure and the WAN created by MPLS. This is under control of either the MPLS customer or the service provider, depending on the contract and/or configuration.

■ **Provider Edge (PE) router:** The edge of the provider network that pops the label off (removes the label from) the MPLS labeled packets, making them normal traffic, and passes them to the CE router. It also adds the MPLS transport labels and passes the traffic to the provider core network. PE routers may be attached to other CE routers and partitioned using a Virtual Routing and Forwarding (VRF) instance to isolate customer traffic and routes from other customers. VRFs are considered as secure as a shared Layer 2 infrastructure (such as Frame Relay or ATM). This router is under the control of the MPLS service provider.

■ **Provider (P) router:** Provides high-speed transport of labeled packets through the provider network to other P routers and PE routers. This router is under the control of the MPLS service provider.

■ **Provider network:** This is the service provider core network. It is the infrastructure of the service provider running one or more Layer 3 routing protocols (usually an Interior Gateway Protocol such as Open Shortest Path First or Intermediate System-to-Intermediate System in conjunction with the EGP, BGP). P routers provide high-speed transport through the core to PE routers. This network is under the control of the MPLS service provider.

■ **Customer network:** The LANs connected by the MPLS infrastructure contain the customer remote sites. This network is under the control of the MPLS customer. Routers in the customer network that are not directly connected to the MPLS network are sometimes defined as "C" routers (for customer).

- **Customer logical WAN:** The logical path, from the customer perspective, traffic takes between the customer sites. May also be referred to as customer WAN, customer network, etc.

- **Attachment circuit (AC):** This is the circuit between the CE router and PE router. This is a Layer 2 WAN, MAN, or LAN circuit. It is often a leased line or Ethernet circuit.

MPLS comes in three types of services:

- **Layer 2 "pseudowire":** The encapsulation of LAN or Layer 2 protocols. It is also called Any Transport over MPLS (AToM). This service allows the service provider to support the customer with a Layer 2 circuit that appears in function to a T1/E1 or other WAN circuit. It encapsulates the Layer 2 frames into MPLS/IP packets. It is useful for running legacy protocols and devices over an MPLS/IP backbone. For example, consider a legacy device that does not support IP and requires a Layer 2 circuit, such as a T1/E1 (potentially a legacy phone system or X.25 device).

- **Layer 2 Virtual Private LAN Service (VPLS):** VPLS allows the service provider's network to imitate a single Ethernet LAN switch to the customer, but over a WAN. The AC is usually a Layer 2 Ethernet connection from a provider-managed router.

- **Layer 3 VPNs:** The direct routing of the customer IP network over the service provider network. This is the most common MPLS application. It presents the least difficulty for the service provider to manage, provides the highest performance (no Layer 2 in Layer 3 encapsulation and decapsulation), and requires the least amount of equipment. This is accomplished through IP configuration on the CE and static or dynamic routing (most common) between the CE and the PE. The AC is a WAN/MAN interface that runs a Layer 2 WAN protocol with TCP/IP to the PE router. Often, this is the only MPLS solution where the customer directly manages the CE device.

Basic Troubleshooting of MPLS Services

Each of the MPLS services requires slightly different verification. As a CCNA looking at an MPLS WAN, basic WAN/LAN troubleshooting skills are applied as they would be in a non-MPLS environment. The amount of troubleshooting that can be performed at a customer network depends on where the handoff is provided to the customer. This could be at the CE or provided by the CE. This will vary per provider, service type, and contract between the customer and the service provider. Appendix B, "Basic L3VPN MPLS Configuration and Verification," provides a brief example of a customer-side MPLS Layer 3 VPN.

The steps to troubleshoot an MPLS WAN are as follows:

Step 1. Check the up/down status of the interface that is handed off from the service provider. Use normal Layer 1/2 troubleshooting techniques, including the **show interfaces** command.

Step 2.   Check the protocol reachability by attempting to find where reachability ends at Layer 3 with the **ping** and **traceroute** commands. With MPLS VPLS or MPLS pseudowire, you may not be running IP, so you may need to look at whatever protocol is being run over the link to see if end-to-end reachability exists.

Step 3.   If you have access to the CE and can ping the PE:

  a. Check to make sure the routing protocol and/or static routes are properly configured.

  b. If using a routing protocol, make sure a neighbor relationship exists and routes exist in the routing table for the provider network.

Step 4.   If you are unable to correct the problem, you may need to contact the service provider. Take notes on what you tested in your troubleshooting and any lights or alarms that you see externally on any equipment.

Chapter Summary

A network can be defined as a LAN, WAN, or MAN. This chapter discussed the concepts of a WAN and a MAN. A WAN can be interconnected over a private or public infrastructure, such as the Internet. A WAN may have more than one access method, including the mixture of public and private interconnections. WANs use a variety of circuits and hardware that are not used in LANs. A MAN is a short-range WAN. A MAN tends to use higher-speed interconnection technologies due to the short distances.

WANs are designed using interconnections. The interconnections may be circuit switched or packet switched. The placement of the interconnections can be direct (point to point), partially meshed, or fully meshed.

WANs are terminated from service providers at the demarcation point (demarc) by specialized hardware that varies by media type. Media types include Frame Relay, ATM, Ethernet, broadband (DSL and cable), and wireless. Each media type has its own unique qualities. Both the media type and equipment the service provider installs at the demarc determines the customer connection at the demarc. This varies by service provider and country.

There are several WAN encapsulation and termination types. HDLC is an industry-standard protocol. Cisco has a proprietary version, which is the default encapsulation for leased lines. PPP is a common Layer 2 protocol for the WAN. There are two components of PPP: LCP, which negotiates the connection, and NCP, which encapsulates traffic. PPP can also bond multiple links at Layer 2, called Multilink PPP. Frame Relay is a packet-switched, connection-oriented data-link technology. Frame Relay can be deployed in mesh, partial mesh, or hub-and-spoke WANs.

Organizations can implement VPNs through the public Internet. This is common because it is less expensive, quicker to deploy, and easier to scale than traditional WANs, while still offering mechanisms for secure communication. VPNs enable mobile workers to access their organizations resources while providing the worker the ability to dynamically change locations. GRE is a tunneling protocol that can encapsulate a wide variety of protocol packet types inside of IP tunnels as a VPN. GRE does not provide encryption and is often used with IPsec.

MPLS is a technology that service providers use to make their networks more efficient. MPLS uses various handoff methods to the customer network. Troubleshooting and configuring the various deployments of MPLS in the WAN utilizes the LAN and WAN techniques discussed in this book and varies based on the implementation process.

Review Questions

Use the questions here to review what you learned in this chapter. The correct answers are located in Appendix A, "Answers to Chapter Review Questions."

1. Which statement or statements about WANs is/are true? (Source: "Understanding WAN Technologies")

   a. WANs generally connect devices that are located over a broader geographical area.
   b. WANs generally connect devices that are close to each other.
   c. WAN stands for World Around Networks.
   d. WANs use connections of various types to provide access to bandwidth over large geographical areas.

2. Which statement or statements about MAN is/are true? (Source: "Metropolitan-Area Networks")

   a. MANs are short-distance WANs.
   b. MANs can't run over 10 MBps.
   c. Radio waves do not work in a WAN.
   d. MAN stands for Mobile Area Network.
   e. MANs require heavier security than WANs because they are metropolitan.

3. Which of the following is/are not a WAN device? (Source: "WAN Devices")

   a. Spectrometer
   b. CSU/DSU
   c. Router
   d. Ethernet hub

4. Which feature does PPP use to encapsulate multiple protocols? (Source: "Point-to-Point Protocol")

   a. NCP
   b. LCP
   c. IPCP
   d. IPXP

5. Which Layer 2 protocol provides authentication? (Source: "Point-to-Point Protocol")

   a. HDLC

   b. PPP

   c. Frame Relay

   d. GRE

6. What is the purpose of LCP? (Source: "Point-to-Point Protocol")

   a. To perform authentication

   b. To negotiate link options

   c. To encapsulate multiple protocols

   d. To specify asynchronous versus synchronous

7. Which two statements best describe CHAP? (Choose two.) (Source: "Point-to-Point Protocol")

   a. CHAP may be performed periodically.

   b. CHAP uses a two-way handshake.

   c. CHAP uses a three-way handshake.

   d. CHAP uses a two-way hash function.

   e. CHAP passwords are sent in plaintext.

8. With CHAP, how does a remote node respond to a challenge message? (Source: "Point-to-Point Protocol")

   a. With a hash value

   b. With a return challenge

   c. With a plaintext password

   d. With an encrypted password

9. Match each Frame Relay operation component on the left with its definition on the right. (Source: "Establishing a WAN Connection Using Frame Relay")

   1. CIR   **a.** VC that is dynamically established on demand and is torn down when transmission is complete

   2. Inverse ARP   **b.** Maximum average data rate

   3. SVC   **c.** Clock speed of the connection to the Frame Relay cloud

   4. local access rate   **d.** Signaling standard between the router and the Frame Relay switch that is responsible for managing the connection and maintaining status between the devices

   5. LMI   **e.** Method of dynamically associating a remote network layer address with a local DLCI

10. What identifies the logical circuit between the router and the local Frame Relay switch? (Source: "Establishing a WAN Connection Using Frame Relay")

   a. DLCI
   b. LMI signal
   c. FECN packet
   d. BECN packet

11. Which characteristic of Frame Relay can cause reachability issues when a single interface is used to interconnect multiple sites? (Source: "Establishing a WAN Connection Using Frame Relay")

   a. Intermittent
   b. Point-to-point
   c. Error-correcting
   d. NBMA

12. Which VC status on a Cisco router indicates that the local connection to the Frame Relay switch is working but the remote router connection to the Frame Relay switch is not working? (Source: "Establishing a WAN Connection Using Frame Relay")

   a. LMI state
   b. Active state
   c. Deleted state
   d. Inactive state

13. Which issue does Frame Relay introduce to IP networks? (Source: "Establishing a WAN Connection Using Frame Relay")

   a. Split horizon
   b. CIDR
   c. Tunnel termination
   d. Lack of security

14. What are two types of VPNs? (Choose two.) (Source: "Introducing Cisco VPN Solutions")

   a. Remote-access
   b. Remote-to-site
   c. Remote-to-remote
   d. Site-to-site

15. Which three are advantages of VPNs over traditional Layer 2 WANs? (Choose three.) (Source: "Introducing Cisco VPN Solutions")

   a. Can be less expensive
   b. Provide scalability
   c. Do not require a service provider
   d. Provide security
   e. Require less knowledge to install and maintain

16. Which command is used to specify GRE tunnel mode as the tunnel interface mode? (Source: "Configuring a GRE Tunnel")

  a. tunnel mode ip gre
  b. tunnel mode gre ip
  c. tunnel gre ip
  d. tunnel gre

17. Which commands could you use to verify that a GRE tunnel is up? (Source: "Configuring a GRE Tunnel")

  a. show ip interface brief
  b. show interface tunnel
  c. show gre tunnel
  d. show tunnel interface

18. A GRE tunnel is considered a separate subnet from the physical infrastructure. (Source: "Configuring a GRE Tunnel")

  a. True
  b. False

19. Which are MPLS router types? ("Understanding MPLS Networking")

  a. P
  b. CE
  c. DE
  d. PE
  e. MX

20. Depending on the service type, MPLS can encapsulate which type(s) of traffic? ("Understanding MPLS Networking")

  a. IPv4
  b. IPv6
  c. ISDN
  d. Any protocol that can run over a T1 or E1
  e. All of the above

Chapter 6

Network Device Management

This chapter contains the following sections:

- Configuring Network Devices to Support Network Management Protocols

- Router Initialization and Configuration

- Cisco IOS Licensing

- Cisco IOS-XR, IOS-XE, and NX-OS

- Chapter Summary

- Review Questions

Technology is a tool to facilitate business. An organization's network is a core component of enterprise technology. When a network fails or operates in a degraded mode, an organization's ability to conduct its business is impaired. This can result in lost business/revenue, customer satisfaction issues, and even create health/safety issues. Therefore, it is critical for an organization to keep their network running optimally.

This chapter examines basic commands, concepts, and processes to determine network operational status. This includes gathering information from devices and links, and managing/understanding Cisco IOS images, configuration files, Cisco IOS licensing, and what devices are operating on a network.

Chapter Objectives

- Understand network management protocols and their applications

- Understand router and IOS architecture

- Manage configuration files and IOS images

- Manage licensing

- Understand Cisco software concepts

Configuring Network Devices to Support Network Management Protocols

Simple Network Management Protocol (SNMP) is an application-layer protocol that provides a message format for communication between managers and agents. The SNMP system consists of an SNMP manager, an SNMP agent, and a Management Information Base (MIB). The SNMP manager can be part of a Network Management System (NMS), such as Cisco Prime Infrastructure. The network device runs an SNMP process. This process is called an agent. The agent has a set of metrics and functions that can be performed within a device. This is called a MIB. Figure 6-1 shows the typical interaction between the SNMP manager and agent.

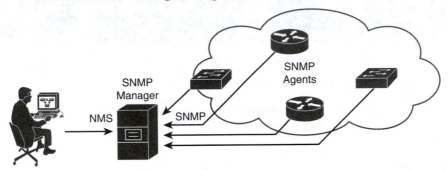

Figure 6-1   *SNMP Manager and Agent*

The agent can be queried, using SNMP, to obtain the values of the metrics defined in the MIB. SNMP managers often make periodic queries. This is known as *polling*. Agents can also send updates to the manger. These updates are called traps. The NMS is programmed to act on, log, or ignore traps or polling data. Polling data is often used in calculations within the NMS to determine any necessary actions (for example, send an alert out via a page or email) or provide reporting. The manager can also send requests to the agent. This can be used to set various values and/or execute commands.

Most Cisco devices support SNMP. This includes routers, switches, firewalls, and server products. Other products support SNMP as well, including operating systems from OS vendors (such as Microsoft) and open source OSs and devices (such as Linux).

Note   For information on how SNMP works on Windows Server, see "How SNMP Works" at http://technet.microsoft.com/en-us/library/cc783142(v=ws.10).aspx.

SNMP Versions

There are three versions of SNMP: SNMPv1, SNMPv2c, and SNMPv3. The major differences are how authentication works (encrypted or plain text) and whether or not an agent allows multiple values to be sent to a manager with a single manager query (bulk retrieval). To summarize these points:

- SNMPv1 and SNMPv2c use a plaintext, community-based password form of security to authenticate communication between managers and agents.

- SNMPv2c introduced a bulk retrieval mechanism and more detailed error message reporting to management stations. The bulk retrieval mechanism supports the retrieval of tables and large quantities of information, minimizing the number of round trips required.

- SNMPv3 primarily introduced security features, such as confidentiality, integrity, and authentication of messages between managers and agents.

Table 6-1 provides a consolidated view of the major differences in the protocol versions.

Table 6-1   *SNMP Version Comparison*

SNMP Version	Security	Bulk Retrieval Mechanism
SNMPv1	Plaintext authentication	No
SNMPv2c	Plaintext authentication	Yes
SNMPv3	Authentication and encryption	Yes

Obtaining Data from an SNMP Agent

It is a good idea to monitor key system resources on a periodic basis. In Figure 6-2, a graph from an open source SNMP manager is being used to poll the CPU of a router every 5 minutes. The output is graphed.

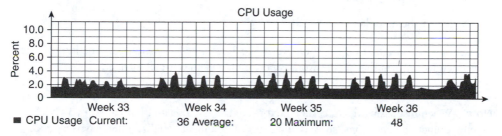

Figure 6-2   *SNMP Monitoring of a Router*

Monitoring and noting the normal operation of key resources in a device allows you to establish a baseline. Most NMSs allow the setting of thresholds. A threshold example would be exceeding 80% of the CPU for 10 minutes. The NMS can then be configured to take action, such as send an email or provide some sort of visual alert. When an agent is polled, the SNMP manager sends a read request, called a GET.

As mentioned earlier, an agent can proactively send an update to the manager in the form of a trap. Figure 6-2 gives an example of a trap collected by a popular commercial NMS program. The trap is called coldStart, which is a common trap generated by a system startup. As you can see from Figures 6-2 and 6-3, the way in which SNMP data is displayed depends on which NMS is acting as the SNMP manager. An NMS just gives a user-friendly representation and display of SNMP data.

Figure 6-3 *Example of an SNMP trap from a Commercial NMS*

Monitoring Polling Data in SNMP

What should be monitored in polling? How do you determine what is normal behavior? These are pretty typical questions. The MIBs are different for every device, and what is considered acceptable behavior varies per mechanism. Monitoring device temperature is one example. The temperature range of a device that is considered "office environment" equipment is different from the temperature range of data center class equipment housed in a controlled environment of a data center. A second example is delay. Acceptable delay for applications varies, as does delay generated by links. An application like VoIP generally requires a delay of less than 150 ms for high-quality, uncompressed voice.

How often should you poll devices? That is not an easy answer. It is dependent on the following conditions:

- The type of polling performed

- Availability needs

- The NMS's capabilities

- Data sampling needs

- Metric being polled

A common configuration is to poll every 2 to 30 minutes, depending on the information needed to confirm that the network is performing in an optimal manner.

Note When discussing delay, certain factors are unavoidable and normal. They vary by environmental conditions, such as link speed. Looking at serialization delay is a good example. Serialization delay is a significant factor in lower-speed links but not in higher-speed links. A 64 kbps link (fractional T1) requires 187 ms for a 1500-byte packet, whereas a 10-GB Ethernet link has a 1.2 microsecond serialization delay. As mentioned previously, serialization delay is the time it takes to clock the packet onto the media.

Monitoring TRAPs in SNMP

What should be monitored in the traps that the NMS receives? How should you determine what is normal? These are pretty typical questions as well. The MIBs are different for every device, and what is considered acceptable behavior varies per device type. An example might be interface state changes. Typically, ports going up and down is a common occurrence on an Ethernet switch. Devices are often rebooted and shut down on a LAN (e.g., a user shuts down their PC when they leave for the day or if it crashes). However, state changes on a WAN interface could mean trouble, because WAN interfaces typically do not go up and down in a stable WAN.

Most SNMP agent devices allow the selective tuning of the traps that are sent out. Cisco IOS Software allows the tuning of the traps that are enabled. Numerous traps are available, and it would be difficult to process all of them. Example 6-1 shows a subset of the available traps when enabling traps globally on a Cisco 871 router.

Example 6-1   *Subset of Cisco IOS traps that Can Be Configured*

```
R1(config)# snmp-server enable traps
  aaa_server            Enable SNMP AAA Server traps
  adslline              Enable ADSL Line-MIB traps
  atm                   Enable SNMP atm traps
  authenticate-fail     Enable SNMP 802.11 Authentication Fail trap
  bgp                   Enable BGP traps
  cnpd                  Enable NBAR Protocol Discovery traps
  config                Enable SNMP config traps
  config-copy           Enable SNMP config-copy traps
  config-ctid           Enable SNMP config-ctid traps
  cpu                   Allow cpu related traps
  deauthenticate        Enable SNMP 802.11 Deauthentication trap
  disassociate          Enable SNMP 802.11 Disassociation trap
  dot11-mibs            Enable dot11 traps
  dot11-qos             Enable SNMP 802.11 QoS Change trap
  eigrp                 Enable SNMP EIGRP traps
  entity                Enable SNMP entity traps
  event-manager         Enable SNMP Embedded Event Manager traps
  firewall              Enable SNMP Firewall traps
  flash                 Enable SNMP FLASH notifications
  frame-relay           Enable SNMP frame-relay traps
  fru-ctrl              Enable SNMP entity FRU control traps
  hsrp                  Enable SNMP HSRP traps
  --More--
<output omitted>
```

Sending Data to an SNMP Agent

The previous section discussed using SNMP for monitoring. This is a very common use for SNMP. However, SNMP can also be used to send commands to a device. The SNMP manager can send an agent a SET command. This allows values to be set, or actions to be taken. An example would be to use SNMP to back up the configuration of a router. The SNMP manager sends a SET to notify the router to send the configuration to a server, such as a Secure File Transfer Protocol (SFTP) server. Figure 6-4 represents the flow of such an action.

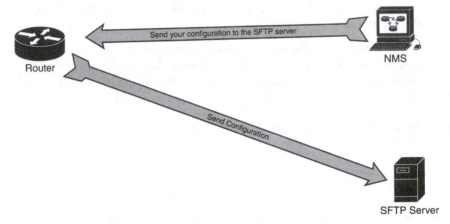

Figure 6-4 *Backup of a Configuration via SNMP*

To send a SET command to an SNMP agent, the device must be configured to allow SNMP write access and must support it. The router in Figure 6-5 is configured for SNMP read-only access, so it does not support the SET command. Most SNMP agents allow configuring read-write mode (GET/SET command support) or read-only mode (GET command only, no SET allowed). Some SNMP agents do not allow configuration of read-write mode or read-only mode. An example of a device that does not support SNMP SET commands is the Cisco ASA Firewall. This device only supports SNMP GET and traps.

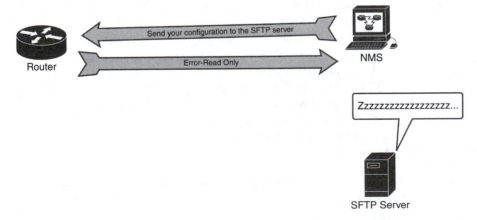

Figure 6-5 *SNMP Read-Only*

SNMP MIBs

A MIB is a collection of information that is organized hierarchically. The data is then accessed using SNMP. Object IDs (OIDs) uniquely identify managed objects in a MIB hierarchy. They can be depicted as a tree, the levels of which are assigned by different organizations. Top-level MIB OIDs belong to different organizations, the example below are Cisco's OIDs. Vendors define private branches, including managed objects, for their own products.

OIDs belonging to Cisco are numbered as follows:

.iso (1).org (3).dod (6).internet (1).private (4).enterprises (1).cisco (9)

Figure 6-6 displays the output of a tool called *snmpget*. The tool can be downloaded from various shareware sites for Windows. It is also packaged as part of the Linux and UNIX operating systems. Using the snmpget application, you can manually obtain values from an SNMP agent. In the case of Figure 6-6, you can get the 5-minute exponentially moving average of the CPU busy percentage. You must specify the parameters an SNMP manager would provide, including the following:

- SNMP version

- Correct community string

- IP address of the network device that you want to query

- OID number

Also, the SNMP community strings authenticate access to the MIB inside the agent. To access a device, the community string definitions must match at least one of the community string definitions on the network device.

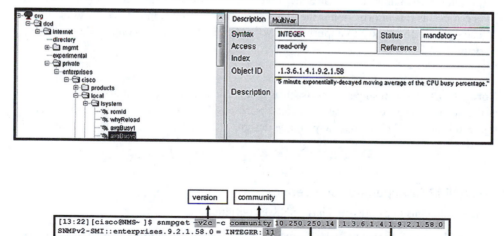

Figure 6-6 *Issuing an SNMP GET to a Device with the Windows snmpget Tool*

The MIB is basically the set of parameters that can be used in the execution of SNMP SET or GET commands against that device and agent. Figure 6-7 shows a website, SNMP Object Navigator, that Cisco hosts to enable you to search, browse, and download MIB data for most Cisco devices (http://tools.cisco.com/Support/SNMP/public.jsp). In Figure 6-7, a search for temperature objects has been executed. However, with the majority of common NMSs, most common MIBs are integrated into the NMS software.

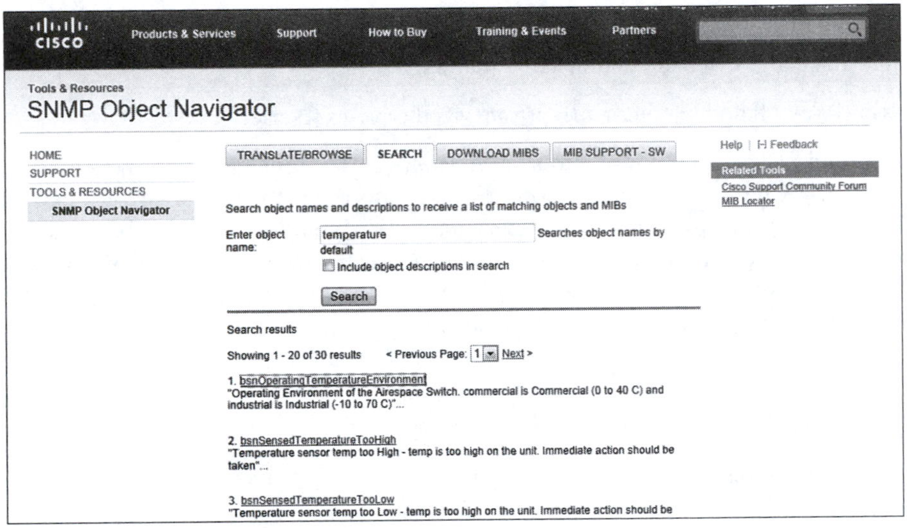

Figure 6-7   *Cisco SNMP Object Navigator*

Network engineers must recognize that the operation of an NMS platform differs per product. Basic knowledge of an SNMP agent, SNMP manager, and composition of a MIB is critical, as this information is the same among all platforms. Individual NMS platforms usually have the ability to import other MIBs that are not already contained in the software.

Note   Most commercial platforms (such as Cisco Prime) and open NMS platforms (such as OpenNMS, Cacti, etc.) operate on similar principals but are configured, used, and customized based on their individually unique design.

Basic SNMP Configuration and Verification

The following steps present a basic SNMP configuration:

Step 1.   Set a community string (password) of **cisco123** and set the SNMP access to read-only (**RO**) or read-write (**RW**). In this example, **RW** is configured.

```
R1(config)# snmp-server community cisco123 RW
```

Step 2.   Set the contact information and location.

```
R1(config)# snmp-server contact Branch-Amherst, NH
R1(config)# snmp-server location Branch-Office
```

Step 3.   Set the trap destination and the community string to use.

```
Branch(config)# snmp-server host 192.168.1.200 trap cisco123
```

Step 4.   Verify.

Step 4a.   Check the configuration for the commands:

```
R1# show running-config | include snmp
snmp-server community cisco123 RW
snmp-server location JT_Office
snmp-server contact Johnny Tiso-Amherst,NH
snmp-server host 192.168.1.200 cisco123
```

Step 4b.   Check the operational state:

```
R1# show snmp
Chassis: FHK140673EM
Contact: Branch-Amherst,NH
Location: Branch_Office
0 SNMP packets input
    0 Bad SNMP version errors
    0 Unknown community name
    0 Illegal operation for community name supplied
    0 Encoding errors
    0 Number of requested variables
    0 Number of altered variables
    0 Get-request PDUs
    0 Get-next PDUs
    0 Set-request PDUs
    0 Input queue packet drops (Maximum queue size 1000)
0 SNMP packets output
    0 Too big errors (Maximum packet size 1500)
    0 No such name errors
    0 Bad values errors
    0 General errors
    0 Response PDUs
    0 TRAP PDUs
SNMP Dispatcher:
   queue 0/75 (current/max), 0 dropped
SNMP Engine:
   queue 0/1000 (current/max), 0 dropped
SNMP TRAP Queue: 0 dropped due to resource failure.

SNMP logging: enabled
    Logging to 192.168.1.200.162, 0/10, 0 sent, 0 dropped.
```

Because SNMP was configured, all of the counters are zero. Notice the output for Chassis. This is set by default and is the system serial number. Table 6-2 defines the commands used in the preceding example.

Table 6-2   *SNMP Configuration Commands Used in Example*

Command	Description
snmp-server community *string* **[RO	RQ]**	Defines the community access string with read-only or read-write privilege. *string* is the password (in this example, cisco123).
snmp-server contact *contact_name*	Sets the system contact string.
snmp-server location *location*	Sets the system location string.
snmp-server host *ip_address* **trap** *community_string*	Sends SNMP traps using the community string to the IP address given.
snmp-server chassis-id *serial_no*	Is set by default to the device serial number. The serial number does not appear in this example but can be changed using this command.
show snmp *additional_options*	Shows the operational state of the SNMP agent on the router. This command allows additional options that are beyond the scope of this text. For a full command option list, see the *Cisco IOS SNMP Support Command Reference* at http://www.cisco.com/en/US/docs/ios-xml/ios/snmp/command/nm-snmp-cr-book.html.

Note   In the configuration examined in the preceding steps, all traps were specified, which is the default. This is most likely not a configuration used in a production network. For more information on configuring traps, see http://www.cisco.com/en/US/tech/tk648/tk362/technologies_tech_note09186a0080094a05.shtml.

The sample configuration illustrates a basic SNMP configuration on router Branch. Community access string cisco123 is configured to permit read-write SNMP access to router Branch. This means that NMS can retrieve and modify MIB objects from router Branch. NMS would retrieve MIB objects, for example, for generating graphs of CPU usage. Any NMS that attempts to gather SNMP information from the router R1 must have **community** set to **cisco123**.

The system contact and location strings of the SNMP agent are also set on the router so that these descriptions can be accessed through the configuration file. Configuring the basic information is recommended because it may be useful when troubleshooting the configuration.

Access control lists (ACL) can also be used to restrict SNMP access to a select group of source IP addresses. In the following example, the NMS is located at 192.168.100.1. An ACL will be applied to the **snmp-server** command to restrict access to the agent from the NMS at that IP address only.

```
access-list 99 permit 192.168.100.1
snmp-server community cisco123 RW 99
```

In this example, the device allows SNMP communication only from the manager at 192.168.100.1. The SNMP manager must use the community string; the ACL just defines which IP addresses(s) an SNMP manager can communicate from.

Syslog Overview

Syslog is a protocol that was initially designed as part of the UNIX operating system. It is defined in RFC 3164. Syslog separates the generation of messages from the storage of messages. This allows a machine to send event notification messages across IP networks to event message collectors (syslog servers) and/or its own buffer or local storage. The default behavior of a Cisco IOS device sends the output from system messages and **debug** privileged EXEC commands to a logging process running within the device.

The logging process controls the distribution of logging messages to various destinations (see Figure 6-8), such as the logging buffer, terminal lines, or a syslog server, depending on device configuration. The process also sends messages to the console by default. Logging services provide a means to gather logging information for monitoring and troubleshooting devices. Most devices, Cisco IOS devices included, allow you to specify which syslog information to capture and where to send the captured syslog messages.

Messages from syslog are assigned a severity level when created. Table 6-3 lists and describes all of the syslog levels.

Table 6-3   *Syslog Logging Levels*

Level	Description
0 – emergency	System is unusable (also called "panic" in some versions of syslog)
1 – alert	Immediate action is needed
2 – critical	Critical condition
3 – error	Error condition
4 – warning	Warning condition
5 – notification	Normal but significant condition
6 – informational	Informational message only
7 – debugging	Appears during debugging only

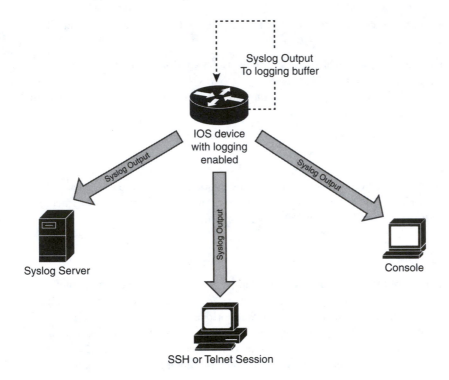

Figure 6-8   *Syslog Destinations*

You can access logged system messages by using the device CLI or by directing them to a properly configured syslog server. The switch or router software saves syslog messages in an internal buffer. System messages can be remotely monitored by viewing the logs on a syslog server or by accessing the device through the network (Telnet or SSH) or the console port. The **terminal monitor** command (disabled by **terminal no monitor** command) allows the monitoring of logging from a network connection.

A standard syslog server generally stores the syslog data in a flat file on the host operating system (in UNIX or Linux, this is /var/log/system.log). There are many commercial and open source syslog servers (quite a few for Windows). There are also NMSs with syslog integrated into the NMS platform. These types of syslog servers and syslog/NMS servers can often take action on, report on, or give custom views of syslog data.

Error messages regarding software or hardware malfunctions are displayed at levels warning (4) through emergency (0). These types of messages mean that the functionality of the device is affected.

Output from the **debug** commands is displayed at the debugging level. Interface up or down transitions and system restart messages are displayed at the notifications level, which is only for information—device functionality is not affected. Syslog servers are preferable to the screen or the log buffer, because in high levels of output, the screen and buffer can be quickly overrun.

Syslog Message Format

Syslog messages generated by Cisco IOS are as follows:

```
seq no:timestamp: %facility-severity-MNEMONIC:description
```

Table 6-4 defines all of the fields, which is followed by an example.

Table 6-4   *Syslog Message Format*

Field	Definition
seq no	Stamps log messages with a sequence number. The **service sequence-numbers** global configuration command must be configured for a sequence number. Configuring this command is a good idea, as it allows for numeration to determine order of log messages.
timestamp	Date and time of message. The **service timestamps log [datetime | log]** global configuration command must be configured. Configuring this command is a good idea, so event times can be determined. Device should also have an accurate time and/or clock configured.
facility	Originating facility of the message (interface, SNMP, etc.).
severity	0–7 severity code; see Table 6-3 for more details.
MNEMONIC	Single-word description of the message.
description	Brief text string defining the message; see Table 6-3 for a list of these messages.

The following example is a syslog message indicating that the FastEthernet0/2 interface has gone up:

```
*Apr 18 10:05:55.423: %LINEPROTO-5-UPDOWN: Line protocol on Interface
FastEthernet0/2, changed state to up
```

The next example is a syslog message indicating that the router has been requested to reload via a **reload** command:

```
*Apr 18 10:09:11.219:: %SYS-5-RELOAD: Reload requested  by console. Reload Reason:
Reload Command.
```

Syslog Configuration

To configure syslog, specify a syslog server host as a destination for syslog messages. Then indicate the message levels by severity and limit the syslog messages sent to syslog server based on the severity. When the syslog command is configured, it does not have to use IP addresses. If the router is configured to use hostnames, the configuration can use hostnames. The router would either need to be configured with a static host name using the **ip host** command or configured to use a DNS server with the **ip name-server** command. Examples of both are listed below:

```
R1(config)# ip host NMS1 10.1.10.100

R1(config)# ip name-server 192.168.50.50
```

The following provides the configuration of R1, shown in Figure 6-9, to send informational traps to the SNMP manager at 10.1.10.100:

```
R1(config)# logging 10.1.10.100
R1(config)# logging trap informational
```

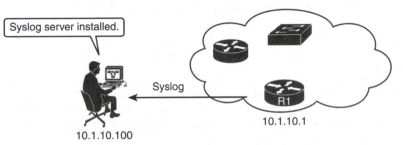

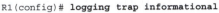

Figure 6-9   *Syslog Example*

The **logging** command identifies a syslog server host to receive logging messages. Figure 6-10 illustrates that if you issue the command more than once, it will add a list of syslog servers that will all receive the logging messages.

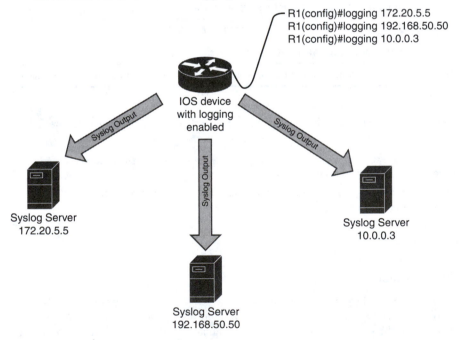

Figure 6-10   *Multiple Syslog Destinations*

NetFlow Overview

NetFlow is a Cisco technology that provides statistics on packets flowing through devices in the network. It allows extremely granular and accurate traffic measurements and high-level aggregated traffic collection from routers, switches, and other NetFlow-capable devices (such as Cisco Nexus and ASA devices).

Cisco IOS sends NetFlow data to an application, called a NetFlow collector. A NetFlow collector can be a free-standing application or part of an NMS. The relationship between a NetFlow-enabled device and the collector is illustrated in Figure 6-11.

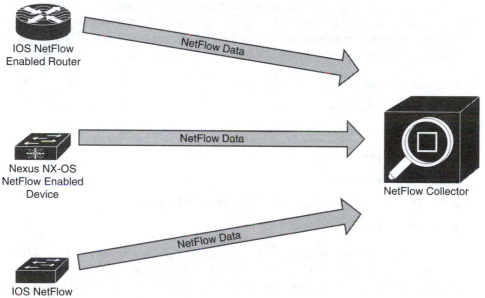

Figure 6-11 *NetFlow Devices and NetFlow Collector*

Some of the purposes for which NetFlow data can be used include the following:

- Analyzing application and network usage

- Analyzing network productivity and utilization of network resources

- Gauging the impact of changes to the network

- Detecting abnormal network behavior

- Long-term trending for network planning

- Identifying potential problem sources

Note   NetFlow version 9, the latest version as of this writing, is now referred to as Flexible NetFlow in some Cisco documentation.

NetFlow is transparent to the existing network, including end stations, application software, and non-NetFlow network devices. NetFlow capture and export are configured and performed independently on each internetworking device. Notably in Figure 6-11, NetFlow operates under both Cisco IOS and Cisco NX-OS.

A NetFlow network flow is defined as a unidirectional stream of packets between a given source and destination. The source and destination are each defined by a network layer IP address and transport layer source and destination port numbers. Specifically, a flow is defined by the combination of seven key fields:

- Source IP address

- Destination IP address

- Source port number

- Destination port number

- Layer 3 protocol type

- ToS (Type of Service; a field in the IP header used for priority)

- Input logical interface

There are several NetFlow collectors and analyzers available both commercially and free. These include Cisco NetFlow Collector (NFC). These tools facilitate the analysis of the traffic on your network by showing the top talkers, top listeners, top protocols, and other key metrics. They allow visibility on traffic types (web, mail, FTP, peer-to-peer, etc.) and patterns (which devices are sending and receiving traffic, by types and volume). Figure 6-12 provides a sample report of data collection and analysis.

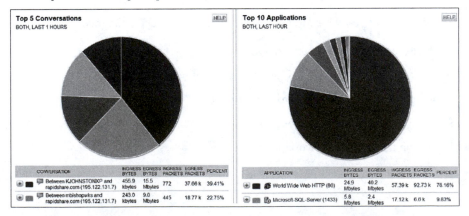

Figure 6-12   *NetFlow Collector Reporting*

NetFlow Architecture

The purpose of the NetFlow collector is to grab flow export data from multiple routers and filter and aggregate the data according to the policies of the customer. The data is collected and stored based on the "cafeteria tray" model (keep what you want and leave the rest). Figure 6-13 graphically represents how the data is filtered and aggregated. Storing this summarized or aggregated view of the data instead of raw flow data minimizes storage requirements.

An organization may use more than one collector. For example, one collector may store a view of the data for analyzing performance and utilization, and another collector may store another view of the data for accounting and billing purposes.

The collector can then be used to feed an analyzer or other reporting tool (if the collector and the reporting/analyzer tool are separate devices/tools).

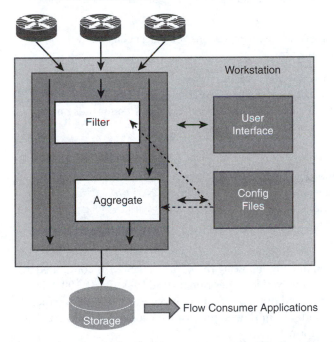

Figure 6-13 *Filtering and Aggregating NetFlow Data*

The NetFlow collector passively listens to specified UDP ports to receive and process exported NetFlow datagrams. The NetFlow collector application provides a solution that scales to accommodate consumption of NetFlow export data from multiple devices in order to support key flow applications, include accounting, billing, and network planning/ monitoring.

A NetFlow consumer application, such as a NetFlow analyzer, takes the data and provides the means to do near real-time visualization and analysis of recorded and aggregated flow data. You can set up a query that can specify the device, the aggregation scheme and the time interval that you wish to view and then retrieve the relevant data. You can then sort and visualize the data in a manner that makes sense for the interpreters of the data (bar charts, pie charts, or histograms of the sorted reports). The information can also be exported to spreadsheets, such as Excel, for more detailed analysis, trending, reporting, and so on.

NetFlow Configuration

The steps to configure NetFlow on a device are as follows:

Step 1.   Configure NetFlow data capture. NetFlow can capture data from ingress (incoming) and egress (outgoing) packets.

Step 2.   Configure NetFlow data export. You need to specify the IP address or host-name of the NetFlow collector, and the UDP port that the NetFlow collector listens to.

Step 3.   Configure the NetFlow data export version. You can specify the version of the NetFlow data export format.

Step 4.   Verify NetFlow operation and statistics. After you have configured NetFlow, you can analyze the exported data on a workstation running an application such as NetFlow Collector (NFC) or using several **show** commands on the router itself.

> **Note**   NetFlow consumes additional system resources, especially memory. If the device has memory constraints, you might want to preset the size of the NetFlow cache so that it contains a smaller number of entries. The default cache size varies with the platform type and Cisco IOS version.

In Figure 6-14, and the configuration directly following the figure, router R1 is configured as a NetFlow device, sending the data to the NetFlow collector at IP address 10.1.10.100, UDP port 99. Traffic that is being either received or transmitted by the interface GigabitEthernet0/1 is captured using the **ip flow** command. The **ip flow-export version** command specifies that the export packet uses the version 9 format.

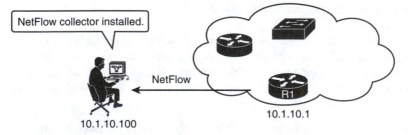

Figure 6-14   *NetFlow Example*

The following commands are used in the configuration of router R1 in Figure 6-14:

```
R1(config)# interface GigabitEthernet0/1
R1(config-if)# ip flow ingress
R1(config-if)# ip flow egress
R1(config-if)# exit
R1(config)# ip flow-export destination 10.1.10.100 99
R1(config)# ip flow-export version 9
```

Table 6-5 describes these commands.

Table 6-5 *Configuration Commands Used in the NetFlow Example*

Command	Description
ip flow {ingress | egress}	Configures NetFlow on the interface. Captures traffic that is being received or being transmitted by the interface.
ip flow-export destination *ip-address udp-port*	Specifies the IP address and UDP port that the NetFlow collector is listening at.
ip flow-export version *version*	Specifies the NetFlow version. Version 9 is the latest as of this writing and is not backward compatible with other versions.

Verifying NetFlow Operation

NetFlow operation can be verified in the device using **show** commands.

The **show ip flow interface** command is used to verify whether NetFlow is enabled on an interface. In Example 6-2, NetFlow is enabled in ingress and not the egress direction on the GigabitEthernet0/1 interface.

Example 6-2 *Verifying Flow on Interface*

```
R1# show ip flow interface
GigabitEthernet0/1
  ip flow ingress
```

The **show ip flow export** command is used to verify the status and statistics for NetFlow accounting data export. In Example 6-3, the configured destination for NetFlow export is 10.1.10.100 using UDP port 99. The version of the configured flow export is version 9.

Example 6-3   *Verifying Flow Statistics and Status*

```
R1# show ip flow export
Flow export v9 is enabled for main cache
    Export source and destination details :
    VRF ID : Default
        Destination(1) 10.1.10.100 (99)
    Version 9 flow records
     43 flows exported in 15 udp datagrams
```

The **show ip cache flow** command is used to display a summary of NetFlow statistics on the device, as shown in Example 6-4. This command displays which protocols use the highest volume of traffic and the path that the traffic takes.

Example 6-4   *Reviewing NetFlow Statistics with* **show ip cache flow**

```
R1# show ip cache flow
<output omitted>
IP Flow Switching Cache, 278544 bytes
   2 active, 4094 inactive, 31 added
   6374 ager polls, 0 flow alloc failures
   Active flows timeout in 30 minutes
   Inactive flows timeout in 15 seconds
IP Sub Flow Cache, 34056 bytes
   2 active, 1022 inactive, 31 added, 31 added to flow
   0 alloc failures, 0 force free
   1 chunk, 0 chunks added
    last clearing of statistics 00:49:48
Protocol     Total Flows  Packets Bytes  Packets  Active(Sec)  Idle(Sec)
-----------  Flows /Sec   /Flow   /Pkt   /Sec     /Flow        /Flow
TCP-Telnet   19    0.0    19      58     0.1      6.5          11.7
TCP-WWW      14    0.0    8       202    0.0      0.0          1.5
TCP-other    2     0.0    9       98     0.0      2.2          8.9

<output omitted>
SrcIf   SrcIPaddress  DstIf     DstIPaddress  Pr  SrcP  DstP  Pkts
Gi0/1   172.16.1.100  Gi0/0.10  10.1.10.100   01  0000  0000  1341
```

Router Initialization and Configuration

When a Cisco router boots, the router executes a set of actions. These actions are performed in a specific order. In the boot process, the router makes a decision regarding the next step in the process. Knowledge of the boot sequence is important when troubleshooting or configuring a device. Carefully managing Cisco IOS images and configuration files reduces device downtime and maintains best practices.

Cisco IOS image files contain the Cisco IOS Software that is required for a Cisco device to operate. The device configuration files contain a set of user-defined configuration commands that customize the functionality of a Cisco device.

Router Internal Component Review

A review of the components of a router is important to help explain and understand how a router boots and how its software works. The major internal components of a Cisco router include

- CPU

- Interfaces

- RAM

- Flash memory

- NVRAM

Figure 6-15 displays a logical diagram of these major components and how they are interconnected.

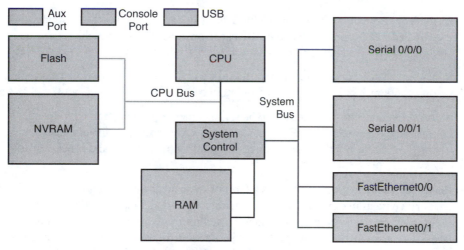

Figure 6-15   *Logical Diagram of Router Components*

Note   Older devices had physical ROM. This was dedicated ROM inside the router. This functionality has been consolidated in the flash memory in routers.

A router is a specialized computer, similar in many ways to a PC. Routers have many of the same hardware and software components that are found in other computers, such as:

■ **Central processing unit (CPU):** The CPU executes operating system instructions, such as system initialization, routing functions, and switching functions.

■ **Random-access memory (RAM):** RAM stores the instructions and data that the CPU needs in order to execute. This read/write memory contains the software and data structures that allow the router to function. RAM is volatile memory and loses its content when the router is powered down or restarted. However, the router also contains permanent storage areas, such as ROM, flash, and NVRAM. RAM is used to store components such as:

  ■ **Operating system:** Cisco IOS Software is copied into RAM during bootup.

  ■ **Running configuration file:** This file stores the configuration commands that Cisco IOS Software is currently using on the router. With few exceptions, all commands that are configured on the router are stored in the running configuration file, which is also known as "running-config."

  ■ **IP routing table:** This file stores information about directly connected and remote networks. It is used to determine the best path to forward the packet.

  ■ **Address Resolution Protocol (ARP) cache:** This cache contains the IP address-to-MAC address mappings, like the ARP cache on a PC. The ARP cache is used on routers that have LAN interfaces such as Ethernet interfaces.

  ■ **Packet buffer:** Packets are temporarily stored in a buffer when they are received on an interface or before they exit an interface.

  ■ **Additional memory caches and tables:** Other memory caches and tables needed for Cisco IOS operation are also contained in RAM. Examples include the NetFlow cache and the Cisco Express Forwarding (CEF) table, and other processes.

■ **Read-only memory (ROM):** ROM is a form of permanent storage. This type of memory contains microcode for basic functions to start and maintain the router. The ROM contains the ROM monitor, which is used for router disaster-recovery functions, such as password recovery. ROM, like a hard drive, is nonvolatile; it maintains the memory contents even when the power is off. ROM is not listed in the diagram because, as stated above, in newer devices the function of ROM has been incorporated into a sectioned-off portion of the flash memory.

■ **Flash memory:** Flash memory is nonvolatile computer memory that can be electrically written and erased. Flash is used as permanent storage for the operating system. In most models of Cisco routers, the Cisco IOS image is permanently stored in flash memory (typically compressed) and copied (and decompressed, if compressed) into RAM during the bootup process, where the CPU then executes it. Some older models of Cisco routers run the Cisco IOS image directly from flash. Flash consists of single in-line memory modules (SIMM) or Personal Computer Memory Card

International Association (PCMCIA) cards, which can be upgraded to increase the amount of flash memory. Flash memory does not lose its contents when the router loses power or is restarted. USB drives can also be used as flash memory.

- **Nonvolatile RAM (NVRAM):** NVRAM does not lose its information when power is turned off. Cisco IOS Software uses NVRAM as permanent storage for the startup configuration (startup-config) file. All configuration changes are stored in the running-config file in RAM, and with few exceptions, Cisco IOS Software implements them immediately. To save those changes in case the router is restarted or loses power, the running configuration must be copied to NVRAM, where it is stored as the startup-config file.

- **Configuration register:** The configuration register is used to control how the router boots. The configuration register value is stored in NVRAM.

- **Interfaces:** Interfaces are the physical connections to the external world for the router, and include the following:

  - Ethernet, Fast Ethernet, and Gigabit Ethernet

  - Asynchronous and synchronous serial

  - USB interface

  - Console and auxiliary serial ports

There are many types of routers and switches. The majority have the same basic components, which may be located in different areas depending on form factor. There are routing devices that contain different architectures, such as the Cisco Carrier Routing System (CRS) series of routers. These types of devices, such as the CRS, are outside the scope of this book and the CCNA certification.

ROM Functions

Three major areas of microcode are generally contained in ROM, as logically represented in Figure 6-16:

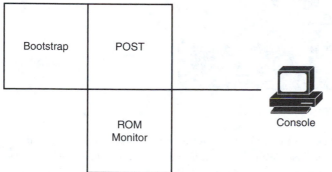

Figure 6-16 *Logical Representation of ROM*

- **Bootstrap code:** This is used to bring up the router during initialization. It reads the configuration register to determine how to boot. If instructed to do so, the ROM loads the Cisco IOS Software.

- **Power-on self-test (POST):** This is the microcode that is used to test the basic functionality of the router hardware and determine which components are present.

- **ROM monitor (ROMmon):** This area includes a low-level operating system that is normally used for manufacturing, testing, troubleshooting, and password recovery. In ROM monitor mode, the router has no routing or IP capabilities.

Router Power-Up Sequence

When a Cisco router boots, it includes a series of steps, such as:

- Performing tests

- Finding and loading the Cisco IOS Software

- Finding and loading configurations

- Running the Cisco IOS Software

Understanding the sequence of events that occurs during the power up (boot) of a router is fundamental and critical to accomplishing operational tasks and troubleshooting. When a router is powered up, the following steps are executed, as shown in Figure 6-17:

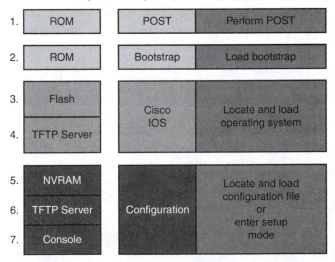

Figure 6-17   *Router Boot Sequence*

Step 1.   Perform POST. This event is a series of hardware tests that verifies that all components of the Cisco router are functional. During this test, the router also determines which hardware is present. POST executes from microcode that is resident in the system ROM.

Step 2.   Load and run bootstrap code. Bootstrap code is used to perform subsequent events, such as locating the Cisco IOS Software, loading it into RAM, and then running it. When the Cisco IOS Software is loaded and running, the bootstrap code is not used until the next time that the router is reloaded or power-cycled.

Step 3.   Find the Cisco IOS Software. The bootstrap code determines the location of the Cisco IOS Software to be run. Normally, the Cisco IOS Software image is located in the flash memory, but it can also be stored in other places, such as a TFTP server. The configuration register and configuration file determine where the Cisco IOS Software images are located and which image file to use.

Step 4.   Load the Cisco IOS Software. Once the bootstrap code has found the proper image, it then loads it into RAM and starts the Cisco IOS Software. Some older routers do not load the Cisco IOS Software image into RAM, but execute it directly from flash memory instead.

Step 5.   Find the configuration. After the Cisco IOS Software is loaded, the bootstrap program searches for the startup-config file in NVRAM.

Step 6.   Load the configuration. If a startup-config file is found in NVRAM, the Cisco IOS Software loads it into RAM as the running configuration and executes the commands in the file, one line at a time. The running-config file contains interface addresses, starts routing processes, configures router passwords, and defines other characteristics of the router. If a configuration does not exist, the router enters the setup utility or attempts an AutoInstall to look for a configuration file from a TFTP server.

Step 7.   Run the configured Cisco IOS Software. When the prompt is displayed, the router is running the Cisco IOS Software with the current running-config file. The network administrator can begin using Cisco IOS commands on this router.

Configuration Register

A Cisco IOS device has a 16-bit configuration register in NVRAM. Each bit has value 1 (on or set) or value 0 (off or clear), and each bit setting affects the router behavior upon the next reload power cycle.

You can use the 16-bit configuration register to

- Force the router to boot into the ROM monitor.
- Select a boot source and default boot filename.
- Control broadcast addresses.
- Ignore the startup-configuration. This is usually done to recover a lost password.
- Change the console line speed.

The lowest 4 bits (the rightmost hexadecimal number) are called the boot field and specify how a router locates the Cisco IOS image file. The default value for the configuration register is 0x2102.

Major configuration register values are as follows:

- **0x2102:** Normal operation. Load the Cisco IOS image from flash and load the default startup configuration file.

- **0x2100:** Load into ROMmon mode.

- **0x2142:** Load Cisco IOS from flash and ignore the startup configuration.

Note   For a listing of configuration register values and how to interpret configuration register values, see "Use of the Configuration Register on All Cisco Routers" at http://www. cisco.com/en/US/products/hw/routers/ps133/products_tech_note09186a008022493f. shtml.

The configuration register is discussed in the next section and in the "Cisco IOS Password Recovery" section later in the chapter.

Changing the Configuration Register

Prior to altering the configuration register, determine how the router is currently loading the software image. The **show version** command displays the current configuration register value. The last line of the display contains the configuration register value, as shown in Example 6-5.

Example 6-5   *Configuring Register Setting*

```
Branch# show version
<output omitted>
Configuration register is 0x2102
```

You can change the default configuration register setting with the **config-register** global configuration command, as shown in Example 6-6. The configuration register is a 16-bit register. The lowest 4 bits of the configuration register (bits 3, 2, 1, and 0) form the boot field. A hexadecimal number is used as the argument to set the value of the configuration register. As stated in the previous section, the default value of the configuration register is 0x2102.

Example 6-6   *Changing the Configuration from the Cisco IOS Command Line*

```
R1# configure terminal
R1(config)# config-register 0x2101
R1(config)# exit
R1# show version
<output omitted>
Configuration register is 0x2102 (will be 0x2101 at next reload)
```

The **show version** command is used to verify changes in the configuration register setting. The new configuration register value takes effect when the router reloads.

In Example 6-6, the **show version** command indicates that the configuration register setting of 0x2101 will be used during the next router reload. The new configuration register value will affect the router to boot the first Cisco IOS image found in flash.

When using the **config-register** command, all 16 bits of the configuration register are set. Be careful to modify only the bits that you are trying to change, such as the boot field, and leave the other bits as they are. Remember that the other configuration register bits perform functions that include selecting the console line speed and determining whether to use the saved configuration in NVRAM.

The configuration register also can be changed in ROMmon mode. The primary reason for changing the configuration register in ROMmon mode is for password recovery. Password recovery is discussed later in this chapter in the "Cisco IOS Password Recovery" section.

Locating the Cisco IOS Image to Load

When a Cisco router boots, it searches for the Cisco IOS image using a specific sequence. It looks for the location that is specified in the configuration register, flash memory, and a TFTP server. Figure 6-18 graphically represents the process of locating the Cisco IOS image.

The bootstrap code is responsible for locating the Cisco IOS Software and uses the following steps:

Step 1.   The bootstrap code checks the boot field of the configuration register.

For example, a configuration register value of 0x2102 (the 0x indicates that the digits that follow are in hexadecimal notation) has a boot field value of 0x2. The rightmost digit in the register value is 2 and represents the lower 4 bits of the register. Table 6-6 displays how different values of the boot field affect locating the Cisco IOS image.

Order of locating Cisco IOS image:

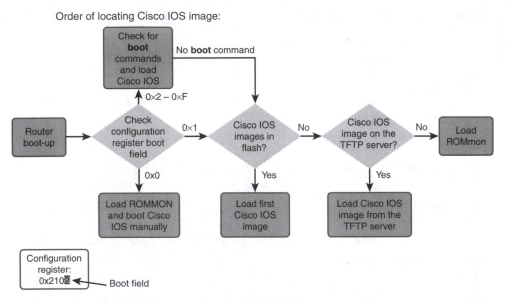

Figure 6-18 *Flowchart for Locating the Cisco IOS Image*

Table 6-6 *Configuration Register Values*

Configuration Register Boot Field Value	Description
0x0	At the next power cycle or reload, the router boots to the ROMmon.
0x1	Boots the first image in flash memory as a system image.
0x2 to 0xf	At the next power cycle or reload, the router sequentially processes each **boot system** command in global configuration mode.

Step 2.   If the boot field value of the configuration register is from 0x2 to 0xF, the bootstrap code parses the startup configuration file in NVRAM for the boot system commands that specify the name and location of the Cisco IOS Software image to load. Several boot system commands can be entered in sequence to provide a fault-tolerant boot plan. The **boot system** command is a global configuration command that allows you to specify the source for the Cisco IOS Software image to load. The following examples show some of the syntax options available.

The following example boots the system boot image from the flash device:

```
Branch(config)# boot system flash:c2900-universalk9-mz.SPA.152-4.M1.bin
```

The following example illustrates a configuration that specifies the TFTP server as the source of the Cisco IOS image, with ROMmon as the backup:

```
Branch(config)# boot system tftp://c2900-universalk9-mz.SPA.152-4.M1.bin
Branch(config)# boot system rom
```

Step 3.   If the configuration has no **boot system** commands, the router defaults to loading the first valid Cisco IOS image in flash memory and runs it.

Step 4.   If a valid Cisco IOS image is not found in flash memory, the router attempts to boot from a network TFTP server using the boot field value as part of the Cisco IOS image filename.

Step 5.   After six unsuccessful attempts to locate the TFTP server, the router loads ROMmon.

Note   The procedure of locating the Cisco IOS image depends on the Cisco router platform and default configuration register values. The preceding process is based on the Cisco 3900 Series, 2900 Series, and 1900 Series Integrated Services Routers.

Loading a Cisco IOS Image File

When the router locates a valid Cisco IOS image file in flash memory, the Cisco IOS image is normally loaded into RAM to run. If the image needs to be loaded from flash memory into RAM, it must first be decompressed. After the file is decompressed into RAM, it is started. When the Cisco IOS Software begins to load, you may see a string of pound signs (#) while the image is being decompressed, as shown in Example 6-7.

Example 6-7   *Cisco IOS Boot*

```
System Bootstrap, Version 15.0(1r)M15, RELEASE SOFTWARE (fc1)
Technical Support: http://www.cisco.com/techsupport
Copyright (c) 2011 by cisco Systems, Inc.
Total memory size = 512 MB - On-board = 512 MB, DIMM0 = 0 MB
CISCO2901/K9 platform with 524288 Kbytes of main memory
Main memory is configured to 72/-1(On-board/DIMM0) bit mode with ECC enabled
Readonly ROMmon initialized
program load complete, entry point: 0x80803000, size: 0x1b340
program load complete, entry point: 0x80803000, size: 0x1b340
IOS Image Load Test
```

```
Digitally Signed Release Software
program load complete, entry point: 0x81000000, size: 0x5d433c0
Self decompressing the image:
################################################################################
################################################################################
################################################################################
################################################################################
################################################################################
################################################################################
################################################################################
############################## [OK]
<output omitted>
```

The **show version** command can be used to help verify and troubleshoot some of the basic hardware and software components of the router. It displays information regarding the version of the Cisco IOS Software that is currently running on the router, the bootstrap program, and information about the hardware configuration, including the amount of system memory. Example 6-8 illustrates the full output of the **show version** command.

Example 6-8   *Running the show version Command on a Cisco 2951 ISR*

```
Branch# show version
cisco IOS Software, C2951 Software (C2951-UNIVERSALK9-M), Version 15.1(4)M4, RELEASE
SOFTWARE (fc1)
Technical Support: http://www.cisco.com/techsupport
Copyright (c) 1986-2012 by cisco Systems, Inc.
Compiled Tue 20-Mar-12 19:11 by prod_rel_team


ROM: System Bootstrap, Version 15.0(1r)M16, RELEASE SOFTWARE (fc1)


Branch uptime is 15 weeks, 3 days, 14 hours, 4 minutes
System returned to ROM by power-on
System restarted at 16:56:38 MST Mon Feb 18 2013
System image file is "flash0:c2951-universalk9-mz.SPA.151-4.M4.bin"
Last reload type: Normal Reload


This product contains cryptographic features and is subject to United
States and local country laws governing import, export, transfer and
use. Delivery of cisco cryptographic products does not imply
third-party authority to import, export, distribute or use encryption.
Importers, exporters, distributors and users are responsible for
compliance with U.S. and local country laws. By using this product you
agree to comply with applicable laws and regulations. If you are unable
to comply with U.S. and local laws, return this product immediately.
```

A summary of U.S. laws governing cisco cryptographic products may be found at:
http://www.cisco.com/wwl/export/crypto/tool/stqrg.html

If you require further assistance please contact us by sending email to
export@cisco.com.

cisco CISCO2951/K9 (revision 1.1) with 479232K/45056K bytes of memory.
Processor board ID FTX1234ABCD
4 Gigabit Ethernet interfaces
2 Serial interfaces
2 terminal lines
2 Channelized T1/PRI ports
1 Virtual Private Network (VPN) Module
1 Services Module (SM) with Services Ready Engine (SRE)
    cisco Wide Area Application Services Software 5.0.3a (b7 Nov 4 2012 12:01:55) in
slot/sub-slot 1/0
DRAM configuration is 72 bits wide with parity enabled.
255K bytes of non-volatile configuration memory.
250880K bytes of ATA System CompactFlash 0 (Read/Write)

License Info:

License UDI:

Device#   PID   SN
----
*0   CISCO2951/K9   FTX1234ABCD

Technology Package License Information for Module:'c2951'

Technology   Technology-package   Technology-package
              Current   Type   Next reboot
----
ipbase   ipbasek9   Permanent   ipbasek9
security   securityk9 Permanent   securityk9
uc   None   None   None
data   None   None   None

Configuration register is 0x2102

The output from the **show version** command includes the following:

- **Cisco IOS version:** The running Cisco IOS version.

```
cisco IOS Software, C2951 Software (C2951-UNIVERSALK9-M), Version 15.1(4)M4,
RELEASE SOFTWARE (fc1)
```

- **ROM bootstrap program:** Version of the system bootstrap software, which is stored in ROM and initially used to boot the router.

```
ROM: System Bootstrap, Version 15.0(1r)M16, RELEASE SOFTWARE (fc1)
```

    Location of Cisco IOS image:

```
System image file is "flash0:c2951-universalk9-mz.SPA.151-4.M4.bin"
```

- **Interfaces:** This section of the output displays the physical interfaces on the router. In this example, the Cisco 2951 router has four Gigabit Ethernet interfaces and two serial interfaces. It also has an optional VPN encryption module and a Cisco Wide Area Application Services (WAAS) module.

```
4 Gigabit Ethernet interfaces
2 Serial interfaces
2 terminal lines
2 Channelized T1/PRI ports
1 Virtual Private Network (VPN) Module
1 Services Module (SM) with Services Ready Engine (SRE)
   cisco Wide Area Application Services Software 5.0.3a (b7 Nov  4 2012
12:01:55) in slot/sub-slot 1/0
```

- **Amount of NVRAM:**

```
255K bytes of non-volatile configuration memory.
```

- **Amount of flash:**

```
250880K bytes of ATA System CompactFlash 0 (Read/Write)
```

- **Configuration register:** The last line of the **show version** command displays the current value of the software configuration register in hexadecimal format. The configuration register is used to modify the default boot behavior of the device. In this example, the default configuration register value is listed.

```
Configuration register is 0x2102
```

Selecting and Loading the Configuration

After the Cisco IOS Software image is loaded and started, the router must be configured to operate properly. Figure 6-19 shows the logic used to locate a configuration file.

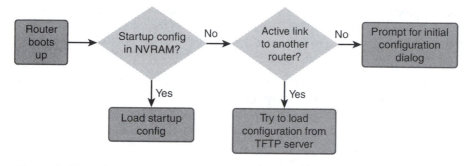

Figure 6-19 *Flowchart for Locating the Configuration File*

If there is an existing saved configuration file (startup-config) in NVRAM, it is executed. If there isn't, the router either begins AutoInstall or enters the setup utility.

If the startup configuration file does not exist in NVRAM, the router may search for a TFTP server. If the router detects that it has an active link to another configured router, it sends a broadcast searching for a configuration file across the active link. This condition causes the router to pause, but you will eventually see a console message like the following one:

```
%Error opening tftp://255.255.255.255/network-confg(Timed out)
%Error opening tftp://255.255.255.255/cisconet.cfg (Timed out)
```

Note   The 255.255.255.255 address in IPv4 is the broadcast address for any local IP subnet the interface is connected to (no matter what the IP address or subnet mask of the interface is). Devices routing IPv4 do not propagate this broadcast.

The setup utility prompts the user at the console for specific design information to create a basic initial configuration on the router, as shown in Example 6-9.

Example 6-9 *Autoconfiguration in an Unconfigured Router*

```
<output omitted>
cisco CISCO2901/K9 (revision 1.0) with 483328K/40960K bytes of memory.
Processor board ID FCZ1642C5XJ
2 Gigabit Ethernet interfaces
1 Serial(sync/async) interface
1 terminal line
DRAM configuration is 64 bits wide with parity enabled.
255K bytes of non-volatile configuration memory.
250880K bytes of ATA System CompactFlash 0 (Read/Write)
--- System Configuration Dialog ---
Would you like to enter the initial configuration dialog? [yes/no]:
```

The **show running-config** and **show startup-config** commands are among the most commonly used Cisco IOS Software EXEC commands, because they show, respectively, the current running configuration in RAM on the router, and the startup configuration file in NVRAM that the router uses on the next restart.

If the words "Current configuration" are displayed, as in Example 6-10, the active running configuration from RAM is being displayed.

Example 6-10   *Running Configuration*

```
Branch# show running-config
Building configuration...
Current configuration : 1318 bytes
!
! Last configuration change at 13:11:38 UTC Thu Mar 28 2013
! NVRAM config last updated at 13:11:38 UTC Thu Mar 28 2013
! NVRAM config last updated at 13:11:38 UTC Thu Mar 28 2013
version 15.2
<output omitted>
```

If there is a message at the top indicating how much nonvolatile memory is being used ("Using 1318 out of 262136 bytes," for example), as shown in Example 6-11, the startup configuration file from NVRAM is being displayed.

Example 6-11   *Startup Configuration*

```
Branch# show startup-config
Using 1318 out of 262136 bytes
!
! Last configuration change at 13:11:38 UTC Thu Mar 28 2013
! NVRAM config last updated at 13:11:38 UTC Thu Mar 28 2013
! NVRAM config last updated at 13:11:38 UTC Thu Mar 28 2013
version 15.2
<output omitted>
```

Cisco IOS File System and Devices

The Cisco IOS File System (IFS) feature provides a single interface for all of the file systems that a router uses. The availability of the network can be at risk if the configuration of a router or the operating system is compromised. This could be malicious, accidental, or due to a hardware failure. To avoid these problems, save, back up, and restore configuration and Cisco IOS images.

IFS allows you to create, navigate, and manipulate directories on a Cisco device. Which directories are available depends on the platform. Cisco IFS, illustrated in Figure 6-20, provides a single interface to all the file systems that a Cisco router uses.

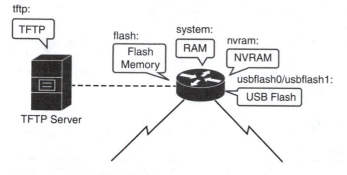

Figure 6-20 *Cisco IFS*

The following are the IFS components:

■ Flash memory files systems

■ Network-accessible file systems: TFTP, Remote Copy Protocol (RCP), and FTP

■ Any other endpoint for reading or writing data (such as NVRAM, the running configuration in RAM, etc.)

An important feature of Cisco IFS is the URL convention that specifies files on network devices and the network. The URL prefix designates the file system.

Example 6-12 displays the output of the **show file systems** command, which lists all of the available file systems on the Cisco 2901 router. This command provides insightful information, such as the amount of available and free memory, the type of file system, and its permissions. Permissions include read-only (as indicated by the "ro" flag), write-only (as indicated by the "wo" flag), and read and write (as indicated by the "rw" flag).

Example 6-12 *Cisco IFS Example*

```
Branch# show file systems
File Systems:

     Size(b)       Free(b)        Type      Flags      Prefixes
*    15998976      5135872        flash     rw         flash:
        -             -           opaque    rw         bs:
        -             -           opaque    rw         vb:
     524288        520138         nvram     rw         nvram:
        -             -           network   rw         tftp:
        -             -           opaque    rw         null:
        -             -           opaque    rw         system:
```

```
-              -              opaque    ro        xmodem:
-              -              opaque    ro        ymodem:
-              -              opaque    wo        syslog:
```

The flash file system has an asterisk preceding it, which indicates the current default file system. The bootable Cisco IOS Software is located in flash; therefore, the pound symbol (#) that is appended to the flash listing indicates a bootable disk. Table 6-7 contains the common prefixes used to denote file repositories:

Table 6-7   *IFS File Repository Types*

Prefix	Description
flash:	Flash memory. This prefix is available on all platforms. For platforms that do not have a device named flash, the flash: prefix is aliased to slot0. Therefore, the flash: prefix can be used to refer to the main flash memory storage area on all platforms.
ftp:	FTP network server.
http:	HTTP network server.
rcp:	RCP network server, an insecure copy program originally designed for the UNIX operating system.
system:	Contains the system memory, including the current running configuration.
tftp:	TFTP network server.
usbflash0, usbflash1	USB flash disk.
nvram:	NVRAM file system.

The **copy** command allows you to move files from different points on Cisco IFS and network servers. It is demonstrated in the next section.

Note   For more information on managing Cisco IFS, see *The Integrated File System Configuration Guide, Cisco IOS Release 15M&T* at http://www.cisco.com/en/US/docs/ios-xml/ios/ifs/configuration/15mt/ifs-15-mt-book.pdf.

Managing Cisco IOS Images

Production internetworks often span wide areas and contain multiple routers and switches. It is prudent to retain a backup copy of the Cisco IOS Software image and configuration in case the system image or configuration in the device becomes corrupted or accidentally erased. Widely distributed routers need a source or backup location. Using a network server allows image and configuration uploads and downloads over the network. The network server can be another router, a workstation, or a host system running TFTP, FTP, SFTP, or one of the other supported protocols.

Storage of Cisco IOS Software images and configuration files on a central server enables control and archive of the number and revision level of Cisco IOS images and configuration files that are required for network operation. Figure 6-21 gives the common example of using a TFTP server for a centralized repository of Cisco IOS images and configuration. The server can accept files from router flash, and transfer files to the router flash.

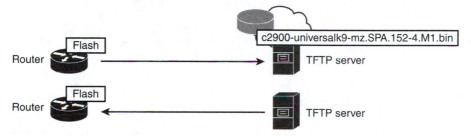

Figure 6-21 *Network Server for Cisco IOS Images and Configuration*

Interpreting Cisco IOS Image Filenames

In preparing to deploy or upgrade a Cisco IOS device, you must select a suitable Cisco IOS image with the correct feature set and required version. The Cisco IOS image file is based on a special naming convention. The name for the Cisco IOS image file contains multiple parts, each with a specific meaning. Understanding this naming convention is important when upgrading and selecting a Cisco IOS image. Figure 6-22 breaks down a sample filename.

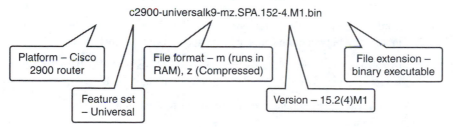

Figure 6-22 *Cisco IOS File Naming*

The filename in Figure 6-22 is explained as follows:

- The first part (c2900) identifies the platform on which the image runs. In this example, the platform is a Cisco 2900 router.

- The second part (universal) specifies the feature set. In this case, "universal" refers to the universal, single image set, which includes IP Base, Security, Unified Communications, and Data feature sets. Each router is activated for the IP Base feature set by default. Other feature sets require activation.

- The third part (mz) indicates where the image runs and if the file is compressed. In Figure 6-22, "mz" shows that the file runs from RAM and is compressed.

- The fourth part (15.2(4)M1) is the version number.

- The final part (bin) is the file extension. This extension indicates that this file is a binary executable file.

Note   The Cisco IOS Software naming conventions, field meaning, image content, and other details are subject to change and have historically changed over time.

Creating a Cisco IOS Image Backup

To maintain network operations with minimum downtime, it is necessary to have procedures in place for backing up Cisco IOS images. That way, you can quickly copy an image back to a router, which may be necessary due to a corrupted image, an erased image, or a hardware replacement. A TFTP or other network server may be used, as shown in Figure 6-23.

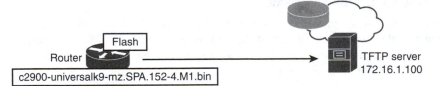

Figure 6-23   *Creating a Cisco IOS Image Backup*

The steps to create a backup of a Cisco IOS image to a TFTP server are as follows. Assume that there is connectivity between the Cisco IOS device and the network server.

Step 1.   Verify that the host operating system on the TFTP server has sufficient disk space to accommodate the Cisco IOS Software image (see Figure 6-24).

Step 2.   Use the **show flash0:** command on the router to determine the size of the Cisco IOS image file:

```
Branch# show flash0:

-#- --length-- -----date/time------ path

1      97794040   Mar 28 1969 00:00:00 +00:00 c2900-universalk9-mz.
SPA.152-4.M1.bin

                                                    <output omitted>
```

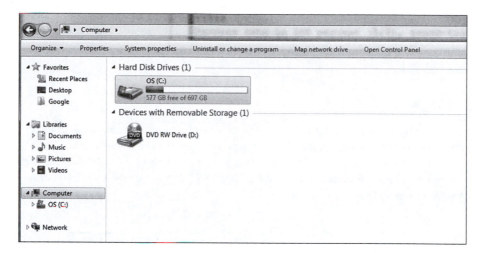

Figure 6-24   *Verifying Disk Space on the Host Operating System*

Step 3.   Copy the image to the TFTP server using the **copy** command:

```
Branch# copy flash0: tftp:
Source filename []? c2900-universalk9-mz.SPA.152-4.M1.bin
Address or name of remote host []? 172.16.1.100
Destination filename []? c2900-universalk9-mz.SPA.152-4.M1.bin
!!!!!!!!!!!!!!!!!!!!
<output omitted>
97794040 bytes copied in 363.468 secs (269058 bytes/sec)
```

Figure 6-25 shows the network server with the Step 3 tftp process running from the Branch router.

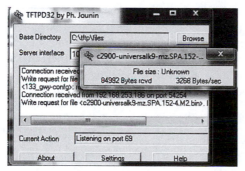

Figure 6-25   *TFTP Network Server Operation*

In the example shown in Figure 6-25, a backup was created of the current image file on the router (c2900-universalk9-mz.SPA.152-4.M2.bin) to the TFTP server at 172.16.1.100. When conducting transfers with the **copy** command, an exclamation point indicates that the copy process is taking place. Each exclamation point displays the successful transfer of ten packets (512 bytes each). A period shows that the copy process timed out. The copy process will retry. However, many periods in a row typically means that the copy process may fail.

Upgrading the Cisco IOS Image

Cisco constantly releases new Cisco IOS Software versions to resolve caveats (software defects) and provide new features. A network server is used for the upgrade process, as shown in the example in Figure 6-26. The network server is running TFTP. Unlike the previous examples, Figure 6-26 reinforces the fact that TFTP can be run over an IPv6 connection as well as an IPv4 connection.

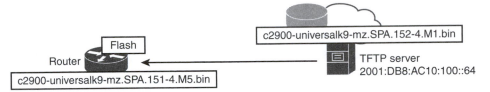

Figure 6-26   *TFTP to Upgrade Cisco IOS Through IPv6*

If the need arises to upgrade or reinstall the Cisco IOS software, the process is essentially the reverse of that given in previous section. On the Cisco IOS device, follow these steps to install the image to the device:

Step 1.   Use Cisco Feature Navigator, shown in Figure 6-27, to determine the correct software for your platform. The Feature Navigator is located at http://tools. cisco.com/ITDIT/CFN/jsp/index.jsp. The Feature Navigator allows software to be released by feature (Research Features) or by version, platform, or product type (Research Software).

Step 2.   Download the file from the Product/Technology Support section of Cisco. com, as shown in Figure 6-28. This page is part of the main support page, *Support and Downloads* at: http://www.cisco.com/cisco/web/support/index. html and appears when clicking the *Downloads* tab. Transfer it to the TFTP server using any file transfer procedures on the host operating system of the TFTP server. If the operating system permits, a direct download from a web browser is sufficient.

Figure 6-27   *Cisco Feature Navigator*

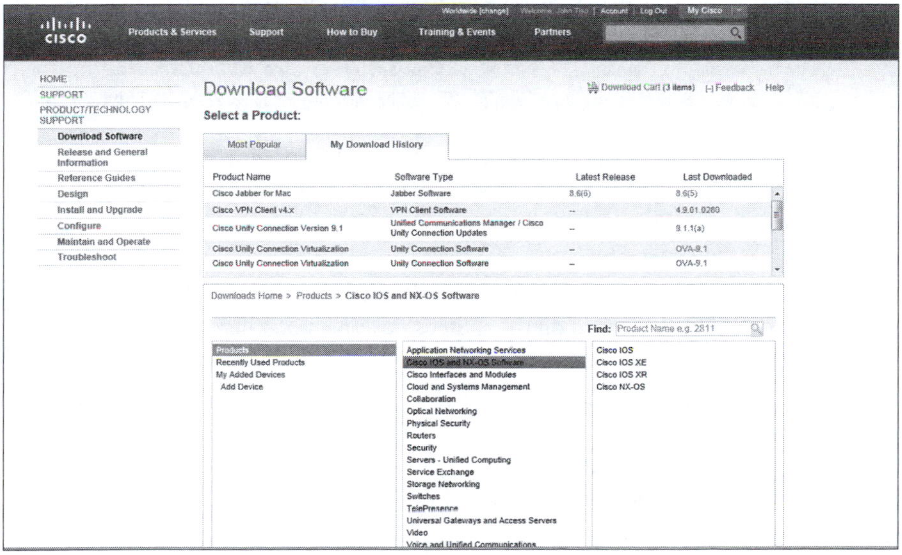

Figure 6-28   *Downloading Software*

Step 3.   Make sure that the network TFTP server is accessible. Ping the TFTP server to test connectivity:

```
Branch# ping ipv6 2001:DB8:AC10:100::64
Packet sent with a source address of 2001:DB8:AC10:100::62
!!!!!
Success rate is 100 percent (5/5), round-trip min/avg/max = 4/4/4 ms
```

Step 4.   Make sure sufficient flash space exists on the router that is being upgraded. You can verify the amount of free flash using the **show flash0:** command:

```
Branch# show flash0:
-#- --length-- -----date/time------ path
<output omitted>
6 3000320 Nov 20 2012 10:03:30 +00:00 cpexpress.tar
7 1038 Nov 20 2012 10:03:36 +00:00 home.shtml
153710592 bytes available (102899712 bytes used)
```

Compare the free flash space with the new image file size.

Step 5.   Copy the Cisco IOS image file from the TFTP server to the router using the **copy** command:

```
Branch# copy tftp: flash0:
Address or name of remote host []? 2001:DB8:AC10:100::64
Source filename []? c2900-universalk9-mz.SPA.152-4.M1.bin
Destination filename []? c2900-universalk9-mz.SPA.152-4.M1.bin
Accessing tftp://2001:DB8:AC10:100::64/c2900-universalk9-mz.SPA.152-4.
M1.bin...
Loading c2900-universalk9-mz.SPA.152-4.M1.bin from
2001:DB8:AC10:100::64 (via GigabitEthernet0/0): !!!!!!!!!!!!!!!!!!!!!!!
<output omitted>
[OK - 97794040 bytes]
97794040 bytes copied in 368.128 secs (265652 bytes/sec)
```

Step 6.   Once the image is saved on the router's flash memory, instruct the router to load the new image during the bootup. Save the configuration.

```
R1config)# boot system flash: c2900-universalk9-mz.SPA.152-4.M1.bin
R1(config)# exit
R1# copy running-config startup-config
        Building configuration...
```

Step 7.   Finally, reload the router to boot the new image.

The new image file (c2900-universalk9-mz.SPA.152-4.M1.bin) is loaded from the TFTP server at 2001:DB8:AC10:100::64 to the router. It uses IPv6 as the transport protocol, to demonstrate that TFTP can also be used across IPv6 networks.

When the image file has been copied to the router, instruct the router to boot the new image file. Use the **boot system** command. Recall that the boot field in the configuration register must be set to 0x2 to 0xF in order for the router to check the **boot** commands. Save the configuration.

Reload the router to boot the router with the new image. Once the router has booted, verify that the new image has loaded by using the **show version** command.

Managing Device Configuration Files

Device configuration files contain a set of user-defined configuration commands that customize the functionality of a Cisco device. Configuration files of a Cisco router are stored in the following locations:

- The running configuration is stored in RAM.

- The startup configuration is stored in NVRAM.

You can copy configuration files from the router to a file server using FTP or TFTP. The running configuration can be backed up before changing its contents, therefore allowing the original configuration file to be restored from the server. The protocol that is used depends on the type of server that is used.

You may want to copy configuration files from a server to the running configuration in RAM or to the startup configuration file in NVRAM of the router for one of the following reasons:

- **To restore a backed-up configuration file:** This might be needed to replace a router with a new device or back out configuration changes.

- **To use the configuration file for another router:** If you are deploying a large number of routers that have similar configurations, you may want to use the same configuration file multiple times. A good example is a multisite WAN where the only difference may be hostnames, SNMP values, and IP addressing. You could use the same configuration file, and then manually change the addressing and names from the console. It is also possible to alter the configuration file with a text editor and save it with a different name on the network server.

- **To use the configuration file to have a "warm spare" for a critical device:** The device could have an identical configuration and be powered off. If the original device fails, you would only need to switch cabling.

- **Version and change control:** Most medium-size to large enterprises have change control procedures to ensure continuity in operations. Archiving configurations before changes is part of change control. This is useful to recover from misconfigurations and also to keep a record of changes that may change network behavior.

Use the **copy running-config startup-config** command after a configuration change is made in the RAM and must be saved to the startup configuration file in NVRAM. Similarly, copy the startup configuration file in NVRAM back into RAM with the **copy startup-config running-config**. However, note that when loading a configuration into the running configuration, the inbound configuration and the current running configurations merge, which may create an undesirable condition in which an inconsistent configuration exists.

Note   You may see the command **wr mem** (short for **write memory**). This is an old Cisco IOS command equivalent to **copy running-config startup-config**. The command is considered deprecated but remains in Cisco IOS.

Use the **erase startup-config** command to delete the saved startup configuration file in NVRAM.

Note   You may see the command **wr erase** (short for **write erase**). This is an old Cisco IOS command equivalent to **erase startup-config**. The command is considered deprecated but remains in Cisco IOS.

Figure 6-29 illustrates how to use the **copy tftp running-config** command to merge the running configuration in RAM with a saved configuration file on a TFTP server.

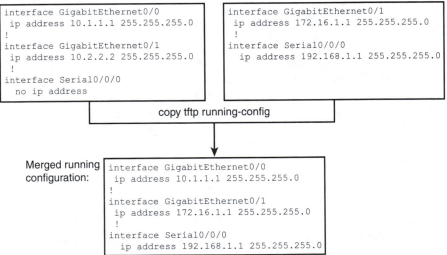

Figure 6-29   *Merging the Configuration*

When a configuration is copied into the running configuration in RAM from any source (including entry from the terminal), the configuration is merged with any existing configuration in RAM. It does not overwrite the existing configuration. Any conflicting commands are overwritten, any new commands are entered, and any commands that are in a default state remain that way unless they are changed by the new configuration.

You can use the TFTP servers to store configurations in a central place, allowing centralized management and updating. Regardless of the size of the network, a copy of the current running configuration should always be kept online as a backup.

The **copy running-config tftp** command allows the current configuration to be uploaded and saved to a TFTP server. The IP address or name of the TFTP server and the destination filename must be supplied.

The **copy tftp running-config** command downloads a configuration file from the TFTP server to the running configuration of the RAM. Again, the address or name of the TFTP server and the source and destination filename must be supplied. A clean configuration can be obtained by erasing the startup configuration and loading the configuration into NVRAM as the startup configuration. The device can then be restarted with a fresh configuration.

Cisco IOS Password Recovery

If you cannot log in to the Cisco IOS device (e.g., because of a lost console password and/or username) or the **enable** password is lost, you must perform a password recovery. The procedure may differ slightly for different platforms, but the tasks remain fundamentally the same: The router is reset to enter ROMmon mode and the configuration register is adjusted to ignore the startup configuration. The router is then restarted and does not read the configuration. The passwords can be reset and the configuration can be merged back in. The configuration register is returned to normal and the system is restarted.

In a password recovery, the configuration register is set to a value that instructs the device to ignore the startup configuration. This includes ignoring the forgotten password(s). Because a user cannot enter privileged EXEC mode in order to change the configuration register, the register has to be changed in ROMmon mode. To enter ROMmon mode, reboot the router and press the Break key to interrupt the boot process to get into ROMmon mode. If your system does not have a Break key, you can use one of the many terminal emulation programs that can emulate a Break key, as shown in the PuTTY example in Figure 6-30.

Follow these steps to perform password recovery:

Step 1. Either switch off or shut down the device.

Step 2. Switch on the router. Press the **Break** key (or send a break sequence with a terminal emulator, as shown in Figure 6-30) within the first 30 seconds after the power is on to interrupt the boot process. This places the device into ROMmon mode, as shown here:

```
rommon 1>
```

Step 3. Set the configuration register to 0x2142. Hexadecimal number of 4 instructs the router to ignore the startup configuration at next reload.

```
rommon 1> confreg 0x2142
```

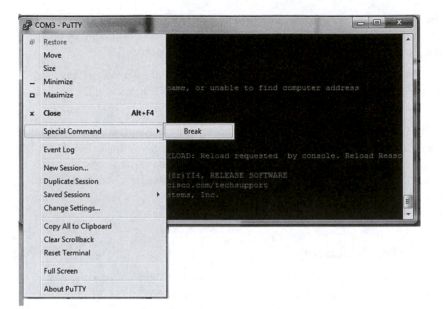

Figure 6-30   *Break Key Emulation*

Step 4.   Reset the device. The device reboots but ignores the startup-config configuration. Do not enter the interactive setup dialog.

```
Would you like to enter the initial configuration dialog? [yes/no]: no
```

Step 5.   Enter privileged EXEC mode. You should be able to do so, because the saved configuration is ignored and an empty configuration without an enable password is loaded.

```
Router> en
Router#
```

Step 6.   Copy startup-config to running-config:

```
Router# copy startup-config running-config
```

Step 7.   The configuration has been successfully merged in. However, because the default state of network interfaces is shut down, the interfaces will need to be enabled with the **no shutdown** command.

```
Router(config-if)# no shutdown
```

Step 8.   Enter configuration mode and set a new enable password. This overwrites the enable password that was merged into the configuration. Because you were already in privileged EXEC mode when the configuration was merged in, you can enter configuration mode and change the password.

```
Router# configure terminal
Router(config)# enable secret newpassword
```

Step 9. Change the configuration register back to its normal value:

```
Router(config)# config-register 0x2102
```

Step 10. Copy running-config to startup-config:

```
Router# copy running-config startup-config
```

Step 11. Optionally, reload the router to verify the configuration changes.

Note Password recovery procedures may slightly deviate based on device. See "Password Recovery Procedures" on Cisco.com for more information: http://www.cisco.com/en/US/products/sw/iosswrel/ps1831/products_tech_note09186a00801746e6.shtml.

Note Tools are available on the Internet that allow the decryption of passwords if you have a copy of the configuration on a network server. However, Cisco doesn't support any of these methods of password recovery. Use them at your own risk, and understand the danger of allowing your password to traverse the public Internet.

Cisco IOS Licensing

The Cisco IOS 15 Software Activation feature is an orchestrated collection of processes and components that activates Cisco IOS Software feature sets by obtaining and validating Cisco IOS Software licenses. With the Cisco IOS Software Activation feature, you can enable licensed features and register licenses.

Historically, Cisco IOS Software was not licensed. If you had enough memory and NVRAM, you could load any Cisco IOS image for your platform. Entitlement was not verified, and it was easy to be out of compliance with your licensing agreements. Interpreting licenses was sometimes difficult, as was identifying which features were included in packages, because multiple Cisco IOS images were built for each feature set. Now, Cisco IOS 15 uses a universal image, called the Universal IOS Image. The technology package removal is an example of the architecture, and feature sets are unlocked via licensing. The Cisco IOS 15 licensing model is discussed in more detail in the upcoming sections.

Licensing Overview

When you order a new router, it is shipped preinstalled with the software image and the corresponding permanent licenses for the packages and features that you specified. The **show license** command in Cisco IOS 15 displays the installed licenses.

The router comes with the evaluation license, also known as a temporary license, for most packages and features supported on it. If you want to try a new software package

or feature, activate the evaluation license for that particular item. If you want to permanently activate a software package or feature on your router, you must get a new software
license.

Software Claim Certificates are used for licenses that require software activation. The
Claim Certificate provides the Product Activation Key (PAK) for your license and important information regarding the Cisco End User License Agreement (EULA). In most cases,
Cisco or your Cisco partner has already activated the licenses ordered at the time of purchase and no Software Claim Certificate is provided.

Because licensing is a major change in Cisco IOS 15, it is important to have a baseline
understanding of its configuration, integration, and verification.

Cisco IOS Licensing and Packaging Prior to Cisco IOS 15

As mentioned, the licensing and packaging of previous versions of Cisco IOS Software
differed from the licensing and packaging of Cisco IOS 15. Prior to Cisco IOS version
15.0, a software image was selected based on a required feature set of the device. There
were eight software packages (images) to satisfy requirements in different service categories. Cisco IOS Software Packaging consisted of eight packages for Cisco routers. Figure
6-31 displays the relationship among the packages, which are defined further in Table 6-8.

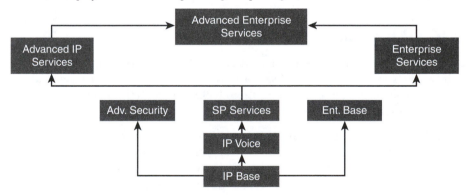

Figure 6-31   *Historic Cisco IOS Packaging*

Table 6-8   *Cisco IOS Pre-IOS 15 Image Packaging*

Software Image/ Package	Features
IP Base	all base level IP data networking features. This is the entry-level Cisco IOS Software image
IP Voice	converged voice and data, VoIP, VoFR, and IP Telephony
Advanced Security	Security and VPN features, including Cisco IOS Firewall, IDS/IPS, IPsec, 3DES, and VPN

Software Image/ Package	Features
SP Services	all IP voice features + SSH/SSL, ATM, VoATM, and MPLS
Advanced IP Services	Advanced Security + SP Services
Enterprise Base	enterprise protocols: multiprotocol support
Enterprise Services	All enterprise base features + all SP services + all IBM networking
Advanced Enterprise Services	All Cisco IOS features that the platform can support

Cisco IOS 15 Licensing and Packaging

With Cisco IOS 15, routers come with a single Cisco IOS image with IP Base activated. Additional feature pack licenses can be installed and activated to expand the feature set of the device. The universal Cisco IOS contains all features and packages. Each package is a grouping of technology-specific features. Multiple technology package licenses can be activated.

Premium features beyond the default IP Base package are grouped into three major Technology Packages: Data, Security, and Unified Communications. These three packages represent the vast majority of features available in Cisco IOS. Figure 6-32 shows the flow of the other packages from the IP Base license.

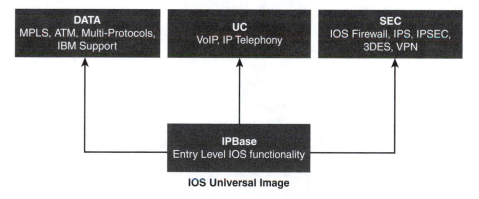

Figure 6-32 *Cisco IOS 15 Packaging*

Table 6-9 lists the technology package licenses from Figure 6-32 that are supported on Cisco ISR G2 platforms.

Table 6-9 *Cisco IOS 15 Packages*

Package	Features
IP Base (ipbasek9)	Entry-level Cisco IOS functionality; prerequisite to all other packages
Data (datak9)	MPLS, ATM, and Multi-Protocol support
Unified Communications (uck9)	VoIP, IP Telephony
Security (securityk9)	Cisco IOS Firewall, IPS, IPsec, 3DES, VPN

Obtaining Licensing

The software activation process is represented in Figure 6-33.

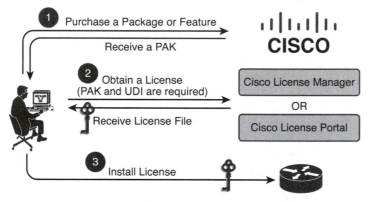

Figure 6-33 *Cisco IOS Software Activation Process*

The following steps describe the software activation process shown in Figure 6-33:

Step 1. Purchase the software package or feature you want to install. A Product Activation Key (PAK) is included.

Step 2. Obtain the license file by using one of the following options:

- **Cisco License Manager (CLM):** An application that is available for download at http://www.cisco.com/go/clm

- **Cisco License Registration Portal:** The web-based portal for getting and registering individual software licenses, available at http://www.cisco.com/go/license

Step 3. Use the Cisco IOS command-line interface to install and manage licenses.

Note If the normal licensing process fails, send an email to licensing@cisco.com. This alias opens a low-severity (severity 4) Cisco Technical Assistance (TAC) Service Request (a.k.a. Case). If you require immediate assistance, open a higher-severity TAC Service Request by contacting the TAC in your part of the world at http://www.cisco.com/en/US/support/tsd_cisco_worldwide_contacts.html.

To obtain the license, you might also need the universal device identifier (UDI). The UDI has two main components: the product ID (PID) and the serial number (SN). PID+":"+SN=UDI. See Example 6-13, which also demonstrates the output from the **show license udi** command that reveals the product ID and serial number of the router (**show running-config** also shows the UDI).

Example 6-13 *Displaying the UDI*

```
Router# show license udi
Device#    PID                SN                      UDI
-------------------------------------------------------------------------------
*0         CISCO2901/K9       FCZ1642C5XD             CISCO2901/K9:FCXX642C5XD
```

Note For more details on license activation, including how to transfer licenses, see "Configuring the Cisco IOS Software Activation Feature": http://www.cisco.com/en/US/docs/ios/csa/configuration/guide/csa_commands.html.

The routers also ship with a small tag that is attached at the factory, an example of which is shown in Figure 6-34.

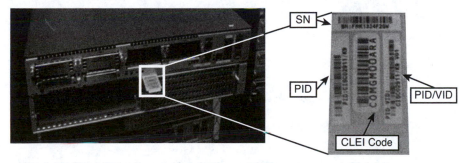

Figure 6-34 *Factory Installed ID Tags*

Table 6-10 explains the fields identified on the tag shown in Figure 6-34.

Table 6-10   *Cisco IOS 15 Packaging*

Field on Tag	Description
CLEI	Common Language Equipment Identifier (CLEI) is a worldwide unique 10-character alphanumeric code that identifies communications equipment in a concise, uniform, feature-oriented language, describing product type, features, source document, and associated drawings and versions.
PID/VID	Product ID/Version ID. The VID is the version of the product. Whenever a product is revised, the VID is incremented.
SN	Chassis Serial Number.
PID	The PID is the name by which the product can be ordered; historically it has been called the "Product Name" or "Part Number." This is the identifier that you would use to order an exact replacement part.

License Verification

Use the **show license** command in privileged EXEC mode to see information about Cisco IOS Software licenses, as shown in Example 6-14.

Example 6-14   *License Verification*

```
Router# show license
Index 1 Feature: ipbasek9
Period left: Life time
License Type: Permanent
License State: Active, In Use
License Count: Non-Counted
License Priority: Medium
Index 2 Feature: securityk9
Period left: Not Activated
Period Used: 0 minute 0 second
License Type: EvalRightToUse
License State: Not in Use, EULA not accepted
License Count: Non-Counted
License Priority: None
<output omitted>
```

The **reload** command indicates the license status before a reboot, as shown in Example 6-15.

Example 6-15 *Restarting the Router and Examining the Licensing*

```
Router# reload

The following license(s) are expiring or have expired.
Features with expired licenses may not work after Reload.
Feature: uc,Status: expiring, Period Left: 7  wks 5  days

Proceed with reload? [confirm]
```

The **show version** command indicates the license type(s) installed. Example 6-16 shows the Security, Unified Communications, and Data packages installed over the IP Base license.

Example 6-16 *Using* **show version** *to Verify Licensing*

```
R1# show version
<output omitted>
License Info:
License UDI:

-------------------------------------------------
Device# PID                      SN
-------------------------------------------------
*0      C3900-SPE150/K9          FHH12259999
Technology Package License Information for Module:'c2900'
-----------------------------------------------------------
Technology    Technology-package       Technology-package
              Current     Type         Next reboot
-----------------------------------------------------------
ipbase        ipbasek9    Permanent    ipbasek9
security      None        None         None
uc            uck9        Permanent    uck9
data          None        None         None
Configuration register is 0x0
```

Permanent License Installation

Example 6-17 shows how to install a permanent UC license on the R1 router that is in Figure 6-35. Let's assume that the license file was obtained from Cisco and stored on the flash of the router or a network server, such as a TFTP server. In this case it is installed on flash, most likely copied to the flash from a network server.

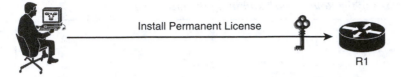

Figure 6-35   *Installing a Permanent License*

Permanent licenses are perpetual; that is, no usage period is associated with them. Once installed, they provide all the permissions needed to access features in the software image. Routers should be shipped with permanent licenses installed by manufacturing. In that case, the activation process is not necessary.

As shown in Example 6-17, the **license install** command is used to install the permanent license to the router in Figure 6-35.

Example 6-17   *Installing a Permanent License*

```
R1# license install flash0:uck9-C2900-SPE150_K9-FHH12250057.xml
Installing licenses from "uck9-C2900-SPE150_K9-FHH12250057.xml"
Installing...Feature:uck9...Successful:Supported
1/1 licenses were successfully installed
0/1 licenses were existing licenses
0/1 licenses were failed to install
upt-3945-1#
*Jul 7 17:24:57.391: %LICENSE-6-INSTALL: Feature uck9 1.0 was installed in this
device.
UDI=C3900-SPE150/K9:FHH12250057; StoreIndex=15:Primary License Storage
*Jul 7 17:24:57.615: %IOS_LICENSE_IMAGE_APPLICATION-6-LICENSE_LEVEL: Module name =
c2900
Next reboot level = uck9 and License = uck9
```

After installing a permanent license, the router needs to be reloaded to finish activation unless an evaluation license for that technology package was active before the permanent license was installed.

Evaluation License Installation

Figure 6-36 shows the basic configuration command for activating an evaluation UC license on the router. Evaluation licenses are temporary, and you use them to evaluate a feature set on new hardware. Temporary licenses are integrated into the router and are limited to a specific usage period (by default, 60 days). You can contact Cisco if you need to extend an evaluation license.

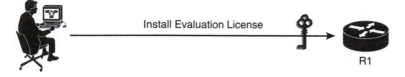

Figure 6-36   *Evaluation License Activation*

Table 6-11 describes the commands for activating an evaluation license. The **license boot module** command followed by a **reload** is used. The evaluation license agreement prints with the command. This process is displayed in Example 6-18.

Table 6-11   *Activation of Evaluation License*

Command	Description
license boot module *module-name* **technology-package** *package-name*	Activates the evaluation license. Use the **?** command with the **module** command to see the module name for your router, and with the **technology-package** command to see the software packages and features supported on your router.
reload	A reload is required to enable the activated license.

Example 6-18   *License Installation Output*

```
Branch (config)# license boot module c2900 technology-package uck9
PLEASE READ THE FOLLOWING TERMS CAREFULLY. INSTALLING THE LICENSE OR
LICENSE KEY PROVIDED FOR ANY CISCO PRODUCT FEATURE OR USING SUCH
PRODUCT FEATURE CONSTITUTES YOUR FULL ACCEPTANCE OF THE FOLLOWING
TERMS. YOU MUST NOT PROCEED FURTHER IF YOU ARE NOT WILLING TO BE BOUND
BY ALL THE TERMS SET FORTH HEREIN.
Use of this product feature requires an additional license from cisco, together with an
additional payment. You may use this product feature
on an evaluation basis, without payment to cisco, for 60 days. Your use
of the product, including during the 60 day evaluation period, is
subject to the cisco end user license agreement
http://www.cisco.com/en/US/docs/general/warranty/English/EU1KEN_.html
If you use the product feature beyond the 60 day evaluation period, you
must submit the appropriate payment to cisco for the license. After the
60 day evaluation period, your use of the product feature will be
governed solely by the cisco end user license agreement (link above),
together with any supplements relating to such product feature. The
above applies even if the evaluation license is not automatically
```

```
terminated and you do not receive any notice of the expiration of the
evaluation period. It is your responsibility to determine when the
evaluation period is complete and you are required to make payment to
Cisco for your use of the product feature beyond the evaluation period.
Your acceptance of this agreement for the software features on one
product shall be deemed your acceptance with respect to all such
software on all Cisco products you purchase which includes the same
software. (The foregoing notwithstanding, you must purchase a license
for each software feature you use past the 60 days evaluation period,
so that if you enable a software feature on 1000 devices, you must
purchase 1000 licenses for use past the 60 day evaluation period.)
Activation of the software command line interface will be evidence of
your acceptance of this agreement.
ACCEPT? [yes/no]: yes
% use 'write' command to make license boot config take effect on next boot
Nov 27 08:44:14.395: %IOS_LICENSE_IMAGE_APPLICATION-6-LICENSE_LEVEL: Module name=
c2900 Next reboot level = uck9 and License = uck9
Nov 27 08:44:15.023: %LICENSE-6-EULA_ACCEPTED: EULA for feature uck9 1.0 has been
accepted. UDI=CISCO2901/K9:FCZ1642C5XD; StoreIndex=1:Built-In License Storage
```

Reload the router after the license is successfully installed, using the **reload** command. Use the **show license** command after the router is reloaded to verify that the license has been installed, as shown in Example 6-19. The EvalRightToUse output indicates an evaluation license.

Example 6-19 *Reviewing License*

```
R1# show license
Index 1 Feature: ipbasek9
Period left: Life time
License Type: Permanent
License State: Active, In Use
License Count: Non-Counted
License Priority: Medium
Index 2 Feature: securityk9
Period left: Not Activated
Period Used: 0 minute 0 second
License Type: EvalRightToUse
License State: Not in Use, EULA not accepted
License Count: Non-Counted
License Priority: None
Index 3 Feature: uck9
Period left: 8 weeks 3 days
```

```
Period Used: 9 minutes 30 seconds
License Type: EvalRightToUse
License State: Active, In Use
License Count: Non-Counted
License Priority:
Low
<output omitted>
```

Backing Up Licenses

The example listed below shows the command for backing up the license on the R1 router depicted in Figure 6-37 using the **license save** command:

```
R1# license save flash:all_licenses.lic
license lines saved ..... to flash:all_licenses.lic
```

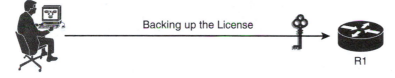

Figure 6-37   *Backing Up Licenses*

Once the **license save** command is executed, copy the license from the flash to a network server via the **copy** command. The process is similar to backing up a Cisco IOS image or configuration. Execute the **copy** command:

```
copy flash:all_licenses.lic tftp
```

Uninstalling Permanent Licenses

Permanent licenses, other than the IP Base license, can be uninstalled. Example 6-20 shows the concept of removing a permanent license from the router in Figure 6-38. This may be done to rehost the license on another platform for various reasons, such as replacement of the old platform. First, disable the technology package and reload the router. Then, after the router reloads, remove the license and reload the router for a second time.

Figure 6-38   *License Removal*

Table 6-12 describes the commands used in Example 6-20.

Table 6-12 *Licensing Commands Description*

Command	Description
license boot module *module-name* **technology-package** *package-name* **disable**	Disables the active license.
license clear *feature-name*	Clears the technology package license from license storage.
no license boot module *module-name* **technology-package** *package-name* **disable**	Clears the actual command from the configuration file, because once it is executed, it does not need to be in the running-config or startup-config.
reload	Reloads the router. A reload is required to make the software license inactive. A second reload is required to remove the license permanently.

Example 6-20 illustrates the two steps to clear an active license from a Cisco 3900 Series Router. In Example 6-20, the two reloads are performed.

Example 6-20 *Two Steps to Removing a Permanent License*

```
R1(config)# license boot module c3900 technology-package uck9 disable
% use 'write' command to make license boot config take effect on next boot
R1# copy running-config startup-config
R1(config)# exit
R1# reload
R1# license clear uck9
*Jul 7 00:34:23.691: %SYS-5-CONFIG_I: Configured from console by console
clear uck9
Feature: uck9
1       License Type: Permanent
License State: Active, Not in Use
License Addition: Exclusive
License Count: Non-Counted
Comment:
Store Index: 15
Store Name: Primary License Storage
Are you sure you want to clear? (yes/[no]): yes
```

```
upt-3945-1#
*Jul 7 00:34:31.223: %LICENSE-6-REMOVE: Feature uck9 1.0 was removed from this
device.
UDI=C3900-SPE150/K9:FHH12250057; StoreIndex=15:Primary License Storage

<Router Restart Output Omitted>
R1 configure terminal
R1(config)# no license boot module c3900 technology uck9 disable
R1(config)# exit
R1# reload
<output omitted>
```

The section, "Cisco IOS Licensing," discussed the new concept of a Universal IOS Image. The technology package removal is an example of the architecture of the Universal IOS Image. In previous Cisco IOS images, only the technology packages to be used in the device were built into the image. All the technology packages are in the Universal IOS Image. This is the reason for the disabling of the technology package *before* the license removal. The technology package remains in the image, but is rendered inoperable.

Rehosting a License

In the scenario shown in Figure 6-39, a router has been damaged by lightning and needs to be replaced. The license needs to be moved to the replacement router. It must be rehosted to the new router using the same CLM or licensing portal that would be used if generating a new license.

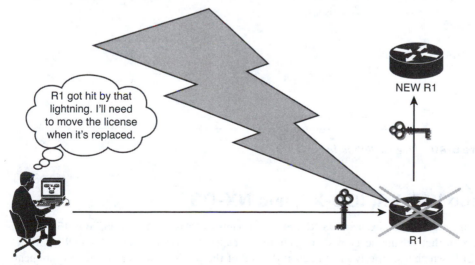

Figure 6-39 *Router Needing to Be Replaced*

To replace the router, perform the following steps:

Step 1. Log in to the Cisco License Administration Portal (http://www.cisco.com/go/license) with your Cisco.com username and password.

Step 2. Go to the Product License Registration page (see Figure 6-40) and choose **Transfer > License for RMA** (for an RMA) or **Transfer > License for Transfer** to move to a new device.

Step 3. Follow the procedures and provide the necessary information (including the PID and SN from both the source and destination devices). Verify the licenses to be transferred and the entitlement information.

Step 4. Once the rehost registration is complete, download the rehost license.

Step 5. Install the rehost license on the replacement (destination) device as if it were a new license.

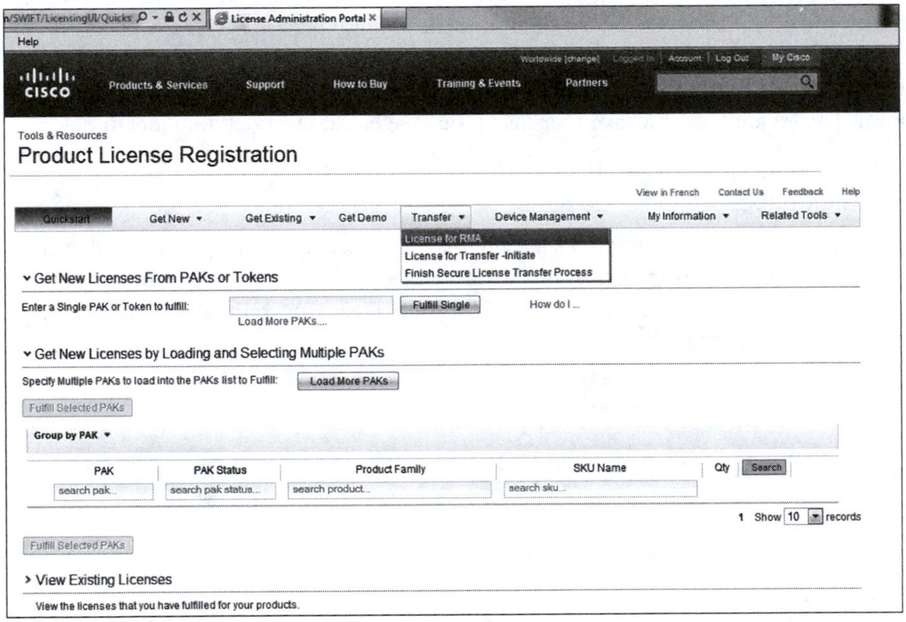

Figure 6-40 *License Rehosting and Transfer*

Cisco IOS-XR, IOS-XE, and NX-OS

Cisco IOS-XR and Cisco IOS-XE are two variants of "classic Cisco IOS," IOS 15. They are both used and developed uniquely for specialized platforms. Cisco IOS-XR is for the CRS, which was briefly mentioned at the end of the section "Router Internal Component Review" earlier in the chapter. Cisco IOS-XE is designed for the Aggregation Services Routers (ASR) 1000 series and the Catalyst 4500E switch. Although Cisco IOS-XR and Cisco IOS-XE have very similar names, they are considerably different.

Cisco NX-OS is the operating system employed by the Cisco Nexus series of data center class switches. The Nexus line is used for core networking as well as Cisco Unified Fabric at the distribution and access layers. Cisco Unified Fabric allows the use of the same hardware for both the Layer 2 and Layer 3 switching of networking protocols and server-to-storage protocols such as Fibre Channel.

This section explores the architecture, features, and usage of Cisco IOS-XR, IOS-XE, and NX-OS. The topic of Cisco IOS-XR, IOS-XE, and NX-OS (and their respective hardware platforms) is out of scope for the CCNA exam; however, as a CCNA, you may run into these platforms in the field. Another reason to cover them is that Cisco has discussed (but has not "road mapped") for some time the option of using Cisco IOS-XE on the full Catalyst line of switches and the Cisco ISR Series. Thus, a high-level understanding of these other Cisco operating systems and the platforms they run on is useful in the job role of a CCNA.

> **Note** For more information on the CRS, ASR, Catalyst 4500E, and Nexus devices, reference their respective technology pages:
>
> - **CRS series of routers:** http://www.cisco.com/en/US/products/ps5763/index.html
>
> - **ASR series of routers:** http://www.cisco.com/en/US/products/ps9343/index.html
>
> - **Catalyst 4500E:** http://www.cisco.com/en/US/prod/collateral/switches/ps5718/ps4324/product_bulletin_c25-619765.html
>
> - **Nexus series of devices:** http://www.cisco.com/en/US/products/ps9441/Products_Sub_Category_Home.html

> **Note** For more information on software packaging for all Cisco operating systems (including Cisco IOS 15 and the other OSs discussed in this section), see the *White Paper: Cisco IOS and NX-OS Software Reference Guide* at http://www.cisco.com/web/about/security/intelligence/ios-ref.html.

Cisco IOS-XR

Cisco IOS-XR is supported only on carrier-class routers (for example, the CRS). It has the same look and feel of Cisco IOS 15, but with additional components to support the unique features of Cisco IOS-XR. Cisco IOS-XR and the platforms it runs on are designed for service providers. Service providers are in the business of "moving packets." Given this, they require a highly scalable and reliable core. They need devices in their core that never drop a packet and that rarely are out of service or run out of system resources. This is a higher level of availability than what an enterprise normally requires when using routing protocols such as EtherChannel, Hot Standby Routing Protocol/

Global Load Balancing Protocol, and Spanning Tree Protocol. The main features of Cisco IOS-XR include the following:

- In-Service Software Upgrade (ISSU), allowing upgrades/patches to Cisco IOS Software without a system reload

- Reload of only parts of the OS (rather than a whole system reload)

- Support for internal physical component redundancy

- Memory isolation and protection between processes (one process should not crash another)

- Redundant hardware components

- Support of very high packet-forwarding speeds

Note For more information on Cisco IOS-XR, see the main page for Cisco IOS-XR Software at http://www.cisco.com/en/US/products/ps5845/index.html.

Cisco IOS-XE

Cisco IOS-XE operates an instance of Cisco IOS 15 over a Linux kernel. This makes Cisco IOS-XE functionally equivalent to Cisco IOS 15. However, the system boot, internal architecture, and certain commands have differences. Highlighting these major differences is beyond the scope of this text.

Cisco IOS-XE has three major features:

- Separation of the management functions of Cisco IOS (control plane) from the forwarding of data packets (data plane), which creates support for:

  - Use of multicore CPUs (because the IOS has been threaded into multiple processes load balancing can occur over the multiple CPU cores)

  - Better reliability, because the data and control planes are isolated from each other

  - ISSU

- The underlying Linux architecture provides Cisco with improved services integration, such as the ability to separate security functions from the core routing software.

- Platform abstraction. This normalizes hardware-specific elements to the Cisco IOS (that is, show commands and configuration commands are less hardware specific).

Note For more information on Cisco IOS-XE, see "What Is Cisco IOS-XE?" at http://www.cisco.com/en/US/prod/collateral/iosswrel/ps9442/ps11192/ps11194/QA_C67-622903.html.

Cisco NX-OS

Cisco NX-OS is a newer operating system developed for the Nexus series of data center class switches. It only runs on the Nexus series and MDS series of data center devices. The code was modeled after Cisco SAN-OS (used in the Cisco Storage Area Networks MDS switches). Cisco SAN-OS is still in service, but only in storage-only applications.

In Cisco NX-OS, many of the commands and features are similar to both Cisco IOS and SAN-OS. However, it is a completely new operating system. It is built around four main concepts:

- **Resiliency:** Cisco NX-OS delivers highly secure, continuous operations which includes:

  - Failure detection

  - Fault isolation

  - Self-healing features

  - Hitless In-Service Software Upgrade (ISSU)

- **Virtualization:** Cisco NX-OS enhances virtual machine portability and converges multiple services, platforms, and networks by providing virtualization and unified fabric.

- **Efficiency:** Operational tools and clustering technologies are integrated into NX-OS that are designed to reduce complexity and offer consistent features and operations.

- **Extensibility:** Cisco NX-OS is designed to scale current and future multiprocessor hardware platforms. It facilitates the integration of new features and evolving standards.

Note For more information on Cisco SAN-OS and its supported devices, see "Cisco SAN-OS Data Sheet" at http://www.cisco.com/en/US/prod/collateral/ps4159/ps6409/ps5989/ps6217/product_data_sheet09186a00801bcfd8_ps4358_Products_Data_Sheet.html.

Note For more information on Cisco NX-OS, see the "Cisco NX-OS Software" page at http://www.cisco.com/en/US/products/ps9372/index.html.

Chapter Summary

This chapter examined four major subjects: network management and management protocols; Cisco IOS image and configuration management; Cisco IOS licensing; and an introduction to Cisco IOS-XE, IOS-XR, and NX-OS.

Network management is a necessary component for developing and maintaining a well-operating and stable network environment. Understanding proper network function, defining normal operation, and identifying abnormalities are key to keeping business continuity for organizations.

An SNMP-managed network consists of three major components: manager, agent, and MIB. An SNMP manager controls and monitors agent devices. Network Management Systems have SNMP manager functions integrated into them. NMSs provide active network monitoring, provide reporting/trending, and allow configuration changes. An SNMP agent is a software module that runs on a network device. A MIB is the definition of the manageable components in an agent.

Syslog is a logging protocol that can be directed to network servers and the system console. It allows visibility into system operations and can capture debugging information. Syslog servers can be used to capture and correlate this data to assist in network management and monitoring.

NetFlow provides the ability to characterize IP traffic and identify its source, traffic destination, timing, and application information. NetFlow information is critical for network availability, performance, and troubleshooting. The monitoring of IP traffic flows increases the accuracy of capacity planning and ensures that resource allocation supports organizational goals. NetFlow helps to determine how to optimize resource usage, plan network capacity, and identify the optimal conditions.

SNMP, syslog, and NetFlow each provide different visibility and roles in network operation. The combination of the three is possible through the utilization of NMS platforms.

Cisco IOS images and configuration files can be transferred to and from network servers. These network servers may run a variety of protocols. The most common is TFTP. Configuration and image file management are important to ensure device uptime, ease of deployment, and ability to recover from failures.

Licensing and packaging of Cisco IOS is a new model in Cisco IOS 15. It is a key area to understand due to its tight integration to device operation and its new model of operation. Cisco IOS 15 uses a universal image, with all features included in the software. Features are enabled through licensing. Licensing and packaging of features has been simplified and can be used incrementally. Licenses require management for deployment, maintenance, and device replacement.

Cisco IOS-XR and IOS-XE are specialized versions of Cisco IOS 15 that run only on limited platforms. Cisco NX-OS is an operating system specific to the Nexus line of data center switches only.

The items discussed in this chapter are all components of serviceability. Serviceability in information technology is considered to be the ease with which networks can operate and troubleshoot. Serviceability is important because it is directly linked to financial costs of network operation, efficiency of staff and resources, and business continuity.

Review Questions

Use the questions here to review what you learned in this chapter. The correct answers are located in Appendix A, "Answers to Chapter Review Questions."

1. The SNMP system consists of which three components? (Choose three.) (Source: "Configuring Network Devices to Support Network Management Protocols")

   a. SNMP manager
   b. SNMP agent
   c. SNMP trap
   d. MIB
   e. Threshold

2. A device is configured with the **snmp-server community Cisco RO** command. An NMS is trying to access this router via SNMP. What kind of access does the NMS have? (Source: "Configuring Network Devices to Support Network Management Protocols")

   a. The NMS can only graph obtained results.
   b. The NMS can graph obtained results and change the hostname of the router.
   c. The NMS can only change the hostname of the device.
   d. The NMS can graph obtained results and perform any administrative function except reload the device.

3. What type(s) of systems can be managed and provide reporting data with SNMP? (Source: "Configuring Network Devices to Support Network Management Protocols")

   a. Windows servers
   b. Linux systems
   c. Cisco routers
   d. Non-Cisco routers
   e. Cisco switches
   f. C, D, and E only
   g. C and E only
   h. All of these answers are correct

4. Which method(s) can be used to ensure only certain manager(s) can communicate with an SNMP agent? (Source: "Configuring Network Devices to Support Network Management Protocols")

   a. ACLs
   b. Community strings
   c. Restricted operation mode (ROM)
   d. Forced consideration
   e. snmp-server restrict *ip_address* command

5. You want to configure the router with IP address 10.1.1.1 to send syslog messages of all severities, including debugging, to the syslog server with IP address 192.168.1.240. Which configuration is correct? (Source: "Configuring Network Devices to Support Network Management Protocols")

   a. logging 10.1.1.1
       logging trap debugging
   b. logging 192.168.1.240
       logging trap all
   c. logging 192.168.1.240
       logging debugging
   d. logging 10.1.1.1
       logging debugging

6. Which management protocol could you use to discover which host generates the highest volume of traffic? (Source: "Configuring Network Devices to Support Network Management Protocols")

   a. SNMP
   b. Syslog
   c. NetFlow

7. Which stage of a Cisco router bootup process occurs last? (Source: "Router Initialization and Configuration")

   a. POST
   b. Find and load Cisco IOS Software
   c. Find and load bootstrap
   d. Find and load configuration

8. Which stage of a Cisco router bootup process verifies that all router components are operational? (Source: "Router Initialization and Configuration")

   a. POST
   b. Find Cisco IOS Software
   c. Find bootstrap
   d. Find configuration

9. Which Cisco router component is used primarily to store the startup-config file? (Source: "Router Initialization and Configuration")

   a. RAM

   b. ROM

   c. NVRAM

   d. Flash memory

   e. Configuration register

10. Which of the following is a low-level operating system normally used for manufacturing, testing, and troubleshooting? (Source: "Router Initialization and Configuration")

   a. POST

   b. Bootstrap

   c. Mini Cisco IOS

   d. ROMmon

11. What happens if the router cannot find a valid startup configuration file in NVRAM during router bootup? (Source: "Router Initialization and Configuration")

   a. The router enters setup mode.

   b. The router attempts to restart.

   c. The router runs ROM monitor.

   d. The router performs a shutdown.

12. Which Cisco IOS command is used to download a copy of the Cisco IOS image file from a TFTP server? (Source: "Managing Device Configuration Files")

   a. copy IOS: tftp:

   b. copy tftp: flash:

   c. copy flash: tftp:

   d. backup flash: tftp:

13. Which Cisco IOS command displays the amount of memory that is available where the Cisco IOS image is stored on your router? (Source: "Managing Device Configuration Files")

   a. show flash

   b. show nvram

   c. show memory

   d. show running-config

14. Where is the running configuration of the router usually stored? (Source: "Managing Device Configuration Files")

   a. BIOS

   b. RAM

   c. NVRAM

   d. Bootflash

15. Which is a type of network server that can support the backup and restoration of configuration files and Cisco IOS images? (Source: "Managing Device Configuration Files")

    a. TFTP

    b. NFS

    c. CIFS

    d. SFTP

16. Which device(s) can contain a copy of a configuration or Cisco IOS image? (Source: "Managing Device Configuration Files")

    a. Internal flash

    b. USB drive

    c. Network server

17. Which technology package license provides basic Cisco IOS functionality for the router? (Source: "Cisco IOS Licensing")

    a. ipbasek9

    b. datak9

    c. uck9

    d. securityk9

18. Which command is used to install a permanent license? (Source: "Cisco IOS Licensing")

    a. install license

    b. license boot module

    c. license install

    d. license load

19. When replacing a failed device, how is licensing handled? (Source: "Cisco IOS Licensing")

    a. A new license ships on the device and just requires the VID to be recoded.

    b. Manufacturing emails the license simultaneously with shipment.

    c. The license must be migrated using Cisco.com and is then installed like a new license.

20. Which is true about evaluation licenses? (Source: "Cisco IOS Licensing")

    a. They are installed using the same process as permanent licenses.

    b. They are good for 120 days by default.

    c. They require a reload to be enabled.

    d. They can overwrite a permanent license.

21. Which of the following statement(s) is/are true about Cisco IOS-XR (Source: "Cisco IOS-XR")

    a. Currently runs on ASR 1000 and Catalyst 4500E only

    b. Runs on carrier-class platforms only (e.g., CRS-1)

    c. Supports ISSU

    d. Runs on any Cisco IOS–capable device

    e. Has no major functional differences from other Cisco IOS versions

    f. Is interchangeable with Cisco IOS-XE

22. Which of the following statement(s) is/are true about Cisco IOS-XE? (Source: "Cisco IOS-XE")

    a. Runs on ASR 1000 and Catalyst 4500E only

    b. Runs on carrier-class platforms only (e.g., CRS-1)

    c. Supports ISSU

    d. Runs on any Cisco IOS–capable device

    e. Has no major functional differences from other Cisco IOS versions

    f. Is interchangeable with Cisco IOS-XR

23. Which of the following statement(s) is/are not true about Cisco NX-OS? (Source: "Cisco NX-OS")

    a. Supports the Catalyst 4500E series and Nexus platforms

    b. Designed for core networking and Unified Fabric implementations

    c. Designed for data center switching

    d. Based on Cisco IOS 15 on a Linux kernel

Chapter 7

Advanced Troubleshooting

This chapter contains the following sections:

- Advanced Router Diagnostics

- Device Debugging

- Chapter Summary

- Review Questions

This chapter examines advanced troubleshooting methods. The first section presents advanced router diagnostics, which includes the collection and processing of data needed for troubleshooting. The second section introduces the debug command and debugging process.

These processes and skills are not directly tested as part of the CCNA certification exam. However, the knowledge that you gain in this chapter will facilitate your certification study and build a foundation for developing advanced skills. A novice network engineer can use the knowledge in this chapter to help better "triage" (or even solve) technical issues before escalating them to Cisco TAC or a more senior engineer. It is also useful knowledge to facilitate troubleshooting that is directed by a TAC or other senior engineer.

Chapter Objectives

- Understand the collection and processing of diagnostic data

- Research Cisco IOS software defects (bugs)

- Understand the syntax and usage of the debugging '**debug**' command for both diagnostics and research purposes

Advanced Router Diagnostics

This section explores the following information on advanced diagnostics:

- How to collect diagnostic information

- How to use a Cisco tool called the Output Interpreter

- How to research bugs and software defects

Collecting Cisco IOS Device Diagnostic Information

Collecting Cisco IOS device diagnostics is important in several scenarios, ranging from router crashes, to unpredictable router behavior, to a request from Cisco TAC. One of the main commands to collect bulk diagnostic data is **show tech-support** (**show tech** for short). This command provides a diagnostic dump of major **show** commands, with no line or page breaks or passwords removed. It is available on Cisco IOS, NX-OS, and the ASA firewall. There are slight differences in what is collected per platform and OS. Example 7-1 provides output of the **show tech** command from a Cisco 2951 Integrated Service Router (ISR). The following list presents the set of major commands run by **show tech** and defines what each command achieves:

- **show version:** Displays the configuration of the system hardware, the software version, the names and sources of configuration files and software images, the router uptime, licensing, serial number(s), and information on how the system has been restarted.

- **show license:** Displays licensing information.

- **show stacks:** Monitors the stack usage of processes and interrupt routines. The **show stacks** output is one of the most important sets of diagnostic information to collect when the router crashes.

- **show running-configuration:** Displays the current running configuration.

- **show interface:** Displays the current state of all interfaces.

- **show controllers:** Displays the controller state that is specific to controller hardware. It is useful for diagnostic tasks.

- **show process cpu:** Provides the current processes running in Cisco IOS and CPU utilization statistics.

- **show processes memory:** Displays information regarding the active processes in the router and the corresponding memory used by each process and by the system as a whole.

- **show buffers:** Provides diagnostic information that can be used to diagnose and identify Cisco IOS bugs related to memory leaks and wedged interfaces (software errors causing input queue overloads).

Executing **show tech**, as shown in Example 7-1, is accomplished in privilege EXEC mode.

Example 7-1   Sample show tech *Command from a Cisco 2951 Router*

```
HQ# show tech-support


----------------- show version -----------------



Cisco IOS Software, C2951 Software (C2951-UNIVERSALK9-M), Version 15.1(4)M4, RELEASE
SOFTWARE (fc1)
Technical Support: http://www.cisco.com/techsupport
Copyright (c) 1986-2012 by Cisco Systems, Inc.
Compiled Tue 20-Mar-12 19:11 by prod_rel_team


ROM: System Bootstrap, Version 15.0(1r)M16, RELEASE SOFTWARE (fc1)


HQ uptime is 8 weeks, 1 day, 17 hours, 15 minutes
System returned to ROM by power-on
System restarted at 19:15:34 PDT Sat Mar 23 2013
System image file is "flash0:c2951-universalk9-mz.SPA.151-4.M4.bin"
Last reload type: Normal Reload
<output truncated>
```

The **show tech** command executes and should be collected in a terminal emulation program's buffer. Additional information on capturing output in a terminal emulation program's buffer is provided later, in the section "Capturing Debugging Output." The **show tech** command is also a useful tool for gathering system information for as-built documentation for a "snapshot in time" of a router.

If you happen to be opening a case (service request) with Cisco TAC, you can proactively upload the data when opening the case. The case-opening tool gives you the option to upload a file, or you can automatically attach any files (such as the **show tech** output file) to an email and send it to attach@cisco.com using the case number as a subject.

Using the Output Interpreter to Detect Issues

To assist you in detecting issues in **show** command output, Cisco offers a tool called Output Interpreter. This tool, shown in Figure 7-1, provides an analysis of **show** commands and output from the **show tech** command. The Output Interpreter is available for use at http://www.cisco.com/cgi-bin/Support/OutputInterpreter/home.pl.

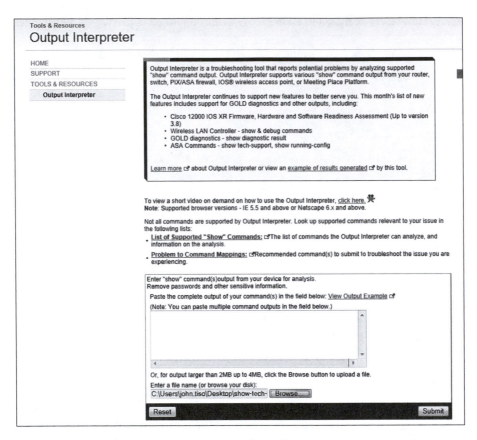

Figure 7-1   *Invoking Output Interpreter from Cisco.com*

You can either copy command output and paste it into Output Interpreter or upload a file to it. In Figure 7-1, a **show-tech** file has been uploaded from the HQ router. Upon submitting the file, the tool analyzes the file. It produces output that can be emailed to the user as well as browsed. Figure 7-2 displays the output with the option chosen to email the analysis with hyperlinks included.

After performing its analysis, as shown in Figure 7-2, the tool reports error conditions, warnings, status information, and helpful resources. These results may include configuration areas that need to be corrected or identification of recognized product defect/bugs.

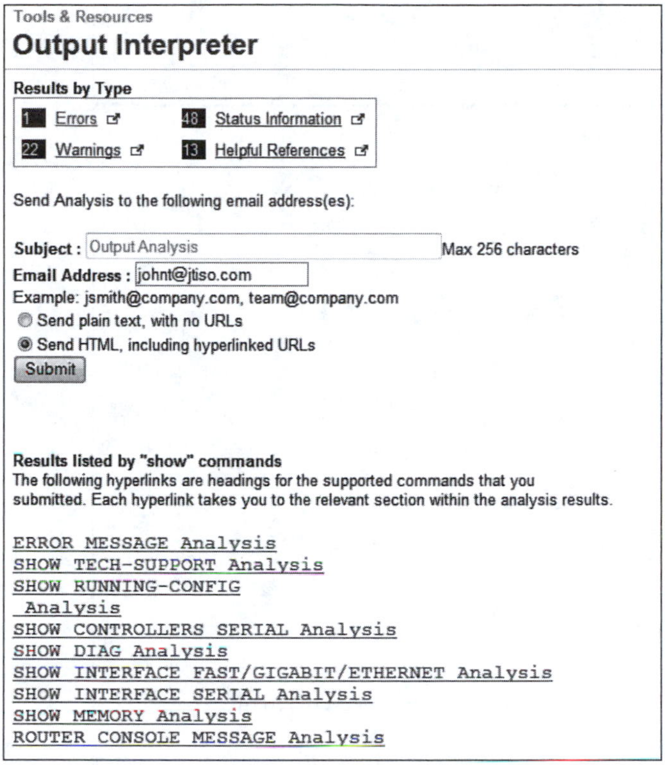

Tools & Resources
Output Interpreter

Results by Type

1	Errors ☞	48	Status Information ☞
22	Warnings ☞	13	Helpful References ☞

Send Analysis to the following email address(es):

Subject : Output Analysis   Max 256 characters
Email Address : johnt@jtiso.com
Example: jsmith@company.com, team@company.com
◯ Send plain text, with no URLs
◉ Send HTML, including hyperlinked URLs
Submit

Results listed by "show" commands
The following hyperlinks are headings for the supported commands that you
submitted. Each hyperlink takes you to the relevant section within the analysis results.

ERROR MESSAGE Analysis
SHOW TECH-SUPPORT Analysis
SHOW RUNNING-CONFIG
 Analysis
SHOW CONTROLLERS SERIAL Analysis
SHOW DIAG Analysis
SHOW INTERFACE FAST/GIGABIT/ETHERNET Analysis
SHOW INTERFACE SERIAL Analysis
SHOW MEMORY Analysis
ROUTER CONSOLE MESSAGE Analysis

Figure 7-2   *Output Interpreter Results*

Researching Cisco IOS Software Defects

Cisco IOS, like any software product, is subject to software defects, often called bugs.
To help you research such bugs, Cisco maintains a tool called the Bug Toolkit, located at
http://tools.cisco.com/Support/BugToolKit/action.do?hdnAction=searchBugs. Figure 7-3
shows the initial screen.

The Bug Toolkit enables you to search Cisco's bug database of defects that are available
for customers to search. Search parameters can be altered to adjust for device type, version and releases, and Cisco IOS versions. In Figure 7-4, the keyword "wedged" was used
as the search parameter. (As mentioned earlier, a wedged interface is a software defect
that causes the interface's input queue to be overrun.) In this search, seven defects were
found that contained the keyword "wedged."

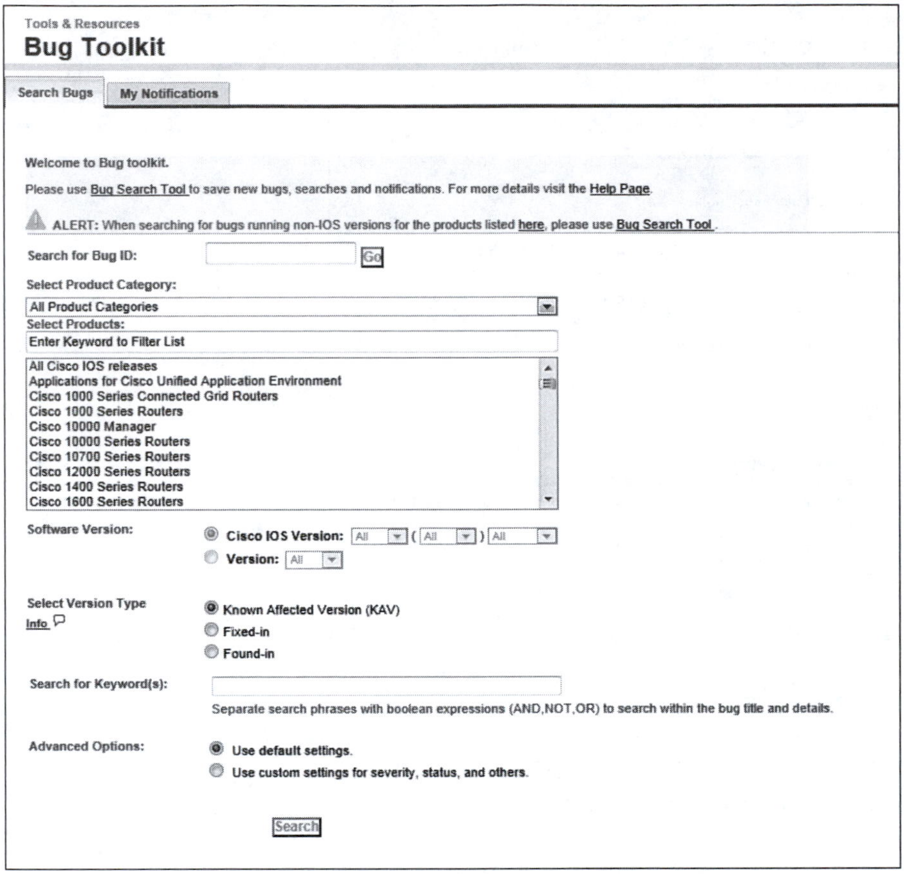

Figure 7-3   *Bug Toolkit from Cisco.com*

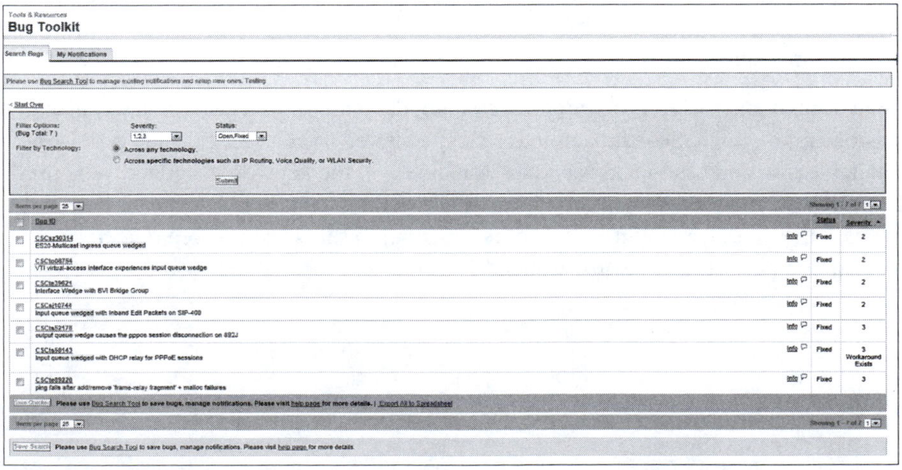

Figure 7-4   *Defect Search in the Bug Toolkit*

Clicking the hyperlink for a bug in the Bug ID column provides the full description of the defect, as shown in the example in Figure 7-5, including the status, whether or not it has been fixed, version(s) fixed in, whether a workaround exists, and the component affected.

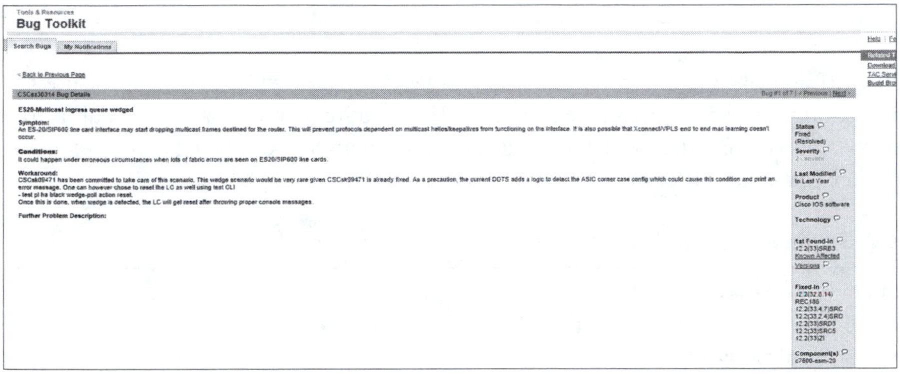

Figure 7-5 *Individual Defect Description in the Bug Toolkit*

To determine if a particular bug is a possible match to your issue, the versions, components, and description should be a match. The next step is to test one of the "fixed-in" versions or try the workaround given. Ideally, you should do your testing in a lab, or open a TAC case for full verification. Keep in mind, the fixed-in version may have other defects, or may require more resources (such as RAM or flash) than your system's capabilities. When in doubt, get help from a more senior engineer or the Cisco TAC.

Device Debugging

The **debug** command is an important tool in Cisco IOS. It is available from privileged EXEC mode. The **debug** command is assigned high priority in the router CPU process. Incorrect usage of the **debug** command can seriously impair the device, interrupt device operation, or create a situation where the device is unusable. Therefore, using the **debug** command is recommended only to troubleshoot specific problems. You should disable it when it is no longer needed. The **debug** command should be reserved for use by advanced engineers or during troubleshooting sessions with Cisco technical support staff. Use of the **debug** command is recommended only during periods of lower network traffic and fewer users.

Capturing Debugging Output

Debugging output can be directed to the console, the AUX port, a VTY, an internal buffer, or a syslog server. The default behavior sends debugging output to the console and not to AUX ports or VTY sessions. The console will always capture debug output, even if it is being captured to another destination. To disable logging at the console, configure the router as shown in Example 7-2.

Example 7-2   *Disable Logging Output to the Console*

```
HQ# configure terminal
Enter configuration commands, one per line.  End with CNTL/Z.
HQ(config)# no logging console
```

Turning off console logging on a production router that is not undergoing troubleshooting is a good idea, as it saves system resources. However, remember that the default is to log at the console, and that reenabling it does not show up in the running or startup configuration. Example 7-3 reenables console logging.

Example 7-3   *Enable Console Logging*

```
HQ# configure terminal
Enter configuration commands, one per line.  End with CNTL/Z.
HQ(config)# logging console
```

To see logging information (including debugs) at a VTY session or the AUX port, execute the **terminal monitor** command:

```
HQ# terminal .monitor
```

Attempting to run the command on a session with the console port will result in an error:

```
HQ# terminal monitor
% Console already monitors
```

When used at a VTY, the **terminal monitor** command only is in effect for the specific VTY session.

A suggested way to capture the output from **debug** commands from the terminal to a file is to enable logging to a file in the terminal-emulation program in use. Figure 7-6 is an example screen from PuTTY, a common terminal emulator.

The key points to note in Figure 7-6 are that PuTTY is configured to capture all session output (All Session Output is selected under Session Logging) and that an output file is selected (in this case, the default filename is selected). This output file can be opened with any text editor. Figure 7-7 shows an output log from the terminal emulator opened in Windows Notepad.

Figure 7-6 *Terminal-Emulation Settings*

Figure 7-7 *Reviewing a Log File in Windows Notepad*

A key point in Figure 7-7 is the first command in the log file, **term len 0**. The full command is **terminal length 0**. This command stops the device from having any pauses in output from a command such as **show running-configuration**. The normal pausing denoted by "—More—" would not be enabled to stop the output.

To direct debugging to a syslog server, configure the router : as shown in the "Syslog Overview" section of Chapter 6, "Network Device Management." The **logging trap** command must be set to the debug level, which is level 7.

Debug output can also be sent to a system-defined buffer. In Figure 7-7, the router has a logging buffer set up. However, it is configured to capture only warnings. The command employed to set up debugging uses the **debug** keyword:

```
HQ(config)# logging buffered 50000 debug
```

In this case, 50000 sets a buffer in RAM (in bytes). The maximum buffer size varies per Cisco IOS version and device type. The buffer runs circularly, so newer messages overwrite older ones after the buffer is filled. The **show logging** command displays the messages in the buffer, oldest messages first. In Example 7-4, debugging is enabled to a log buffer. The **debug ip packet** command is executed. This creates a log entry on each IP packet that goes through the device. The sample debug command is run, the **ping** command that is executed fails, and the logging buffer output produced from running the **ping** command is reviewed via the **show logging** command. The ping fails, and the debug reports that the packets are not routable. The debug messages also show no source IP address, IP: s=0.0.0.0. In Example 7-6, the logging buffer is cleared with the **clear logging** command.

Example 7-4   *Enabling a Debug*

```
HQ# debug ip packet
IP packet debugging is on
HQ# ping 192.168.1.250


Type escape sequence to abort.
Sending 5, 100-byte ICMP Echos to 192.168.1.250, timeout is 2 seconds:
.....
Success rate is 0 percent (0/5)
HQ# show logging
Syslog logging: enabled (0 messages dropped, 2 messages rate-limited,
                0 flushes, 0 overruns, xml disabled, filtering disabled)


No Active Message Discriminator.


No Inactive Message Discriminator.


    Console logging: disabled
    Monitor logging: level debugging, 0 messages logged, xml disabled,
                     filtering disabled
    Buffer logging:  level debugging, 25 messages logged, xml disabled,
                     filtering disabled
    Logging Exception size (4096 bytes)
```

```
      Count and timestamp logging messages: disabled
      Persistent logging: disabled

No active filter modules.

ESM: 0 messages dropped

    Trap logging: level informational, 32 message lines logged

Log Buffer (50000 bytes):

*May  4 05:46:22.043: IP: s=0.0.0.0 (local), d=192.168.1.250, len 100, unroutable
*May  4 05:46:24.039: IP: s=0.0.0.0 (local), d=192.168.1.250, len 100, unroutable
*May  4 05:46:26.040: IP: s=0.0.0.0 (local), d=192.168.1.250, len 100, unroutable
*May  4 05:46:28.040: IP: s=0.0.0.0 (local), d=192.168.1.250, len 100, unroutable
*May  4 05:46:30.040: IP: s=0.0.0.0 (local), d=192.168.1.250, len 100, unroutable
HQ#
```

In Example 7-5, there is no active IP interface.

Example 7-5   *Verifying Interface Status After Reviewing the Debug*

```
HQ# show ip interface brief
Interface            IP-Address      OK?   Method      Status        Protocol
FastEthernet0        192.168.1.1     YES   manual      up            down
<output omitted>
```

Example 7-6   *Clearing the Logging Buffer*

```
HQ# clear logging
Clear logging buffer [confirm] y
```

Note   Example 7-4 uses an extremely high overhead **debug** command. Using **debug ip packet** easily overwhelms a device. This can occur even in a router experiencing low utilization, as the CPU is engaged for *every IP packet* that goes through the router. For demonstration purposes, the router is accessed from the console and has all of its interfaces shut down to both artificially generate the error and limit utilization on the router.

Caution Executing the **debug all** command turns on all possible debugging. Do not execute this command on any device that has any production or important activity, as it will severely impact and/or interrupt device operation.

Verifying and Disabling Debugging

Use the **show debug** command to show which debugging is active in the system, as shown in Example 7-7.

Example 7-7 *Determining Which Debugging Is Enabled*

```
HQ# show debug
Generic IP:
  IP packet debugging is on for access list 150
fastethernet:
  Fast Ethernet events debugging is on
```

In this case, IP packet debugging is on for an access list and Fast Ethernet events debugging is on.

Debugs can be disabled through either an **undebug** command or a **no debug** command (they are functionally equivalent and completely interchangeable). The command can be used to shut off a specific debugging command or all debugging in the system (**undebug all** or **no debug all**).

In Example 7-8, the debugging used in the previous section is disabled by using the **undebug** command.

Example 7-8 *Disabling a Specific Debug with* **undebug**

```
HQ# undebug ip packet
IP packet debugging is off
```

Example 7-9 disables debugging used in the previous section using the **no debug** command.

Example 7-9 *Disabling a Specific Debug with no* **debug**

```
HQ# no debug ip packet
IP packet debugging is off
```

Example 7-10 shows that the **debugging** command has disabled only the IP packet debugging, and the remainder of the debugging is still enabled.

Example 7-10   *Checking the Enabled Debugs*

```
HQ# show debug
fastethernet:
  Fast Ethernet events debugging is on
```

To disable all debugging in the system, use either the **undebug all** command or **no debug all** command, as shown in Example 7-11.

Example 7-11   *Disabling All Debugging in the System*

```
HQ# undebug all
All possible debugging has been turned off
HQ# no debug all
All possible debugging has been turned off
```

When executing a **show debug** command, as shown in Example 7-12, only a blank line is displayed when no debugging is enabled.

Example 7-12   *All System Debugging Disabled*

```
HQ# show debug
<blank line feed>
HQ#
```

Limiting Debugging Output

Many debugging commands can be operated in a conditional mode or restricted by a modifier. Examples include a condition on an interface or use of an ACL. Only certain debugging commands can be used with an ACL or set up conditionally. The Cisco IOS *Debug Reference Guides,* which are IOS software version specific, can be reviewed to find the usage of a specific debugging command.

> **Note**   The full set of Cisco IOS 15.0 reference guides, including the *Debug Comm and Reference*, can be found at the *Cisco IOS 15 Command References* page at: http://www.cisco.com/en/US/products/ps10591/prod_command_reference_list.html.

ACL Triggered Debugging

Let's look at an example of a **debug ip packet** command. Figure 7-8 shows a simple network that will be used in this section.

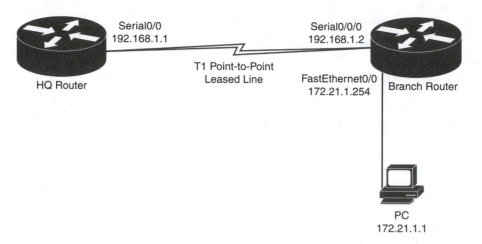

Figure 7-8   *Simple Network Example*

As noted at the end of the "Capturing Debugging Output" section, **debug ip packet** is a high-overhead **debug** command. However, you can use an ACL to reduce the output generated from the command. With an ACL, the packets matching the ACL are the only ones that the debugging is run against. Examples 7-13 through 7-16 present the steps to enable the debugging with the ACL.

Example 7-13   *Examining the* **debug ip packet** *Command Options*

```
HQ# debug ip packet ?
  <1-199>          Access list
  <1300-2699>      Access list (expanded range)
  detail           Print more debugging detail
  <cr>
```

The first step to enable the command is to set up an ACL that limits the traffic. An extended access list that limits pings to the PC at the address 172.21.1.1 is provided in Example 7-14.

Example 7-14   *Configuring an ACL to Support the* **debug** *command*

```
HQ(config)# access-list 150 permit icmp any host 172.21.1.1 echo
HQ(config)# access-list 150 permit icmp host 172.21.1.1 any echo-reply
```

Prior to enabling any **debug** command, run a check to make sure that the ACL is enabled and has the correct syntax. In Example 7-15 the ACL is validated.

Example 7-15 *Validating the ACL*

```
HQ# show access-lists
Extended IP access list 150
    10 permit icmp any host 172.21.1.1 echo
    20 permit icmp host 172.21.1.1 any echo-reply
```

The **debug** command can now be enabled using the access list, as shown in Example 7-16.

Example 7-16 *Enabling* **debug ip packet** *with an ACL to Limit the Debugging*

```
HQ# debug ip packet 150
IP packet debugging is on for access list 150
```

In Example 7-17, first the log is cleared. Clearing out any previous output before running this example makes it easier to isolate the debugging information that is desired. Next, in Example 7-17, a **ping** is run to an address that is not covered by the ACL (to demonstrate that it is not logged), and then a **ping** is run to the host that matches the ACL, 172.21.1.1. Then, the log is reviewed to show the pings.

Example 7-17 *Clearing the Log in Preparation for Debugging, and Executing* **ping** *Commands to Verify the ACL Debugging Is Working*

```
HQ# clear log
Clear logging buffer [confirm]y
HQ# ping 192.168.1.2

Type escape sequence to abort.
Sending 5, 100-byte ICMP Echos to 192.168.1.2, timeout is 2 seconds:
!!!!!
Success rate is 100 percent (5/5), round-trip min/avg/max = 1/5/20 ms
HQ# ping 172.21.1.1

Type escape sequence to abort.
Sending 5, 100-byte ICMP Echos to 172.21.1.1, timeout is 2 seconds:
!!!!!
Success rate is 100 percent (5/5), round-trip min/avg/max = 1/3/4 ms
HQ# show logging
<output omitted>
Log Buffer (50000 bytes):

May 19 22:55:59.310: IP: s=192.168.1.1 (local), d=172.21.1.1 (Serial0), len 100,
sending
May 19 22:55:59.310: IP: s=192.168.1.1 (local), d=172.21.1.1 (Serial0), len 100,
sending full packet
```

```
May 19 22:55:59.310: IP: s=172.21.1.1 (Serial0), d=192.168.1.1, len 100, input
feature,
MCI Check(64), rtype 0, forus FALSE, sendself FALSE, mtu 0, fwdchk FALSE
May 19 22:55:59.310: IP: tableid=0, s=172.21.1.1 (Serial0), d=192.168.1.1 (Serial0),
routed via RIB
May 19 22:55:59.310: IP: s=172.21.1.1 (Serial0), d=192.168.1.1 (Serial0), len 100,
rcvd 3
May 19 22:55:59.314: IP: s=172.21.1.1 (Serial0), d=192.168.1.1, len 100, stop
process pak for forus packet
May 19 22:55:59.314: IP: s=192.168.1.1 (local), d=172.21.1.1 (Serial0), len 100,
sending
May 19 22:55:59.314: IP: s=192.168.1.1 (local), d=172.21.1.1 (Serial0), len 100,
sending full packet
May 19 22:55:59.314: IP: s=172.21.1.1 (Serial0), d=192.168.1.1, len 100, input
feature,
MCI Check(64), rtype 0, forus FALSE, sendself FALSE, mtu 0, fwdchk FALSE
May 19 22:55:59.314: IP: tableid=0, s=172.21.1.1 (Serial0), d=192.168.1.1 (Serial0),
routed via RIB
May 19 22:55:59.314: IP: s=172.21.1.1 (Serial0), d=192.168.1.1 (Serial0), len 100,
rcvd 3
May 19 22:55:59.314: IP: s=172.21.1.1 (Serial0), d=192.168.1.1, len 100, stop
process pak for forus packet
May 19 22:55:59.314: IP: s=192.168.1.1 (local), d=172.21.1.1 (Serial0), len 100,
sending
May 19 22:55:59.318: IP: s=192.168.1.1 (local), d=172.21.1.1 (Serial0), len 100,
sending full packet
May 19 22:55:59.318: IP: s=172.21.1.1 (Serial0), d=192.168.1.1, len 100, input
feature,
MCI Check(64), rtype 0, forus FALSE, sendself FALSE, mtu 0, fwdchk FALSE
May 19 22:55:59.318: IP: tableid=0, s=172.21.1.1 (Serial0), d=192.168.1.1 (Serial0),
routed via RIB
May 19 22:55:59.318: IP: s=172.21.1.1 (Serial0), d=192.168.1.1 (Serial0), len 100,
rcvd 3
May 19 22:55:59.318: IP: s=172.21.1.1 (Serial0), d=192.168.1.1, len 100, stop
process pak for forus packet
May 19 22:55:59.318: IP: s=192.168.1.1 (local), d=172.21.1.1 (Serial0), len 100,
sending
May 19 22:55:59.318: IP: s=192.168.1.1 (local), d=172.21.1.1 (Serial0), len 100,
sending full packet
May 19 22:55:59.322: IP: s=172.21.1.1 (Serial0), d=192.168.1.1, len 100, input
feature,
MCI Check(64), rtype 0, forus FALSE, sendself FALSE, mtu 0, fwdchk FALSE
May 19 22:55:59.322: IP: tableid=0, s=172.21.1.1 (Serial0), d=192.168.1.1 (Serial0),
routed via RIB
May 19 22:55:59.322: IP: s=172.21.1.1 (Serial0), d=192.168.1.1 (Serial0), len 100,
rcvd 3
May 19 22:55:59.322: IP: s=172.21.1.1 (Serial0), d=192.168.1.1, len 100, stop
process pak for forus packet
```

```
May 19 22:55:59.322: IP: s=192.168.1.1 (local), d=172.21.1.1 (Serial0), len 100,
sending

May 19 22:55:59.322: IP: s=192.168.1.1 (local), d=172.21.1.1 (Serial0), len 100,
sending full packet

May 19 22:55:59.322: IP: s=172.21.1.1 (Serial0), d=192.168.1.1, len 100, input
feature,

MCI Check(64), rtype 0, forus FALSE, sendself FALSE, mtu 0, fwdchk FALSE

May 19 22:55:59.322: IP: tableid=0, s=172.21.1.1 (Serial0), d=192.168.1.1 (Serial0),
routed via RIB

May 19 22:55:59.322: IP: s=172.21.1.1 (Serial0), d=192.168.1.1 (Serial0), len 100,
rcvd 3

May 19 22:55:59.322: IP: s=172.21.1.1 (Serial0), d=192.168.1.1, len 100, stop
process pak for forus packet
```

Reviewing the logging output shows that 30 lines of output were generated by a single **ping** command. The **ping** to 192.168.1.2 does not appear in the output, as expected in the debug, because the ACL conditionally picks 172.21.1.1 only.

Another statistic to review is the ACL, to see how many hits occurred during the test. Example 7-18 clears the ACL counters, runs a **ping** to 172.21.1.1, and reviews the ACL counters.

Example 7-18 *Reviewing ACL Counters*

```
HQ# clear access-list counters

HQ# ping 172.21.1.1

Type escape sequence to abort.
Sending 5, 100-byte ICMP Echos to 172.21.1.1, timeout is 2 seconds:
!!!!!
Success rate is 100 percent (5/5), round-trip min/avg/max = 1/2/4 ms
HQ# show access-lists
Extended IP access list 150
    10 permit icmp any host 172.21.1.1 echo (10 matches)
    20 permit icmp host 172.21.1.1 any echo-reply (25 matches)
```

Note that the ACL counters are higher than the number of ICMP packets sent in Example 7-18. ACL counters begin when the ACL is assigned to the process (or at system startup, if it is in the startup configuration).

If the ACL is removed prior to the disabling of the debugging, the system automatically disables the debugging. This is shown in Example 7-19.

Example 7-19   *Disabling an ACL Assigned to a Debugging Session Without Disabling Debugging*

```
HQ# configure terminal
Enter configuration commands, one per line.  End with CNTL/Z.
HQ(config)# no access-list 150
IP packet debugging is off
Turning off all possible debugging on ACL 150
```

Conditionally Triggered Debugging

Figure 7-9 illustrates a simple network that is referenced in this section. All debugging output is assumed to be running to the console.

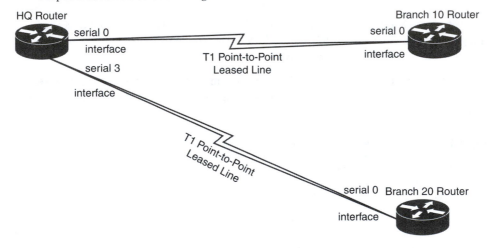

Figure 7-9   *Simple WAN Example*

Using the routers in Figure 7-9, this section reviews the effects of limiting a debugging command to a specific interface. In Example 7-20, **debug serial interface** is run on the HQ router. In Example 7-20, there is no traffic running through the HQ router other than HDLC keepalives on the serial lines.

Example 7-20   *Enabling Debugging on All Serial Interfaces*

```
HQ# debug serial interface
Serial network interface debugging is on
*May 20 22:22:22.851: Serial0: HDLC myseq 28, mineseen 28*, yourseen 41, line up
*May 20 22:22:22.855: Serial3: HDLC myseq 26, mineseen 26*, yourseen 27, line up
*May 20 22:22:44.851: Serial0: HDLC myseq 29, mineseen 29*, yourseen 42, line up
*May 20 22:22:44.855: Serial3: HDLC myseq 27, mineseen 27*, yourseen 28, line up
```

Looking at the debug output, the HDLC keepalives are identified for serial interfaces 0 and 3. Example 7-21 shows that only serial interface 3 is set.

Example 7-21   *Enabling Conditional Debugging on the Serial Interface*

```
HQ# debug interface serial 3
Condition 1 set
```

The **debug** output in Example 7-22 shows output on matching the single interface only.

Example 7-22   *Debugging Output After Setting the Condition on Serial Interface 3 Only*

```
<output omitted>
*May 20 22:22:32.895: Serial3: HDLC myseq 32, mineseen 32*, yourseen 33, line up
*May 20 22:22:54.895: Serial3: HDLC myseq 35, mineseen 35*, yourseen 48, line up
```

The debugging for serial interface 3 is the only output. Now, the condition can be removed without disabling serial debugging. This is accomplished by turning off the debugging on the interface, which removes the condition from the debugging. Example 7-23 shows the removal of the condition, followed by a warning that all serial line debugging will be reenabled.

Example 7-23   *Removing the Debugging Condition While Debugging Is Still Enabled*

```
HQ# undebug interface serial 3
This condition is the last interface condition set.
Removing all conditions may cause a flood of debugging
messages to result, unless specific debugging flags are first removed.
Proceed with removal? [yes/no]: y
Condition 1 has been removed
```

The preferred method is to turn off the serial debugging or all debugging before removing the conditional trigger. Otherwise, as the warning in Example 7-23 indicates, all serial debugging is reenabled, potentially causing a service-impacting issue.

Troubleshooting an Issue with Debugging

In this section, OSPF failure is diagnosed using debugging. Figure 7-10 provides a very simplistic network using two routers. Branch and HQ are connected by a Fast Ethernet link on the same subnet. Both interfaces are in area 0 and are using OSPF authentication with a plaintext authentication key.

FastEthernet0/0   FastEthernet0/0
192.168.1.1   192.168.1.2
OSPF Area 0   OSPF Area 0

HQ Router   Branch Router

Figure 7-10 *HQ and Branch Routers*

In Figure 7-10, the HQ and Branch routers can't establish a neighbor relationship. Begin the troubleshooting process with the following steps and configurations:

Step 1.   Check to see if there are OSPF neighbors:

```
HQ# show ip ospf neighbor
<blank line>
```

Step 2.   Ping the router that should be a neighbor:

```
HQ# ping 192.168.1.2
Type escape sequence to abort.
Sending 5, 100-byte ICMP Echos to 192.168.1.2, timeout is 2 seconds:
!!!!!
Success rate is 100 percent (5/5), round-trip min/avg/max = 1/1/4 ms
```

Step 3.   Check the configuration to make sure OSPF is configured properly:

```
HQ# show running-config
<output omitted>

router ospf 100
 area 0 authentication
 network 192.168.1.1 0.0.0.0 area 0
<output omitted>
interface FastEthernet0/0
 ip address 192.168.1.1 255.255.255.0
 ip ospf authentication-key kati
<output omitted>
```

Step 4.   Once steps 1-3 have been completed, now run debugging on the **adj** (for adjacency) keyword and you immediately see a key mismatch:

```
HQ# debug ip ospf adj
OSPF adjacency events debugging is on
HQ#
*May  4 06:45:31.760: OSPF: Rcv pkt from 192.168.1.2, FastEthernet0/0 :
Mismatch Authentication Key - Clear Text
```

Step 5. Check the configuration on Branch and notice that the key is wrong on the interface:

```
HQ# show running-config
<output omitted>
router ospf 100
   area 0 authentication
   network 192.168.1.2 0.0.0.0 area 0
<output omitted>
interface FastEthernet0/0
 ip address 192.168.1.2 255.255.255.0
 ip ospf authentication-key katie
<output omitted>
```

The configuration displayed in Step 5 quickly determines the issue with the **debug** command.

Verifying Protocol Operation with Debugging

The **debug** command is a good tool to use when you are trying to learn more about protocols and functions. Protocols are important because they support fundamental design, implementation, and troubleshooting techniques. The **debug** command is a good tool to run in a controlled environment (such as a lab) to gain a better understanding of how underlying protocols function. It can be an excellent study aid. As an example, this section shows how to verify a PPP connection with CHAP authentication. Figure 7-11 provides a simple configuration of two routers running PPP with CHAP-level authentication.

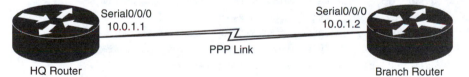

Figure 7-11 *PPP with CHAP Authentication Example*

Example 7-24 is the same as the example for CHAP with PPP used in the "Configuring PPP Authentication with CHAP" section of Chapter 5, "Understanding WAN Technologies." The only difference in these examples would be the router names (Chapter 5 uses RouterA and RouterB, for device names. In this example, Branch and HQ were used). Example 7-24 provides the configuration for the Branch and HQ routers.

Example 7-24 *Configuration for the Branch and HQ Routers*

```
Router(config)# hostname HQ
HQ(config)# username Branch password Cisco123
HQ(config)# interface serial 0/0/0
HQ(config-if)# ip address 10.0.1.1 255.255.255.0
```

```
HQ(config-if)# encapsulation ppp
HQ(config-if)# ppp authentication chap


Router(config)# hostname Branch
Branch(config)# username HQ password C1sco123
Branch(config)# interface serial 0/0/0
Branch(config-if)# ip address 10.0.1.1 255.255.255.0
Branch(config-if)# encapsulation ppp
Branch(config-if)# ppp authentication chap
```

Debugging is run against the PPP authentication, as shown in Example 7-25. This allows the examination of how the actual CHAP exchange occurs.

Example 7-25 *Running debug from the HQ Router to Examine CHAP Operations*

```
HQ# debug ppp authentication
Oct 23 11:08:10.642: %LINK-3-UPDOWN: Interface Serial0/0/0, changed state to
up
Oct 23 11:08:10.642: Se0/0/0 PPP: Using default call direction
Oct 23 11:08:10.642: Se0/0/0 PPP: Treating connection as a dedicated line
Oct 23 11:08:10.642: Se0/0/0 PPP: Session handle[CC000003] Session id[5]
Oct 23 11:08:10.642: Se0/0/0 PPP: Authorization required
Oct 23 11:08:10.674: Se0/0/0 CHAP: O CHALLENGE id 4 len 28 from "HQ"
Oct 23 11:08:10.718: Se0/0/0 CHAP: I CHALLENGE id 1 len 28 from "Branch"
Oct 23 11:08:10.718: Se0/0/0 CHAP: Using hostname from unknown source
Oct 23 11:08:10.718: Se0/0/0 CHAP: Using password from AAA
Oct 23 11:08:10.718: Se0/0/0 CHAP: O RESPONSE id 1 len 28 from "HQ"
Oct 23 11:08:10.722: Se0/0/0 CHAP: I RESPONSE id 4 len 28 from "Branch"
Oct 23 11:08:10.722: Se0/0/0 PPP: Sent CHAP LOGIN Request
Oct 23 11:08:10.726: Se0/0/0 PPP: Received LOGIN Response PASS
Oct 23 11:08:10.726: Se0/0/0 PPP: Sent LCP AUTHOR Request
Oct 23 11:08:10.726: Se0/0/0 PPP: Sent IPCP AUTHOR Request
Oct 23 11:08:10.726: Se0/0/0 LCP: Received AAA AUTHOR Response PASS
Oct 23 11:08:10.726: Se0/0/0 IPCP: Received AAA AUTHOR Response PASS
Oct 23 11:08:10.726: Se0/0/0 CHAP: O SUCCESS id 4 len 4
Oct 23 11:08:10.742: Se0/0/0 CHAP: I SUCCESS id 1 len 4
Oct 23 11:08:10.746: Se0/0/0 PPP: Sent CDPCP AUTHOR Request
Oct 23 11:08:10.746: Se0/0/0 CDPCP: Received AAA AUTHOR Response PASS
Oct 23 11:08:10.746: Se0/0/0 PPP: Sent IPCP AUTHOR Request-if)#
Oct 23 11:08:11.742: %LINEPROTO-5-UPDOWN: Line protocol on Interface
Serial0/0/0, changed state to up
```

The authentication is shown. The highlighted areas display the two-way CHAP challenge/response authentication exchange. This explains how debugging in Cisco IOS also provides information on router operations.

Chapter Summary

This chapter provided some advanced troubleshooting and information gathering techniques. Collecting diagnostic information is an important skill. Proper documentation is needed to be able to fully diagnose and troubleshoot issues. Collecting diagnostic information is also very useful to establish network baselines and document normal operating conditions and configurations.

The Cisco Output Interpreter and Cisco Bug Toolkit can help you to narrow down problems significantly. If conditions do not exactly match a known bug, or the problem is diagnosed incorrectly, a software upgrade may not resolve a problem. The condition could be misdiagnosed, the wrong code selected, or another or new bug may exist in the new code loaded. Cisco IOS Software upgrades should be reviewed thoroughly and lab tested, if possible, before deployment. An engineer should always understand that software upgrades may introduce an unknown variable into a new environment.

Performing debugging on a Cisco router is a powerful tool. Exercise caution when using the **debug** tool because it can create an unstable situation or make a situation worse. Prior to performing any debugging in a production environment, know from testing what the debugging might cause.

Review Questions

Use the questions here to review what you learned in this chapter. The correct answers are located in Appendix A, "Answers to Chapter Review Questions."

1. Which of the following is true of the **show tech-support** command? (Source: "Collecting Cisco IOS Device Diagnostic Information")

   a. Can be provided to Cisco as a means to review the router operational state
   b. Doesn't provide any licensing or useful information to the network administrator
   c. Contains the startup configuration
   d. Contains password information, so it must be secured

2. Which of the following is accurate about the Output Interpreter? (Source: "Using the Output Interpreter to Detect Issues")

   a. Comes on a DVD with a new router and only runs under Microsoft Windows
   b. Is a web application on Cisco's website to examine **show** commands
   c. Only works with the **show technical-support** command
   d. Can be purchased from Cisco on DVD when ordering equipment

3. A known bug can be looked up by using which of the following? (Source: "Researching Cisco IOS Bugs and Defects")

   a. Cisco TAC only

   b. The Bug Toolkit

   c. The **show defect bugid** command in the router

4. Which of the following allows an SSH or Telnet session to see debugging and other Cisco IOS messages? (Source: "Capturing Debugging Output")

   a. The **terminal monitor** command

   b. The **logging console** command

   c. Adding **terminal monitor** to the running configuration

   d. Adding **logging console** command to the running configuration

5. Which command(s) can disable debugging? (Source: "Verifying and Disabling Debugging")

   a. **undebug all**

   b. **no debug all**

   c. **no debug** *debug_command_enabled*

   d. **undebug** *debug_command_enabled*

6. Which of the following can limit debugging output? (Source: "Limiting Debugging Output")

   a. Using an ACL if the debugging command permits

   b. Using conditional debugging if the debugging command permits

   c. Using partial debugging if the debugging command permits

   d. Using the **debug limit** *debugging_command_enabled* command

7. Which statement is correct about the impact of debugging on system performance? (Source: "Device Debugging")

   a. Debugging does not impact system performance.

   b. Debugging always has some impact on system performance. Some commands have more impact than others.

   c. Debugging impacts the system only if the system is busy.

   d. Debugging impacts the system only if the **debug all** command is enabled.

8. Debugging only shows errors in the process/protocol being monitored. True or False? (Source: "Verifying Protocol Operation with Debugging")

   a. True

   b. False

   c. Only if the **debug all** command is enabled

Answers to Chapter Review Questions

Chapter 1

1. A
2. A and E
3. C
4. C
5. A
6. C
7. A and D
8. C
9. B
10. D
11. C
12. D
13. B
14. B
15. False
16. C

Chapter 2

1. C
2. 1. b
   2. c
   3. a
   4. e
   5. d
3. C
4. D
5. B
6. E
7. A and C
8. D

Chapter 3

1. B and C
2. B
3. C
4. C
5. E
6. C
7. C
8. B
9. C
10. 1. b
    2. d
    3. c
    4. a
11. A and E
12. 1. b
    2. a
    3. d
    4. c
13. B
14. A
15. False

16. B and D

17. C and D

18. A

19. B, D, and G

20. A

21. A

22. 1. c
   2. d
   3. a
   4. b

Chapter 4

1. C

2. 1. b
   2. c
   3. a

3. B

4. A

5. B

6. C

7. B and D

8. A, B, and D

9. B and C

10. D

11. A and C

12. A

13. C

14. D

15. C

16. D

17. A

18. A

19. B

Chapter 5

1. A and D
2. A
3. A and D
4. A
5. B
6. B
7. A and C
8. A
9. 1. b
   2. e
   3. a
   4. c
   5. d
10. A
11. D
12. D
13. A
14. A and D
15. A, B, and D
16. B
17. A and B
18. A
19. A, B, and D
20. E

Chapter 6

1. A, B, and D
2. A
3. H
4. A and B
5. B
6. C
7. D
8. A
9. C

10. D

11. A

12. B

13. A

14. B

15. A and D

16. A, B, and C

17. A

18. C

19. C

20. C

21. B and C

22. A and C

23. A and D

Chapter 7

1. A

2. B

3. B

4. A

5. A, B, C, and D

6. A and B

7. B

8. B

Appendix B

1. B

2. A

3. B

4. D

Basic L3VPN MPLS Configuration and Verification

This appendix contains the following sections:

- L3VPN MPLS Configuration and Validation Example

- Summary

- Review Questions

When configuring L3VPN (Layer 3 VPN) MPLS, the service provider normally supplies the basic, initial configuration for the CE even if the CE is managed by the customer. The customer sends its traffic through the CE to the PE. The CE is the customer edge router, and the PE is the provider edge router. The PE labels the traffic and sends it into the service provider's MPLS network.

When using Virtual Private LAN Services (VPLS) or Pseudowire, the circuit handed to the customer does not require MPLS configuration, as it appears to be either an Ethernet Connection or as T1/E1. So, to the customer, the circuit is configured, monitored, and managed as a leased line.

However, with L3VPNs, the customer may have administrative control of the Layer 3 IP connection between the CE and PE. In this case, either static routes or a routing protocol is used. Often, the provider establishes a BGP relationship between the CE and the PE. The CE then runs the customer's IGP as well as BGP to the service provider. The BGP routes are redistributed into the customer's IGP for reachability to the remote sites, or the customer may use static routing. The customer's IGP or static routes are redistributed into BGP.

This appendix discusses MPLS from the customer side only.

Appendix Objectives

- Introduce basic L3VPN MPLS concepts from an MPLS customer perspective

- Introduce the configuration of a simple L3VPN MPLS CE device

- Introduce basic L3VPN MPLS monitoring

L3VPN MPLS Configuration and Validation Example

Figure B-1 shows a typical L3VPN implementation of a service provider's MPLS backbone to connect a headquarters and three branches in a hub-and-spoke network. The branches have flat networks with only one to two subnets connected directly to the CE. The headquarters has multiple LAN segments that are routed via OSPF.

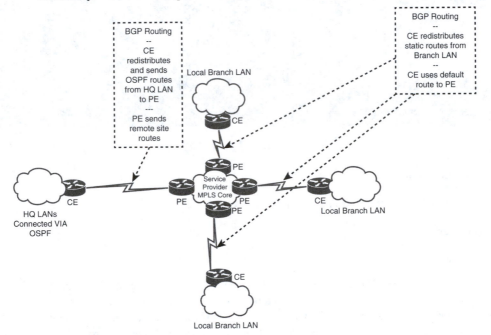

Figure B-1   *Typical Hub-and-Spoke L3VPN*

Example B-1 shows configuration of the BGP on the HQ CE.

Example B-1   *BGP on CE to PE on HQ Router*

```
router bgp 65222
! AS number for the customer site
 neighbor 192.168.253.1 remote-as 65333
! BGP peer/PE router
 neighbor 192.168.253.1 default-originate
! Send a default route for the customer network to the PE. This will be contained
within the VRF.
```

Example B-2 illustrates the customer IGP on a typical CE.

Example B-2 *Sample IGP Configuration for the CE*

```
router ospf 100
 router-id 172.15.0.254
 redistribute bgp 65222 metric-type 1 subnets
! Inject the VRF site routes into OSPF
 network 10.74.28.0 0.0.0.255 area 0
```

Once the routing protocols are configured and the routing protocols converge, the **show ip bgp neighbors** command confirms that the neighbor relationship is established, as demonstrated in Example B-3.

Example B-3 *Checking BGP Neighbor Relationship from CE to PE*

```
HQ_CE# show ip bgp neighbors
BGP neighbor is 192.168.253.1,  remote AS 1888, external link
  BGP version 4, remote router ID 10.248.23.254
  BGP state = Established, up for 8w4d
  Last read 00:00:33, last write 00:00:18, hold time is 135, keepalive interval is
45 seconds
  Neighbor sessions:
    1 active, is not multisession capable (disabled)
<output truncated>
```

The **show ip route** command guides the BGP routes to the remote sites and the OSPF routes to the local LANs, as demonstrated in Example B-4.

Example B-4 *Verifying Routes on the CE*

```
HQ_CE# show ip route
Codes: L - local, C - connected, S - static, R - RIP, M - mobile, B - BGP
       D - EIGRP, EX - EIGRP external, O - OSPF, IA - OSPF inter area
       N1 - OSPF NSSA external type 1, N2 - OSPF NSSA external type 2
       E1 - OSPF external type 1, E2 - OSPF external type 2
       i - IS-IS, su - IS-IS summary, L1 - IS-IS level-1, L2 - IS-IS level-2
       ia - IS-IS inter area, * - candidate default, U - per-user static route
       o - ODR, P - periodic downloaded static route, H - NHRP, l - LISP
       + - replicated route, % - next hop override


      10.0.0.0/8 is variably subnetted, 373 subnets, 8 masks
O        10.1.0.0/17 [110/41] via 10.12.0.6, 6d04h, GigabitEthernet0/1
                     [110/41] via 10.12.0.4, 6d04h, GigabitEthernet0/0
```

```
O          10.4.132.0/26 [110/51] via 10.12.0.6, 2d22h, GigabitEthernet0/1
                         [110/51] via 10.12.0.4, 2d22h, GigabitEthernet0/0
O          10.12.0.2/31 [110/3] via 10.12.0.6, 6d04h, GigabitEthernet0/1
                         [110/3] via 10.12.0.4, 6d04h, GigabitEthernet0/0
C          10.12.0.4/31 is directly connected, GigabitEthernet0/0
L          10.12.0.5/32 is directly connected, GigabitEthernet0/0
C          10.12.0.6/31 is directly connected, GigabitEthernet0/1
L          10.12.0.7/32 is directly connected, GigabitEthernet0/1
B          10.18.0.0/24 [20/0] via 192.168.253.1, 5d00h
B          10.43.0.0/16 [20/0] via 192.168.253.1, 5w4d
B          10.73.129.0/24 [20/0] via 192.168.253.1, 5d00h
<output truncated>
```

Example B-5 shows the configuration of the CE in a typical branch. The configuration is pretty simple because only two subnets are directly connected to the PE, an IGP is not needed, and the connected routes can be redistributed into BGP. The CE has a default (0.0.0.0) route to the local PE.

Example B-5 *Simple Branch BGP Configuration*

```
router bgp 65223
! AS number used for the customer site
 redistribute connected
! Send the directly connected LAN routes to the provider instead of using a routing
protocol
 neighbor 192.168.253.93 remote-as 65334
!PE router is the neighbor, using the AS number in the command
```

Summary

MPLS is a complex subject that has been covered extensively in many books. As a CCNA, you should have at least rudimentary knowledge of an L3VPN configuration and how to apply it (even though it is not tested on the CCNA exams), as you may need to do this as part of your job.

Review Questions

Use the questions here to review what you learned in this appendix. The correct answers are located in Appendix A, "Answers to Chapter Review Questions."

1. MPLS Pseudowire requires a direct BGP connection from the customer to the service provider WAN.

   a. True
   b. False

2. L3VPN MPLS connects the customer LANs via which router type?

   a. CE
   b. PE
   c. P
   d. PN
   e. All of the above

3. MPLS L3VPN requires the customer to route its LANs with a dynamic routing protocol.

   a. True
   b. False

4. Which statement(s) is/are true about L3VPN MPLS?

   a. A dynamic routing protocol is required.
   b. The CE hands off a clear-channel Ethernet or T1/E1 to the customer network.
   c. The CE to PE connection uses MPLS labels.
   d. Dynamic routing, static routing, or connecting all LANs directly to the CE are valid configurations.

Glossary of Key Terms

This glossary defines many of the terms and abbreviations related to networking. It includes all the key terms used throughout the book. As with any growing technical field, some terms evolve and take on several meanings. Where necessary, multiple definitions and abbreviation expansions are presented. This glossary also includes some terms that were not covered in the book, but that you may find interesting and useful.

A

access control list (ACL)   A list kept by Cisco routers to control access to or from the router for a number of services. For example, ACLs prevent packets with a certain IP address from leaving a particular interface on the router.

access layer   The access layer in the three-layer hierarchical network model describes the portion of the network where devices connect to the network and includes controls for allowing devices to communicate on the network.

access server   A communications processor that connects asynchronous devices to a LAN or WAN through network and terminal-emulation software. Performs both synchronous and asynchronous routing of supported protocols. Sometimes called a network access server.

administrative distance   The metric that routers use to select the best path when there are two or more different routes to the same destination from two different routing protocols. It is often referred to as the reliability or trustworthiness of a routing protocol. The lower the administrative distance, the more preferred the protocol is. The interface of a connected route has the lowest administrative distance of 0, followed by static routes at 1. Administrative distances can be manually changed in the configuration of a router.

advanced distance vector routing protocol   A distance vector routing protocol that has the capability to operate on more than a monolithic, periodic routing update. Examples are incremental updates and a composite metric. EIGRP is placed in this category.

Advanced Encryption Standard (AES)   The National Institute of Standards and Technology (NIST) adopted AES to replace the existing DES encryption in cryptographic devices. AES provides stronger security than DES and is computationally more efficient than 3DES. AES offers three different key lengths: 128-, 192-, and 256-bit keys.

application-specific integrated circuit (ASIC)   A development process for implementing integrated circuit designs that are specific to the intended application, as opposed to designs for general-purpose use. For example, ASIC is used in Cisco Express Forwarding to route packets at a higher speed than an individual CPU could support.

Area Border Router   In OSPF, connects one or more nonbackbone areas to the backbone.

asymmetric encryption   Uses different keys for encryption and decryption. Knowing one of the keys does not allow a hacker to deduce the second key and decode the information. One key encrypts the message, and a second key decrypts it. It is impossible to encrypt and decrypt with the same key.

asymmetric routing   When traffic from the source and the return traffic from the destination take different paths.

asynchronous   A form of communication that does not require clocking. The start of each character is individually signaled by the transmitting device. An RS-232 serial line is an example of where asynchronous communication occurs.

Asynchronous Transfer Mode (ATM)   An international standard for cell relay in which multiple service types (such as voice, video, or data) are conveyed in fixed-length (53-byte) cells. Fixed-length cells allow cell processing to occur in hardware, thereby reducing transit delays. ATM is designed to take advantage of high-speed transmission media such as E3, T3, and SONET.

attenuation   Loss of communication signal energy.

Authentication Header (AH)   Provides data authentication and integrity for IP packets passed between two systems. It verifies that any message passed between two systems has not been modified during transit. It also verifies the origin of the data. AH does not provide data confidentiality (encryption) of packets. Used alone, the AH protocol provides weak protection.

auto-MDIX   An optional feature of Catalyst switches. When the auto-MDIX feature is enabled, the switch detects the required cable type for copper Ethernet connections and configures the interface pin-outs accordingly, enabling the use of either a crossover cable or a straight-through cable for connections to a 10/100/1000 port on the switch, regardless of the type of device on the other end of the connection.

Automatic Private IP Addressing (APIPA)   Certain Windows clients have this feature, with which a Windows computer can automatically assign itself an IP address in the 169.254.*x*.*x* range if a DHCP server is unavailable or does not exist on the network.

autonomous system (AS)   A group of routers under a single administrative control. This group normally runs a single Interior Gateway Protocol, such as EIGRP or OSPF. However, the AS may run more than one routing protocol.

Autonomous System Boundary Router (ASBR)   In OSPF, a router that exchanges routes between OSPF and another routing domain via route redistribution. Routes are injected into OSPF from an ASBR. An ASBR communicates the OSPF routes into another routing domain. The ASBR runs OSPF and another routing protocol.

Autonomous System Number (ASN)   A unique number used by routing protocols to define the AS. The EIGRP routing protocol uses an ASN to identify its peer routers. Other Interior Gateway Protocols do not use an explicit ASN. However, the Exterior Gateway Protocol, Border Gateway Protocol (BGP), uses a unique ASN for each AS. This is used in routing and the exchange of routing information. The public Internet uses ASNs to identify unique organizations that are publically registered, with a block reserved for use in private networks. ASNs range from 0 to 65535. In public registration, ASNs 0, 23456, and 65535 are reserved for administrative use. ASN numbers 64512 through 65534 are reserved for use for private networks and are not for use on the public Internet.

AutoSecure   Uses a single command to disable nonessential system processes and services, eliminating potential security threats.

B

backbone   The part of a network that acts as the primary path for traffic that is most often sourced from and destined for other networks. In OSPF, this is known as area 0.

backup designated router (BDR)   In OSPF, a backup to the designated router (DR) in case the DR fails.

Backward Explicit Congestion Notification (BECN)   A bit set by a Frame Relay network in frames traveling in the opposite direction of frames encountering a congested path. The DTE receiving frames with the BECN bit set can request that higher-level protocols take flow control action as appropriate.

Basic Rate Interface (BRI)   An ISDN interface composed of two B channels and one D channel for circuit-switched communication of voice, video, and data.

bearer (B) channel   In ISDN, a full-duplex 64-kbps channel used to send user data.

bit-oriented   A class of data link layer communication protocols that can transmit frames regardless of frame content. Compared with byte-oriented protocols, bit-oriented protocols provide full-duplex operation and are more efficient and reliable.

black hat   Someone who uses his knowledge of computer systems to break into systems or networks that he is not authorized to use, usually for personal or financial gain. A cracker is an example of a black hat.

Bootstrap Protocol (BOOTP)   A protocol used by a network node to determine the IP address of its Ethernet interfaces to affect network booting.

bot   An application that runs automated tasks.

bottom-up troubleshooting   You start with the physical components of the network and move up through the layers of the OSI model until you find the cause of the problem. Bottom-up troubleshooting is a good approach to use when you suspect a physical problem.

bridge protocol data unit (BPDU)   A frame used by STP to exchange information on bridge IDs, root path costs, topology changes, and STP timers. There are three types of BPDUs: Configuration BPDUs, Topology Change Notifications (TCN), and Topology Change Notification Acknowledgements (TCA).

broadband   A transmission system that multiplexes multiple independent signals onto one cable. In telecommunications terminology, any channel having bandwidth greater than a voice-grade channel (4 KHz). In LAN terminology, a coaxial cable on which analog signaling is used. Also called wideband.

broadcast domain   A logical section of a network in which all data link layer broadcasts are contained.

broadcast storm   A condition where broadcasts are flooded endlessly, often due to a looping at Layer 2 (bridge loop).

buffer   A storage area used to handle data in transit. Buffers are used in internetworking to compensate for differences in process speed between network devices. Bursts of data can be stored in buffers until they can be handled by slower processing devices. Also known as a packet buffer.

C

cable   A transmission medium of copper wire or optical fiber wrapped in a protective cover.

cable analyzer   A multifunctional handheld device that is used to test and certify copper and fiber cables for different services and standards. The more sophisticated tools include advanced troubleshooting diagnostics that measure distance to performance defect (NEXT, RL), identify corrective actions, and graphically display crosstalk and impedance behavior.

cable modem (CM)   Enables you to receive data at high speeds. Typically, the cable modem attaches to a standard 10BASE-T Ethernet card in the computer.

cable modem termination system (CMTS)   A component that exchanges digital signals with cable modems on a cable network. A headend CMTS communicates with cable modems that are located in the subscriber homes.

cable television   A communication system in which multiple channels of programming are transmitted to homes using broadband coaxial cable. Formerly called community antenna television (CATV).

cable tester   A specialized handheld device designed to test the various types of data communication cabling. Cable testers can be used to detect broken wires, crossed-over wiring, shorted connections, and improperly paired connections.

call setup time   The time required to establish a switched call between DTE devices.

carrier sense multiple access with collision avoidance (CSMA/CA)   Media access method that requires WLAN devices to sense the medium for energy levels and wait until the medium is free before sending.

Catalyst Operating System (CatOS)   The first operating system on the Catalyst line of switches prior to Cisco IOS Software. It is no longer supported and it has been deprecated in favor of IOS.

cell   1) The basic unit for ATM switching and multiplexing. Cells contain identifiers that specify the data stream to which they belong. Each cell consists of a 5-byte header and 48 bytes of payload. 2) In wireless technology, a cell is the area of radio range or coverage in which the wireless devices can communicate with the base station. The cell's size depends on the speed of the

transmission, the type of antenna used, and the physical environment, as well as other factors.

cell relay   A network technology based on the use of small, fixed-size packets, or cells. Because cells are fixed length, they can be processed and switched in hardware at high speeds. Cell relay is the basis of many high-speed network protocols, including ATM, IEEE 802.6, and SMDS.

central office (CO)   A local telephone company office to which all local loops in a given area connect and in which circuit switching of subscriber lines occurs.

Challenge Handshake Authentication Protocol (CHAP)   A security feature supported on lines using PPP encapsulation that prevents unauthorized access. CHAP does not itself prevent unauthorized access; it merely identifies the remote end. The router or access server then determines whether that user is allowed access.

channel   1) A communication path. Multiple channels can be multiplexed over a single cable in certain environments. 2) In IBM, the specific path between large computers (such as mainframes) and attached peripheral devices.

channel service unit (CSU)   A digital interface device that connects end-user equipment to the local digital telephone loop. Often mentioned with DSU as CSU/DSU.

channel service unit/data service unit (CSU/DSU)   A piece of equipment that combines the CSU and DSU functions required by digital lines, such as T1 or T3 carrier lines. The CSU provides termination for the digital signal and ensures connection integrity through error correction and line monitoring. The DSU converts the T-carrier line frames into frames that the LAN can interpret, and vice versa.

circuit   A communications path between two or more points.

circuit switching   A switching system in which a dedicated physical circuit path must exist between sender and receiver for the duration of the "call." Used heavily in the telephone company network. Circuit switching can be contrasted with contention and token passing as a channel access method, and with message switching and packet switching as a switching technique.

Cisco Discovery Protocol (CDP)   A media- and protocol-independent device-discovery protocol that runs on all Cisco-manufactured equipment, including routers, access servers, bridges, and switches. Using CDP, a device can advertise its existence to other devices and receive information about other devices on the same LAN or on the remote side of a WAN.

Cisco Express Forwarding (CEF)   A Cisco proprietary protocol that allows high-speed packet switching in ASICs, rather than using a CPU. CEF offers "wire speed" routing of packets and load balancing.

Cisco IOS helper address   An address configured on an interface to which broadcasts received on that interface are sent.

Cisco Router and Security Device Manager (SDM)   A web-based device-management tool designed for configuring LAN, WAN, and security features on Cisco IOS Software–based routers.

classless interdomain routing (CIDR)   A technique supported by BGP4 and based on route aggregation. CIDR allows routers to group routes to reduce the quantity of routing information carried by the core routers. With CIDR, several IP networks appear to networks outside the group as a single, larger entity. With CIDR, IP addresses and their subnet masks are written as four octets, separated by periods, followed by a slash and a two-digit number that represents the subnet mask.

Clear to Send (CTS)   A circuit in the EIA/ TIA-232 specification that is activated when the DCE is ready to accept data from the DTE.

clock skew   A clock's frequency difference, or the first derivative of its offset with respect to time. Also referred to as clock drift.

coaxial cable   A cable consisting of a hollow cylindrical conductor that surrounds a single inner wire conductor. Two types of coaxial cable are currently used in LANs: 50-ohm cable, which is used for digital signaling, and 75-ohm cable, which is used for analog signaling and high-speed digital signaling.

collision domain   A section of a network segment in which all data link layer frame collisions are contained.

committed information rate (CIR)   The rate at which a Frame Relay network agrees to transfer information under normal conditions, averaged over a minimum increment of time. CIR, measured in bits per second, is one of the key negotiated tariff metrics.

communications line   The physical link (such as a wire or telephone circuit) that connects one or more devices to one or more other devices.

community antenna television (CATV)   A communication system in which multiple channels of programming are transmitted to homes using broadband coaxial cable.

community string   A text string that acts as a password and is used to authenticate messages sent between a management station and a router containing an SNMP agent. The community string is sent in every packet between the manager and the agent.

configuration register   In Cisco routers, a 16-bit user-configurable value that determines how the router functions during initialization. The configuration register can be stored in hardware or software. In hardware, you set the bit position by specifying a hexadecimal value using configuration commands.

congestion   Traffic in excess of network capacity.

connectionless   A term used to describe data transfer without the existence of a virtual circuit.

connection-oriented   A term used to describe data transfer that requires the establishment of a virtual circuit.

console cable   Used for connecting to the AUX and console ports of a Cisco router. Most commonly RS-232, but USB cables are available also.

control plane   Handles the interaction of the router with the other network elements, providing the information needed to make decisions and control the overall router operation. This plane runs processes such as routing protocols and network management.

convergence   The speed and capability of a group of switches running STP to agree on a loop-free Layer 2 topology for a switched LAN.

core layer   The backbone of a switched LAN. All traffic to and from peripheral networks must pass through the core layer. It includes high-speed switching devices that can handle relatively large amounts of traffic.

core router   In a packet-switched star topology, a router that is part of the backbone and that serves as the single pipe through which all traffic from peripheral networks must pass on its way to other peripheral networks.

cracker   Someone who tries to gain unauthorized access to network resources with malicious intent.

customer premises equipment (CPE)   Terminating equipment, such as terminals, telephones, and modems, supplied by the telephone company, installed at customer sites, and connected to the telephone company network.

cut-through switching   An Ethernet frame switching approach that streams data through a switch so that the leading edge of a packet exits the switch at the egress port before the packet finishes entering the ingress port. A device using cut-through packet switching reads, processes, and forwards packets as soon as the destination address is read and the egress port determined.

cycles per second   A measure of frequency.

D

data center class switches   High-performance and scalable devices that provide a network core, consolidation of services and servers, and interconnection of technologies. Usually contain redundant components and require specialized heating and cooling.

data communications   The sending and receiving of data between two endpoints. Data communications require a combination of hardware (CSU/DSUs, modems, multiplexers, and other hardware) and software.

data communications equipment (DCE)   Data communications equipment is the EIA expansion of DCE. Data circuit-terminating equipment is the ITU-T expansion. The devices and connections of a communications network that comprise the network end of the user-to-network interface. The DCE provides a physical connection to the network, forwards traffic, and provides a clocking signal used to synchronize data transmission between DCE and DTE devices. Modems and interface cards are examples of DCE.

Data Encryption Standard (DES)   Developed by IBM, DES uses a 56-bit key, ensuring high-performance encryption. DES is a symmetric key cryptosystem.

data-link connection identifier (DLCI)   A value that specifies a PVC or SVC in a Frame Relay network. In the basic Frame Relay specification, DLCIs are locally significant (connected devices might use different values to specify the same connection). In the Local Management Interface (LMI) extended specification, DLCIs are globally significant (DLCIs specify individual end devices).

Data Over Cable Service Interface Specification (DOCSIS)   An international standard developed by CableLabs, a nonprofit research and development consortium for cable-related technologies. CableLabs tests and certifies cable equipment vendor devices, such as cable modems and cable modem termination systems, and grants DOCSIS-certified or qualified status.

data plane   Handles packet forwarding from one physical or logical interface to another. It involves different switching mechanisms such as process switching and Cisco Express Forwarding (CEF) on Cisco IOS Software routers.

data service unit (DSU)   A device used in digital transmission that adapts the physical interface on a DTE device to a transmission facility such as T1 or E1. The DSU is also responsible for such functions as signal timing. Often combined in the same device with a CSU as a CSU/DSU.

Data Set Ready (DSR)   An EIA/TIA-232 interface circuit that is activated when DCE is powered up and ready for use.

data stream   All data transmitted through a communications line in a single read or write operation.

data VLAN   A VLAN that is configured to carry only user-generated traffic. In particular, a data VLAN does not carry voice-based traffic or traffic used to manage a switch.

decryption   The reverse application of an encryption algorithm to encrypted data, thereby restoring that data to its original, unencrypted state.

dedicated line   A communications line that is indefinitely reserved for transmissions, rather than switched as transmission is required.

default gateway   The route that the device uses when it has no other explicitly defined route to the destination network. The router interface on the local subnet acts as the default gateway for the sending device.

default VLAN   The VLAN that all the ports on a switch are members of when a switch is reset to factory defaults. All switch ports are members of the default VLAN after the initial boot of the switch. On a Catalyst switch, VLAN 1 is the default VLAN.

delta (D) channel   A full-duplex 16-kbps (BRI) or 64-kbps (PRI) ISDN channel.

demarcation point (demarc)   The point where the service provider or telephone company network ends and connects with the customer's equipment at the customer's site.

demilitarized zone (DMZ)   The interface of a firewall where the publicly accessible segment exists. The host on the outside may be able to reach the host on the public services segment, the DMZ, but not the host on the inside part of the network.

denial-of-service (DoS) attack   An attack designed to saturate network links with illegitimate data. This data can overwhelm an Internet link, causing legitimate traffic to be dropped.

designated port (DP)   In Spanning Tree Protocol, the switch port that receives and forwards frames toward the root bridge as needed.

designated router (DR)   In OSPF, a router on a multiaccess network segment that coordinates all routing updates on the segment.

DHCP for IPv6 (DHCPv6)   Dynamic Host Configuration Protocol for IPv6.

DHCP relay agent   A component that relays DHCP messages between DHCP clients and DHCP servers on different IP networks.

DHCPACK   Unicast message sent by a DHCP server in response to a device sending a DHCPREQUEST. This message is used by the DHCP server to complete the DHCP process.

DHCPDISCOVER   Broadcast messages sent by a client device to discover a DHCP server.

DHCPOFFER   Unicast message returned by the DHCP server in response to a client device sending a DHCPDISCOVER broadcast message. This message typically contains an IP address, subnet mask, default gateway address, and other information.

DHCPREQUEST   Broadcast message sent by a client device in response to a DHCP server's DHCPOFFER message. This message is used by the device to accept the DHCP server's offer.

Diffie-Hellman (DH)   An algorithm to securely derive shared keys across an untrusted network infrastructure. Diffie-Hellman is used to generate keys to be used in the ciphers specified in IPsec transforms. IPsec uses these transforms in conjunction with DH keys to encrypt and decrypt data as it passes through the VPN tunnel.

digital multimeter (DMM)   A test instrument that directly measures electrical values of voltage, current, and resistance. In network troubleshooting, most multimedia tests involve checking power-supply voltage levels and verifying that network devices are receiving power.

digital subscriber line (DSL)   An always-on connection technology that uses existing twisted-pair telephone lines to transport high-bandwidth data and that provides IP services to subscribers. A DSL modem converts an Ethernet signal from the user device into a DSL signal, which is transmitted to the central office.

Dijkstra's algorithm   The shortest path first algorithm. Used in OSPF and IS-IS link-state routing protocols for calculation of the SPF tree. Named after the inventor of the algorithm, Dutch computer scientist Edsger Dijkstra.

Discard Eligible (DE)   Also known as tagged traffic. If the network is congested, tagged traffic can be dropped to ensure delivery of higher-priority traffic.

Distance Vector Routing Protocol   A type of routing protocol where a router's routing table is based on hop-by-hop metrics and is only aware of the topology from a viewpoint of its directly connected neighbors. EIGRP and RIP are examples of distance vector routing protocols.

distributed DoS (DDoS) attack   Designed to saturate network links with illegitimate data. This data can overwhelm an Internet link, causing legitimate traffic to be dropped. DDoS uses attack methods similar to standard DoS attacks, but it operates on a much larger scale. Typically, hundreds or thousands of attack points attempt to overwhelm a target.

distribution layer   In the three-layer hierarchical network design model, the distribution layer is the layer that invokes policy and routing control. Typically, VLANs are defined at this layer.

divide-and-conquer troubleshooting   You start by collecting users' experiences with the problem and document the symptoms. Then, using that information, you make an informed guess about the OSI layer at which to start your investigation. After you verify that a layer is functioning properly, assume that the layers below it are functioning, and work up the OSI layers. If an OSI layer is not functioning properly, work your way down the OSI layer model.

Domain Name System (DNS)   A form of hostname to IP address name resolution. The primary form of name resolution used on the public Internet.

drop cable   Generally, a cable that connects a network device (such as a computer) to a physical medium. A type of attachment user interface (AUI).

DS0 (digital signal level zero)   A framing specification used to transmit digital signals over a single channel at 64 kbps on a T1 facility.

DSL access multiplexer (DSLAM)   The device located at the provider's central office (CO). Concentrates connections from multiple DSL subscribers.

DUAL (diffusing update algorithm)   The algorithm that EIGRP uses to obtain a loop-free topology, and that allows all EIGRP routers involved in a topology change to synchronize at the same time.

dual stacking   A common transition mechanism to enable the smooth integration of IPv4 to IPv6.

dynamic 6to4 tunneling   Automatically establishes the connection of IPv6 islands through an IPv4 network, typically the Internet. It dynamically applies a valid, unique IPv6 prefix to each IPv6 island, which enables the fast deployment of IPv6 in a corporate network without address retrieval from the ISPs or registries.

dynamic auto   A DTP setting whereby the local switch port advertises to the remote switch port that it is able to trunk but does not request to go to the trunking state. After a negotiation, the local port ends up in trunking state only if the remote port trunk mode has been configured to be on or desirable. If both ports on the switches are set to auto, they do not negotiate to be in the trunking state; they negotiate to be in the access (nontrunk) mode state.

dynamic desirable   A DTP setting whereby the local switch port advertises to the remote switch port that it is able to trunk and asks the remote switch port to go to the trunking state. If the local switch port detects that the remote switch port has been configured in on, desirable, or auto mode, the local switch port ends up in trunking state. If the remote switch port is in the nonegotiate mode, the local switch port remains a nontrunking port.

Dynamic Host Configuration Protocol (DHCP)   Makes the process of assigning new IP addresses almost transparent. DHCP assigns IP addresses and other important network configuration information dynamically.

dynamic NAT   Uses a pool of public addresses and assigns them on a first-come, first-served basis. When a host with a private IP address requests access to the Internet, dynamic NAT chooses an IP address from the pool that is not already in use by another host.

Dynamic Trunking Protocol (DTP)   A Cisco proprietary protocol that negotiates both the status and encapsulation of trunk ports between two devices.

dynamic VLAN   VLAN port membership modes are either static or dynamic. Dynamic VLANs are not widely used in production networks. Dynamic port VLAN membership is configured using a special server called a VLAN Membership Policy Server (VMPS).

E

E1   A wide-area digital transmission scheme used predominantly in Europe that carries data at a rate of 2.048 Mbps. E1 lines can be leased for private use from common carriers.

E3   A wide-area digital transmission scheme used predominantly in Europe that carries data at a rate of 34.368 Mbps. E3 lines can be leased for private use from common carriers.

Encapsulating Security Payload (ESP)   Provides a combination of security services for IPsec-processed IP packets. Examples of the services offered by ESP include data confidentiality, data origin authentication, data integrity, and data confidentiality.

encapsulation   The process of placing higher-layer protocols into lower-layer protocols for transport. Placing an IP packet into an HDLC frame for transport across a leased line is an example.

encryption   Applying a specific algorithm to data to alter its appearance, making it incomprehensible to those who are not authorized to see the information.

end-system configuration table   Contains baseline records of the hardware and software used in end-system devices such as servers, network management consoles, and desktop workstations. An incorrectly configured end system can have a negative impact on a network's overall performance.

enterprise network   A large and diverse network connecting most major points in a company or other organization. Differs from a WAN in that it is privately owned and maintained.

EtherChannel   A technology that was originally developed by Cisco as a LAN switch-to-switch technique of grouping more than one Fast Ethernet, Gigabit Ethernet, or 10-Gigabit Ethernet ports into one logical channel.

Ethernet   The main media used in local-area networking. There are many varieties of this media implementation at various speeds.

EUI-64 (Extended Universal Identifier 64)   An IPv6 address format created by taking an interface's MAC address (which is 48 bits long) and inserting another 16-bit hexadecimal string (FFFE) in the OUI (first 24 bits) of the MAC address. To ensure that the chosen 48-bit address is a unique Ethernet address, the seventh bit in the high-order byte is set to 1 (equivalent to the IEEE U/L, Universal/Local bit).

Excess Burst Size (BE)   A negotiated tariff metric in Frame Relay internetworks. The number of bits that a Frame Relay internetwork attempts to transmit after the committed burst (BC) is accommodated. In general, BE data is delivered with a lower probability than BC data, because BE data can be marked as DE by the network.

exchange identification (XID)   Request and response packets exchanged before a session between a router and a Token Ring host. If the parameters of the serial device contained in the XID packet do not match the host's configuration, the session is dropped.

extranet   A WAN connection between separate entities, such as business partners, that offers limited, specific usage applications. May be either VPN or leased line based.

F

feasible distance (FD)   In EIGRP, the best metric along a path to a destination network, including the metric to the neighbor advertising that path.

feasible successor   In EIGRP, a path whose reported distance is less than the feasible distance (current best path).

firewall   A router or access server designated as a buffer between any connected public network and a private network. A firewall router uses access lists and other methods to ensure the security of the private network.

firmware   Software instructions set permanently or semipermanently in ROM. On Cisco Catalyst switches, the firmware provides a means of booting the switch with these instructions, which are unaffected by a power loss.

Flash   Technology developed by Intel and licensed to other semiconductor companies. Flash memory is nonvolatile storage that can be electrically erased and reprogrammed. Flash allows software images to be stored, booted, and rewritten as necessary.

Forward Explicit Congestion Notification (FECN)   A bit set by a Frame Relay network to inform the DTE receiving the frame that congestion occurred in the path from source to destination. DTE receiving frames with the FECN bit set can request that higher-level protocols take flow-control action as appropriate.

fragmentation   The process of breaking a packet into smaller units when transmitting over a network medium that cannot support the packet's original size.

Frame Relay   An industry-standard switched data link layer protocol that handles multiple virtual circuits using HDLC encapsulation between connected devices. Frame Relay is more efficient than X.25, the protocol for which it is generally considered a replacement.

Frame Relay access device (FRAD)   Any network device that provides a connection between a LAN and a Frame Relay WAN.

frequency   The number of cycles, measured in hertz, of an alternating current signal per unit of time.

full duplex   The capability of a port for simultaneous data transmission and reception.

full-mesh topology   A network in which each network node has either a physical circuit or a virtual circuit connecting it to every other network node. A full mesh provides a great deal of redundancy, but because it can be prohibitively expensive to implement, it is usually reserved for network backbones.

G

gateway   A special-purpose device that performs an application layer conversion of information from one protocol stack to another. The term *gateway* also is used to refer to a router or an interface on a router that enables users in an organization to connect to the Internet.

Generic Routing Encapsulation (GRE)   A tunneling protocol developed by Cisco that can encapsulate a wide variety of protocol packet types inside IP tunnels. This creates a virtual point-to-point link to Cisco routers at remote points over an IP internetwork. By connecting multiprotocol subnetworks in a single-protocol backbone environment, IP tunneling using GRE allows network expansion across a single-protocol backbone environment.

Global Load Balancing Protocol (GLBP)   A Cisco proprietary protocol that provides both redundancy and load balancing of data. This is through the use of multiple routers. Routers present a shared GLBP address that end stations use as a default gateway.

global routing prefix   Part of the IPv6 address that is a hierarchically structured value assigned to a site.

H

hacker   A general term that has historically been used to describe a computer programming expert. More recently, this term is often used in a negative way to describe an individual who attempts to gain unauthorized access to network resources with malicious intent.

half duplex   Refers to the transmission of data in just one direction at a time. At any given instant, the device can transmit or receive, but not both simultaneously.

hash   Contributes to data integrity and authentication by ensuring that unauthorized persons do not tamper with transmitted messages. A hash, also called a message digest, is a number generated from a string of text. The hash is smaller than the text itself. It is generated using a formula in such a way

that it is extremely unlikely that some other text will produce the same hash value.

hashed message authentication code (HMAC)   A data integrity algorithm that guarantees the message's integrity.

headend   The endpoint of a broadband network. All stations transmit toward the headend; the headend then transmits toward the destination stations.

High-Level Data Link Control (HDLC)   A bit-oriented synchronous data link layer protocol developed by ISO. Derived from SDLC, HDLC specifies a data encapsulation method on synchronous serial links using frame characters and checksums.

High-Speed Serial Interface (HSSI)   A network standard for high-speed (up to 52 Mbps) serial connections over WAN links.

Hot Standby Router Protocol (HSRP)   A Cisco proprietary protocol for use in the redundancy of routers. The routers present a common IP address that end stations employ as the address for the router. One router is the active HSRP router and one acts as a standby in case of gateway failure.

hub   1) Generally, a term used to describe a device that serves as the center of a star topology network. 2) A hub-and-spoke WAN, where the hub (headend) of the WAN serves as the termination point for multiple remote sites. Often seen in WANs based on Frame Relay. 3) A Layer 2 Ethernet device that terminates and connects multiple Ethernet devices to the LAN segment.

hybrid routing protocol   An invalid classification of Layer 3 routing protocols. Often used as an incorrect classification for EIGRP. This term classifies a routing protocol that uses the features of both a link-state protocol and a distance vector protocol.

I

IANA (Internet Assigned Numbers Authority)   An organization operated under the auspices of the ISOC as part of the IAB. IANA delegates authority for IP address-space allocation and domain-name assignment to the NIC and other organizations. IANA also maintains a database of assigned protocol identifiers used in the TCP/IP stack, including autonomous system numbers.

IEEE 802.11   An IEEE specification developed to eliminate problems inherent in the proprietary WLAN technologies. It began with a 1-Mbps standard and has evolved into several other standards, including 802.11a, 802.11b, and 802.11g.

IEEE 802.11b   The IEEE WLAN standard for 11 Mbps at 2.4 GHz.

IEEE 802.11g   The IEEE WLAN standard for 54 Mbps at 2.4 GHz.

IEEE 802.11n   The IEEE WLAN standard for 248 Mbps at 2.4 or 5 GHz. As the latest standard, 802.11n is a proposed amendment that builds on the previous 802.11 standards by adding multiple input, multiple output (MIMO).

IEEE 802.1Q   The IEEE networking standard that supports VLANs over Ethernet. It defines the standard for tagging VLAN traffic so that multiple VLANs can be separately transported over a common link. This is known as VLAN trunking.

IEEE 802.16   The WiMAX standard. It allows transmissions of up to 70 Mbps and has a range of up to 30 miles (50 km). It can operate in licensed or unlicensed bands of the spectrum from 2 to 6 GHz.

inside global address   Used with NAT, a valid public address that the inside host is given when it exits the NAT router.

inside local address   Used with NAT, this usually is not an IP address assigned by an RIR or service provider and is most likely an RFC 1918 private address.

Integrated Services Digital Network (ISDN)   A communication protocol, offered by telephone companies, that permits telephone networks to carry data, voice, and other source traffic.

Internet Control Message Protocol (ICMP)   Chiefly used by TCP/IP network operating systems to send error messages indicating, for instance, that a requested service is not available or that a host or router could not be reached.

Internetwork Packet Exchange (IPX)   A NetWare network layer (Layer 3) protocol for transferring data from servers to workstations. IPX is similar to IP and XNS.

Inter-Switch Link (ISL)   A Cisco proprietary protocol that maintains VLAN information as traffic flows between switches and routers, or switches and switches. ISL is used by trunk ports to encapsulate Ethernet frames between network devices.

inter-VLAN routing   The process of routing data between VLANs within a switched LAN.

intrusion detection system (IDS)   Detects attacks against a network and sends logs to a management console.

intrusion prevention system (IPS)   Prevents attacks against the network and should provide active defense mechanisms in addition to detection, including prevention and reaction. Prevention stops the detected attack from executing. Reaction immunizes the system from future attacks from a malicious source.

Inverse Address Resolution Protocol (ARP)   A method of building dynamic routes in a network. Allows an access server to discover the network address of a device associated with a virtual circuit.

IP multicast   Enables single packets to be copied by the network and sent to a specific subset of network addresses. These receivers subscribe to the multicast group, which correlates to the destination multicast address in the transmission from the source.

IP Next Generation (IPng)   Now known as IPv6, a network layer IP standard used by electronic devices to exchange data across a packet-switched internetwork. It follows IPv4 as the second version of the Internet Protocol to be formally adopted for general use. IPv6 includes support for flow ID in the packet header, which can be used to identify flows.

IP Security (IPsec)   A protocol suite for securing IP communications that provides encryption, integrity, and authentication. IPsec spells out the messaging necessary to secure VPN communications, but it relies on existing algorithms.

IPv6 global unicast address   A globally unique address that can be routed globally with no modification. It shares the same address format as an IPv6 anycast address. The IANA assigns global unicast addresses.

J

J1   A wide-area digital transmission scheme used predominantly in Japan that carries data at a rate of 1.544 Mbps. J1 lines can be leased for private use from common carriers.

jabber   The condition in which a network device continually transmits random, meaningless data onto the network.

jitter   A variation in the delay of received packets. Applications with real-time needs, like VoIP, can be very sensitive to jitter. Jitter is usually caused by variable delays in the network caused by congestion.

jitter buffer   A buffer in router memory to decrease the effects of jitter.

K

K values (EIGRP)   Values used in EIGRP composite metric calculation. The K values allow manual manipulation of the EIGRP composite metric.

keepalive interval   The amount of time between each keepalive message sent by a network device.

knowledge base   An information database used to assist in the use or troubleshooting of a product. Online network device vendor knowledge bases have become indispensable sources of information. When vendor-based knowledge bases are combined with Internet search engines such as Google, a network administrator has access to a vast pool of experience-based information.

L

LACNIC (Latin America and Caribbean Internet Addresses Registry)   One of five Regional Internet Registries (RIR). LACNIC is a not-for-profit membership organization that is responsible for distributing and registering Internet address resources throughout Latin America and part of the Caribbean region.

Layer 2 switch   A device that operates at the data link layer of the OSI model. A Layer 2 switch transparently forwards and filters frames based on the destination MAC address.

leased line   A transmission line reserved by a communications carrier for a customer's private use. A leased line is a type of dedicated line.

Link Access Procedure, Balanced (LAPB)   A data link layer protocol in the X.25 protocol stack. LAPB is a bit-oriented protocol derived from HDLC.

Link Access Procedure for Frame Relay (LAPF)   As defined in the ITU Q.922, specifies Frame Mode Services in the Frame Relay network.

Link Aggregation Control Protocol (LACP)   An industry-standard protocol that aids in the automatic creation of EtherChannel links.

Link Control Protocol (LCP)   A protocol that establishes, configures, and tests datalink connections for use by PPP.

link-state routing protocol   A routing protocol classification where each router has a topology database based on an SPF tree through the network, with knowledge of all nodes. OSPF and IS-IS are examples of linkstate routing protocols.

local-area network (LAN)   A high-speed network for connecting equipment that is in close proximity to each other. This equipment is typically owned by the organization hosting it.

local loop   A line from the premises of a telephone subscriber to the telephone company CO.

Local Management Interface (LMI)   A keepalive mechanism that provides status information about Frame Relay connections between the router (DTE) and the Frame Relay switch (DCE).

logical topology   Describes the arrangement of devices on a network and how they communicate with one another.

loop-avoidance mechanism   A method to keep a network loop free. STP is a Layer 2 method. Layer 3 distance vector routing protocols use methods such as split horizon.

M

man-in-the-middle (MITM) attack   Carried out by an attacker who positions himself between two legitimate hosts. The attacker may allow the normal transactions between hosts to occur, and only periodically manipulate the conversation between the two.

maximum transmission unit (MTU)   The largest size of packets that an interface can transmit without the need to fragment. The MTU varies per media type. Standard Ethernet packets have an MTU size of 1500 bytes for the payload and 18 bytes for the header and checksum. Other media types such as ATM, FDDI, and HSSI all can support larger MTUs than Ethernet.

mesh   A network topology in which devices are organized in a manageable, segmented manner with many, often redundant, interconnections strategically placed between network nodes.

Message Digest 5 (MD5)   An algorithm used for message authentication. MD5 verifies the integrity of the communication, authenticates the origin, and checks for timeliness.

metropolitan-area network (MAN)   A network that spans a metropolitan area. Generally, a MAN spans a larger geographic area than a LAN but a smaller geographic area than a WAN.

microfilter   A device that prevents certain router frequencies from traveling over the telephone line and interfering with telephone calls.

microwave   Electromagnetic waves in the range 1 to 30 GHz. Microwave-based networks are an evolving technology gaining favor due to high bandwidth and relatively low cost.

modem   A device that converts digital and analog signals. At the source, a modem coverts digital signals to a form suitable for transmission over analog communication facilities. At the destination, the analog signals are returned to their digital form. Modems allow data to be transmitted over voice-grade telephone lines.

Multichassis EtherChannel (MEC)   A Cisco proprietary technology that allows an EtherChannel bundle to be split across multiple Catalyst 6500 chassis. Part of the Cisco VSS features.

multilayer switch   A switch that is also capable of routing packets, in addition to switching Layer 2 frames.

Multiprotocol Label Switching (MPLS)   A high-performance packet-forwarding technology that integrates the performance and traffic management capabilities of data link layer (Layer 2) switching with the scalability, flexibility, and performance of network layer (Layer 3) routing.

N

NAT overloading   Sometimes called Port Address Translation (PAT). Maps multiple private IP addresses to a single public IP address or a few addresses.

NAT pool   A list of public IP addresses used in NAT.

native VLAN   A native VLAN is assigned to an IEEE 802.1Q trunk port. An IEEE 802.1Q trunk port supports tagged and untagged traffic coming from many VLANs. The 802.1Q trunk port places untagged traffic on the native VLAN. Native VLANs are set out in the IEEE 802.1Q specification to maintain backward compatibility with untagged traffic common to legacy LAN scenarios. A native VLAN serves as a common identifier on opposing ends of a trunk link. It is a security best practice to define a native VLAN to be a dummy VLAN distinct from all other VLANs defined in the switched LAN. The native VLAN is not used for any traffic in the switched network.

Network Address Translation (NAT)   A mechanism for translating private addresses into publicly usable addresses to be used within the public Internet. An effective means of hiding actual device addressing within a private network. Used extensively with the exhaustion of IPv4 public addresses.

network baseline   Used to efficiently diagnose and correct network problems. A network baseline documents what the network's expected performance should be under normal operating conditions. This information is captured in documentation such as configuration tables and topology diagrams.

network configuration table   Contains accurate, up-to-date records of the hardware and software used in a network. The network configuration table should provide the network engineer with all the information necessary to identify and correct the network fault.

Network Control Protocol (NCP)   Used to establish and configure different network layer protocols.

network documentation   Provides a logical diagram of the network and detailed information about each component. This information should be kept in a single location, either as hard copy or on the network on a protected website. Network documentation should include a network configuration table, an end-system configuration table, and a network topology diagram.

network interface   The demarcation point between the telco's network and the customer's analog phone lines.

network interface device (NID)   Connects the customer premises to the local loop at the demarcation point.

Network Management System (NMS)   Responsible for managing at least part of a network. An NMS is generally a reasonably powerful and well-equipped computer, such as an engineering workstation. NMSs communicate with agents to help keep track of network statistics and resources.

Network Security Wheel   Helps you comply with a security policy. The Security Wheel, a continuous process, promotes retesting and reapplying updated security measures on a continuous basis.

network topology   See topology.

network topology diagram   A graphical representation of a network that illustrates how each device is connected and its logical architecture. A topology diagram has many of the same components as the network configuration table. Each network device should be represented on the diagram with consistent notation or a graphical symbol. Also, each logical and physical connection should be represented using a simple line or other appropriate symbol. Routing protocols also can be shown.

nonbroadcast multiaccess (NBMA)   A term describing a multiaccess network that does not support broadcasting (such as X.25 or Frame Relay) or in which broadcasting is not feasible (for example, an SMDS broadcast group or an extended Ethernet that is too large).

nondesignated port (NDP)   In Spanning Tree Protocol, a switch port that is not forwarding (blocking) data frames and is not populating its MAC address table with the source addresses of frames that are seen on the attached segment.

nonvolatile RAM (NVRAM)   RAM that retains its contents when a device is powered off. In Cisco products, NVRAM is used to store configuration information.

Novell IPX   See Internetwork Packet Exchange (IPX).

null modem   A small box or cable used to join serial computing devices directly, rather than over a network.

NX-OS   An operating system designed by Cisco for the Nexus line of data center switching products. It has many similarities to Cisco IOS, but is a unique operating system.

O

office environment equipment   Equipment designed for operation in an office, rather than a data center. Equipment temperature range, noise, and emissions operate within the guidelines of an acceptable office environment as defined by the U.S. Department of Labor Occupational Safety and Health Administration (OSHA). Form factor and power requirements are suitable for a standard office.

one-step lockdown wizard   Tests your router configuration for potential security problems and automatically makes any necessary configuration changes to correct any problems found.

Open Shortest Path First (OSPF)   A scalable, link-state routing protocol used by many networks inside companies.

optical time-domain reflectometer (OTDR)   Pinpoints the distance to a break in a fiber-optic cable. This device sends signals along the cable and waits for them to be reflected. The time between sending the signal and getting it back is converted into a distance measurement. The TDR function normally is packaged with data cabling testers.

OSI (Open Systems Interconnection) model   A seven-layer model for describing the functions of computer networking. This model is used to teach and troubleshoot networks.

outside global address   A reachable IP address used in NAT and assigned to hosts on the Internet.

P

packet-switched network   Uses packet-switching technology to transfer data.

packet switching   A networking method in which nodes share bandwidth with each other by sending packets.

partial mesh topology   A network in which some network nodes are organized in a full mesh and others are connected to only one or two other nodes in the network. A partial mesh does not provide the level of redundancy of a full-mesh topology, but it is less expensive to implement. Partial-mesh topologies generally are used in the peripheral networks that connect to a fully meshed backbone.

passphrase   A sentence or phrase that translates into a more secure password. The phrase should be long enough to be hard to guess but easy to remember and type accurately.

Password Authentication Protocol (PAP)   An authentication protocol that allows PPP peers to authenticate one another. The remote router attempting to connect to the local router is required to send an authentication request. Unlike CHAP, PAP passes the password and username in the clear (unencrypted). PAP does not itself prevent unauthorized access, but merely identifies the remote end. The router or access server then determines if that user is allowed access. PAP is supported only on PPP lines.

password recovery   The process of legitimately accessing a device when the password is unknown.

permanent virtual circuit (PVC)   A virtual circuit that is permanently established. PVCs save bandwidth associated with circuit establishment and are torn down in situations where certain virtual circuits must exist all the time.

Per-VLAN Spanning Tree (PVST)   A Cisco proprietary STP implementation that maintains a spanning-tree instance for each VLAN configured in the network. PVST relies on Inter-Link Switch (ISL) for VLAN trunk encapsulation.

Per-VLAN Spanning Tree Plus (PVST+)   PVST+ provides the same functionality as PVST, including PortFast, and adds support for IEEE 802.1Q. PVST+ is not supported on non-Cisco devices.

phisher   Someone who uses email or other means to trick others into providing sensitive information, such as credit card numbers or passwords. A phisher masquerades as a trusted party that has a legitimate need for the sensitive information.

physical topology   The mapping of a network that shows the physical layout of equipment, cables, and interconnections.

ping   A command used to verify Layer 3 connectivity. Ping sends an ICMP echo request to the destination address. When a host receives an ICMP echo request, it responds with an ICMP echo reply to confirm that it received the request.

point of presence (POP)   A point of interconnection between the communications facilities provided by the telephone company and the building's main distribution facility.

point-to-multipoint connection   A connection used to connect LANs to service provider WANs that allows a topology where one connection has a direct link to all other WAN links, but the other WAN links are not connected to each other.

point-to-point connection   A connection used to connect LANs to service provider WANs and to connect LAN segments within an enterprise network.

Point-to-Point Protocol (PPP)   A successor to SLIP. Provides router-to-router and host-to-network connections over synchronous and asynchronous circuits.

Port Address Translation (PAT)   Sometimes called NAT overloading. Maps multiple private IP addresses to a single public IP address or a few addresses.

Port Aggregation Protocol (PAgP)   A Cisco proprietary protocol that aids in the automatic creation of EtherChannel links.

port forwarding   The act of forwarding a network port from one network node to another. This technique, sometimes called tunneling, can allow an external user to reach a port on a private IP address (inside a LAN) from the outside through a NAT-enabled router.

portable network analyzer   A portable device that is used to troubleshoot switched networks and VLANs. By plugging in the network analyzer anywhere on the network, a network engineer can see the switch port to which the device is connected and the average and peak utilization.

preshared key (PSK)   A secret key that is shared between the two parties using a secure channel before it needs to be used. PSKs use symmetric key cryptographic algorithms. A PSK is entered into each peer manually and is used to authenticate the peer. At each end, the PSK is combined with other information to form the authentication key.

Primary Rate Interface (PRI)   An ISDN interface to primary rate access. Primary rate access consists of a single 64-Kbps D channel plus 23 (T1) or 30 (E1) B channels for voice or data.

primary station   In bit-synchronous data link layer protocols such as HDLC and SDLC, a station that controls the transmission activity of secondary stations. Also performs other management functions such as error control through polling or other means. Primary stations send commands to secondary stations and receive responses.

protocol analyzer   Decodes the various protocol layers in a recorded frame and presents this information in a relatively easy-to-use format.

public switched telephone network (PSTN)   A general term referring to the variety of telephone networks and services in place worldwide. Also called the plain old telephone service (POTS).

Q

quality of service (QoS)   A measure of performance for a transmission system that reflects its transmission quality and service available.

R

radio frequency (RF)   A generic term referring to frequencies that correspond to radio transmissions. Cable TV and broadband networks use RF technology.

Rapid Per-VLAN Spanning Tree Plus (Rapid PVST+)   A Cisco implementation of RSTP. It supports one instance of RSTP for each VLAN.

Rapid Spanning Tree Protocol (RSTP)   RSTP, specified by IEEE 802.1w, is a dramatic improvement to IEEE 802.1D, providing very fast spanning-tree convergence on a link-by-link basis using a proposal and agreement process independent of timers.

read-only memory (ROM)   Nonvolatile memory that can be read, but not written to, by the microprocessor.

reassembly   The putting back together of an IP datagram at the destination after it has been fragmented at either the source or the intermediate node.

Regional Internet Registry (RIR)   An organization overseeing the allocation and registration of Internet number resources in a particular region of the world. There are currently five RIRs.

reported distance   In EIGRP, the total metric along a path to a destination network as advertised by a neighbor.

RFC 1918, Address Allocation for Private Internets   Allocates private IP addresses that are a reserved block of numbers that can be used by anyone. ISPs typically configure their border routers to prevent privately addressed traffic from being forwarded over the Internet.

RIPE (Réseaux IP Européens) Network Coordination Centre   One of five Regional Internet Registries. RIPE is a not-for-profit membership organization that is responsible for distributing and registering Internet address resources throughout Europe, the Middle East, and parts of Central Asia.

Rivest, Shamir, and Adleman (RSA)   An asymmetric key cryptosystem. The keys use a bit length of 512, 768, 1024, or larger.

ROMMON (ROM monitor)   The system bootstrap that loads the Cisco IOS code. ROMMON is a basic set of instructions that is used to load the Cisco IOS Software. ROMMON mode can be manually entered for system maintenance and for configuration password recovery.

route summarization   The process of combining contiguous network blocks into a single route.

router   A device used to route packets between TCP/IP subnets.

router-on-a-stick   A term used to describe the topology of a Layer 2 switch trunked to an interface on a router for the purposes of inter-VLAN routing. In this topology, the router interface is configured with one logical subinterface for each VLAN.

Routing Information Protocol next generation (RIPng)   RIP for IPv6.

routing table   The table, stored in a router or other internetworking device, that keeps track of routes of network destinations and metrics associated with those routes.

RS-232   The traditional name for a series of standards for serial binary single-ended data and control signals connecting between DTE and DCE. Commonly used on older PCs. Most modern PCs require a USB to RS-232 conversion connection. The light blue cable for connection to AUX/console ports that comes with Cisco routers is RS-232 based. See console cable.

RSA signature   Uses the exchange of digital certificates to authenticate the peers. The local device derives a hash and encrypts it with its private key. The encrypted hash (digital signature) is attached to the message and is forwarded to the remote end. At the remote end, the encrypted hash is decrypted using the public key of the local end. If the decrypted hash matches the recomputed hash, the signature is genuine.

S

SAN-OS   The Cisco operating system that runs the dedicated storage SAN switches from the MDS line of switches, predating NX-OS.

Secure Hash Algorithm 1 (SHA-1)   Uses a 160-bit secret key. The variable-length message and the 160-bit shared secret key are combined and are run through the HMAC-SHA-1 hash algorithm. The output is a 160-bit hash. The hash is appended to the original message and is forwarded to the remote end.

Secure Shell (SSH)   A protocol that allows data to be exchanged over a secure channel between two computers. A secure form of Telnet.

security policy   A policy for an organization that informs users, staff, and managers of their obligations for protecting technology and information assets.

Serial Line Internet Protocol (SLIP)   A standard protocol for point-to-point serial connections using a variation of TCP/IP. A predecessor of PPP.

signaling   The process of sending a transmission signal over a physical medium for purposes of communication.

small office/home office (SOHO)   Generally, an office in a home or small building with ten or fewer workers who have limited connectivity and IT needs.

SNA Control Protocol   Part of the family of Network Control Protocols (NCP), specifically for SNA. Used to establish and configure different network layer protocols.

SONET (Synchronous Optical Network) A high-speed (up to 2.5 Gbps) synchronous network specification developed by Bellcore and designed to run on optical fiber. STS-1 is the basic building block of SONET. Approved as an international standard in 1988.

spammer An individual who sends large quantities of unsolicited email messages. Spammers often use viruses to take control of home computers and use them to send bulk messages.

spanning-tree algorithm (STA) Used by STP to create a spanning tree.

Spanning Tree Protocol (STP) Bridge protocol that utilizes the spanning-tree algorithm, enabling a learning bridge to dynamically work around loops in a network topology by creating a spanning tree. Bridges exchange BPDU messages with other bridges to detect loops, and then remove the loops by shutting down selected bridge interfaces. Refers to both the IEEE 802.1 Spanning-Tree Protocol standard and the earlier Digital Equipment Corporation Spanning-Tree Protocol on which it is based. The IEEE version supports bridge domains and allows the bridge to construct a loop-free topology across an extended LAN. The IEEE version is generally preferred over the Digital Equipment Corporation version. *See also* BPDU and spanning-tree algorithm.

split horizon A rule used by Layer 3 distance vector routing protocols that indicates that routes should not be advertised out the same interface that they arrive on.

splitter Separates the DSL traffic from the POTS traffic.

star topology A LAN topology in which endpoints on a network are connected to a common central switch by point-to-point links.

stateless autoconfiguration A plug-and-play IPv6 feature that enables devices to connect themselves to the network without any configuration and without any servers (such as DHCP servers). This key feature enables the deployment of new devices on the Internet, such as cell phones, wireless devices, home appliances, and home networks.

Static NAT Uses a one-to-one mapping of local and global addresses, and these mappings remain constant. Static NAT is particularly useful for web servers or hosts that must have a consistent address that is accessible from the Internet. These internal hosts may be enterprise servers or networking devices.

statistical time-division multiplexing (STDM) A technique whereby information from multiple logical channels can be transmitted across a single physical channel. Statistical multiplexing dynamically allocates bandwidth only to active input channels, making better use of available bandwidth and allowing more devices to be connected than with other multiplexing techniques.

storage area network (SAN) The networking of interconnected storage devices to computers/servers. This includes tape arrays/drives and disk arrays/drives.

subnet ID A 16-bit subnet field that individual organizations can use to create their own local addressing hierarchy. This field allows an organization to use up to 65,535 individual subnets.

switched virtual circuit (SVC) A virtual circuit that is dynamically established on demand and that is torn down when transmission is complete. SVCs are used in situations where data transmission is sporadic.

symmetric key encryption   Encryption algorithms such as DES and 3DES require a shared secret key to perform encryption and decryption. Each of the two computers must know the key to decode the information. With symmetric key encryption, also called secret key encryption, each computer encrypts the information before sending it over the network to the other computer. Symmetric key encryption requires knowledge of which computers will be talking to each other so that the same key can be configured on each computer.

synchronization   The establishment of common timing between sender and receiver.

Synchronous Data Link Control (SDLC)   An SNA data link layer communications protocol. A bit-oriented, full-duplex protocol that has spawned numerous similar protocols, including HDLC and LAPB.

systematic approach   A troubleshooting method that analyzes the network as a whole rather than in a piecemeal fashion. A systematic approach minimizes confusion and cuts down on time that would be wasted with trial and error.

T

T1   A digital WAN carrier facility. T1 transmits DS-1 formatted data at 1.544 Mbps through the telephone switching network, using AMI or B8ZS coding.

T3   A digital WAN carrier facility. T3 transmits DS-3 formatted data at 44.736 Mbps through the telephone switching network.

TACACS/TACACS+   An authentication protocol, developed by the Defense Data Network (DDN) community, that provides remote-access authentication and related services, such as event logging. User passwords are administered in a central database rather than in individual routers, providing an easily scalable network security solution.

T-carrier   A TDM transmission method that usually refers to a line or cable carrying a DS-1 signal.

TCP/IP model   This model predates the OSI model and describes the technologies used to allow TCP/IP to function for internetworking.

telephony   The science of converting sound to electrical signals and transmitting it between widely removed points.

teleworker   An employee who enjoys some flexibility in working location and hours. The daily commute to an office is replaced by telecommunication links.

TFTP server   Trivial File Transfer Protocol is a simplified version of FTP that allows files to be transferred from one computer to another over a network. The TFTP server stores and receives the uploaded files for download at the user's request.

time-division multiplexing (TDM)   A technique in which information from multiple channels can be allocated bandwidth on a single wire based on preassigned time slots. Bandwidth is allocated to each channel regardless of whether the station has data to transmit.

Time to Live (TTL)   The field in an IP header that indicates how long a packet is considered valid; each routing device that an IP packet passes through decrements the TTL by 1.

top-down troubleshooting   You start with the end-user applications and move down through the layers of the OSI model until you find the cause of the problem. You test end-user applications of an end system before tackling the more specific networking pieces. Use this approach for simpler problems or when you think the problem is with a piece of software.

topology   The arrangement of various elements in the network. It can be used to define physical items, such as a cabling infrastructure, or a logical construct, such as router location in OSPF. Often represented as a diagram. See network topology diagram.

traffic engineering   Enables the performance optimization of pathing through a network through traffic classification, path choice, and classes of service.

transaction   A result-oriented unit of communication processing.

transmission link   A network communications channel consisting of a circuit or transmission path and all related equipment between a sender and a receiver. Most often used to refer to a WAN connection.

Triple DES (3DES)   A newer variant of DES that encrypts with one key, decrypts with a different key, and then encrypts a final time with another key. 3DES provides significantly more strength to the encryption process.

Trivial File Transfer Protocol (TFTP)   A simplified version of FTP that allows files to be transferred from one computer to another over a network in clear text without authentication.

Trojan horse   A type of virus in which the application is written to look like something else, when in fact it is an attack tool. An example of a Trojan horse is a software application that runs a simple game on a workstation. While the user is occupied with the game, the Trojan horse mails a copy of itself to every address in the user's address book. The other users receive the game and play it, thereby spreading the Trojan horse to the addresses in each address book.

trunk   Used to create multiple network cables or ports in parallel to increase the link speed beyond the limits of any single cable or port.

tunneling   An architecture that is designed to provide the services necessary to implement any standard point-to-point encapsulation scheme.

U–V

Universal Asynchronous Receiver/Transmitter (UART)   An integrated circuit, attached to a computer's parallel bus, used for serial communications. The UART translates between serial and parallel signals, provides transmission clocking, and buffers data sent to or from the computer.

V.35   The ITU-T standard for synchronous communications between a NAD and a packet network. Originally specified to support data rates of 48 kbps, it now supports speeds of up to 2.048 Mbps using a 34-pin rectangular connector.

variance   The feature in EIGRP that allows uneven-cost load balancing.

virtual circuit (VC)   A logical circuit created to ensure reliable communication between two network devices. A virtual circuit is defined by a VPI/VCI pair, and it can be either permanent (PVC) or switched (SVC). Virtual circuits are used in Frame Relay and X.25. In ATM, a virtual circuit is called a virtual channel.

virtual LAN (VLAN)   A group of hosts with a common set of requirements that communicate as if they were attached to the same wire, regardless of their physical location. A VLAN has the same attributes as a physical LAN, but it allows for end stations to be grouped together even if they are not located on the same LAN segment. Network reconfiguration can be done through software instead of physically relocating devices.

virtual link (OSPF)   Used when OSPF areas are not directly connected to the OSPF backbone, area 0, a logical construct for connecting the remote area to the backbone area when a direct link does not exist.

virtual port channel (vPC)   A technology used by Nexus switches that allows a single EtherChannel bundle to be split across Nexus chassis in an active-active manner.

virtual private network (VPN)   A means to securely and privately transmit data over an unsecured and shared network infrastructure (such as the public Internet).

Virtual Router Redundancy Protocol (VRRP)   An industry-standard protocol, similar to the Cisco proprietary protocol HSRP, that presents a common IP address that end stations use as a default gateway. VRRP uses an active-standby approach to router redundancy.

Virtual Switching System (VSS)   A Cisco technology that allows two Catalyst switches to be linked under one supervisor engine. The paired switches appear as one switch in the internetwork, and allow features like Multichassis EtherChannel.

virus   Malicious software that is attached to another program to execute a particular unwanted function on a workstation.

VLAN ID (VID)   The parameter in the IEEE 802.1Q tag that indicates the VLAN

the frame is associated with. A Catalyst 2960 switch supports up to 4096 VLAN IDs.

VLAN trunk   An Ethernet point-to-point link between an Ethernet switch interface and an Ethernet interface on another networking device, such as a router or a switch, carrying the traffic of multiple VLANs over the singular link. A VLAN trunk allows you to extend the VLANs across an entire switched LAN.

VLAN Trunking Protocol (VTP)   A Cisco proprietary Layer 2 protocol that enables a network manager to configure a single switch so that it propagates VLAN configuration information to other switches in the network, as well as synchronizes the information with the switches in the VTP domain.

Voice over IP (VoIP)   The capability to carry normal telephony-style voice over an IP-based Internet with POTS-like functionality.

voice VLAN   A specialized Catalyst switch VLAN with an accompanying Catalyst CLI command set. Voice VLANs are designed for and dedicated to the transmission of voice traffic involving Cisco IP phones or Cisco softphones. QoS configurations are applied to voice VLANs to prioritize voice traffic.

VTP advertisements   Messages transmitted between Catalyst switches to share and synchronize VLAN configuration details in the switched LAN.

VTP client   Participates in VTP operation, but does not permit creating, changing, or deleting of VLANs on the client itself. A VTP client stores VLAN information for the VTP domain only while the switch is powered on. A switch reset deletes the VLAN information. A switch must be manually configured to change its mode from VTP server to VTP client.

VTP configuration revision number   A number that indicates the current state of the VLAN information on the switch. The number enables the synchronization of VLAN information within the VTP domain.

VTP domain   A set of Catalyst switches with the same VTP domain name; all switches in a VTP domain share the same synchronized VLAN information.

VTP modes   VTP has three operating modes: server, client, and transparent. The operating mode determines how the switch uses and shares VLAN information within the VTP domain.

VTP password   The VTP password must match on all switches in a VTP domain. The password secures the information in the VTP domain and prevents a rogue switch added to a network from compromising VLAN information.

VTP pruning   Prevents unnecessary transmission of VLAN information from one VLAN across all trunks in a VTP domain. VTP pruning permits switches to negotiate which VLANs have active associations with ports on the portion of the network connected to the opposing end of a trunk link and, hence, prune the VLANs that are not actively associated with ports on that portion of the network. VTP pruning is disabled by default.

VTP server   Advertises the VTP domain VLAN information to other VTP-enabled switches in the same VTP domain. VTP servers store the VLAN information for the entire domain in NVRAM. The server is where VLANs can be created, deleted, or renamed for the domain. It may take multiple subset advertisements to fully update the VLAN information.

VTP transparent mode   VTP transparent mode switches forward VTP advertisements to VTP clients and VTP servers, but does not originate or otherwise process VTP advertisements. VLANs that are created, renamed, or deleted on a VTP transparent mode switch are local to that switch only.

VTP version   VTP has three versions: version 1, version 2, and version 3.

W–X

white hat   Someone who looks for vulnerabilities in systems or networks and then reports them to the system's owners so that they can be fixed. This person is ethically opposed to the abuse of computer systems. A white hat generally focuses on securing IT systems, whereas a black hat (the opposite) wants to break into them.

wide-area network (WAN)   A data communications network that serves users across a broad geographic area and often uses transmission devices provided by common carriers. Frame Relay, SMDS, and X.25 are examples of WANs.

Wi-Fi Alliance   Offers certification for interoperability between vendors of 802.11 products. It helps market a WLAN technology by promoting interoperability between vendors. Certification includes all three 802.11 RF technologies and Wi-Fi Protected Access (WPA).

wildcard mask   A 32-bit quantity used in conjunction with an IP address to determine which bits in an IP address should be ignored when comparing that address to another IP address. A wildcard mask is specified when setting up access lists.

WiMAX (Worldwide Interoperability for Microwave Access)   Described in the IEEE standard 802.16, WiMAX offers high-speed broadband service with wireless access. It provides broad coverage like a cell phone network rather than using small Wi-Fi hotspots.

wiring closet   A specially designed room used to wire a data or voice network. Wiring closets serve as a central junction point for the wiring and wiring equipment that is used to interconnect network devices.

worm   Executes code and installs copies of itself in the memory of the infected computer, which can, in turn, infect other hosts.

X.25   An ITU-T standard that defines how connections between DTE and DCE are maintained for remote terminal access and computer communications in packet data networks (PDN). X.25 specifies LAPB, a data link layer protocol, and PLP, a network layer protocol. Frame Relay has to some degree superseded X.25. X.25 was often used in applications that required guaranteed data delivery, such as financial applications.

Index

SYMBOLS

% (percent sign), 83

. (dot), 54

: (colons), 75

A

aborted transmissions, 62

ABRs (Area Boundary Routers), 152

abstraction, platform, 330

access

    CE (Customer Edge) routers, 264

    local access rates, 235

    MIBs (Management Information Bases), 275

    NADs (network access devices), 195

    remote-access VPNs, 253

    SNMP (Simple Network Management Protocol), 276

    WANs (wide-area networks), 194

access control lists. *See* ACLs

access servers, CDP (Cisco Discovery Protocol), 58

ACLs (access control lists)

    counters, reviewing, 355

    debugging, triggering, 351-356

    filtering, 122

    IPv4 (Internet Protocol version 4), 50, 71-72

    IPv6 (Internet Protocol version 6), 84-86

    OSPF (Open Shortest Path First), 167

    SNMP (Simple Network Management Protocol), 279

    validation, 353

ACs (attachment circuits), 263

activating PPP (Point-to-Point Protocol) links, 221

active routers, 37

AD (advertised distance), 102

Adaptive Security Appliance. *See* ASAs

adding VLANs (virtual LANs), 5

Address Resolution Protocol. *See* ARP

addresses

Frame Relay, mapping, 240-243

IP (Internet Protocol), DRs/BDRs, 149

IPv6 (Internet Protocol version 6), troubleshooting, 75-76

MAC (Media Access Control), 10, 23, 58

unicast, troubleshooting, 76-77

adjacencies, neighbors, 147-149

administrative distance, routing protocols, 95-98

advantages of link-state routing protocols, 144

advertised distance. *See* AD

advertisements

EIGRP (Enhanced Interior Gateway Protocol), 126

LSAs (link-state advertisements), 144-145

verification, 172

agents, SNMP (Simple Network Management Protocol), 270. *See also* SNMP

obtaining data from, 271

sending data to, 274

aggregation, NetFlow, 285

algorithms

DUAL, 99, 125

dynamic routing, 92

SPF (shortest path first), 94, 145

analog phone line interfaces, 201

analyzing STP (Spanning Tree Protocol), 24-26

Antireplay protection, 256

applications. *See also* tools

Cisco IOS. *See* IOS

hypervisor, 72-74

point-to-point networks, 191

Telnet, 55

terminal-emulation program, 346

WAAS (Wide Area Application Services), 300

applying

ACLs (access control lists), 71

Output Interpreter, 341

architecture

CRS (Carrier Routing System), 291

NetFlow, 285-286

redundancy, 12

WANs (wide-area networks), 188

Area Boundary Routers. *See* ABRs

areas

IDs, 148

NSSAs (not-so-stubby areas), 156

OSPF (Open Shortest Path First)

structures, 150

types, 150-153

stub, 155-156

totally stub, 157

ARP (Address Resolution Protocol), 51, 57

caches, 290

inverse, 236

AS (autonomous systems), 92, 119

ASAs (Adaptive Security Appliance), 253

ASBRs (Autonomous System Boundary Routers), 152-153

ATM (Asynchronous Transfer Mode), 198

attachment circuits. *See* ACs

Attempt state, 166

authentication

CHAP (Challenge-Handshake Authentication Protocol), 222-223, 359

EIGRP (Enhanced Interior Gateway Protocol), 114-115

IPSec, 256

OSPF (Open Shortest Path First), 149

PAP (Password Authentication Protocol), 222

SNMP (Simple Network Management Protocol), 271

autoconfiguration, 301

automatic network summarization, 123

automatic trunk negotiation, 8

Autonomous System Boundary Routers. *See* ASBRs

autonomous systems. *See* AS

auto-summary command, 124

avoidance, loops, 13

B

BackboneFast, 21, 28

backbones, router configuration, 151

backing up licenses, 325

back-to-back routers, integrated CSU/DSU, 209-216

backup designated routers. *See* BDRs

bandwidth

EIGRP (Enhanced Interior Gateway Protocol), 103

metrics, 126

reduced bandwidth usage, 99

redundancy, 29-35

references

modification, 147

verification, 176

serial interfaces, 212

bandwidth bandwidth_kbps command, 224

bandwidth bandwidth_kilobits command, 213

Barker, Keith, 72

basic connectivity, testing, 51

BDRs (backup designated routers), 149

BGP (Border Gateway Protocol), 93, 128

bidirectional communication, 147-148

BIDs (bridge IDs), 14, 17, 22

blocking ports, 14

booting routers, 292-293, 302

bootstrap code, 292, 295

Border Gateway Protocol. *See* BGP

BPDU Guard, 28

BPDUs (bridge protocol data units), 13, 16, 21

Branch Routers

EIGRP (Enhanced Interior Gateway Protocol)

configuration, 105

IPv6 configuration, 133

Frame Relay configuration, 248

GRE tunnel configurations, 259

OSPFv3 (Open Shortest Path First version 3), 178

point-to-multipoint configuration, 248

point-to-point Frame Relay, 246

SNMP configuration, 278

Break key emulation, 314

bridge IDs. *See* BIDs

Bridge Priority field, 23

bridge protocol data units. *See* BPDUs

bridging loops, 18, 26

broadband, 198

broadcasts

replication, 238

storms, 13

buffers, packets, 290

Bug Toolkit, 344

building

LSDBs (links-state databases), 149-150

redundant switches topologies, 11

C

cablelength command, 217

cables. *See also* connections

crossover, 196, 209

Ethernet, 199

fiber optic, 187-207

modems, 194, 202

serial, 195

troubleshooting, 50

caches

ARP (Address Resolution Protocol)

RAM (random-access memory), 290

viewing, 57

memory, 290

calculations, metrics, 128

CAPEX (capital expenditure), 193

Carrier Routing System. *See* CRS

carrier transitions, 61

CDP (Cisco Discovery Protocol), 13, 58-60

CE (Customer Edge) routers, 262

central processing units. *See* CPUs

Challenge-Handshake Authentication Protocol. *See* CHAP

channel-group channel-no timeslots timeslot-list speed command, 217

channel service unit/data service unit. *See* CSU/DSU

channels, viewing ports, 35

CHAP (Challenge-Handshake Authentication Protocol), 198, 222-223, 359

configuration, 227

PPP (Point-to-Point Protocol), 225-227

character output, ping command, 54

checking routing for networks output, 120

CIDR (classless interdomain routing), 76

CIR (committed information rate), 235

circuit-switched communication links, 204

circuits

ACs (attachment circuits), 263

T1/E1, 200-201

Cisco Discovery Protocol. *See* CDP

Cisco Feature Navigator, 308

Cisco IOS File System. *See* IFS

Cisco IOS Software. *See* IOS

Cisco IOS-XE, 330

Cisco IOS-XR, 329-330

Cisco License Manager. *See* CLM

Cisco Licenses Registration Portal, 318

Cisco NX-OS, 331

Cisco Prime Infrastructure, 270

Cisco Unified Border Element. *See* CUBE

Cisco Virtual Office. *See* CVO

Claim Certificates, 316

classful routing, 94-95

classification of routing protocols, 93

classless interdomain routing. *See* CIDR

classless routing, 94-95, 99

CLE (Common Language Equipment), 319

clientless VPNs (virtual private networks), 206

CLM (Cisco License Manager), 318

clockrate clock_rate_bits command, 213

clockrate clock_rate_bps command, 224

codes

bootstrap, 292, 295

IPv6 neighbor discovery table, 82

collecting IOS device diagnostic information, 340-341

Collector (NetFlow), 283

collisions, 61

colons (:), 75

commands

auto-summary, 124

bandwidth

bandwidth_kbps, 224

bandwidth_kilobits, 213

cablelength, 217

channel-group channel-no timeslots timeslot-list speed, 217

clockrate

clock_rate_bits, 213

clock_rate_bps, 224

controller type slot/port, 217

copy, 304

debug, 352

debug ip packet, 348, 352

EIGRP (Enhanced Interior Gateway Protocol), 105, 130-131

encapsulation

frame-relay, 246, 249

ppp, 224, 227

encapsulation frame-relay [cisco | ietf], 244

EXEC, 302

frame-relay

interface dlci dlci, 244-246

lmi, 250

map, 252

map protocol protocol_address dlci, 244-246, 249

pvc, 251

framing framing_type, 217

GET, 274

hostname hostname, 227

interface

    interface, 244

    interface.subinterface point-to-multipoint, 249

    interface.subinterface point-to-point, 246

    serial interface_number, 213

    serial port/mod, 224, 227

    tunnel<tunnel_number>, 259

ip address

    ip_address subnet_mask, 244

    ip_v4_address subnet_mask, 224, 227

ip default-network, 67

ip flow , 287

ip flow-export

    destination ip-address udp-port, 287

    version version, 287

ip host name ip_address, 69

ip ospf

    cost cost, 160

    process_id area-id area_id, 170

ipv6

    router ospf process-id, 179

    router ospf process-id are area-id, 179

license boot module, 323

linecode code_type, 217

netsh interface ipv6 show neighbor Windows, 80

network-clock-select priority t1_or_e1 slot/port, 217

network network wildcard_mask area area_id, 160

no debug, 350

no shutdown, 213, 224

OSPFv3 (Open Shortest Path First version 3), 179

passive-interface interface, 171

ping, 51

    EIGRP (Enhanced Interior Gateway Protocol), 118

    extended, 53

    IPv6 (Internet Protocol version 6), 79

    output characters, 54

    static name resolution, 69

    triggering ACL (access control list) debugging, 355

    troubleshooting ACLs (access control lists), 72

ppp authentication chap, 227

redistribute, 153

reload, 320

router-id router_id, 179

router ospf process_id, 160

serial interfaces, 213

SET, 274

show

    access-lists, 71

    buffers, 340

    cdp neighbors, 59

    controllers, 340

    debug, 350

    etherchannel port-channel, 35

    etherchannel summary, 34

    flash0:, 306

    glbp, 41

    interface, 60, 104, 340

    interface interface switchport, 10

interface port-channel, 34

interfaces, 7, 62, 249

ip cache flow, 288

ip eigrp neighbors, 106-107

ip eigrp topology, 110-111

ip flow interface, 287

ip interface, 168, 260

ip interface brief, 260

ip ospf interface, 170, 175

ip ospf neighbor, 172

ip protocols, 120, 170

ip route, 63-65, 108-109, 173

ipv6 eigrp neighbors, 134

license, 320, 340

license udi, 319

mac address-table, 58

process cpu, 340

processes memory, 340

running-config, 302, 340

snmp additional_options, 278

spanning-tree, 25

stacks, 340

startup-config, 302

tech, 341

version, 298, 321, 340

vlan, 5

shutdown, 227

snmp-server

    chassis-id serial_no, 278

    community string [RO | RQ], 278

    contact contact_name, 278

    host ip_address trap community_string, 278

    location location, 278

switchport

    access vlan, 5

    nonegotiate interface, 9

terminal monitor, 346

traceroute, 51,

tracert, 52

tunnel

    destination ip_address, 259

    mode gre ip, 259

    source ip_address, 259

undebug, 350

username username password password, 227

vlan

    global configuration, 4

    vlan_id, 10

committed information rate. See CIR

Common Language Equipment. See CLE

Common Spanning Tree. See CST

components

    BPDUs (bridge protocol data units), 16

    EIGRP (Enhanced Interior Gateway Protocol), 99, 115-118

    end-to-end IPv4 (Internet Protocol version 4), 48-50

    end-to-end IPv6 (Internet Protocol version 6), 78-80

    IFS (Cisco IOS File System), 303

    Interface and Hardware Component Configuration Guide,

    PPP (Point-to-Point Protocol), 220

    routers, 289-291

confidentiality, 256, 271

configuration

ABRs (Area Boundary Routers), 153

ACLs (access control lists), 71

CHAP (Challenge-Handshake Authentication Protocol), 227

Cisco IOS, 300-302

EIGRP (Enhanced Interior Gateway Protocol), 105-106

   authentication, 114-115

   IPv6 (Internet Protocol version 6), 133-135

   verification, 106-108

EtherChannel, 33-34

file management, 311-313

GRE (Generic Routing Encapsulation) tunnels, 256-261

hypervisor, 74

integrated CSU/DSU, 215-216

IOS traps, 273

L3VPN (Layer 3 VPN), 369-372

merging, 312

multilink PPP (Point-to-Point Protocol) over serial lines, 228-232

NetFlow, 286-287

network device management, 270

NMS (Network Management System), 272

OSPF (Open Shortest Path First), multiarea IPv4 implementation, 158-160

OSPFv3 (Open Shortest Path First version 3), 178-179

point-to-multipoint, 247-249

PPP (Point-to-Point Protocol), 223-227

registers, 291-295

routers

   backbones, 151

   normal areas, 151

running configuration files, 290

serial interfaces, WANs, 209-214

SNMP (Simple Network Management Protocol), 276-279

switches, 4

syslog, 281

trunks, 7

VLANs (virtual LANs), 3

WANs (wide-area networks), 243-244, 249-252

congestion, troubleshooting, 61

connections

basic connectivity, testing, 51

CPE (customer premises equipment), 194

Frame Relay, 185, 198

IPv4 (Internet Protocol version 4)

   CDP (Cisco Discovery Protocol), 58-60

   troubleshooting, 48

   verifying, 51-58

IPv6 (Internet Protocol version 6), 78-80

Layer 3, 63

physical connection issues, 60-63

routing domains, 93

switch-to-switch connectivity, 6

troubleshooting, 47

WANs (wide-area networks), 187

consoles, CDP (Cisco Discovery Protocol) messages, 60

controller type slot/port command, 217

conventions, IPv6 (Internet Protocol version 6) addresses, 75-76

convergence

distance vector protocols, 94

rapid, 99

STP (Spanning Tree Protocol), 21

converting optical fiber, 194

copy command, 304

copy tftp running-config command,

core routers, WANs (wide-area networks), 193

costs

interfaces, 175

OSPF (Open Shortest Path First) modification, 147

counters, reviewing ACLs (access control lists), 355

CPE (customer premises equipment), 193

CPUs (central processing units), 290

crashes, 340. *See also* troubleshooting

CRC (cyclic redundancy check), 61

crossover cables, 196, 209

CRS (Carrier Routing System), 291

CST (Common Spanning Tree), 20

CSU/DSU (channel service unit/data service unit), 61, 212

integrated CSU/DSU

back-to-back routers, 216-209

configuration, 215-216

integrated modules, 214

WANs (wide-area networks), 192-193

CUBE (Cisco Unified Border Element), 40

current paths, identification of, 63-66

Customer Edge. *See* CE

customer logical WANs, 263

customer networks, 262

customer premises equipment. *See* CPE

CVO (Cisco Virtual Office), 205

cyclic redundancy check. *See* CRC

D

data centers, troubleshooting, 86

data circuit-terminating equipment. *See* DCE

data integrity, 256

data-link connection identifiers. *See* DLCIs

data structures, link-state routing protocols, 145-146

data terminal equipment. *See* DTE

database descriptors. *See* DBDs

databases

LSDBs (links-state databases), 144, 145

MAC (Media Access Control), 13

VLANs (virtual LANs), 5

DBDs (database descriptors), 149, 164

DCE (data circuit-terminating equipment), 193, 196, 213

dead intervals, 148

debug command, 352

debug ip packet command, 348, 352

debugging

devices, 345

capturing output, 345-350

conditionally triggered, 356-357

limiting output, 351

protocol operations, 359-361

triggering ACLs (access control lists), 351-356

troubleshooting, 357-359

verification, 350-351

IP (Internet Protocol) packets, 350

dedicated communication links, 204

dedicated link extranets, 211

default administrative distances, 96

default configuration, switches, 4

default gateways,

IPv4 (Internet Protocol version 4), 66

IPv6 (Internet Protocol version 6), 81-83

redundancy, 36-41

defects, researching IOS, 343-345

delay

EIGRP (Enhanced Interior Gateway Protocol), 103

metrics, 126

polling data, monitoring in SNMP, 272

DELAY code, 82

deployment

HSRP (Hot Standby Router Protocol), 39-40

VPNs (virtual private networks), 252

description message, 281

designated port. *See* DP

designated routers. *See* DRs

desired paths, identification of, 63-66

destination networks, path selection, 146

detection, applying Output Interpreter, 341

devices, 269. *See also* network device management

debugging, 345

capturing output, 345-350

conditionally triggered, 356-357

limiting output, 351

protocol operations, 359-361

triggering ACLs (access control lists), 351-356

troubleshooting, 357-359

verification, 350-351

IOS, collecting diagnostic information, 340-341

IPSec (IP Security), 255-256

NADs (network access devices), 195

UDIs (universal device identifiers), 319

VLANs (virtual LANs), 2. *See also* VLANs

VoIP (Voice over IP), 58

WANs (wide-area networks), 192-195

diagnostics. *See also* troubleshooting

device information, collecting IOS, 340-341

routers, 340

digital subscriber line. *See* DSL

disabling

automatic summarization, 124

debugging, 350-351

ports, 14

disadvantages of link-state routing protocols, 153

discovery, neighbors, 238

distance vector protocols, 93

distances

AD (advertised distance), 102

administrative, routing protocols, 95-98

FD (feasible distance), 102

distribute lists, filtering, 122

DLCIs (data-link connection identifiers), 235

DNS (Domain Name Server), 50

dynamic name resolution, 69

hostname validation, 55

lookup, 69

troubleshooting, 68

domains

classful routing, 95

routing, 92

dot (.), 54

Down state, 166

DP (designated port), 14, 19

drops, queues, 60

DRs (designated routers), 149

DSL (digital subscriber line), 198

modems, 193

termination, 201

DTE (data terminal equipment), 193, 196, 213

DTP (Dynamic Trunking Protocol), 8-9

DUAL algorithm, 99, 125

dynamic name resolution, 69-71

dynamic routing, overview of, 92-106

Dynamic Trunking Protocol. *See* DTP

E

echo requests (ICMP), 51

EGP (Exterior Gateway Protocol), 93

EIA/TIA-232 interfaces, 195

EIGRP (Enhanced Interior Gateway Protocol), 91

authentication, 114-115

configuration, 105-108

dynamic routing, 92-106

features, 98-115

interfaces, enabling, 120

IPv6 (Internet Protocol version 6)

command syntax, 130-131

configuration, 133-135

feasible successors, 128-129

implementation, 124-136

load balancing, 129

theory of operation, 124

troubleshooting, 135

verification, 131-132

load balancing, 110-112

metrics, 103-104, 126

neighbors, 118-121, 134

packet types, 100-101

passive interfaces, 108-111

path selection, 101, 126

traffic sharing, 113-114

troubleshooting, 115-124

automatic network summarization, 123

components, 115-118

route filtering, 122-124

routing tables, 121

unadvertised routes, 121

variance, 112-113

emulation

Break key, 314

terminal-emulation program, 346

enabling

debugging, 348

EIGRP (Enhanced Interior Gateway Protocol) interfaces, 120

encapsulation

GRE (Generic Routing Encapsulation), 256-261

serial lines, 219

encapsulation frame-relay [cisco | ietf] command, 244

encapsulation frame-relay command, 246, 249

encapsulation ppp command, 224, 227

encryption, 256

end-to-end connections

IPv4 (Internet Protocol version 4) components, 48-50

IPv6 (Internet Protocol version 6) components, 78-80

End User License Agreement. *See* EULA

Enhanced Interior Gateway Protocol. *See* EIGRP

entries, troubleshooting inaccurate routing, 124

environments, virtual

IPv4 (Internet Protocol version 4), 72-74

IPv6 (Internet Protocol version 6), 86

errors

CRC (cyclic redundancy check), 61

Ethernet, 62

framing, 62

input, 61

user-reported, 49

EtherChannel

bandwidth, increasing, 29-35

configuration, 33-34

protocols, 31

LACP (Link Aggregation Control Protocol), 32-33

PAgP (Port Aggregation Protocol), 31-32

verification, 34-35

Ethernet, 198

cable, 199

crossover cables, 196

interfaces, trunks, 6

links, troubleshooting, 62

Metro, 209

EULA (End User License Agreement), 316

evaluation license installation, 273-322

exchange protocols, 164

exchange state, 166

EXEC command, 302

EXEC mode, 314, 341

exstart state, 166

extended ping, 53

Extended System ID field, 23

extensibility (Cisco NX-OS), 331

Exterior Gateway Protocol. *See* EGP

extranets, 209

F

facility message, 281

failures. *See also* troubleshooting

link-state routing protocols, 144

STP (Spanning Tree Protocol), 26-28

FD (feasible distance), 102

feasible successors, 128-129

features of EIGRP (Enhanced Interior Gateway Protocol), 98-115

fiber optic cabling, 207-187

filenames, interpreting Cisco IOS images, 305-306

files

configuration, managing, 311-313

repositories, 304

running configuration, 290

filters

BPDUs (bridge protocol data units), 21

NetFlow, 285

routes, troubleshooting EIGRP, 122-124

flash memory, 290, 303

Flexible NetFlow. *See* NetFlow

flow

control, Layer 2, 197

interfaces, NetFlow, 287

messages, CHAP, 222

SFTP (Secure File Transfer Protocol), 274

flowcharts, troubleshooting EIGRP, 115

formatting. *See also* configuration

IPv6 (Internet Protocol version 6) addresses, 56-76

syslog messages, 281

Frame Relay

connections, 185, 198

WANs (wide-area networks), 233

configuration, 243-244

mapping addresses, 240-243

overview of, 233-236

point-to-multipoint configuration, 247-249

point-to-point subinterface configuration, 245-246

signaling, 239-240

topologies, 236-237

troubleshooting, 237-239

verifying configuration, 249-252

frame-relay interface dlci dlci command, 244-246

frame-relay lmi command, 250

frame-relay map command, 252

frame-relay map protocol protocol-address dlci command, 244-246, 249

frame-relay pvc command, 251

frames, multiple frame transmission, 13

framing errors, 62

framing framing_type command, 217

FTP (File Transfer Protocol), 303

full-mesh networks

Frame Relay, 236

WANs (wide-area networks), 189-191

full state, 166

functions of WANs (wide-area networks), 186

G

Gateway Load-Balancing Protocol. *See* GLBP

gateways, default

IPv4 (Internet Protocol version 4), 66

IPv6 (Internet Protocol version 6), 81-83

redundancy, 36-41

Generic Routing Encapsulation. *See* GRE

GET command, 274

GLBP (Gateway Load-Balancing Protocol), 40-41

global key chains, 115

global unicast addresses, 76

GRE (Generic Routing Encapsulation), 256-261

groups, standby, 37

guards, BPDUs (bridge protocol data units), 21

H

HDLC (High-Level Data Link Control) protocol, 197, 218-220

Hello

intervals, 148

protocol, 163

hierarchies, link-state routing protocols, 150

High-Level Data Link Control protocol. *See* HDLC protocol

hops, 94

hostname hostname command, 227

hostnames

ping command, 69

validation, 55

hosts

nslookup, 70

operating systems, verification, 307

Hot Standby Router Protocol. *See* HSRP

HQ Routers

EIGRP (Enhanced Interior Gateway Protocol)

configuration, 105

IPv6 configuration, 133

Frame Relay configuration, 248

GRE tunnel configurations, 259

OSPFv3 (Open Shortest Path First version 3), 178

point-to-multipoint configuration, 248

point-to-point Frame Relay, 246

HSRP (Hot Standby Router Protocol), 37-38

interface tracking, 38

in IPv6, 40

load balancing, 39

in service deployments, 39-40

hub-and-spoke networks

Frame Relay, 237

L3VPNs, 370

WANs (wide-area networks), 188-189

hypervisor, 72-74

I-J

IANA (Internet Assigned Numbers Authority), 76

ICMP (Internet Control Messaging Protocol), 51

identification of paths

IPv4 (Internet Protocol version 4), 63-66

IPv6 (Internet Protocol version 6), 81

IDs

areas, 148

routers, 148

tags, 319

IFS (Cisco IOS File System), 302

IGP (Interior Gateway Protocol), 91-93

images, IOS

loading, 297-300

locating to load, 295-297

managing, 305

upgrading, 308-311

implementation

EIGRP (Enhanced Interior Gateway Protocol), 91

IPv6 (Internet Protocol version 6), 124-136

troubleshooting, 115-124

EtherChannel, 31

scalable medium-sized networks, 1

configuring trunks, 7

creating VLANs (virtual LANs), 4-6

DTP (Dynamic Trunking Protocol), 8-9

overview of VLANs (virtual LANs), 2

troubleshooting VLANs (virtual LANs), 9-10

trunk operations, 6-7, 10-11

scalable multiarea networks with OSPF, 143

VPNs (virtual private networks), 185

INCMP (Incomplete) code, 82

incoming filtering, 122

increasing bandwidth with EtherChannel, 29-35

infrastructure

Cisco Prime Infrastructure, 270

MPLS (Multiprotocol Label Switching), 261-264

INIT state, 166

input

errors, 61

queue drops, 60

In-Service Software Upgrade. *See* ISSU

installing Cisco IOS

evaluation license, 273-322

permanent licenses, 321-322

integrated CSU/DSU

back-to-back routers, 209-216

configuration, 215-216

modules, 214

Integrated Service Router. *See* ISR

Integrated Services Digital Network. *See* ISDN

integrity, 256, 271

interconnections, 191. *See also* connections

interface interface command, 244

interface interface.subinterface point-to-multipoint command, 249

interface interface.subinterface point-to-point command, 246

interface serial interface_number command, 213

interface serial port/mod command, 224, 227

interface tunnel<tunnel_number>
    command, 259
interfaces
  analog phone lines, 201
  authentication, configuration, 114
  costs, 175
  EIA/TIA-232, 195
  EIGRP (Enhanced Interior Gateway
    Protocol)
      enabling, 120
      verification, 134
  EtherChannel. *See* EtherChannel
  Ethernet trunks, 6
  LMIs (Local Management
    Interfaces), 236, 249
  multilink PPP (Point-to-Point
    Protocol), 230-232
  NetFlow, 287
  OSPF (Open Shortest Path First),
    148
  passive
      *EIGRP (Enhanced Interior
        Gateway Protocol), 108-111*
      *OSPF (Open Shortest Path
        First), 170*
  resets, 61
  routers, 291
  serial, 209-214
  status, 63
  tracking, 38
  V.35, 195
  WICs (WAN interface cards), 196
Interior Gateway Protocol. *See* IGP
Intermediate System-to-Intermediate
    System. *See* IS-IS
internal component review, routers,
    289-291

Internet Assigned Numbers Authority
    (IANA), 76
Internet-based extranets, 210
Internet Control Messaging Protocol.
    See ICMP
Internet Protocol. *See* IP
Internet Protocol version 4. *See* IPv4
Internet Protocol version 6. *See* IPv6
interpreting Cisco IOS image file-
    names, 305-306
intervals, 148
inverse ARP (Address Resolution
    Protocol), 236
IOS
  configuration, 300-302
  defects, researching, 343-345
  devices, collecting diagnostic infor-
    mation, 340-341
  images
      interpreting filenames, 305-306
      loading, 297-300
      locating to load, 295-297
      managing, 305
      upgrading, 308-311
  licensing, 315
      backing up, 325
      *Cisco IOS 15 licensing and
        packaging, 316*
      *evaluation license installation,
        273-322*
      obtaining, 318-319
      overview of, 315
      *permanent license installation,
        321-322*
      prior to Cisco IOS 15, 316-317
      rehosting, 327-328

uninstalling permanent licenses, 325-327

verification, 287-321

loading, 293

password recovery, 313

trap configuration, 273

IP (Internet Protocol)

addresses, DRs/BDRs, 149

packets, debugging, 350

ports to Telnet, 55

routing tables, 67, 290

ip address ip_address subnet_mask command, 244

ip address ip_v4_address subnet_ mask command, 224, 227

ip default-network command, 67

ip flow-export destination ip-address udp-port command, 287

ip flow-export version version com- mand, 287

ip flow command, 287

ip host name ip_address command, 69

ip ospf cost cost command, 160

ip ospf process_id area-id area_id command, 170

IPSec (IP Security), 255-256

IPv4 (Internet Protocol version 4)

EIGRP (Enhanced Interior Gateway Protocol), 125

multiarea IPv4 implementation, 154

troubleshooting

ACLs (access control lists), 71-72

CDP (Cisco Discovery Protocol), 58-60

connections, 48

default gateway issues, 66

end-to-end components, 48-51

identification of paths, 63-66

name resolution issues, 68

physical connection issues, 60-63

verifying connections, 51-58

virtual environments, 72-74

IPv6 (Internet Protocol version 6)

EIGRP (Enhanced Interior Gateway Protocol)

command syntax, 130-131

configuration, 133-135

feasible successors, 128-129

implementation, 124-136

load balancing, 129

theory of operation, 124

troubleshooting, 135

verification, 131-132

HSRP (Hot Standby Router Protocol), 40

troubleshooting, 75

ACLs (access control lists), 84-86

construction of addresses, 75-76

default gateway issues, 81-83

end-to-end connections, 78-80

identification of paths, 81

name resolution issues, 83

neighbor discovery in, 80-82

unicast addresses, 76-77

virtual environments, 86

ipv6 router ospf process-id are area- id command, 179

ipv6 router ospf process-id command, 179

ISDN (Integrated Services Digital Network), 199

IS-IS (Intermediate System-to-Intermediate System), 93

isolation, memory, 330

ISR (Integrated Service Router), 340

ISSU (In-Service Software Upgrade), 330

ITU-T (International Telecommunication Union-Telecommunication), 195

K

K values, 127
EIGRP (Enhanced Interior Gateway Protocol), 103

keys
chains, 114
PAK (Product Activation Key), 316-318

L

L3VPN (Layer 3 VPN) configuration, 369-372

LACP (Link Aggregation Control Protocol), 32-33

LANE (LAN Emulation), 198

last-mile links, 207

late collisions, 61

Layer 2
flow control, 197
MPLS (Multiprotocol Label Switching), 263
WANs (wide-area networks), 197-199

Layer 3
connections, troubleshooting, 63
MPLS (Multiprotocol Label Switching), 263
reachability, 168

Layer 3 VPN. See L3VPN

layouts. See formatting

learning, 14

leased dark fiber, 208

leased lines, 212

levels of syslog logging, 279

license boot module command, 323

licensing, Cisco IOS, 315
backing up, 325
Cisco IOS 15 licensing and packaging, 316
evaluation license installation, 273-322
obtaining, 318-319
overview of, 315
permanent license installation, 321-322
prior to Cisco IOS 15, 316-317
rehosting, 327-328
uninstalling permanent licenses, 325-327
verification, 287-321

linecode code_type command, 217

lines, serial, 63

Link Aggregation Control Protocol. See LACP

link-state acknowledgments. See LSAcks

link-state advertisements. See LSAs

link-state protocols, 94

link-state requests. See LSRs

link-state routing protocols, 144-146, 150

link-state updates. *See* LSUs

links

circuit-switched communication, 204

dedicated communication, 204

EtherChannel, 31

Ethernet, troubleshooting, 62

last-mile, 207

packet-switched communication, 205

point-to-point, 6

PPP (Point-to-Point Protocol), 221

serial communication, 210

switched communication, 204

WANs (wide-area networks), 203

links-state databases. *See* LSDBs

Linux, 330

listening, 14

lists

ACLs (access control lists). *See* ACLs

distribute, filtering, 122

LMIs (Local Management Interfaces), 236, 249

load balancing

EIGRP (Enhanced Interior Gateway Protocol), 99, 103, 110-112, 129

GLBP (Gateway Load-Balancing Protocol), 40-41

HSRP (Hot Standby Router Protocol), 39

loading

Cisco IOS images, 297-300

IOS, 293

state, 166

local access rates, 235

Local Management Interfaces. *See* LMIs

locations

Cisco IOS images to load, 295-297

VLANs (virtual LANs), 2

logging, syslog. *See* syslog

lookup, DNS (Domain Name Server), 69

loopback

plugs, T1 lines, 216

unicast addresses, 76

loop-free classless routing, 99

loops

avoidance, 13

bridging, 18, 26

guards, 21

STP (Spanning Tree Protocol), 13

LSAcks (link-state acknowledgments), 150

LSAs (link-state advertisements), 144-145

OSPF (Open Shortest Path First), 153

OSPFv3 (Open Shortest Path First version 3), 177-178

LSDBs (links-state databases), 144-145, 149-150

LSRs (link-state requests), 149

LSUs (link-state updates), 150

M

MAC (Media Access Control)

addresses, 10, 23, 58

Address fields, 23

databases, troubleshooting, 13

management, 269. *See also* network device management

Management Information Bases. *See* MIBs

managers, SNMP (Simple Network Management Protocol), 270

MANs (metropolitan-area networks), 207-209

maps
  addresses, Frame Relay, 240-243
  topologies, 145

masks
  networks, 148
  subnet
    classful routing, 94
    VLSMs (variable-length subnet masks), 99

MEC (MultiChassis EtherChannel), 31

Media Access Control. *See* MAC

memory
  caches, 290
  flash, 290, 303
  isolation, 330
  NVRAM (nonvolatile RAM), 291
  RAM (random-access memory), 290
  ROM (read-only memory), 290

merging configurations, 312

messages
  CDP (Cisco Discovery Protocol), 60
  description, 281
  dynamic routing, 92
  facility, 281
  flow, 222
  MNEMONIC, 281
  seq no, 281

severity, 281

syslog, 279-281

timestamp, 281

metrics
  calculations, 128
  EIGRP (Enhanced Interior Gateway Protocol), 103-104, 126
  OSPF (Open Shortest Path First), 146-147
  viewing, 112

Metro Ethernet, 209

metropolitan-area networks. *See* MANs

MIBs (Management Information Bases), 270
  polling data, monitoring, 272
  SNMP (Simple Network Management Protocol), 275-276

mismatch
  trunks, 11
  VLANs (virtual LANs), 59

MNEMONIC message, 281

modems. *See also* connections
  cable, 194
  DSL (digital subscriber line), 193
  WANs (wide-area networks), 192

modes
  DTP (Dynamic Trunking Protocol), 8
  EXEC, 314, 341
  LACP (Link Aggregation Control Protocol), 33
  PAgP (Port Aggregation Protocol), 32
  read-only, 274

modification
  bandwidth references, 147
  configuration registers, 294

neighbors, 123

OSPF (Open Shortest Path First) costs, 147

modules

integrated CSU/DSU, 214

protocol-dependent, 99

WAAS (Wide Area Application Services), 300

monitoring

polling data in SNMP, 272

traps in SNMP, 273

Morris, Scott, 72

MPLS (Multiprotocol Label Switching), 199-200, 261-264

multiarea IPv4 implementation

OSPF (Open Shortest Path First), 154

components of troubleshooting, 165-168

configuration, 158-160

neighbors, 168-172

neighbor states, 162-165

NSSAs (not-so-stubby areas), 156

planning implementation, 158

single-area vs., 155

stub areas, 155-156

totally stub areas, 157

troubleshooting, 162

verification, 160-162

OSPFv3 (Open Shortest Path First version 3), 176-180

multicast replication, 238

MultiChassis EtherChannel. *See* MEC

multilink PPP (Point-to-Point Protocol) over serial line configuration, 228-232

multiple frame transmission, 13

multiple syslog destinations, 282

Multiprotocol Label Switching. *See* MPLS

N

NADs (network access devices), 195

name resolution

dynamic name resolution, 69-71

IPv4 (Internet Protocol version 4), 68

IPv6 (Internet Protocol version 6), 83

static name resolution, 68-69

NAT (Network Address Translation), 74, 94

navigation, Cisco Feature Navigator, 308

NBMA (nonbroadcast multiaccess) networks, 166, 238

NDP (nondesignated port), 14

negotiation, automatic trunk, 8

neighbors

adjacencies, 147-149

discovery, 99

Frame Relay, 238

in IPv6 (Internet Protocol version 6), 80-82

EIGRP (Enhanced Interior Gateway Protocol), 106, 118-121, 134

link-state routing protocols, 145-146

modification, 123

OSPF (Open Shortest Path First), 168-172

states, multiarea OSPF, 162-165

NetFlow, 283-288

architecture, 285-286

configuration, 286-287

verification, 287-288

netsh interface ipv6 show neighbor Windows command, 80

network access devices. *See* NADs

Network Address Translation. *See* NAT

network-clock-select priority t1_or_e1 slot/port command, 217

network device management, 269

Cisco IOS-XE, 330

Cisco IOS-XR, 329-330

Cisco NX-OS, 331

configuration, 270

IOS licensing, 315

backing up, 325

Cisco IOS 15 licensing and packaging, 316

evaluation license installation, 322-273

obtaining, 318-319

overview of, 315

permanent license installation, 321-322

prior to Cisco IOS 15, 316-317

rehosting, 327-328

uninstalling permanent licenses, 325-327

verification, 287-321

routers, 288

Cisco IOS password recovery, 313

configuration files, 311-313

configuration registers, 293-295

IFS (Cisco IOS File System), 302

internal component review, 289-291

interpreting Cisco IOS image filenames, 305-306

loading Cisco IOS images, 297-300

locating Cisco IOS images to load, 295-297

managing Cisco IOS images, 305

power-up sequences, 292-293

ROM (read-only memory), 291-292

selecting/loading configurations, 300-302

upgrading Cisco IOS images, 308-311

SNMP (Simple Network Management Protocol)

configuration, 276-279

message formats (syslog), 281

MIBs (Management Information Bases), 275-276

NetFlow, 283-288

obtaining data from agents, 271

overview of syslog, 279-280

polling data, monitoring in, 272

sending data to agents, 274

syslog configuration, 281

traps, monitoring in, 273

versions, 270-271

network interface cards. *See* NICs

Network Management System. *See* NMS

network network wildcard_mask area area_id command, 160

networks. *See also* connections

automatic summarization, 123

customer, 262

destination, path selection, 146

failures, troubleshooting, 63

interfaces, analog phone lines, 201

ISDN (Integrated Services Digital Network), 199

MANs (metropolitan-area networks), 207-209

masks, 148

MPLS (Multiprotocol Label Switching), 261-264

NBMA (nonbroadcast multiaccess), 166

provider, 241

PVST+ (Per-VLAN Spanning Tree Plus), 21-23

scalable medium-sized. *See* scalable medium-sized networks

SONET (Synchronous Optical Network), 198

two-router IPv6, 133

VPNs (virtual private networks). *See* VPNs

WANs (wide-area networks), 185-186. *See also* WANs

wireless, 194, 199

Nexus Operating System. *See* NX-OS

NICs (network interface cards), 6

NMS (Network Management System), 270

configuration, 272

traps, monitoring, 273

no debug command, 350

no shutdown command, 213, 224

nonbackbone areas, 151

nonbroadcast multiaccess. *See* NBMA

non-Cisco equipment, running CDP on, 58

nondesignated port. *See* NDP

nonvolatile RAM. *See* NVRAM

normal areas, 151

notation, CIDR (classless interdomain routing), 76

not-so-stubby areas. *See* NSSAs

nslookup

IPv4 (Internet Protocol version 4), 70

IPv6 (Internet Protocol version 6), 84

NSSAs (not-so-stubby areas), 156

numbers, AS (autonomous systems), 119

NVRAM (nonvolatile RAM), 291-293

NX-OS (Nexus Operating System), 340

O

Object IDs. *See* OIDs

obtaining IOS licensing, 318-319

OIDs (Object IDs), 275

one-line summary per channel group, 35

Open Shortest Path First. *See* OSPF

operating expense. *See* OPEX

operating systems

Cisco NX-OS, 331

host verification, 307

RAM (random-access memory), 290

operations

protocols, verification, 359-361

trunks, 6-7

OPEX (operating expense), 193

optical fiber converters, 194

optimizing redundancy, 29-35

options

OSPF (Open Shortest Path First), 149

WANs (wide-area networks)

links, 203

private connection, 204-205

public connection, 205-207

OSPF (Open Shortest Path First), 93

areas

structures, 150

types, 150-153

AS (autonomous systems), 151

costs, modification, 147

link-state routing protocols, 144-146

LSAs (link-state advertisements), 153

LSDBs (links-state databases), building, 149-150

metrics, 146-147

multiarea IPv4 implementation, 154

components of troubleshooting, 165-168

configuration, 158-160

neighbor states, 162-165

NSSAs (not-so-stubby areas), 156

planning implementation, 158

single-area vs.,155

stub areas, 155-156

totally stub areas, 157

troubleshooting, 162

verification, 160-162

neighbors

adjacencies, 147-149

troubleshooting, 168-172

overview of, 144

path selection, troubleshooting, 174-176

routing tables, troubleshooting, 172-174

scalable multiarea networks, implementation, 143

OSPFv3 (Open Shortest Path First version 3), 176-180

output

characters, ping command, 54

debugging

capturing, 345-350

limiting, 351

queue drops, 61

Output Interpreter, applying, 341

P

P (Provider) routers, 262

packaging

Cisco IOS 15 licensing and, 316

prior to Cisco IOS 15, 316-317

packet-switched communication links, 205

packets

buffers, 290

DBDs (database descriptors), 149

IP (Internet Protocol), debugging, 350

LSAcks (link-state acknowledgments), 150

LSDBs (links-state databases), updating, 149

LSRs (link-state requests), 149

LSUs (link-state updates), 150

metrics. *See* metrics

NetFlow, 284

types, EIGRP, 100-101

PAgP (Port Aggregation Protocol), 31-32

PAK (Product Activation Key), 316, 318

PAP (Password Authentication Protocol), 198, 222

partial-mesh networks

Frame Relay, 236

WANs (wide-area networks), 189

passive-interface interface command, 171

passive interfaces

EIGRP (Enhanced Interior Gateway Protocol), 108-111

OSPF (Open Shortest Path First), 170

Password Authentication Protocol. *See* PAP

password recovery, IOS, 313

paths

identification of

IPv4 (Internet Protocol version 4), 63-66

IPv6 (Internet Protocol version 6), 81

selection

destination networks, 146

EIGRP (Enhanced Interior Gateway Protocol), 101, 126

OSPF (Open Shortest Path First), troubleshooting, 174-176

PCMCIA (Personal Computer Memory Card International Association), 291

percent sign (%), 83

permanent IOS license installation, 321-322

permanent virtual circuits. *See* PVCs

PE (Provider Edge) routers, 262

Personal Computer Memory Card International Association. *See* PCMCIA

Per-VLAN Spanning Tree Plus. *See* PVST+

physical connection issues, troubleshooting, 60-63

physical interfaces. *See* interfaces

physical locations, VLANs (virtual LANs), 2

PIDs (product IDs), 319

ping command, 51

ACLs (access control lists)

triggering debugging, 355

troubleshooting, 72

EIGRP (Enhanced Interior Gateway Protocol), troubleshooting, 118

extended, 53

IPv6 (Internet Protocol version 6), 79

output characters, 54

static name resolution, 69

placement of routers, troubleshooting, 87

plain old telephone system (POTS), 194

planning OSPF multiarea IPv4 implementations, 158

platform abstraction, 330

plugs, loopback, 216

point-to-multipoint configuration, 247-249

point-to-point links, 6

point-to-point networks, WANs, 191

Point-to-Point Protocol. *See* PPP

point-to-point subinterface configuration, 245-246

polling data, monitoring in SNMP, 272

populating routing tables, 64

Port Aggregation Protocol. *See* PAgP

Portfast, 20, 28

ports

 channels, viewing, 35

 disabled, 14

 EtherChannel, 34

 IP (Internet Protocol), Telnet to, 55

 MAC (Media Access Control) address tables, 58

POST (power-on self-test), 292

POTS (plain old telephone system), 194

power-on self-test. *See* POST

power-up sequences, routers, 292-293, 302

PPP (Point-to-Point Protocol), 198

 configuration, 223-227

 WANs (wide-area networks), 220-221

ppp authentication chap command, 227

prevention, bridging loops, 18

priority routers, 149

private connection options, WANs, 204-205

private dark fiber, 208

private (link-local) unicast addresses, 76

privileged EXEC mode, 314

PROBE code, 82

processes, dynamic routing, 92

Product Activation Key. *See* PAK

protocol-dependent modules, 99

protocols

 ARP (Address Resolution Protocol), 51, 57, 236

 BGP (Border Gateway Protocol), 93, 128

 CDP (Cisco Discovery Protocol), 13, 58-60

 CHAP (Challenge-Handshake Authentication Protocol), 198, 359

 distance vector, 93

 DTP (Dynamic Trunking Protocol), 8-9

 EIGRP (Enhanced Interior Gateway Protocol). *See* EIGRP

 EtherChannel, 31

 exchange, 164

 FTP (File Transfer Protocol), 303

 GLBP (Gateway Load-Balancing Protocol), 40-41

 HDLC (High-Level Data Link Control), 197

 Hello, 163

 HSRP (Hot Standby Router Protocol), 37-38

  interface tracking, 38

  in IPv6, 40

load balancing, 39

in service deployments, 39-40

IGP (Interior Gateway Protocol), 91, 93

LACP (Link Aggregation Control Protocol), 32-33

link-state, 94

operations, verification, 359-361

PAgP (Port Aggregation Protocol), 31-32

PAP (Password Authentication Protocol), 198

PPP (Point-to-Point Protocol), 198

RIP (Routing Information Protocol), 93

routing, 92

administrative distances, 95-98

classification of, 93

Frame Relay, 237-239

hierarchies, link-state, 150

link-state, 144-146

OSPF (Open Shortest Path First). See OSPF

RTP (Reliable Transport Protocol), 99

SDLC (Synchronous Data Link Control), 197

SFTP (Secure File Transfer Protocol), 274

SNMP (Simple Network Management Protocol), 270

STP (Spanning Tree Protocol), 12

analysis, 24-26

failures, 26-28

types, 20-21

WANs (wide-area networks)

CHAP (Challenge-Handshake Authentication Protocol), 222-223

HDLC (High-Level Data Link Control), 218-220

Layer 2, 197-199

PAP (Password Authentication Protocol), 222

PPP (Point-to-Point Protocol), 220-221

Provider. *See* P

Provider Edge. *See* PE

provider networks, 241

Pseudowire, 369

public connection options, WANs, 205-207

PVCs (permanent virtual circuits), 235, 251

PVST+ (Per-VLAN Spanning Tree Plus), 20-23

Q

QoS (quality of service), 61

WANs (wide-area networks), 200

queries, nslookup, 70

queues, drops, 60

R

RAM (random-access memory), 290

rapid convergence, 99

Rapid STP. *See* RSTP

RCP (Remote Copy Protocol), 303

RCS (Real Time Control System), 191

reachability, 92

Frame Relay, 237-239

Layer 3, 168

OSPF (Open Shortest Path First), 168

REACH (Reachable) code, 82

read-only memory. *See* ROM

read-only mode, SNMP, 274

Real Time Control System. *See* RCS

recovery

neighbor discovery, 99

passwords, IOS, 313

redistribute command, 153

reduced bandwidth usage, 99

redundancy

bandwidth, increasing with EtherChannel, 29-35

Cisco IOS-XR, 330

default gateways, 36-41

topologies

overview of, 12-15

switches, 11

WANs (wide-area networks), 191

references, bandwidth

modification, 147

verification, 176

Regional Internet Registries (RIR), 76

registers, configuration, 291-295

registration, Cisco Licenses Registration Portal, 318

rehosting IOS licenses, 327-328

relationships, neighbors, 168

reliability, EIGRP, 103

Reliable Transport Protocol. *See* RTP

reload command, 320

remote-access VPNs, 253

Remote Copy Protocol. *See* RCP

remote sites, interconnections, 191

repositories, files, 304

Request for Comments. *See* RFCs

researching Cisco IOS software defects, 343-345

reserved unicast addresses, 76

resets, interfaces, 61

resiliency, 331

restarting routers, 321

results, applying Output Interpreter, 341

reviewing

ACL (access control list) counters, 355

EIGRP (Enhanced Interior Gateway Protocol) neighbors, 134

licenses, 318

STP (Spanning Tree Protocol), 24-26

RFCs (Request for Comments), 91

RIP (Routing Information Protocol), 93

RIR (Regional Internet Registries), 76

RJ-45 straight-through cable, 196

ROM (read-only memory), 290-292

ROMmon (ROM monitor), 292, 313

Root Guard, 21, 28

root port. *See* RP

router-id router_id command, 179

router ospf process_id command, 160

routers

ABRs (Area Boundary Routers), 152

active, 37

ARP (Address Resolution Protocol) caches, 57

ASBRs (Autonomous System Boundary Routers), 152-153

autoconfiguration, 301

backbone configuration, 151

back-to-back, integrated CSU/DSU, 209-216

Branch Routers

   EIGRP configuration, 105

   EIGRP IPv6 configuration, 133

   Frame Relay configuration, 248

   GRE tunnel configurations, 259

   OSPFv3 (Open Shortest Path First version 3), 178

   point-to-multipoint configuration, 248

   point-to-point Frame Relay, 246

   SNMP configuration, 278

CDP (Cisco Discovery Protocol), 58

CE (Customer Edge), 262

HQ Routers

   EIGRP configuration, 105

   EIGRP IPv6 configuration, 133

   Frame Relay configuration, 248

   GRE tunnel configurations, 259

   OSPFv3 (Open Shortest Path First version 3), 178

   point-to-multipoint configuration, 248

   point-to-point Frame Relay, 246

IDs, 148

interfaces, 291

ISR (Integrated Service Router), 340

neighbor OSPF, 147

network device management, 288

   Cisco IOS password recovery, 313

   configuration files, 311-313

   configuration registers, 293-295

   IFS (Cisco IOS File System), 302

   internal component review, 289-291

   interpreting Cisco IOS image filenames, 305-306

   loading Cisco IOS images, 297-300

   locating Cisco IOS images to load, 295-297

   managing Cisco IOS images, 305

   power-up sequences, 292-293

   ROM (read-only memory), 291-292

   selecting/loading configurations, 300-302

   upgrading Cisco IOS images, 308-311

normal area configuration, 151

P (Provider), 262

PE (Provider Edge), 262

placement, troubleshooting, 87

priority, 149

restarting, 321

sources, determination of, 172

standby, 37

troubleshooting, 340

   applying Output Interpreter, 341

*collecting IOS device informa-
    tion, 340-341*

*researching Cisco IOS software
    defects, 343-345*

types, 150-153

virtual, redundancy, 36

WANs (wide-area networks), 192

routes

feasible successor, 103

filtering, troubleshooting EIGRP,
    122-124

path selection, 101

unadvertised, troubleshooting
    EIGRP, 121

routing

classful, 94-95

classless, 94-95

CRS (Carrier Routing System), 291

domains, 92

dynamic, overview of, 92-106

entries, troubleshooting inaccurate,
    124

GRE (Generic Routing
    Encapsulation), 256-261

protocols, 92

administrative distances, 95-98

classification of, 93

Frame Relay, 237-239

hierarchies, link-state, 150

link-state, 144-146

*OSPF (Open Shortest Path
    First). See OSPF*

tables, 92

IP (Internet Protocol), 67

*OSPF (Open Shortest Path
    First), 172-174*

*reviewing using passive inter-
    faces, 109*

Unicast, 64

updating, 95, 108

Routing Information Protocol. *See*
RIP

RP (root port), 14, 17

RSTP (Rapid STP), 20

RTP (Reliable Transport Protocol), 99

rules, ACLs (access control lists), 85

running

configuration files, RAM, 290

traceroute, 52

runts, 61

S

scalable medium-sized networks

DTP (Dynamic Trunking Protocol),
    8-9

implementing, 1

trunks

configuring, 7

operations, 6-7

troubleshooting, 10-11

VLANs (virtual LANs)

creating, 4-6

overview of, 2

troubleshooting, 9-10

**scalable multiarea networks, OSPF
    implementation, 143**

scaling delay, 127

**SDLC (Synchronous Data Link
    Control) protocol, 197**

**searching Cisco IOS images to load,
    295-297**

Secure File Transfer Protocol. *See* SFTP

Securing the Data Plane Configuration Guide Library, Cisco IOS Release 15M&T, 72

security

  IPSec (IP Security), 255-256

  SNMP (Simple Network Management Protocol), 271

  VPNs (virtual private networks), 185

selection

  Cisco IOS configurations, 300-302

  DP (designated port), 19

  paths, 101, 146. *See also* paths, selection

sending data to SNMP agents, 274

seq no message, 281

serial cabling, WANs, 195

serial communication links, 210

serial encapsulation, WANs, 232

serial interfaces, WANs, 209-214

serial lines, 63

  encapsulation, 219

  multilink PPP (Point-to-Point Protocol) configuration, 228-232

serial numbers. *See* SNs

servers

  SFTP (Secure File Transfer Protocol), 274

  Telnet, 55

service provider demarcation points, WANs, 200

services

  HSRP (Hot Standby Router Protocol), 39-40

  ISDN (Integrated Services Digital Network), 199

WAAS (Wide Area Application Services), 300

WANs (wide-area networks), 187

SET command, 274

settings. *See* configuration

severity message, 281

SFTP (Secure File Transfer Protocol), 274

sharing traffic, EIGRP, 113-114

shortest path first. *See* SPF

show commands

  show access-lists command, 71

  show buffers command, 340

  show cdp neighbors command, 59

  show controllers command, 340

  show debug command, 350

  show etherchannel port-channel command, 35

  show etherchannel summary command, 34

  show flash0: command, 306

  show glbp command, 41

  show interface command, 60, 104, 340

  show interface interface switchport command, 10

  show interface port-channel command, 34

  show interfaces command, 7, 62, 249

  show ip cache flow command, 288

  show ip eigrp neighbors command, 106-107

  show ip eigrp topology command, 110-111

  show ip flow interface command, 287

show ip interface brief command, 260

show ip interface command, 168, 260

show ip ospf interface command, 170, 175

show ip ospf neighbor command, 172

show ip protocols command, 120, 170

show ip route command, 63-65, 108-109, 173

show ipv6 eigrp neighbors command, 134

show license command, 320, 340

show license udi command, 319

show mac address-table command, 58

show process cpu command, 340

show processes memory command, 340

show running-config command, 302, 340

show snmp additional_options command, 278

show spanning-tree command, 25

show stacks command, 340

show startup-config command, 302

show tech command, 341

show version command, 298, 321, 340

show vlan command, 5

shutdown command, 227

signaling, Frame Relay, 239-240

SIMMs (single in-line memory modules), 291

Simple Network Management Protocol. *See* SNMP

single-area OSPF, 155

single in-line memory modules. *See* SIMMs

site-to-site VPNs, 253

SNMP (Simple Network Management Protocol), 270

 network device management

  configuration, 276-279

  message formats (syslog), 281

  MIBs (Management Information Bases), 275-276

  NetFlow, 283-288

  obtaining data from agents, 271

  overview of syslog, 279-280

  polling data, monitoring in, 272

  sending data to agents, 274

  syslog configuration, 281

  traps, monitoring in, 273

 versions, 270-271

snmp-server chassis-id serial_no command, 278

snmp-server community string [RO | RQ] command, 278

snmp-server contact contact_name command, 278

snmp-server host ip_address trap community_string command, 278

snmp-server location location command, 278

SNs (serial numbers), 319

software. *See also* applications

 Cisco IOS. *See* IOS

 defects, researching, 343-345

licenses. *See* licensing

VPNs (virtual private networks), 205

SONET (Synchronous Optical Network), 198

sources, determination of routers, 172

Spanning Tree Protocol. *See* STP

SPF (shortest path first), 94, 145

split horizons, 238

spoke networks, 188. *See also* hub-and-spoke networks

STALE code, 82

standby

groups, 37

routers, 37

state, 13

starting routers, 292-293, 302

states

HSRP (Hot Standby Router Protocol), 38

multiarea OSPF neighbors, 162-165

static name resolution, 68-69

statistics, NetFlow, 288

status

interfaces, 63

NetFlow, 288

protocols, verification of EIGRP neighbors, 118

STP (Spanning Tree Protocol), 12

analysis, 24-26

failures, 26-28

types, 20-21

structures, OSPF areas, 150

stub areas, 155-156

subinterfaces

NBMA (nonbroadcast multiaccess) networks, 238

point-to-point configuration, 245-246

subnet masks

classful routing, 94

VLSMs (variable-length subnet masks), 99

summarization, automatic network, 123

SVCs (switched virtual circuits), 235

switched communication links, 204

switched virtual circuits. *See* SVCs

switches

CDP (Cisco Discovery Protocol), 58

default configuration, 4

MPLS (Multiprotocol Label Switching), 200, 261-264

redundancy, 11-15

WANs (wide-area networks), 185, 192

switchport access vlan command, 5

switchport nonegotiate interface command, 9

switch-to-switch connectivity, 6

Synchronous Data Link Control protocol. *See* SDLC protocol

Synchronous Optical Network. *See* SONET

syslog

configuration, 281

messages, formatting, 281

overview, 279-280

T

T1 lines

crossover cables, 209

integrated CSU/DSU, 215

loopback plugs, 216

WANs (wide-area networks), 200-201

tables

MAC (Media Access Control) addresses, 10, 58

routing, 92

IP (Internet Protocol), 67

OSPF (Open Shortest Path First), 172-174

reviewing using passive interfaces, 109

Unicast, 64

TAC (Technical Assistance), 339, 345

tags, ID, 319

Technical Assistance. *See* TAC

Telnet, 55

to IP ports, 55

IPv6 (Internet Protocol version 6) connections, 67

terminal-emulation program, 346

terminal monitor command, 346

termination

cable modems, 202

DSL (digital subscriber line), 201

WANs (wide-area networks), 203

testing basic connectivity, 51

timestamp message, 281

Time to Live. *See* TTL

tools

Bug Toolkit, 344

nslookup

IPv4 (Internet Protocol version 4), 70

IPv6 (Internet Protocol version 6), 84

ping command, 51-53

traceroute, 51

IPv6 (Internet Protocol version 6), 79

running, 52

topologies

EtherChannel, 29-35

IPv6 (Internet Protocol version 6), 135

maps, 145

redundancy

overview of, 12-15

switches, 11

STP (Spanning Tree Protocol), 15

WANs (wide-area networks)

Frame Relay, 236-237

full-mesh networks, 189-191

hub-and-spoke networks, 188-189

partial-mesh networks, 189

point-to-point networks, 191

totally stub areas, 157

traceroute, 51

IPv6 (Internet Protocol version 6), 79

running, 52

tracert command, 52

tracking interfaces, 38

traffic sharing, EIGRP, 113-114

transitions

  carrier, 61

  from exstart to full state, 162

transmissions, aborted, 62

traps, monitoring SNMP, 273

triggering debugging

  ACLs (access control lists), 351-356

  conditionally, 356-357

troubleshooting, 339

  ACLs (access control lists), 71-72

  cables, 50

  connections, 47

  data centers, 86

  default gateways, 66

  devices, debugging, 345, 357-359

  DNS (Domain Name Server), 50

  EIGRP (Enhanced Interior Gateway Protocol), 115-124

    automatic network summarization, 123

    components, 115-118

    IPv6 (Internet Protocol version 6), 135

    neighbors, 118-121

    route filtering, 122-124

    routing tables, 121

    unadvertised routes, 121

  Ethernet links, 62

  IPv4 (Internet Protocol version 4), 48

    ACLs (access control lists), 71-72

    CDP (Cisco Discovery Protocol), 58-60

    default gateway issues, 66

    end-to-end components, 48-51

    identification of paths, 63-66

    name resolution issues, 68

    physical connection issues, 60-63

    verifying connections, 51-58

    virtual environments, 72-74

  IPv6 (Internet Protocol version 6), 75

    ACLs (access control lists), 84-86

    construction of addresses, 75-76

    default gateway issues, 81-83

    end-to-end connections, 78-80

    identification of paths, 81

    name resolution issues, 83

    neighbor discovery in, 80-82

    unicast addresses, 76-77

    virtual environments, 86

  Layer 3 connections, 63

  MPLS (Multiprotocol Label Switching),

  name resolution issues

    dynamic name resolution, 69-71

    static name resolution, 68-69

  NBMA (nonbroadcast multiaccess) networks, 238

  OSPF (Open Shortest Path First)

    components, 165-168

    multiarea IPv4 implementation, 162

    neighbors, 168-172

    path selection, 174-176

    routing tables, 172-174

  overview of, 86

routers, 340
>   *applying Output Interpreter, 341*
>   *collecting IOS device information, 340-341*
>   *placement, 87*
>   *researching Cisco IOS software defects, 343-345*
>   STP (Spanning Tree Protocol), 24-26
>   trunks, 10-11
>   virtual environments, 72-74
>   VLANs (virtual LANs), 9-10
>   VPNs (virtual private networks), 74
>   WANs (wide-area networks)
>   *Frame Relay, 237-239*
>   *serial encapsulation, 232*

trunks, 1
>   configuration, 7
>   operations, 6-7
>   troubleshooting, 10-11

TTL (Time to Live), 13

tunnel destination ip_address command, 259

tunnel mode gre ip command, 259

tunnel source ip_address command, 259

tunnels, GRE (Generic Routing Encapsulation), 256-261

two-router IPv6 networks, 133

two-way state, 166

types
>   OSPF (Open Shortest Path First) areas, 150-153
>   of packets, 100-101
>   of routers, 150-155
>   STP (Spanning Tree Protocol), 20-21

of unicast addresses, 76

of VPNs (virtual private networks), 253

U

UDIs (universal device identifiers), 319

unadvertised routes, troubleshooting EIGRP, 121

undebug command, 350

unicast addresses, troubleshooting, 76-77

Unicast routing tables, 64

uninstalling permanent licenses, 325-327

universal device identifiers. *See* UDIs

unspecified unicast addresses, 76

updating
>   packets, LSDBs, 149
>   passive interfaces, 108
>   routing, 95

upgrading
>   Cisco IOS images, 308-311
>   ISSU (In-Service Software Upgrade), 330

UplinkFast, 20

username username password password command, 227

user-reported errors, 49

utilities. *See* tools

V

V.35 interfaces, 195

validation
>   ACLs (access control lists), 353
>   hostnames, 55

L3VPN (Layer 3 VPN), 370-372

serial line encapsulation, 219

values

configuration register, 294-295

K, 103, 127

variable-length subnet masks. *See* **VLSMs**

variance, EIGRP (Enhanced Interior Gateway Protocol), 112-113

VCs (virtual circuits), 235

verification

advertisements, 172

bandwidth references, 176

CHAP (Challenge-Handshake Authentication Protocol) configuration, 227

devices, debugging, 350-351

EIGRP (Enhanced Interior Gateway Protocol)

configuration, 106-108

IPv6 (Internet Protocol version 6), 131-132

AS numbers, 119

EtherChannel, 34-35

GRE (Generic Routing Encapsulation) tunnels, 260

host operating systems, 307

IOS licensing, 287-321

IPv4 (Internet Protocol version 4) connections, 51-58

IPv6 (Internet Protocol version 6)

addresses, 80

connections, 79-80

L3VPN (Layer 3 VPN), 369

NetFlow, 287-288

OSPF (Open Shortest Path First) multiarea IPv4 implementation, 160-162

OSPFv3 (Open Shortest Path First version 3), 179-180

protocol operations, 359-361

SNMP (Simple Network Management Protocol), 276-279

VLANs (virtual LANs), configuration, 4-6

WANs (wide-area networks), Frame Relay, 249-252

versions of SNMP (Simple Network Management Protocol), 270-271

video collaboration, 191

viewing

ARP (Address Resolution Protocol) caches, 57

metrics, 112

port channels, 35

routing tables, 67

UDIs (universal device identifiers), 319

VLANs (virtual LANs), 5

virtual circuits. *See* **VCs**

virtual environments

IPv4 (Internet Protocol version 4), 72-74

IPv6 (Internet Protocol version 6), 86

virtual LANs. *See* **VLANs**

Virtual Private LAN Services. *See* **VPLS**

virtual routers, redundancy, 36

virtualization, Cisco NX-OS, 331

vlan global configuration command, 4

vlan vlan_id command, 10

VLANs (virtual LANs)

configuration, 3

creating, 4-6

mismatch, 59

overview of, 2

troubleshooting, 9-10

VLSMs (variable-length subnet masks), 99

voice collaboration, 191

VoIP (Voice over IP) devices, 58

VPLS (Virtual Private LAN Services), 369

VPNs (virtual private networks), 74

clientless, 206

implementation, 185

software, 205

WANs (wide-area networks)

GRE (Generic Routing Encapsulation) tunnels, 256-261

IPSec (IP Security), 255-256

MPLS (Multiprotocol Label Switching), 261-264

overview of, 252-255

W

WAAS (Wide Area Application Services), 300

WAN interface cards. *See* **WICs**

WANs (wide-area networks), 185-186

architecture, 188

CHAP (Challenge-Handshake Authentication Protocol), 222-223

core routers, 193

customer logical, 263

devices, 192-195

extranets, 209

Frame Relay, 233

configuration, 243-244

mapping addresses, 240-243

multipoint/point-to-point, 244

overview of, 233-236

point-to-multipoint configuration, 247-249

point-to-point subinterface configuration, 245-246

signaling, 239-240

topologies, 236-237

troubleshooting, 237-239

verifying configuration, 249-252

full-mesh networks, 189-191

HDLC (High-Level Data Link Control) protocol, 218-220

hub-and-spoke networks, 188-189

integrated CSU/DSU

back-to-back routers, 216-209

configuration, 215-216

modules, 214

ISDN (Integrated Services Digital Network), 199

Layer 2 protocols, 197-199

MANs (metropolitan-area networks), 207-209

MPLS (Multiprotocol Label Switching), 200

options

link, 203

private connection, 204-205

overview of, 186-188

PAP (Password Authentication Protocol), 222

partial-mesh networks, 189

point-to-point networks, 191

PPP (Point-to-Point Protocol), 220-221

    configuration, 223-227

    multilink over serial line configuration, 228-232

public connection options, 205-207

routers, 192

serial cabling, 195

serial encapsulation, troubleshooting, 232

serial interface configuration, 209-214

service provider demarcation points, 200

switches, 192

T1 line loopback plugs, 216

T1/E1, 200-201

termination

    cable modem, 202

    DSL (digital subscriber line), 201

    Ethernet, 203

VPNs (virtual private networks)

    GRE (Generic Routing Encapsulation) tunnels, 256-261

    IPSec (IP Security), 255-256

    MPLS (Multiprotocol Label Switching), 261-264

    overview of, 252-255

X.25, 199

WICs (WAN interface cards), 196

Wide Area Application Services. *See* **WAAS**

wide-area networks. *See* **WANs**

wireless access points, CDP, 58

wireless networks, 194, 199

    MANs (metropolitan-area networks), 209

X-Z

X.25, 199

zeros, IPv6 (Internet Protocol version 6) addresses, 75

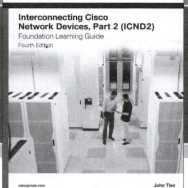

FREE
Online Edition

Safari Books Online

Your purchase of **Interconnecting Cisco Network Devices, Part 2 (ICND2) Foundation Learning Guide** includes access to a free online edition for 45 days through the **Safari Books Online** subscription service. Nearly every Cisco Press book is available online through **Safari Books Online**, along with thousands of books and videos from publishers such as Addison-Wesley Professional, Exam Cram, IBM Press, O'Reilly Media, Prentice Hall, Que, Sams, and VMware Press.

Safari Books Online is a digital library providing searchable, on-demand access to thousands of technology, digital media, and professional development books and videos from leading publishers. With one monthly or yearly subscription price, you get unlimited access to learning tools and information on topics including mobile app and software development, tips and tricks on using your favorite gadgets, networking, project management, graphic design, and much more.

Activate your FREE Online Edition at
informit.com/safarifree

STEP 1:   Enter the coupon code: NBUANXA.

STEP 2:   New Safari users, complete the brief registration form.
            Safari subscribers, just log in.

If you have difficulty registering on Safari or accessing the online edition,
please e-mail customer-service@safaribooksonline.com